To Lucy

With my very
Best Wishes

Alex Leger.

23rd Sept 2016

BLUE PETER
BEHIND THE BADGE

ALEX LEGER

BLUE PETER: BEHIND THE BADGE
The untold story of the nation's favourite children's programme

First published by
Lauren Productions Ltd 2012

ISBN 978-0-9573808-0-6

Designed by Henry Leger
Printed and bound by Butler Tanner and Dennis Ltd, Frome, Somerset

A CIP catalogue record of this book is available from the British Library.

CONTENTS

ILLUSTRATION CREDITS

The photographs in this book are all from my private collection and reproduced with the kind permission of *Blue Peter* and the BBC, with the exception of the following pages:

7, 9, 12, 15, 19, 27, 28, 32, 36, 42, 45, 117: copyright BBC
41: reproduced with the permission of James Walker Photography
85: permission is being sought and any help would be gratefully received.
123, 125 and 126: reproduced with the kind permission of Peter Brown
192 and 195: MOD Crown copyright reproduced under the terms of the open licence agreement with kind permission of Group Captain Jon Fynes RAF
220: reproduced with the permission of British Airways
232, 235 and 236 (large photograph): reproduced with kind permission of Sightsavers/Felicia Webb
244, 245, 246, 247, 248, 252: reproduced with kind permission of Simon Thomas
257: reproduced with the kind permission of Judy Leden and Chris Dawes
267, 270 and 342: MOD Crown copyright reproduced under the terms of the open licence agreement with the permission of the RAF Falcons
Front cover, 314 and 316: reproduced with the kind permission of Nicola Baker
323: reproduced with the permission of Robbie Shone – www.shonephotography.com
341 (two photographs): reproduced with permission from www.Skydiveelsinore.com
345 and 346: reproduced with permission of Tony Gussin, *North Devon Gazette*
Front cover, 354 and 356: reproduced with the kind permission of Rob Franklin
355: reproduced with the kind permission of Ash Mills

I acknowledge the kindness of Chris Capstick, who took all the photographs on pages 278, 280, 281, 282, 285, 286, 304 and 307.

The documents on the following pages are reproduced with the kind permission of Tim Levell, editor, *Blue Peter*:
24: The Nelson's Column shooting script (page 1)
108: Biddy Baxter's last programme (title page signed by Biddy)
186: programme script (title page signed by all presenters) to celebrate 35th anniversary
318: Blue Peter Melbourne filming schedule (title page)

Every effort has been made to fulfil requirements with regard to copyright material. The author and publisher will be glad to rectify any omissions at the earliest opportunity.

ACKNOWLEDGEMENTS

This book has been a labour of love. It has been necessary to draw a line under a way of life that, for me, has come to an end. And it would not have been possible without the support of so many people who believe in *Blue Peter* as much as I do.

Top of the list to thank is my wife Lynn and my children Hannah and Henry, who put up with my absences for 36 years and who listened patiently as I battled to find the right words. 'Thank you' is barely adequate.

My stories are about people and in particular the many *Blue Peter* presenters who helped by reading and verifying their bits of the text. I am grateful to those who gave me quotes to bring to life the events that we shared. My thanks go to John Noakes, Peter Purves, Lesley Judd, Simon Groom, Christopher Wenner, Tina Heath, Sarah Greene, Peter Duncan, Janet Ellis, Mark Curry, Yvette Fielding, John Leslie, Diane Louise Jordan, Anthea Turner, Tim Vincent, Stuart Miles, Katy Hill, Richard Bacon, Romana D'Annunzio, Konnie Huq, Simon Thomas, Matt Baker, Liz Barker, Zoe Salmon, Gethin Jones, Andy Akinwolere, Helen Skelton, Joel Defries and Barney Harwood. It is their history as well as mine.

I have also been assisted by the programme's producers, in particular Biddy Baxter and Edward Barnes, who gave me details about how the programme developed in the early years. Other producers have given me their memories, which have added value to the storylines. I am indebted to John Adcock, Lewis Bronze (who followed Biddy as programme editor), Michael Cook and Crispin Evans. I would particularly thank Richard Marson, who read the early version of the text not once but twice. My thanks also to Tim Levell who approved the book on behalf of the BBC.

As well as the programme's producers I am indebted to Bill Yates, Henry Farrar, John McIntyre, Graham Banks, Mike Milburn and also Godfrey Johnson, who bore witness to many of the events, for their help in vetting the storylines. Sara Vernon, Trevor Williams, Hannah Leger, Jean Rowton, and Sadru Banji also persevered with the text and gave me much needed support and guidance with its structure and emphasis.

My thanks also go to Ros Jesson, Anne Askwith and Colin Gamm, who copy-edited the book, Duncan Lamont, who cast a legal eye over the text and Henry, my son, who patiently designed the book.

FOREWORD

I wanted expert witnesses to my endeavours and I am grateful that Matt Baker and Simon Thomas have kindly agreed to testify on my behalf:

Matt: It was impossible to be a *Blue Peter* presenter without wondering whether you'd survive an Alex Leger film shoot. He famously wrote on one of my risk assessments 'presenter may die' in such a matter-of-fact fashion, it seemed almost normal to him. When Alex was directing a scuba-diving feature in the Red Sea, I suffered an equipment failure on a World War II wreck and had to use my buddy's emergency air supply. Alex merely took this in his stride because I was still alive and we'd got the pictures he needed. Editors used to live in fear of getting a call that a presenter had had an accident but thankfully we all came through with nothing more than scrapes, bruises and exhaustion.

What no one could accuse Alex of was not caring, especially about *Blue Peter*. He lived and breathed the programme for 36 years and took no prisoners. He had no time for egos and just wanted the best. Nothing was too extreme, too challenging or too much of an obstacle. Can you believe, he even got the head of antiquities in Egypt to close the Pyramids while the public was actually queueing to get in, so we could film without interruption.

Simon: I likened Alex to a 'champagne cork' because by the time he'd gone through the rigours of getting to a shoot, he was ready to pop and heaven help anyone who wasn't ready to jump into action when he shouted 'Action!' And his 'Action!' was easily the loudest in TV! His energy was boundless and infectious. He made us work till we dropped but we knew the end result would actually make us look good. Over the years Alex made more than 600 *Blue Peter* films, which prompted the praise from John Leslie, 'Never in the field of *Blue Peter* filming has one man done so much for so many, for so long'.

But if there's one refrain uttered by Alex with relentless regularity that makes me chuckle to this day, it's his hallmark director's call; 'That was very nice, but can we do that just one more time...'

Matt Baker

Simon Thomas

(Above): John Noakes begins his record-breaking skydive from the back of a C130 Hercules. This was the film that made me want to join the *Blue Peter* team

Prologue

Most of us have grown up with *Blue Peter*. Its daredevil presenters have often become household names. Many have come and gone over the programme's 54-year history. Since joining *Blue Peter* in 1975, when there were still just three television channels in the UK, I managed to notch up 36 years with Auntie's favourite children's programme. No other person has worked longer for *Blue Peter*.

It was a 'think it/do it' job that embraced a huge variety of experiences, with no room for Monday-morning blues.

Whether I was walking the deck of the *Mary Rose*, flying with the Red Arrows or feasting on tarantulas in Cambodia, I always knew that something else, equally engaging, was just around the corner.

Twenty-five years ago friends often told me 'You have a fantastic job' and I got on with it. Today directors are likely to be asked lots of questions beforehand, including the all-important one: 'How much will it cost?'

For several decades health and safety considerations have worn away at budgets and have struck at the heart of achievable risk taking. Long gone are the days when personal harnesses were seen as an optional extra. Much more time has to be devoted to safety and in a fast-moving magazine programme like *Blue Peter* there is never enough time. Location safety costs have spiralled out of all proportion to the programme's budget. Challenges with real jeopardy, once accepted as part of the bread and butter of the programme, have become a luxury.

So, even though the aims and formula of the programme have remained the same, technology, safety and broadcasting trends have made it a very different programme to watch. In some ways it is a microcosm of how the BBC has adapted to the ever-changing needs of its audiences and new legislation. For me, the difference between the 1970s and now is immense.

I have been asked many times to write this book and it is time to leave a record for my family and for anyone interested in working at the coal face of popular TV, as well as the many thousands of loyal viewers. I have been lucky. Film-making means I have a visual record of the past years, and a list of dates when the filming took place.

Rather as with a written diary, I have had only to remember the occasion, or watch the archives – some with cringing embarrassment and others with a sense of professional pride – to recall every last detail of the struggle to get it right. There was no such thing as an easy assignment. I have selected only those events that are indelibly etched on to my memory. When what happened off camera was as entertaining, if not more so, as what happened on camera.

I began with John Noakes, Peter Purves and Lesley Judd, and then worked with every one of the 27 presenters that followed. There was Simon Groom, with whom I had more adventures in far-flung places than any other; Peter Duncan, who later became Chief Scout; John Leslie, who for a while was romantically entwined with Catherine Zeta-Jones; Katy Hill, who survived aerobatics with the Red Arrows; Simon Thomas, who returned to the Solomons with me to fulfil a lifetime ambition; Matt Baker, whose determination gave a whole new meaning to 'having a go'; and Helen Skelton, whose resilience in the face of physical challenges is a record all by itself.

There are memories of both presenters and contributors, and memories also of the programme's editors, of whom there have been only six in over fifty years. They took the blame when things went wrong and played a pivotal role in shaping the programme.

In its heyday the programme attracted a regular six to eight million viewers of all ages and was, for many, a life-changing experience. It gained a well-deserved reputation as the leading children's programme. After all, most of us have a 'favourite *Blue Peter* moment'.

Blue Peter: Behind the Badge documents the changes over decades of broadcasting. Inevitably, it also provides something of a historical record.

This book is my very own selection of the highs and lows, the tears and laughter, the downright dangerous and, of course, the special friendships on my long and rewarding journey with *Blue Peter*.

1

Dicing with death:
the perfect *Blue Peter* CV

When presenter Gethin Jones left *Blue Peter*, he made a short farewell speech in a crowded studio at Television Centre just after transmission. His parting shot was that 'Director Alex Leger wrote on the risk assessment for the shoot, "Gethin may die." ' The assembled collection of BBC staff, freelancers and friends didn't seem that surprised. Quite a few laughed out loud.

It may seem like an extraordinary thing to suggest. I hear you say, 'If it's that dangerous, why do it at all?'

But the simple fact is that *Blue Peter* is all about exciting challenges and risk is inevitable. It's about managing that risk. And therein lies the tale – like one afternoon in the Coral Sea around the Solomon Islands that still makes me shudder. I was visiting the islands prior to a filming expedition.

We raced – throttle wide open – until the storm hit us like a sledge-hammer. Waves broke all around and above us, and the rain was so fierce we couldn't see for more than a few yards in any direction. My companions were two islanders, and they navigated by the roll of the waves and a lifetime of experience. Rainwater built up in the bottom of the canoe so fast I took my hat off and started bailing. Lightning hit the wave tops with massive thunderclaps and, frighteningly, every time it happened, the outboard motor missed a beat.

And then the motor stopped altogether. The crew looked concerned. 'Big problem, Alex.'

The fuel line had a blockage or something, and they furiously started to fix it. The canoe was rolling dangerously and shipping water from the waves. My Melanesian friends had gone from jet black to a shade of grey. The water was brown and angry as it boiled with white waves. I had heard that sharks sometimes came to the surface in a storm because they got disorientated in the poor visibility. I wondered if any had spotted our drifting craft.

Then it dawned on me that we were moving rapidly with the current down the length of Guadalcanal towards the open Pacific, where there

(Left): Alex Leger on a recce in the Solomons. This 'canoe' trip started in flat calm seas before it became a living nightmare

was no chance of a rescue.

Unpleasant thoughts crowded my mind as waves slopped over the sides of the canoe. I looked anxiously to the stern, where my companions struggled with the repairs, and wondered if I should lend a hand. I had a powerful urge to do something to save my life.

Then the outboard restarted. As they looked up from the spluttering motor I saw them calm down. I followed their gaze and turned to glimpse the lights of the Point Cruz Yacht Club in Honiara, which were much further away and off to one side than they had been. They were a flickering beacon of hope in the deepening gloom.

Half an hour at full speed and we hit the yacht-club beach. I stepped ashore. Ten minutes later the heavens opened and it poured with torrential rain until daybreak. Shortly after we'd landed, all the lights went out and the whole town was plunged into darkness. I walked off the beach clutching my lifejacket, the sand firm and reassuring after the rocking canoe. I felt sick. Without lights we wouldn't have stood a chance.

It was 23 November 2001, nearly a year into the new millennium, and not for the first time I marvelled at how the unexpected could still deal a lethal hand. And working on *Blue Peter* meant that every day was full of the unexpected.

Looking back to my early life and well before *Blue Peter*, hits, misses and near-death experiences began even before I joined the programme, and they were the reason I survived. A few of them stick in my mind.

At eight years old I hit a patch of ice and fell off my bike. The car behind took some hair out of my head with its front wheel. At 15 I added ether to a home-made explosive and several weeks later, in the summer heat, it spontaneously exploded while hidden in a suitcase under my bed. Mercifully I wasn't in bed at the time.

Years later, in the University Air Squadron, while flying solo in an RAF Chipmunk, I had an engine failure and landed safely in a field. Others that year were not so lucky. After university, and in the army, I was firing mortar parachute illumination bombs in a wood at night. With each bomb the mortar tube came more upright. The last bomb all but took my helmet off.

So by the time I started on *Blue Peter* I had learnt the hard way that disasters can happen. Not a bad lesson to learn, as it turned out, and during 36 years of directing risky films my luck has held.

When I joined the BBC (April 1973) I didn't know that I wanted to go into television. The right degree had got me a job in the BBC Management Services Group as a very junior consultant, yet everywhere I went I met people who wished they were making television programmes. Their enthusiasm was infectious.

I had written a diary about my experiences as a teacher in the Solomon Islands during a year with Voluntary Service Overseas after I left school, and used it as the basis for an idea for a documentary programme. I sent it to the editor of *The World About Us*, an exploration programme that went out on a Sunday night.

It was sent back a few weeks later with a kind note suggesting I send it to a BBC department known as Further Education. My instinct told me that would be a waste of time. Then a contact in the BBC's documentary unit told me of a series that was planned about local customs around the world. It was called *Tribal Eye*. They were thinking of going to the Solomon Islands. I got in touch.

I pitched up in their offices at Kensington House off Shepherd's Bush Green in a pinstripe suit, carrying a briefcase with my rejected pro-gramme idea, a hand-made head comb inlaid with trochus shell as proof I had actually been there, and some photographs. I was uneasy because I had been told that David Attenborough, who was going to present the series, was going to be there as well as the producer, Michael McIntyre. Anna, the researcher, met me in the BBC reception and escorted me along a corridor past door after open door revealing film-cutting rooms and mounds of unravelled 16 mm film. The whole building throbbed with excitement. Timorously I followed through a maze of stairs and passages until, suddenly, there was the great man himself. My fears subsided. He was charming and welcoming and he made me feel special.

The plan was for us all to go for lunch and he quizzed me about the Solomons. 'Where are the interesting places ... where should we go ... what could we do ... what is there to film?'

The production team had some knowledge but David (he wasn't 'Sir' in those days) needed convincing.

I was upbeat and told them what I knew. They were polite but not really interested. I struggled to think of something that might catch their attention. Suddenly I remembered the Moro Movement and they perked up.

The Moro Movement had been founded by a local man, Moro, when he received a vision that Western influences were wrong. Their community at Makaruka on Guadalcanal have a Stone Age-like culture and to this day they prefer to walk about naked or clad in traditional tree-bark loincloths and reject influences from Western society. Talking to the *Tribal Eye* team, I admitted that I didn't know much about them, I just knew that the community existed and roughly where it was.

While Michael, the programme producer, and Anna quizzed me more for *Tribal Eye*, I gave David my *World About Us* programme idea and he leafed through it. At the end he said, 'Do you think you could direct this?'

I was flabbergasted and said I didn't know. The truth was that while I was ambitious to promote ideas, the thought of directing anything myself hadn't really crossed my mind. I knew so little about how it was done.

Walking back to the Tube station in the summer sun, I suddenly thought, Why not? It was like a bolt from the blue.

August 1975

The only way to get into television production was to get 'an attachment' and these were offered by each department for a period of six months.

I applied for three training attachments for what was then known as a 'production assistant'. I applied to Schools', Further Education and Children's (*Blue Peter*). I got outright rejections from the first two and an interview from the last. So *Blue Peter* it was. In trepidation I caught the London underground to White City and BBC Television Centre, the Corporation's other spiritual home. At the time it was the biggest television programme factory in the world.

Biddy Baxter, the formidable boss of *Blue Peter*, and her producer, Rosemary Gill, were on the selection board. From the start I got them muddled up and mistook Rose for Biddy. Whoever asked the questions, I deferentially angled my replies to Rose. I was only partly aware of the other lady, who I thought was Rose, trying to attract my attention. They seemed very interested in my ideas and particularly one about bee-keeping at Buckfast Abbey in Devon. This was subsequently featured in the *Blue Peter Annual* under the title 'Sticky Habits'.

I passed selection and have often thought that the only reason I got the attachment was because Biddy was determined to get her own back for my rudeness.

I was wrong. It was actually on the advice of Edward Barnes, who had produced *Blue Peter* and was at that time heading for higher things. He advised Biddy that because I had been in the army I could probably get things done and should be good at managing people. The film-making bit, he surmised, could be taught later.

So, despite the fact I had absolutely no television experience, a rarity

(Above and left):
The *Blue Peter* office at
Television Centre in the
early 1980s

for candidates in those days, I was given the chance to prove myself. I owe my exciting life, a rich pattern of experiences at the coal face of television, to Edward Barnes.

10 November 1975
5th Floor, East Tower, BBC Television Centre, London

When I arrived in the *Blue Peter* office on my first day it was a shock to realise my earlier mistake. I needn't have worried. Biddy was charming, although I soon learned she could be anything but, if the situation demanded it.

Overdressed in a brown striped suit with fashionably wide lapels, I knew instantly that I had misjudged the dress code. Television production was a very different place from administration, and jeans or similar were the order of the day. My office suit bit the dust and I don't remember ever wearing it again.

The *Blue Peter* office was surprisingly small. Every desk was covered with piles of press cuttings and strange souvenirs of previous filming exploits. There were bits of finished 'makes' (when the presenters 'made' something out of everyday objects, often using the now infamous 'sticky-backed plastic') and trophies dating back 15 years. The trophies were hideous and in amongst them, and all over the office, there were objects sent in by viewers, everything from cushions to paintings and small sculptures. Huge, ungainly typewriters and bottles of Tipp-Ex filled every other desk. It was worn out and glamorous at the same time – and incredibly untidy.

Although I sensed that the real action wasn't in the office, I knew it would be a while before I would be let off the leash.

The latter part of 1975 and early 1976 was a trial period and I spent most of it in the studio under Biddy's critical eye. She was a powerful leader and had made *Blue Peter* a household name. From the start I was in awe of its status and her reputation.

She was glamorous in a determined way. Immaculately dressed in figure-hugging ensembles, she wore stiletto heels rather as I would handle a knife. In idle moments she would gouge the carpet as her mind analysed one problem after another. She wore her hair in a severe bun that was her hallmark, and there was a rumour that if it was set free, it would fall to her waist.

I learnt to listen very carefully to what she had to say because she meant exactly what she said. I watched with amusement when middle-aged male contributors tried to patronise or flirt with her. They were never in her league and she would make mincemeat of them without mercy.

Biddy was the constant subject of conversation in the *Blue Peter* office, and not just because all our futures depended on her. She was a colourful character and capable of extraordinary actions and comments – from falling in a horse trough when filming with Princess Anne during the Rags Appeal for the charity Riding for the Disabled, to spending hours on the telephone explaining to potential contributors why the programme needed to be the first to feature their idea. She knew that children's attention easily wandered and exclusivity was essential. The high audience viewing figures were testament to this.

In Biddy's words: 'Children don't appreciate an idea can be treated in different ways by different programmes. We always have to be first because of their low boredom threshold.'

She had begun her BBC career in radio as a trainee studio manager. Reminiscing about her experiences, she said she was good at creating sound effects but admitted that that was where her technical expertise ended. Looking back, she says, 'I left before I was found out.'

Even so, I noticed she had a keen ear and as part of her job was to guide the presenters on their performances, incorrect nuances of speech or inappropriate tone of delivery seldom escaped her.

I later learned how she got the job. It was a tribute to the BBC's unusual way of working where so-called 'rules' were to be obeyed and broken at the same time. Biddy was from radio and knew nothing about television.

She was a graduate entry to the corporation from Durham University. She cut her teeth as a trainee radio studio manager and then applied for training attachments to other departments. She became producer of junior English programmes in radio, and then moved to children's television programmes, where she worked on *Watch with Mother*, *The Hot Chestnut Man*, which featured Johnny Morris, and Ray Alan's *Mikki the Martian*.

It just so happened that the very day that Biddy's attachment ended in television a permanent producer job was advertised, and it was for *Blue Peter*.

The founding producer, John Hunter Blair, had become ill with heart disease from which the management had hoped he would eventually recover, so the programme was handed over to whatever producer was at a loose end in the department. This resulted in the programme gradually going downhill. When it became evident that John Hunter Blair was not going to return, his job was advertised. Permanent jobs were like hen's teeth so the vacancy was inundated with experienced and talented applicants. Many had been waiting patiently for years for this opportunity.

It came as a blow to quite a few of them that a complete outsider who 'hadn't the vaguest clue about television' (Biddy's words, not mine) got it. Biddy was 28 years old.

Unfortunately she couldn't be released from her work in radio for several months. So Leonard Chase, a good experienced producer, was put in charge to fill the gap with Edward Barnes, one of the unsuccessful candidates, as his production assistant. When Biddy arrived, Edward was asked to stay on, with the job of nursing the interloper from radio.

He accepted his role with good grace despite his disappointment. The programme was beginning to find its way when Biddy was summoned for jury service, which left Edward holding the fort. Fortunately he remembered working with a talented assistant floor manager, Rosemary Gill, and it was arranged for her to fill the gap. Rosemary never returned to her old department and the team of three that created the 'new' *Blue Peter* was formed.

Biddy's story reminds me of my own gate-crashing of the BBC television production empire. I wonder sometimes whether with the new politically correct ways of working, the decision-making that gave both Biddy and me jobs is less likely these days.

Biddy was an only child and had been brought up near Loughborough. It was no accident that the *Leicester Mercury* was a feature of our daily reading as, 17 years later, every day we scoured the national and provincial papers for possible stories.

Biddy, Edward and Rosemary knew that a flow of fresh new ideas was essential. They were determined to use suggestions from viewers – the problem was how to get hold of them. A rich vein of creativity was waiting to be tapped, and how they found it is a story all by itself.

Edward decided that the programme needed a strong symbol to grab the viewers' attention and Tony Hart, a well-known children's programmes artist, was asked to design one. He came up with the blue galleon that is now so familiar, and Edward immediately recognised its importance. He knew that the programme's new identity had to be prominently displayed wherever it was possible to do so. The distinctive blue ship appeared on all the office stationery, the photos of the pets and presenters and, most importantly of all, in the *Blue Peter* studio and on the *Blue Peter* badge.

Biddy decided that they wouldn't be given away but must be won by viewers of all ages. The badge would be awarded for good ideas for the programme, drawings, paintings, interesting letters and poems. This meant that even a four-year-old could win a badge by sending in a drawing, and many did.

To get the badges manufactured the programme needed more money. The budget for each programme in those early days was just £180. (To give you an idea of how little the programme budget was, decades later it was nearer to £60,000 per programme.)

Biddy decided to go and see Donald Baverstock, who was then Assistant Controller of Television Programmes and controlled the purse-strings, and ask for the extra cash. Having been refused an appointment, undeterred she approached his office on the sixth floor of Television Centre and, seeing it was open, she walked in. Baverstock's inner sanctum was through another door to her left and she knocked on it. She entered and proceeded to launch her pitch for extra funds to pay for badges that would generate programme ideas. It worked.

'I think we ought to do this,' Baverstock said, and he summoned Joanna Spicer, his formidable head of Resources.

Spicer was not impressed. 'But, Donald, how can you justify this expense?' she asked.

Baverstock replied, 'It's for ideas for the programme.'

It was an unassailable answer and *Blue Peter* got the money. This open communication between the viewers and the programme resulted in a flood of ideas and contributions of all kinds to the programme. Each badge winner was entered into an index, against which all subsequent letters were checked – so a piece of news given in the first letter would be remembered, recorded and used in the reply. This way Biddy was able to sign letters in reply that made the viewers feel as if they had a personal relationship with the programme. If a second letter was received, the card index was again checked in case there was a reference that could be used. The letters became personal and treasured possessions to the young correspondents.

Biddy remembered all too well her bitter disappointment when as a six-year-old she had written to Enid Blyton twice and received exactly the same letter on both occasions.

Fairness was at the core of the programme and that was why competitions were judged in different age groups: 7s and under; 8s, 9s and 10s; and 11s and over. Later on, for the annual appeal, recyclable items would be requested and not cash so even the poorest viewer could contribute.

Biddy Baxter *was Blue Peter*. And because programme ideas were so important, she carried them about in shopping bags that bulged with letters, press cuttings and publicity handouts. Every morning I would arrive to see press cuttings marked with black felt-tip pen with instructions to her team – 'For Thurs' or 'See me' – in Biddy's large handwriting and laid prominently on each desk.

Only Biddy decided what went into each programme and every

(Right): Legendary *Blue Peter* editor Biddy Baxter at her desk in 1986

transmission was carefully planned. Biddy and Edward had a weekly meeting to decide what went into each programme. Everything was carefully thought through. We, her production team of seven, were in fierce competition to get our own ideas accepted. For every dozen I put forward, maybe only one would get aired.

Television was, and still is, a fickle business. I had joined a highly motivated team, every member of which was fighting for their survival because each of us was only as good as our last item. We had a higher audience than the nine o'clock news and a prestigious reputation to keep up.

Programme ideas came from everywhere – personal experiences as well as viewers' letters, people who phoned in, publicity handouts and the newspapers. And then there were the home-made presents and drawings that viewers sent to the presenters. And from day one I was expected to pull my weight.

(Left): Biddy Baxter, Edward Barnes and Rosemary Gill in the early 1970s

(Above): The team winds down in the *Blue Peter* office in room E101, BBC East Tower, Television Centre in June 2011 before moving north to Media City in Salford

2

Biddy digs her heels in...

8 December 1975
Greenland Dock, London

Presenter Lesley Judd used to be a dancer, which was great for impromptu studio challenges, and she was the perfect older sister role to the younger viewers. She was pretty without being glamorous and a lovely person. Her only flaw was that she smoked.

One day she was sent a dress from Senegal and when it was unpacked a strange creature emerged from its hem. I took it away to be identified at the Natural History Museum. It turned out to be a golden tortoise beetle. Our specimen was alive and made a brief appearance on the programme. It was my first item, and my first responsibility.

I wrote a script, the first of thousands, and tried to imitate the colloquial style of the programme. I told the story of how the beetle had fallen out of the garment and on to the office floor. It didn't surprise me that the script was then almost completely rewritten by Rose. But for a short studio item it went well.

After transmission I put the beetle somewhere safe and forgot about it. A week later Biddy decided to do a follow-up story and demanded its return. I was filled with blind panic. For the life of me I could not remember where I had put it. I searched high and low without success and dreaded the moment when I would have to confess that I did not know where it was.

Meanwhile I was ordered to watch another director, Crispin Evans, direct a film about the Clothes Horse Race Appeal Depot, which had been hastily set up in Greenland Dock in the East End.

At the beginning of the day there was nothing in the huge warehouse to suggest a centre of activity, and then a lorry with all the clothes and tables arrived. I watched, astonished, as a second-hand clothes sorting depot took shape. It was my first experience of 'improvisation'.

During the day, while we filmed ladies sorting piles of clothes, it

got colder and colder. I had a motorbike with a top box filled with clothing for bad weather. It was so cold I opened the box to find a warm top to survive the ride home. Imagine my delight when I discovered what was lurking inside an envelope at the bottom of the box – the very beetle that had gone missing. And it was still alive! You can imagine my relief that I didn't have to face a roasting from Biddy back in the office.

I had several other near misses in those first six months and was warned by the other directors that it was 'Three strikes and you're out'. Teasing or not, I believed every word of it.

23 February 1976
Knightsbridge

I was asked to set up a four-to-five-minute item about the artist L.S. Lowry, who was rumoured to be dying. I found archive film, organised some of his works from a gallery in Knightsbridge, checked their insurance cover, and wrote a script. The gallery owner was happy to lend us the paintings to show in the studio. I was all set and waited for Biddy to set a date.

Then Lowry died. Immediately L.S. Lowry was part of the programme and I was despatched to collect the paintings. Biddy wanted everything in place to rehearse in the studio after lunch. At 11 o'clock I booked a black cab and set off on my errand.

I had allowed an hour or so spare, which was fortunate because when I pitched up in Knightsbridge, the gallery owner had upped the value of the paintings from two million to ten million pounds. The BBC insurance cover was no longer enough. He would not release the pictures without written confirmation that the upper figure was acceptable. Time was running out and I rang the office for help.

I waited anxiously, thinking that my chances of staying on the programme had just been reduced by a third, but within half an hour the extra cover was approved and a despatch rider arrived with the letter of confirmation. I took the four irreplaceable Lowry paintings, precariously balanced against the back seat of a black cab, to the studio, where easels were waiting for them. There was a uniformed BBC security guard to watch over them and no one mentioned the insurance debacle. Thankfully, it was another good item 'on screen'.

All new members had to do their time on the studio floor. At the bottom of the pile of jobs were the 'makes' and items about the *Blue Peter* garden with the legendary Percy Thrower. Lesley often got to do the 'makes' and one of my jobs was to hand her the bits and pieces as she stood behind the 'make' table doing the 'making'. We chatted in between rehearsals and she tipped me off when she thought I had forgotten something. I had more to learn than most, so I spent a lot of time fiddling about with 'sticky-backed plastic' and in the garden, chatting to Percy.

Margaret Parnell, a freelance contributor who invented the makes, would send in her latest idea in various stages of production so they could be 'made' from scratch. Costly, desirable items could be made out of everyday objects like discarded packaging. The viewer could 'have' without having to 'spend' if they put in a bit of effort.

Margaret's imagination was unbounded and her practical mind meant that even an idiot like me could follow the instructions. All I had to do was write a script. At first, I found scriptwriting incredibly boring work and it was a relief to hand it over to Biddy (Biddy wrote the Monday programme script and Rose the Thursday one).

(Above): The massed bands of the Royal Marines performing live in Studio 3 at Television Centre

'Thank you, darling,' she would say – and then proceed to rewrite it completely.

Biddy's scripts were incredibly messy affairs. She wrote with a ballpoint or black felt-tip pen and happily scrawled away, covering yards of old yellow script paper using huge letters. I was always curious to see how much of my original remained. Quite often all that she would allow was a single word – 'and' – and it would be sticky-taped triumphantly in the middle of acres of her untidy writing like a scalp.

On the studio day I would get in early and arrange all the stages of the make, ready to hand in to the presenter. Studio rehearsals would begin promptly at 10.30 a.m. Lighting technicians would crash about, winding the huge lights up and down and adjusting their angles and gels which gave the lights different colours. Sound engineers would have loud conversations into their headsets with no one in particular, and the cameras would glide about, 'blocking' the shots. And in amongst all this we would practise the make.

Biddy knew the make was pivotal for the success of the programme. She wanted the viewers to be able to copy everything we did, so clarity and simplicity were important. We practised it again and again. Every little detail was examined, improved and rehearsed, and I fought to keep up.

Lesley was building a model ranch, and fencing made of cotton thread stretched between matchstick fence posts. I got a message from the gallery relayed by the floor manager.

'How many fence posts can you do? Any chance of a few more?'

I was confident I could do anything within reason and replied, 'As many as you like.'

I should have known better. On demand, the fencing fairly leapt along the side of the farmyard. I looked anxiously at my dwindling store of matchsticks.

Just when I would have had to capitulate, the floor manager said, 'That's enough of that.' And we moved on to the next stage.

'Here's one I made earlier' took on a whole new meaning.

I fell foul of studio protocol more than once. Unaware just how wide the camera angles were, I managed to hand in a piece of the 'make' to Lesley at the wrong moment. There was a muted gasp from the floor manager when my arm from the shoulder down was transmitted to six million viewers.

Linking all the different items in each show was, and still is, an art. For the record it was Biddy who coined the phrase 'And now for something completely different' and not Monty Python.

Crispin Evans, who worked with me on the programme at that time, described the presentation process as a bit like an art gallery where the programme items are hung in the gallery to the greatest effect. And it took a lot of planning and thought.

Every so often the quiet of the studio would be shattered by the sound of Biddy's high heels clattering on the metal steps as she left her eyrie in the gallery and swooped down to the studio floor. She wasn't

(Right): John Noakes with Shep as a puppy

(Far right): Lesley Judd on location in Brazil in 1977

one for small talk so there was only one reason: something wasn't going according to plan. We would all feel our pulses quicken.

Looking back, I now appreciate her constant attention to detail. It's a wearisome business and she must have felt that on occasions she was bashing her head against a brick wall. Everything in every show mattered equally and she would shower as much praise or criticism on a studio item about a pet fish as she would on a film about Lesley Judd descending the Bishop's Rock Lighthouse and nearly falling into the boiling seas.

There were lots of *Blue Peter* style dos and don'ts that were easy to understand and not so easy to interpret. How quickly you picked them up could be the difference between staying and leaving.

I'll give you some examples. It was right to assume that the presenter would have met the contributor before the filming started, so to feature them meeting and shaking hands as if for the first time would be misleading, so we didn't do it.

And because the programme assumed that contributors were always the presenter's friends it would have been natural for the contributor to say 'as I told you before' (because they had already talked about what they were going to do) but, because it sounded odd, we would edit it out.

Other principles were easier to follow, such as giving the presenter a role and something to do. And to avoid repetition there would be no demonstrations on camera about 'how to do it' by the contributor. So, for example, when Peter Purves joined a firefighting team, he would help fight the fire and the contributor would tell him what to do as he did it for the first time, so his mistakes became part of the film.

If the presenter joined a group he or she had to look as if they belonged but stand out at the same time so the viewers could spot them. The much-coveted *Blue Peter* badges were useful, yet not the complete answer. Sometimes a bit of red day-glo tape would help, or a different coloured jumpsuit in the same style.

Interviews on the move, only making films with interesting contributors – there were dozens of things to ponder, and there was only one *Blue Peter* way of doing it. Understanding the rules was easy. Interpreting them in a myriad of different situations wasn't, and in the 1970s and 1980s you either 'got it' or you didn't.

Biddy lived and breathed *Blue Peter* and that was the reason it was the nation's favourite children's programme for so long. She was blessed with inexhaustible energy and determination, and because she cared so much, we did too. Scratch the surface of any of the 'true believers' in the office at that time, and you found a fanatic.

Love her or hate her, room E514 in the East Tower was a temple to the followers of Biddy Baxter. And the sacrifices were made twice a week on a Monday and Thursday at five past five on BBC1.

(Right): Loughborough Carillon, the location of Alex's first *Blue Peter* shoot

3

Losing my *Blue Peter* virginity

One of the more bizarre conundrums is how *Blue Peter* got its name. The more mundane and least satisfactory explanation I was given was that blue was the favourite colour of the programme's first producer, John Hunter Blair, and that his favourite boy's name was Peter.

The romantic in me favours the accepted motive – the very happy coincidence that there's a flag of the same name that is hoisted for 24 hours every time a ship is about to leave port to warn the crew of the impending departure. It's a blue square with a white square centre, and subsequent producers were quick to adopt the idea that each programme set out on a voyage of discovery.

23–24 March 1976

Loughborough

I'll never forget my first film. Directing on location meant a huge increase in responsibility and it loomed like a great black jagged rock in an otherwise smooth sea. Uneasily I looked everywhere for a clue about how to do it.

I asked the most experienced director on the programme about the shooting script and he said, 'So long as it has a beginning, a middle and an end, you'll be fine.'

Another said, 'Shoot every set-up wide and then shoot it close, and then if you've got time shoot the action again. They might get it right the third time round.'

The producer, John Adcock, told me that the cameraman would probably make most of the decisions for me and to consider carefully whatever the presenters suggested because if their advice wasn't good I could waste a lot of time, and there was never enough of that.

John had taken over the responsibility for all *Blue Peter* film making from Edward Barnes, who had established the house style. (Much later

Edward told me that when he started they only had a budget for one day of shooting on 35 mm silent film and he exchanged this for two days on 16 mm with sound for the same budget!) He used the old current affairs programme *Tonight* as a template to work from.

Now it was John, an affable, kindly man who smiled when he told you off, who was to be my mentor. Other budding film-makers of that time agree with me that he was a most effective, excellent teacher. Over the next few years he guided me through the subtleties of film-making and saved me from many dreadful mistakes.

So, shortly before my very first film, I was left wondering what being a film director was really all about. Surely it couldn't be a simple as sounded? I was right – it wasn't.

We had booked into the Bull's Head in Loughborough and after a fretful night worrying about not having brought a *Blue Peter* badge, and not being able to find Peter Purves, who had disappeared from his hotel room, I pitched up at the shooting location, heart racing with anxiety. The badge problem was huge because it was unthinkable to shoot a film without one.

The film idea was my suggestion and was in two parts. It was all to do with bells.

The first part was about casting a replica of the Liberty Bell in Taylor's Bell Foundry, and the second about playing the Loughborough Carillon. A carillon is like a piano except the player uses a clenched fist to punch wooden levers to ring huge bells in a bell tower. The carillon tower in Loughborough is an unsightly square brick construction in the middle of a park.

Reg Pope was the cameraman. He was a familiar and much respected figure on the location sets of BBC Comedy. He worked on productions such as *Some Mothers Do 'Ave 'Em*, *Terry and June* and *The Goodies*. You would have thought he would have had a sense of humour but he seemed to me tough, grey-haired and rather wild, and I saw no sign of one.

In the days of film, before videotape cameras were invented, the cameraman wielded a mysterious art. It was a mixture of experience and gut reaction. Lights were positioned to produce magical results. Their reputation was always on the line, as was mine, but this director would be in no position to argue. On that bleak morning I made my first contact with a real BBC crew and they could see I knew nothing.

Reg was not pleased. We were going to shoot the second part first, and the Carillon was at the top of a long flight of steps.

'How are we going to get the equipment up there?' he asked. The crew looked uncomfortable.

'There's a trapdoor at the top so let's get a rope and haul it up.'

There was a huge pile of equipment: a 'two-man' set of lights that included some big ones, miles of cables, and heaven knows what else.

Anyone could see that a rope was a daft idea and I said so. I grabbed the heaviest box and said, 'Don't worry, I'll do it.'

(Right): Head foundryman Roy Carnall with Peter Purves in Taylor's bell foundry, Loughborough

(Below): Bells waiting to be tuned

(Bottom right): Peter Purves watches as Roy Carnall pours molten metal into a bell mould

Experience had taught me there's no arguing with action, and I was barely halfway up before the rest of the crew joined in. Reg arrived at the top, carrying the film camera, and I pretended not to notice. They weren't happy, but at least they were on side.

After that it all went well, even if the filming itself did happen more by accident than design. Reg was amazingly helpful and did most of the directing for me. And, most important of all, my assistant, Denise, produced a *Blue Peter* badge.

It got better. Over lunch Reg thawed. He told me a horrific story of when he was a newsman in South Africa during some riot or other. He had taken refuge in a hotel lavatory to escape the bloodletting and had survived for three days by drinking the water out of the cistern.

'Didn't they find you?' I asked.

'When you are as scared as I was, you keep very quiet.'

There were other moments. After casting the copy of the 1776 Liberty Bell, the head foundryman Roy Carnall and Peter dug out the earthen core from inside the bell.

'What's in this?' asked Peter.

'Lots of things, including horse manure,' he replied. There was a small pause while they worked on.

'Of course, what we are doing now is the donkey work.'

That was the first of thousands of small moments that I would learn to treasure. I also knew for certain that I had joined the best of the best, working with the sixty-odd film crews that were based at the BBC's Ealing Film Studios.

About the time they were closed down, Reg retired and tragically died of a heart attack the same day. For me it was a salutary lesson about the stresses and strains of working in television. By then I had worked with him on several occasions and I felt very sad.

A director's first film is their nemesis and I watched mine near fruition. Get it wrong and a promising career could be dashed. Get it right and you get an undeserved reputation as a genius. Either way is trouble and luckily I escaped both, and I was definitely not on the 'genius to watch' list.

During 1975 and 1976 I survived a number of studio items and my film-directing career had been launched with a succession of fairly inauspicious stories: excavated Roman waterfronts in Lower Thames Street, London; the Cabinet War Rooms under Whitehall; and the racehorse Red Rum as he received a civic reception in his home town, Southport.

I found an ally in John Noakes, who could not get over the fact that I had sacrificed a career in management consultancy to go into television. His boyish behaviour and youthful appearance made him appear more naive than he really was. He was a joy to work with because there was almost nothing I could do to advise him. John had a formula and he stuck to it. Whatever the circumstance and whoever the contributor, it was always three questions followed by a joke. He thought long and hard to get the joke ready before each interview.

Every director got a break every now and again and mine was in the shape of Nelson's Column. Edward, who was by then deputy head of Children's Programmes, drove past it on his way to work every day and had noticed a ladder being put up the side of it. I was despatched to investigate.

(Above): John Noakes lowers himself over the edge of the pedestal of Nelson's Column

29 April 1977

Trafalgar Square

A few days later I was in Trafalgar Square, watching John Noakes climbing up the Column to help clear the pigeon droppings from Lord Nelson and his plinth on the top. Terry Doe was the climbing cameraman and I did my best to remain in control from the ground. I didn't want to interrupt the action with my walkie-talkie, so it was agreed that they would check in every half an hour. Terry and John would effectively direct the film between themselves.

I mused that, close up, the Column was a lot bigger than it appeared and a great deal taller. There was no room for me at the top even if I had felt the need to climb up, which I didn't. The previous day vertigo had struck me less than halfway up when in a rash moment I thought to give it a go.

Over three decades of filming later I still have no head for heights.

Luckily John suffered from no such affliction but climbing 140 feet vertically on a thin wooden ladder would test his strength and resolve.

(Above): Cameraman Terry Doe films John as he completes the climb

(Right): John fearlessly approaches the pedestal overhang at the top of Nelson's Column

Before the climb he was taught how to conserve his strength by resting every so often with one leg hooked inside the ladder to anchor him.

The climb went well and John confidently progressed up the Column. But near the top there was a very nasty surprise. To get over the edge of Nelson's plinth he had to hang on to the ladder as it leaned outwards at an angle of about twenty degrees as he climbed the last six or eight feet or so.

Moments after John had reached the plinth I got a call from the sound recordist.

'He'll have to do it again. You won't like what you've got so far.'

'Why?' I asked.

'Believe me, it's not transmittable.'

I had no idea what was wrong and the sound recordist was reluctant to discuss it. It could have been a technical hitch. He was perched with Mike Cook, another assistant producer who worked on the programme, and the second cameraman on top of a 100-foot platform hoist on the north side of the square. There was no easy way of checking what was wrong and time was of the essence. I had no option but to ask John to do it again.

To my surprise and relief John complied without a murmur of complaint. Not for the first time I marvelled at his courage.

After an hour or so I noticed a number of photographers gathered around the base of the Column. I counted no fewer than nine and they all had telescopic lenses. The press had got wind of the story. I felt mildly spooked and asked my assistant Denise whether I should be worried. She knew considerably more about these things than I did.

'No way,' she replied.

In the early afternoon dark clouds gathered and threatened bad weather. John felt exposed and worried about a lightning strike. After half an hour they went away, and he had other things to worry about.

He was preparing to go over the edge of the plinth again, this time in a bosun's chair. No safety harness, just a rope brake. The steeplejack told him to face the column, kneel down and ease himself backwards over the edge. John was never short of words:

'You don't have to tell me to kneel down – I'm already praying,' he said, flashing his engaging smile.

It all happened before health and safety became the huge issue it now is. Today we would have to employ rope specialists and additional qualified safety staff to 'mind the minders' who would be minding us. Then it was common sense that ruled and while today's rules were probably broken we never planned to do anything then or since that would knowingly put anyone in any danger.

Later that afternoon I returned to find Biddy, Edward and Rose looking at the late edition of the *Evening Standard,* which had a picture of John dusting Nelson's hat on the front page. Other newspapers followed. It was publicity on a huge scale.

The film became one of John Noakes' finest hours and it was submitted (unsuccessfully) as the BBC's entry to the Monte Carlo 'hard news' award. I really had very little to do with the final production and had only directed a couple of shots in the entire film. My boss, John Adcock, had personally supervised the edit. However, on paper I was the director with another assistant producer, Mike Cook, and it did me no harm at all because half the country had seen it.

Lady luck was definitely with me that autumn because later that month something even more extraordinary happened to me, which was to change my life.

Biddy was ill.

During the entire time that I worked with Biddy I have only known her to take a day off twice. The day in question was 15 December 1977. I was in charge of a family of St Bernard dogs. There were half a dozen pups and much to the disgust of the camera crew they defecated everywhere. The cameramen refused to move their camera pedestal mounts across the affected areas. My job that day was to clean up the dog mess the moment it appeared, to preserve harmony on the studio floor.

Biddy was a strict taskmaster. If your job was to clean up the dog poo, that's what you did and there was no slacking off. But Biddy wasn't there and Edward Barnes was. And he was much more amenable.

On the studio floor I spotted a stunningly beautiful girl who spent most of her time upstairs in the control gallery where the director and editor sat. Normally I would have avoided the gallery yet I was very curious to find out more about this amazing person.

Unusually after programme transmission, production began again because we had to record the studio links for 'Review of the Year', which featured the highlights of *Blue Peter*'s output for the previous twelve months. With no dogs to look after, and no Biddy to worry about, I joined the production team – and our striking visitor – in the studio control gallery. I managed to engage her in conversation and discovered her name was Lynn Bearham. She was on the BBC's first graduate trainee personnel course.

'How long are you here for?' I asked hopefully.

'I'm on attachment for eight hours,' came the reply. 'What do you do?' she asked.

I replied cheerfully, 'I clear up the dog shit.' I wondered what effect my words would have.

'That's very interesting.'

She wasn't put off, and she wasn't being polite, but did she really mean it? At face value I hardly had the most glamorous of jobs so it was a very good sign. Too many people feigned friendship because of 'production' status and it appeared she definitely wasn't one of those. As the evening wore on I couldn't believe my good luck. Here was a girl who was genuinely interested in people – and in particular she was making time for me.

We were married 18 months later.

(Right): Lynn Leger chatting to Rosemary Gill at an end-of-series party

Proj. No.: 03347/9338   NELSON'S COLUMN FILM

                                Directors: Alex Leger
                                            Michael Cook

                                Presenter: John Noakes

                                (JOHN JOINS AT BASE OF
                                COLUMN AND MEETS REG
                                (STEEPLEJACK))

LS NELSON   COMMENTARY:
TILT DOWN TO
SHOW JOHN
JOINING LS

2-SHOT &   JOHN:
FOLLOW JOHN'S
GAZE. TILT UP   Hello! Have I got to climb
TO LADDER.
FOLLOW UP COLUMN   up that ladder ... ?
TO OVER-HANG

                                 COMMENTARY:

                                 Steeplejacks always work with the

                                 minimum of equipment. Instead of

                                 scaffolding they had attached

                                 a tiny wooden ladder up the side

                                 of the column.

- 1 -

(Above): The original shooting script for climbing Nelson's Column. Note the gap left for commentary information due to pressing deadline

4

Noakes: trouper to the end

25–26 October 1977

Southampton

I had twigged that action films made great viewing and I focused on finding more to do. I found a newspaper report about a brand-new fire engine called the 'crew safety vehicle' and Biddy gave me the go-ahead to film it. The idea was to set fire to a derelict building and then use the CSV to rush to the scene with Peter Purves and put the fire out. Peter always threw himself into everything. He was John Noakes's straight man and however hard he tried to be 'hip', he wasn't. He was the consummate professional and on more than one occasion when I asked him to do a second take, I couldn't tell him why.

At first all went well. The fire got going nicely and the crew safety vehicle raced to the scene. Peter grabbed a hose with a fireman and got to work. I watched from the sidelines as the action unfolded.

What I didn't know – and no one had told me – was that they planned to turn the hose from a jet to a fine spray and then close with the blaze to put it out. It was all very exciting and, like the firefighters, the film crew followed the action. Too closely, as it turned out, and, unlike the fire crew, they weren't wearing protective clothing.

Water from the hoses had loosened the upper part of the building and at the critical moment three bricks fell off the top of the building. My career should have ended at that moment. Two bricks missed and the third hit the top of the magazine on the film camera, which just happened to be a fraction higher than the cameraman's head. The film magazine was a write-off but Tony Leggo's head – and my career – was intact.

Back at the office the incident was discussed in detail and I knew my employment had come within a hair's-breadth of a premature end, not to mention a headline in the newspapers.

Nowadays elaborate safety precautions make directors think

carefully about risk, and as a result accidents are much less likely to happen. But risks are still very much part of the whole business of filming and give it a frisson of uncertainty.

Blue Peter always kept an eye on *Magpie*, the programme's opposition on ITV. Their studios were at Teddington Lock and because of its semi-rural setting they were able to have a garden just outside their studio. This seemed like an idea that was worth pinching but the *Blue Peter* studio was in the middle of the steel and concrete of the Television Centre complex – where on earth could we possibly develop a garden? Edward remembered there was a grassy area between the BBC canteen and the outer walls of Television Centre, and, as only Biddy could, she claimed the land for *Blue Peter*.

From that moment it was known throughout the BBC and to millions of viewers as the *Blue Peter* garden. So much of my time was spent there that it felt like a second home. The ritual of the morning video recordings (when the garden items were pre-recorded on to videotape) became second nature to me. And my education about the world of 'live' TV prospered because I was entrusted to supervise the videotape edits after the morning recording was over. At first the magic of invisible editing was to me just that – pure magic – and it took about a year before I could predict, deep in the basement of Television Centre, how the VT engineer would cover up a stumble or a recording break.

However, outside in the garden, and with the legendary Percy Thrower at the helm, things were less mysterious. If I didn't know what to do I asked his advice, and he was never short of ideas. The gardening calendar of planting, weeding, harvesting and tidying up continued unabated. I began to worry that it was all a bit repetitious but was reassured that the whole point was to show how a little effort, clearly explained, could yield huge rewards.

So I plugged away writing probably the most boring scripts in my entire career and waited to be admonished for my lack of imagination. But chastisement never came. It soon became clear that I was just Percy's messenger because Biddy overflowed with ideas herself and thrived on the challenge. She turned my unimaginative, boringly instructive accounts into lively action and reminded me that it was 'bricks out of straw', which pretty well summed it all up. Later and outside, often in the pouring rain, John, Pete and Lesley would dutifully hang on Percy's every word as they planted yet another row of beans, even though they had heard it all before.

One day Biddy and Edward called in Percy Thrower and asked, during lunch in the canteen for his advice about how to extend the garden. Percy gave it a few minutes' thought and then pulled out of his pocket a small brown envelope for triple-folded A4 paper. He began to sketch. We craned our necks to get our first view of his outline plan for an Italian sunken garden.

We all agreed it was a good idea because it would become a place where programme content other than garden subjects could be introduced.

It would also have a pond and therefore increase the programme's scope. Within a few weeks the builders moved in and we filmed their progress.

Our filming was so disruptive that the cost mushroomed. Work had to stop while we filmed the different stages as and when presenters became available. Even so, I remember that the cost was about £7,000, which, considering the value to the programme, was still good value.

One day I had some visitors from my army days and they wanted to see how the programme worked. I was put on my guard because it was my old adjutant and his two young sons. In the army the adjutant was the man to fear the most because he made sure that the colonel, the big boss, got what he wanted. I had treated him with cautious respect while I was in the army, but now out of it and showing them around the *Blue Peter* studio, we were suddenly old friends and he beamed unnervingly with goodwill.

During a break in rehearsals I thought to get them some fresh air and took my small party for a short walk around the ring road that circumnavigated the studios to the now famous *Blue Peter* garden. The Italian sunken garden was finished and I was looking forward to showing it off. We turned the corner by the restaurant block and I noticed with some surprise that there was an upturned chair in the middle of the pond. And that was not all that was wrong.

'It is supposed to be like this?' the eldest son asked.

The penny dropped as I saw that the garden was in a complete mess, even if it was superficial. We had had some unwelcome visitors. Vandals had struck!

'No, certainly not,' I replied, and immediately began to clear it up. I reported our find to the office and we all joined in putting things right again. It didn't take long and soon things were almost back to normal. Then we had a visitor.

'Stop! Biddy wants to make a feature of it.' Our clean-up was halted in its tracks. The cry came from the floor assistant from the studio, out of breath and agitated. The vandalised *Blue Peter* garden was about to make national news.

Two days later, when I returned to witness the morning recording to

show the clean-up in detail, I was amused to see that all my hard work had been undone and the garden had been 'vandalised' (out of necessity) for a second time.

In 2012 Percy's Italian sunken garden followed the programme when it was moved lock, stock and barrel to Media City in Salford.

(Above): The much-loved *Blue Peter* garden, designed by Percy Thrower, shortly after completion in 1978

9–10 May 1978
RAF Lossiemouth, Forres, Scotland

Perhaps more than any other presenter, action man John Noakes epitomised the spirit of *Blue Peter*. His cheeky-chappy, jovial, on-screen persona made him a national institution. So it is with great fondness that I recall the times we worked together on the show.

I had arranged to make a film with John and the RAF Nimrod patrols that policed the fishing in the North Sea. We had arrived and were next to the main runway, preparing to film a Nimrod take-off. Rain was falling like a fine mist. The cameraman had been allocated one of the new Aaton film cameras that were replacing the old Arriflex models. The Nimrod came thundering down the runway and flashed past, blowing a huge gale of misty rain in our direction. The electrics in the camera shorted out and it stopped working. No matter what we did, we could not get the camera to restart.

I told the RAF what had happened. An hour later a C130 Hercules was tasked to fly us down to RAF Brize Norton to pick up a replacement.

Even taking into account the power of the programme, I was surprised. Today, 31 years later, the RAF would charge us a fee just to be there, and Hercules aircraft are all but unobtainable. Looking back, I think it likely that they might have thought that the chance to film with John was too good an opportunity to miss.

26 June 1978
John Noakes's last appearance

This was a day never to be forgotten in *Blue Peter* history. I had the honour of making John's last film. It was about the weather ship that left Gourock in Scotland on its voyage into the Atlantic to record data used today to explain climate change.

True to form, John saved my bacon by turning an otherwise rather dull event into something worth watching. Using all his personality and good humour, he transformed what was essentially just a simple process into what we might call today 'info-entertainment', all the time being sensitive towards the contributors so as not to belittle what they did. When it was approaching four o'clock he saw that I could be running out of time and whispered into my ear that I should bin a whole sequence in favour of getting shots of the ship steaming along. These, we both knew, were essential for the storyline.

As it was, we left the ship too late to catch the London shuttle back to Heathrow and had to spend the night in Glasgow. It was my first experience of the violence that rampaged through the city's streets at night. I lay in my bed in the hotel in Sauchiehall Street and listened to periodic blood-curdling screams and the sounds of smashing glass.

At six I got up and went down to Reception to find it full of policemen, getting warm. They told me to stay inside until after eight. It wasn't safe and they were staying put.

Like all the films, the sounds and commentary were mixed (or 'dubbed') the morning of transmission, and I was surprised to have the debonair Edward Barnes, who had once produced the programme and was now head of department, for company in the dubbing theatre. John hated reading commentary and he would need several goes to get it right. He would stumble over his words and I would share his frustration as he fought angrily to get it done. He never swore, while I might have. He kept his anger well and truly bottled up but we all knew what he was feeling.

As it was his last film, I wondered if I should brace myself for a tiresome moment, but it never came. His last dub 'ordeal' passed off remarkably smoothly and we all heaved a sigh of relief. I liked John and he had never been less than entirely helpful to me.

Even so he was still a bit of a puzzle. John was imaginative in everything he did and he had the capacity to be entertaining by just being himself so I have no doubt that he understood the perils of the many challenges he faced. And after he left the programme he wrote children's books, showing a creative side of his personality that I had not expected. Why, then, when he took on some exceptionally daring exploits, did he show no fear?

I asked him to tell me how he coped and he just said, 'I was afraid of nothing.' And maybe that is the simple answer and even though I find it hard to understand, I should just accept it. He really did not know what fear was, even though he knew that people died doing just what he agreed to do.

So, for me, John is still an enigma. Why he and I got on so well I will never know because we were so very different. But I am glad that we did and I marvel at the respect he gave me. And who could forget what became like an endearing catchphrase, 'Get down, Shep'? Or, of course, the indomitable force of the charming eccentric action man that was John Noakes.

(Above): John Noakes with his inseparable canine companion Shep

5

In at the deep end

In the famously hot summer of 1976 Monica Sims, the then head of Television Children's Programmes, took sabbatical leave for several months and Edward, who was her deputy, became acting head. One of his first assignments was a routine meeting with the Controller of BBC1, Bryan Cowgill. Looking at the audience figures, Cowgill remarked that children's programmes were doing very well on weekday afternoons but badly on Saturday mornings. Edward told him it was because there was no money allocated for Saturday mornings so they were mostly repeats.

'You come up with the programme and I will come up with the money,' said Cowgill.

Edward remembered that the previous year under a different controller, Rosemary Gill had suggested a programme based on the letters that regularly came into *Blue Peter,* which could be used as a vehicle to enable children to swap items with one another – a TV 'swap shop'. Edward had previously devised a programme called *Z Shed,* hosted by a young disc jockey from Radio 1 (Noel Edmonds), which encouraged children to ask for advice about a variety of problems, ranging from too much homework to bullying. They could write letters or telephone 'live' into the programme and this was the first time a phone-in had been used in children's television. This element had worked well; Noel was a genius at creating a rapport with children of all ages.

Edward, Biddy and Rose discussed how these ingredients could be developed into a seamless, three-hour Saturday morning programme and Edward decided that Biddy should be the editor and Rose should take her place as editor of *Blue Peter.* Biddy, however, decided she couldn't desert *Blue Peter* and so it was Rose who took these bare ingredients and added an enormous amount more to create the great Saturday morning programme *Multi-Coloured Swap Shop.* It subsequently dominated Saturday-morning television and became a ratings winner.

The upshot of this was that Biddy, in her indomitable way, took over the writing of all the scripts, which I thought quite mad even if it was the way she wanted it.

Peter Purves left in March 1978, and with both John and Pete gone, the loss of two such big personalities meant life for Lesley Judd was difficult.

Change was well and truly in the air. Lesley had been offered a job at Southern TV, which suited her because her boyfriend was unwell and lived in Hampshire. She agreed to stay on a further six months to ease in Simon and Chris and it was a very demanding time for her. To me, Lesley was the last of the 'old school' and she instinctively knew what was needed in every situation. Making a film about Red Rum at Southport, she interviewed the jockey and, because he was very hard to understand, she repeated his replies. Only when it came to the edit did I realise how helpful she had been. In truth, working with her as a director, there was very little I could advise. When she left, all that changed and I was very sorry to see her go.

She left the programme in 1979 and the once well-oiled presenting machine, which was already running lumpily, almost stalled from the shock. Change had come at a price. Directors were suddenly required to judge and direct presenter performance because Simon and Chris were new to television; only Tina Heath, a successful actress who took Lesley's place on the team, came with any experience.

Tina, petite and friendly, will be likely to be better remembered as the first *Blue Peter* presenter to become pregnant while working

on the show and have a live ultrasound scan to prove it. This was not only breaking new ground in children's television: it was simply ground-breaking television in those days.

Tina came to *Blue Peter* through her starring role as Lizzie Dripping in a successful children's drama series. She was an accomplished actress and her experience of television was essential to support the other two.

Watching her at work, I thought that she seemed vulnerable, even if she was very capable. Yet she must have felt the pressures of the live programme. Like it or not, she was the bedrock of the studio presentation and items with long, detailed information came her way more often than not. For the boys, learning the script was a huge task because it's a technique that takes years of practice.

Christopher Wenner, who had joined the programme six months before, seemed to find it particularly hard to remember his words. Good looking, public-school educated, he would screw his eyes up with the effort of trying to remember what came next and we kept our fingers crossed that he wouldn't 'dry'.

On location and sticking resolutely to the prescribed film script, Chris could struggle to remember even three sentences in a row. After a few films I learnt to make his speeches as short as possible and allow at least thirty minutes' recording time for each one.

Filming behind the scenes with *The Onedin Line*, a popular BBC drama serial with Peter Gilmore who starred as James Onedin, we spent well over an hour in Falmouth dock trying to get one 'piece to camera' (as they are called in the industry) 'in the can'.

Chris had a mental block and nothing could dislodge it. I should have put the offending lines into out-of-vision commentary (which is where, on reflection, they belonged) but I was young, determined and inexperienced. So the struggle continued, and we got there in the end.

Several days later, looking at the 'rushes' in the *Blue Peter* cutting room on the second floor of the East Tower in Television Centre, I saw seagulls come and go in the background and the clouds arrive and depart as the minutes passed and take followed take. It was like a slow-motion time lapse of all life in that little corner of Cornwall and I wondered if I had acted wisely by being so persistent. I hasten to say that Chris was not alone with this affliction and other presenters would get mental blocks, but not all as regularly as he did.

The shoot had an unexpected bonus both for me and for Chris. During a second day's shooting we had to spend a day out at sea off Brightlingsea on the *Soren Larsen*, the square-rigged sailing ship that was the other star of the show. We filmed on and around the vessel as the winds filled all her sails and she cruised (to all intents and purposes) the oceans of the world.

(Left): Christopher Wenner, Tina Heath and Simon Groom in the studio, celebrating Goldie's birthday

The shots were stunning and were later used in *The Onedin Line*'s programme titles. At their request I gave our original negative film to the programme's producers, and they trawled through it to glean numerous useful 'cutaways'. It was a small thing, but even this faint whiff of the heady world of greasepaint gave me great satisfaction.

Chatting to Chris that day (16 May 1980) he told me that he was thinking of leaving the programme. He asked what he should do if he wanted to produce documentaries. In truth, I thought he didn't stand a hope in hell, just as I didn't, in the deeply competitive world of documentary film-making and I glibly suggested that he would stand the best chance if he went where few others dared to go, namely war zones. Several years later Chris did just that and carved out a prestigious career as a war reporter!

He began in San Salvador, where there was a vicious drugs war, and moved on to other places, including East Timor, where he won an award for a particularly daring piece of reporting and film-making. As a result of the latter I heard that he had to use the name Max Stahl, using a combination of his middle name and his mother's maiden name, because he would have been arrested if he had returned under his original one.

He met and married Liz Trubridge, who was an assistant on the programme. She went on to become a successful drama producer and she produced the prestigious ITV drama series *Downton Abbey*.

I bumped into her during the period when Chris was under cover with the drug gangs that had turned Bierut into another war zone. She had not heard from him in over a fortnight and was concerned for his safety. Needless to say, he survived.

Chris was hard not to like.

9–10 June 1979

Topsham, Devon

In a rash moment I suggested that we make a film for *Blue Peter* about a local custom at my home town in Devon where I was brought up. 'Mud football' had been played as a joke by the salmon fishermen and the sailing club. The 'pitch' was the brown, glistening mudflats that appeared every 12 hours at low tide. Not for nothing is Topsham nicknamed 'Topsham-on-the-Mud'.

Biddy and Rose loved the idea and they pursued me ruthlessly for a date. Spurred on by the joy of actually making a film about my beloved Topsham, I found energy I didn't think I had and organised the whole event from scratch. Everything from the crash barriers, helpfully collected free of charge by a local truck driver, to the public commentary, which was taken off my hands by volunteers from Topsham Round Table. Even the town crier was roped in.

Chris excelled himself by throwing himself into the spirit of it all and, no longer tongue-tied, he happily ad-libbed liberally to camera. I over-heard my great-uncle Roscoe (retired Colonel of the Royal Engineers) asking the cameraman, Mike Coles, how I was getting on. I didn't catch Mike's reply.

The teams taped up their trousers so they wouldn't get too bogged down in the goo, and ran down the high street to the mudflats below the church steps. In a natural arena where the road runs parallel to the river, the spectacle unfolded until the tide turned.

Back in the office Rose loved the film because it was about a local community. I learned that grass-roots items were to be treasured because they were her favourites. Later, visiting my mum back home, I found that just about everyone I knew in Topsham had seen it and approved. It was a great relief because had the reverse been true, I would never have lived it down.

It had been an exhausting film to organise and shoot. I had learned that, more often than not, the best film subjects do not come from a publicity handout or from high-profile events. The Topsham mud football was new information and vivid entertainment for the viewers. We had letters from potential competitors for the following year's event sent in from all over the UK.

4 February 1980
Marlow, Buckinghamshire

By now Tina had been on the show for several months and yet our paths hadn't crossed. Then along came a story about Margaret Beer, who bred death's-head hawkmoths, and to my delight Tina was to present it.

Margaret was a very good talker and on the day of the shoot the stage was set for some interesting moth conversation against a backdrop of what I hoped would be spectacular moth action.

Tina's questioning was so good that the flow of information was seamless. She listened carefully to Margaret's answers and there wasn't a point made that wasn't turned into a line in the plot. Even the moths looked good.

Back on the second floor of the East Tower at Television Centre in the cutting room, the film was put together with very little effort. We had nearly nine minutes of chat and informative pictures. No commentary was necessary, and therein was the flaw.

I was obsessed with the perfect symmetry of the film, undisturbed as it was with words that did not come from the spontaneous interaction between the two. I failed to see the major fault with it. The overall film lacked, for want of a better word, punctuation. There were no dramatic pauses or moments that could only have been signposted by a well-written line or two. It was also probably two or three minutes too long. Not because the information wasn't valuable: there was just so much of it.

Looking back at the film a year later, I saw with dismay that my 'perfect' film was a duologue. Not a bad duologue, but a duologue all the same. It was a lesson well learnt.

Tina was calm and unflappable, and she had a great reputation for being utterly professional. That was how she appeared to us but in reality she was like a swan fighting the current, and all the effort was out of sight. Years later I asked her about this time and she replied:

> As an actor, taking on the job of presenting *Blue Peter* is shockingly hard. Actors are used to learning scripts. Most actors feel that if a line has been written in a certain way, that initially doesn't feel 'comfortable', it is our job to tease out the writer's intention and to understand how to deliver the line. Having that frame of mind, with regard to the seemingly relentless amount of print on every script page with my name alongside it, was the stuff of nightmares for someone who sought to be word perfect. The fear of brain freeze was ever-present.

15–18 April 1980
Westminster Abbey

(Above): Actress Tina Heath, who joined the programme as a presenter in 1979

Every so often we would make historical films written by the programme's historian Dorothy Smith, and Westminster Abbey in the heart of London was chosen to be one of them. By now Tina was well into her pregnancy and quite naturally very sensitive to anything that could harm her unborn child. I did not consider how much the unborn baby would grow in just a few weeks while the film was being planned. And therein lay my mistake.

I had to negotiate every part of the shoot very carefully with the Abbey staff and this took more time than was prudent. They warned me that no lighting stands could be used because they might scratch the priceless and ancient floor tiles. Yet some light was essential because it was, in Devon-speak, a bit dimpsy inside.

After research we chose to use 'faster' film stock in the camera because it would work better in low light. We also looked for the most muscular lighting technician at Ealing Film Studios who would be able to carry several heavy battery lamps at the same time. Each battery weighed about twenty pounds and we had ordered ten of them.

On the day Nigel Meakin, of Michael Palin's travels fame, was the cameraman and a nicer man you couldn't hope to meet. Nigel quickly moved between set-ups and Tina was word perfect as usual. John, the lighting tech, surprised us all by walking about with three batteries over each of his massive arms and without a word of complaint.

We saved the best sequence until last. And this was the climb up the tower.

No *Blue Peter* film was complete without going to the top of whatever building was being filmed. I blindly followed this practice without due consideration for poor Tina's condition. She was by now heavily pregnant. She could barely walk, let alone climb a daunting series of long ladders to the top of the tower.

So it was an understandably very cross Tina who eventually appeared on the ancient windswept tower roof. I did my best to placate her and realised too late that it had been unreasonable to ask her to make the climb. She recovered enough of her composure to deliver her usual polished performance. I thought I had got away with it but back in the cutting room John Adcock observed that Tina 'didn't look best pleased'! I believed that was an understatement of how she really felt. She told me:

> Unlike the chap carrying all of those batteries up to the summit of the Abbey, I could not lay my burden down, even for a second! Oh, happy days! Indeed, as I recall it was a further six weeks before Jem arrived – beautifully timed at 3.30 p.m. on a Monday, giving the 'scoop' to that day's programme, at 5 p.m. I recall Biddy sending congratulations to me on my perfect timing and professional delivery!

Blue Peter *office, E514 East Tower, Television Centre*

Every Tuesday morning the production team of seven or eight producers and assistant producers would gather in a half-circle around Biddy to hear the audience figures from the previous week. Immaculately dressed in a figure-hugging dress and high heels as always, she sat, legs crossed, as she studied the charts.

She equated a high audience with a good programme and, while she was probably right, I always suspected that a good viewing figure was often the result of the previous programme. It was almost as if viewers had said to their friends, *You should have watched* Blue Peter *last night. Lesley Judd nearly had her collar ripped off by a chimpanzee.* And more people would tune in for the next programme just in case.

At university in the late 1960s, I used to watch, provided something really good happened every month or so. If there was a run of five or six dull programmes I would switch off until something hit the headlines. I thought it reasonable to assume that regular viewers behaved the same way so the pressure was always on to keep the surprises coming.

By now I had produced a dozen films and hadn't killed anyone. I also had a permanent job on the programme, and following the pattern of all assistant producers it was time for the next challenge – studio direction.

For sheer power and adrenalin there isn't a lot that can beat a 'live' studio. As a novice it was frightening to see an experienced studio director in full swing, calling the shots during a live transmission.

A team of about forty camera, lighting and sound technicians pooled their expertise while the director coordinated the whole operation through the vision mixer, who cut or switched between the cameras.

For a *Blue Peter* programme there were usually five cameras and they performed a sort of ballet on the studio floor as they changed shots. What was seen by millions of viewers was the direct result of what the director said in the studio gallery. It was a huge responsibility and one that kept me awake at night. Studio days had to be meticulously planned.

Bringing together each programme took a full day in the studio and it was quite a palaver. It began with the programme script that Biddy would finish writing the day before (with the exception of Monday's show, which was always finished on Friday). Only then did the director get hold of it. His or her job was to plan and position the set with the help of the set designer, and then mark on the script which camera would get what shot for each passage in the script.

The director would also have to edit the video inserts from the studio recordings. Hours were spent in the basement of Television Centre where all the video editing equipment was housed. The format was clunky two-inch 'quadruplex' tape, so called because it required four magnetic recording heads and nearly 5,000 feet of tape just to record an hour of television. It may have revolutionised the industry when it was first introduced in the 1950s but the scale of the material meant it was impossible to preview the tape in anything but real time. We relied on the assistants to record the precise timings of everything on the tape. Miss the junction and valuable minutes would be spent watching the tape spooling through in real time, hunting for the required piece. On studio days, when there was a morning recording, the director often worked through lunch to get the inserts ready.

I asked the most experienced director, Ian Oliver, whether he thought I was capable of directing the studio. Ian was renowned for going 'off piste'. He would call the camera shots as he went along and made up many of them at the last minute. He really did fly by the seat of his pants. So when I posed my question his reply was both humorous and serious.

'Can you spell "As directed"?'

'Olly' would write 'As directed' as the total camera instruction for pages of Biddy's detailed script. His point was that to be a good director you had to look for extra shots that would add to the overall presentation. Rather like a pilot of a plane, it was wise to keep one eye on the flight instruments for stability yet keep the other on where you were going. Too much attention to the instruments and the flight would become mechanical and unimaginative. So it was with studio direction.

12 November 1979
Studio 3, Television Centre

My first studio direction day was the usual mixed bag: a school tapestry; the airbrushing of a portrait of Jack and Jill (the cats) to be finished live; a Rolls Royce mobile picture gallery; and an interview with John Pilger, a well-known Australian television journalist.

The day progressed as each shot was blocked and the cameramen rehearsed the shot that I had allocated to them. The composition of each shot was discussed and changed, and the *Blue Peter* ship, in the form of a large Perspex cut-out, suspended from the studio roof, was framed in the back of every shot.

Like all new directors at the time I had absolutely no practical training and was quickly thrown in at the deep end. Whether or not I would direct another studio would depend on how quickly I caught on.

We stuck to the rehearsal timetable and everything was surprisingly easy until the moment that run-through (dress rehearsal) was over. And then it all got very complicated and stressful.

The timings for each item had to total exactly 24 minutes, the 'live' slot allocated to us on BBC1. Some items were too long and had to be trimmed. This was done by cutting sections of the script, and the assistant could calculate how many seconds each trim saved. I could cope with this, but Biddy had something more drastic in mind. She wanted to change the order of presentation.

Everything we had rehearsed during the day had to be revised because the handovers, from one item to another, were completely different. Some shots had to be reallocated to different cameras. It was a bit like trying to keep a dozen plates spinning at the same time.

My mind was still reeling from the rehearsals and to change it all at the last minute was almost the last straw. Minutes flashed by as I worked out as many of the alterations as I could. Panic surged through me as live transmission loomed.

Olly leaned over my shoulder and advised me to tell the camera crew about the script and shot changes only up as far as the seven-minute film, and then do the rest while the film was being transmitted 'on air'.

'Off piste' Olly was in his element. I think he was aching to take over. I wish I could have enjoyed it as much as he did.

'Five minutes to transmission,' the studio assistant called.

There was a gallery clock facing me and at two minutes, two little cue dots appeared in the top left corner of the screen. The last minute lasted an eternity and at ten seconds the dots disappeared, the assistant counted down to zero and we were live on BBC1.

I can't remember much of what followed except that I had a lot of help from the vision mixer and Olly hardly chipped in at all. To my surprise Biddy was not upset when it was all over. She rushed out of the gallery to tackle the presenters about what they'd done wrong.

'See you in the bar. Thank you, everyone,' Olly said over the studio communication system.

I started to tell the crew how grateful I was but I was talking to myself. The communications had gone dead as the crew unplugged everything and hurled themselves into a frenzy of packing up. It was the quickest I had seen them move all day.

By six o'clock the BBC bar was crammed and I was buying drinks for everyone. As I began to unwind I realised that Biddy had treated the whole day as normal, which in itself was a huge compliment. She wasn't one to ignore things that went wrong.

The studio was always the most important part of the show because it played the part of a sitting room, the inside of a house where the family gathered to watch. The films were what happened outside. A great deal of thought went into the look of the studio because it was the hub where everything happened.

For the first 35 years the studio set consisted of shelf units and seating units, which were freestanding furniture items that could be placed anywhere on a grey-painted studio floor within a white cyclorama (single-coloured backdrop). It meant that within seconds the space could be used by a marching band or a troupe of Chinese acrobats. The whole set was lit to peak white.

It was cheap, flexible, distinctive and effective. The huge *Blue Peter* logo, which was suspended from the studio roof, hung against the cyclorama and was tethered to the studio floor to stop it blowing about in the air-conditioning. It was part of the style to keep it in the back of every shot, and it wasn't an easy thing to do. It was a bit like a Chinese puzzle, fiddling with camera angles, and it made an otherwise simple task much more difficult.

In 1982 the shelf units and the single central *Blue Peter* ship were abandoned in favour of a substantial set with ship emblems on every shelf unit. It made directing a lot easier.

In 1990 a black cyclorama and subdued lighting were a major change. They gave the programme a more modern feel yet I mourned the loss of simplicity and the distinctiveness of the earlier style.

Following the usual pattern, I directed studios in blocks of four, six, even twelve programmes at a time – without a break – every Monday and Thursday. It was rather like playing a musical instrument, using your mind rather than your fingers. In time I grew to like the buzz yet it never really satisfied me. In truth I found the confines of the studio a bit restricting and I missed the risk of film direction. And the proximity of Biddy, who always sat at the end of the control gallery, was a burden because she constantly monitored and commented on everything that went on. That was her job.

Although her demands were not unreasonable, she was impatient and I would struggle to keep up. Towards the end it was bit like a race, with me crashing away trying to get ahead of the 'Keep the dog's paws in,' and other comments.

It came to a head one day when I was given a drama-trained vision

(Above): Alex calls the shots directing a live programme from Studio 3's control gallery alongside vision mixer Hilary Briegel (left), production assistant Denise Evans and Biddy Baxter (far right)

mixer who instinctively cut after key words and not, as Biddy preferred, before or on them. The particular key word was 'this'. Biddy would insist on the shot being changed a millisecond before 'this' so whatever 'this' was, it was in vision instantly. And I agreed with her. Try as I might, I could not get the vision mixer to push the button at the desired moment. I was truly between a rock and a hard place and it was very frustrating.

Transmission arrived like Armageddon, as it always did, and at the end Biddy stood up and said, 'That show was a mess and peppered with late cuts.'

Something in me snapped. Angrily I blurted out that I'd had enough and didn't want to direct her poxy little programme anyway. The gallery went dead quiet and Biddy glared at me, red-hot colour in her cheeks. I knew I had gone far too far. Then, aware that everyone was listening, she turned and swept out of the gallery.

In truth I didn't mean it and I spent the night ruminating on my likely future outside children's programmes. Others had been sacked for less.

The next day I arrived outside the office at a quarter to nine to find Biddy struggling with the key.

'Sorry, Biddy. Didn't mean what I said. Got carried away,' I said. To my surprise Biddy was quite light-hearted about it all.

'Don't worry, darling, we all say things we don't mean.' And that was it. No instant dismissal. Nothing.

I escaped the studio as soon as I could.

(Above); Celebrating 25 years of *Blue Peter*. Biddy runs through the programme with presenters Peter Duncan, Janet Ellis and Simon Groom

6

Marching orders

All through the latter half of 1977 working conditions became more and more of an issue with the show workers who built and struck the studio sets. Long and irregular hours were the nub of the problem. Unlike producers and assistant producers (who were then called production assistants), they had a choice. They could work for ITV or in corporate television. Eventually, in December/January 1978, there was a strike.

It was a huge dilemma for the *Blue Peter* team. Should we cross the picket line? We weren't members of the union and jobs like ours were as rare as hen's teeth. Also, we were expected to give our all. That was the price we paid and many had started their careers in the theatre, where life was really tough. We sympathised, and had other thoughts. It may seem like the cowardly option but I arranged to be out on location when the picket line was in place. Everyone heaved a sigh of relief when eventually the strike was settled.

In between directing the studio I was out and about with the rest of the team, directing more films, and I quickly found out that crews and their directors also worked until they dropped. It soon became evident that the BBC did not have a bottomless pit of cash. In an effort to keep programme costs down, yet more and more work was loaded into each filming day so 13-to-15-hour days were not infrequent. Camera crews began to resent the amount of time they spent on the road.

I was in no position to resent anything. I worked as hard as I could because there were plenty of other would-be directors who wanted my job. Perhaps this was no bad thing. I have always believed that a certain amount of paranoia helps to keep people on their toes.

At the end of a filming day, as I drove back from location to arrive home late at night, my legs and knees would ache unbearably. It wasn't as a result of rushing about because directing meant a lot of standing still and patience. It was the stress of feeling the minutes tick by and not being able to do a thing about it. There was a constant fear that we would not finish the filming in time. Being able to run about would have been a welcome release.

It didn't end there. Every six months or so I would collapse with the cumulative stress and endure 48 hours of continuous vomiting while the tensions eased. My anxious wife, Lynn, learnt to steer well clear and wait. Then after my body had done its thing, miraculously, I would be ready to crack on, as they say. It happened so regularly that after a while we got used to it.

I was not alone. Almost everyone in the production team expected to be ill every time the programme came off the air for the summer break. We all cared passionately about the output and it was this passion that produced the memorable moments that shaped young lives. The cost, however, was far from palatable: days of stomach-wrenching unpleasantness. And the film crews suffered collateral damage from our determination.

On 23 May 1978 I directed a film in London about the Post Office underground railway. Lesley Judd travelled its length in a carriage scarcely bigger than her seat, and we faithfully retraced the journey overland, fighting the rush-hour traffic. The resulting film, which ended with the Wombles of Wimbledon Common singing 'Underground, overground, wombling free' to images of both journeys, was not one of my finest moments. It was a 16-hour day and exhausting, yet still cheaper to us than spreading it over two separate days.

The inevitable happened. Money or no money, the crews could take it no longer. Rather than strike, BBC Ealing film crews began a work to rule. For a short period in September 1978 everything had to be done in a ten-hour day. It was a huge relief all round. Suddenly two days filming were better than one, and life was bearable once more. However, the bouts of vomiting brought on by stress continued well into the 1980s.

16 February 1979
RAE Farnborough

We often featured challenges of derring-do around the world, launching the expeditions in the studio before they set off. One day Biddy gave me a press release about a brand-new challenge.

A large hangar at the Royal Aircraft Establishment at Farnborough was the opening scene for a historic expedition that was to become part of my life for the next three years. It was also where lifelong friendships started.

There were crowds of people, photos being taken and lots of 'kit' to look at. Transglobe was planning to make history by becoming the first team to circumnavigate the globe about its polar axis. My contact was team member Oliver Shepard, who was charming and confident.

The expedition leader was the larger-than-life adventurer Sir Ranulph Fiennes, already a household name and latterly described by

The Guinness Book of Records as the 'world's greatest living explorer'. His wife was no shrinking violet either. In fact, Ginny Fiennes was the first woman to receive the Polar Medal. During the media melee she was perched uncomfortably on her husband's lap as the photographers snapped away.

She may have looked nervous about all the press attention yet I was soon to learn that Ginny was as single minded as Biddy, and just as scary to do business with.

The Transglobe Expedition was meant for *Blue Peter*. It was everything that we looked for in a studio item. There was adventure, adversity, discovery, and the expedition members were charming and completely honest. Like Biddy, Ginny was always true to her word. I signed them up to bring their equipment – everything I had seen – to the studio. I think Ginny complied because it was the most outrageous request she had ever received.

'Alex, do you really mean *all* our equipment?' She rang me twice to confirm I actually meant it.

We compromised, but not by much. They filled the studio with a cardboard house, skidoos and piles of kit. Ranulph Fiennes and his team – Charles Burton, Oliver Shepard and Simon Grimes – got dressed up in wolfskins and sweated under the studio lights. Biddy took a shine to Ginny and pledged that the programme would follow the expedition until they returned in three years' time.

As agreed, I made a film about their ship the MV *Benjamin Bowring* in London Docks and watched them depart. With Ginny's help and cooperation from Radio Portishead we set up a telephone link and rang them up for live reports from both Poles. To get in touch I had to alert Radio Portishead and ask them to tell Ginny, when she next reported in, to ring us on a certain day at a certain time, which was always an hour before our live transmission. Ginny and I would then

(Right): The Transglobe team in the studio. (from left to right): Oliver Shepard, Simon Grimes, Sir Ranulph and Ginny Fiennes with the expedition mascot Bothy, Christopher Wenner and Charles Burton

chat until the moment for 'run-through', when the show was practised for the last time. Half an hour later, on transmission, Ran – as he preferred to be called – would come on line and join in. After a few of these lengthy calls I felt Ginny was a friend.

On one occasion when they were at Alert in the Arctic I got her on the phone and she sounded tense.

'Can't talk because we need the battery power. We had a fire last night and there's a lot to sort out. Talk again soon. Sorry, Alex.'

I can hear her voice even now. They had lost half their equipment and heaven knows what else in a terrible fire that had destroyed their storage hut. I marvelled at her nerve because Ran was out on the ice with the others and she was alone apart from Simon Grimes, who was her assistant. The dwindling battery power for the radio was all she had between the most isolated spot in the world and help.

When the Transglobe team returned in triumph, sailing up the Thames to Greenwich in August 1982, *Blue Peter*'s was the only film crew that was allowed on board. I was amused when a *BBC News* reporter asked whether he could borrow my crew for his report. It nearly choked him. There was a lot of snobbery in television, and *News* thought they were rather grand.

While Ran and Prince Charles toured the ship I was summoned to join the guests on the quarterdeck. To my amazement I found myself in conversation with Armand Hammer, the film producer, whose *House of Horror* had been the meat and drink of my cinema-going youth.

Very sadly Ginny died in February 2004 and Ran asked me to help him create a video record of her life. Ginny had never been one for the limelight and I am sure, if she was looking down on us, she would have been very embarrassed, but pleased at the same time.

The same week the MV *Benjamin Bowring*, with the Transglobe Expedition team, steamed up the Thames, our first child, Lauren, was born.

16–17 September 1981

Mont St-Michel

The programme's historian, Dorothy Smith, the wife of long-time *Blue Peter* producer Edward Barnes, was a kindly, motherly figure and very good to beginners like me. She was a useful source of information and I often posed my own problems in a casual way knowing she would discuss them with Edward. As Edward was head of department, they would disappear.

In later years the programme's researchers would fulfil the historian role, but those days were yet to come and Dorothy was the only researcher the programme had. Her scripts focused on contemporary storylines, as well as the historical. One of these was about the twin islands of St

(Above): Simon Groom on the Transglobe ship MV *Benjamin Bowring* on her return to Greenwich

Michael's Mount in Cornwall and Mont St-Michel in France. For me it meant going abroad to film for the very first time.

To make it economically possible we had to find other stories to film while we were there. I noticed that Mont St-Michel was just around the bay from Cancale, a centre for oyster farming. Sarah Greene was the presenter; a charming young lady with theatre in her soul and a winning smile even when she was telling you off.

An essential part of every *Blue Peter* film is the taking part, so swallowing an oyster was essential for the plot. No one had warned Sarah about this and it came as an unpleasant surprise to me when on location she told me she couldn't eat one because she was allergic to oysters. Two years previously she had ended up in hospital and had been told never to risk eating one again.

Now, I love oysters and I am constantly surprised by the number of people who can't or won't eat them. I was so driven by the need to succeed I was not as sympathetic as I should have been. The cameraman, Kevin 'Ripples' Rowley (because of his muscular build), was a bit of lady's man and not on my side. He had been quick to go to Sarah's defence over the oysters and Sarah had to all but pull him off me.

Sarah, however, was adamant. Not a single oyster was going to pass her lips. Nothing I said could persuade her otherwise.

'You'll have to explain that you can't eat oysters,' I said. 'The viewers deserve to know.'

Sarah's resistance was as strong as an unopened oyster's.

'No.'

This was getting tricky because if she wasn't going to eat one then at least she should explain why.

'Why not?'

My attempts to elicit a response proved futile.

That evening we were surrounded by the locals, who were literally tossing oysters down by the dozen. I got an idea.

The next day at breakfast I tackled Sarah again.

'What if you say that while you can't eat oysters yourself, you admire the style of those who can – and then we show lots of locals literally tossing them back. Make a feature of it.'

Sarah considered this for some time. She knew that we had to do something to keep faith with the programme style.

'All right.'

After the oyster episode, I always warned the presenters what they were going to be asked to do. And I had learned the hard way not to get too attached to the script.

Sarah had studied drama at university with award-winning director Anthony Minghella (who directed *The English Patient* amongst other films), and had worked in repertory theatre in Manchester and Birmingham before joining *Blue Peter*. I liked her very much despite her resistance to oysters.

I remember one studio day there was a very uncomfortable young man (younger than me anyway) lurking about in a light grey-blue suit.

(Below): Sarah Greene signing autographs at the Cat Show at Olympia

He was a friend of Sarah's and he was obviously very keen on her. I recognised him from an ITV children's programme, *CBTV*, because I had seen him present a film item about scarecrows. I thought he was good and told him so. Sarah grabbed him from me and disappeared.

That was the first time I met Mike Smith, and a nicer man you couldn't hope to meet. Biddy had also spotted him and, according to Mike, had said to Sarah, 'Is that your bank manager?'

Sarah and Mike were married in 1989. Mike now owns a helicopter company specialising in aerial photography and quite often we meet at *Blue Peter* reunions. It brings back very happy memories. Three decades after the oyster-eating episode, Mike bought an old Porsche and Sarah was amused to see that the cameraman in France, Kevin Rowley, had been a previous owner.

Then in early 1983 my world fell apart.

7

A mountain to climb

21 February 1983
St Mary's Hospital, Roehampton

We had been married for three years when Lynn and I suffered a major tragedy. Lauren, our baby of just six months, died of pulmonary atresia, which means she was born without a pulmonary artery between her heart and her lungs. What she needed, and couldn't get, was a heart-lung transplant. We went into a kind of hell and I took several weeks off.

When I returned to the office, Biddy could see that my heart wasn't really in the programme any more and I'm sure she understood my misery. It could not have been easy for her because I believe I might have become something of a liability. With only a small team of four or five to keep the programme going, she desperately needed me 'on side' and working productively. She told me later that, believing that 'the only antidote to grief was to immerse you in something else', she had looked about for a solution.

Meanwhile, I was so lost in myself that I had even lost my fear of her, which is saying something. Our lives were so empty without our beloved child.

But life went on. And then, two months after Lauren's death and only a few weeks after returning to work in the office, something happened to bring me back to normality.

18 April 1983
Television Centre, London

Biddy came into the office one Monday morning, looked at me and said, 'Etna's erupting. Go and film it. I want it for next Thursday.' Meaning next Thursday's programme.

Then she sat down and added, 'And I don't want to pay for flights or excess baggage.'

Mount Etna was a volcano that had been erupting in Sicily. It is the largest volcano in Europe and one of the most explosive in the world. In 1983, Etna vented its fury for 130 days.

The fame of the programme at that time was such that everyone could see the benefit of *Blue Peter* publicity. So airlines would give us free tickets and quite often an excess baggage allowance as well. It was an arrangement that had mutual benefits. And so it was for the flights out to Sicily.

Nowadays, when we go abroad, money always changes hands.

22–24 April 1983
Mount Etna, Sicily

As the sun went down that Friday night, I found myself about half a mile below the summit of Mount Etna, mesmerised by a hissing sea of molten rock as it flowed down the slope a few yards away. The sheer power of nature spewing its guts out on to the surface of the earth was mind-boggling. Simon Groom was the presenter and he was just as overwhelmed:

> There was a terrifying inevitability about the lava flow: we filmed it moving inexorably down the hillside, burning and devouring everything in its path...

(Left and above): The lava flow from Mount Etna

By this time we had made several films together and I found him good company. Tall, rangy and quick to smile, he was just the kind of presenter I preferred to have with me on an erupting volcano. Simon could always be relied on to know his words and deliver them with conviction. And that night, within a few metres of instant death, speed was important.

> I remember getting as close to the lava flow as I could and performing a classic *Blue Peter* trick: frying some eggs and bacon – in record time!

Much farther down the volcano there were sudden flares of yellow flame as trees were instantly incinerated. Even though we had been up since dawn, travelling, we could have stayed and watched it all night.

The lava rock flowed like runny porridge and glowed red hot as it twisted and turned. It hissed and crackled where it met the cold earth. A low bank had built up at the side and kept the flow going in one direction. The lethal, red-hot stream seemed intent on its course and I thought we were safe until I asked why one of our guides had his eyes constantly on the summit.

'There may be a "bomb" (explosion) and then the flow could change direction. We will need all the warning we can get,' he replied.

As I looked up there was a series of puffs of smoke where I supposed the crater was. I could feel his anxiety mount. The police urged us to get a move on.

We hurriedly completed the filming and retraced our steps back to the hotel and safety.

The next day things began slowly because it was well nigh impossible to find anywhere to eat. All the hotels and cafés had weddings lined up; there was one every half an hour. An erupting volcano is considered very propitious for giving birth to lots of children and we had to wait for over three hours before we got served.

Much later we set off to find the advancing wall of lava. This was easier said than done. It took us another three hours to locate it because most of the roads had been blocked off by molten rock. After turning round endless times to try out different routes, we came across a sight that was even more incredible than the one we'd seen the night before.

At the face of the flow the wall of lava had ramped up as it had cooled. Piling up on itself, it had become a mini-cliff about ten to twelve feet high. Great lumps of red-hot rock were detaching themselves and rolling forward, setting fire to shrubs, fences and the like. It was mesmerising and rather disturbing. Simon stood in front of the wall and poured out his thoughts.

'It's menacing because the lava is faster at the edges. It feels almost as if we're being encircled,' he said.

We were all worried about being trapped.

'It's incredible to think that the lava is as hot as it is two weeks after being spewed out of the centre of the earth,' he said to camera. Later he

(Left): Simon Groom at
the face of the advancing
wall of lava

told me about the challenge of presenting such a sight:

> If I'm honest, I generally work better with a script, but oc-
> casionally you have to 'busk it' – and this was one of those
> occasions. Not difficult, when you're standing in front of a
> ten-foot wall of molten lava, which is advancing towards
> you.

We filmed a bungalow being slowly crushed and buried under
the advance. All its contents had been salvaged. Even the windows and
doors had been removed. It was as if we were watching a condemned
prisoner on death row face an inescapable and imminent execution.
It was disturbing to realise that we were powerless. There was nothing
man could do to alter the will of nature. Simon remembers:

> I was wearing a T-shirt and my bare arms were clearly
> burned from the intense heat. I've never understood to this
> day how the heat from the lava – two weeks after the initial
> eruption, and so far down the hillside from where it had
> originally spewed out of the centre of the earth – was so
> intense. We watched it creep over the lawn of a bungalow
> before, inevitably, the building – once someone's home –
> was flattened.

For me Etna was a strangely healing experience. The lava flow was
just too extraordinary. It even momentarily blotted out my grief for my
daughter. It was mind-blowing power from the centre of the earth and
it actually eclipsed the pain that I felt. It put everything into perspective.
Before Etna I had thought life was pointless; after Etna I was curious
again.

8

Jumping for joy

In the 1980s we had a very small production team. There were seven of us directly involved in getting the show together. Three decades later the *Blue Peter* team would comprise 30 people, making a smaller number of programmes. One thing that has never changed, and this was drummed into us from day one, has been the need to make every penny count. So in 1980, as now, the programme couldn't afford to make a single film that was below par. Every item mattered.

We all lived with the nightmare of not making the grade because Biddy did not tolerate failure. Every film idea put forward had to work. Woe betide the director who got it wrong.

Blue Peter was a good programme to work on if you liked flying. I flew with the famous Red Arrows on more than one occasion, had several other flights in the Hawk and another in the Harrier. I also had a lesson in the Tucano while we waited for a large formation to assemble for the Queen's Golden Jubilee flypast in 2002. At the time I asked the instructor how I was doing and he said I was doing rather better than some of his students. This was a bit worrying because despite some four hundred hours in the Tiger Moth and Chipmunk aircraft some thirty years earlier, I know I have no natural ability as a pilot.

Neither was another of our presenters, Janet Ellis, a natural when it came to the dizzy world of aeronautical antics.

She seemed older and wiser than her years and she had a motherly look, which I thought was reassuring. When she auditioned for the programme Biddy suggested she follow in the footsteps of John Noakes. It was agreed with the RAF Falcons that Janet would join the freefall parachuting team as part of a record-breaking challenge and would become the first female to freefall from 20,000 feet. I was given the task of making it all happen. I was excited even if she wasn't.

7–8 June 1983
RAF Brize Norton

I went down to Number 1 Parachute Training School at RAF Brize Norton to work out a plan. As I drove through the base, Hercules C130 aircraft taxied close to the road and the smell of Avgas was everywhere. In their spartan offices the Falcons made me welcome. The team coach was Flight Sergeant Ally MacDonald, a no-nonsense Scot, and he introduced me to a young parachute instructor, Sergeant Nigel Rogoff, or 'Roggy' for short. In his mid- to late twenties, good looking and with a cheerful smile, Roggy turned out to have quite a sense of humour. It was agreed that they would do a double act. Roggy would do the lesson and Ally would put Janet right after she had 'had a go'.

I told Janet what we had planned and she looked a bit doubtful. In a rash moment I said, 'Don't worry, I'll do the first two jumps with you.'

After that from day one it wasn't just Janet who had misgivings.

Everything went well. Roggy was made for television and Janet did exactly what she was told. She had blind faith in his ability so she was just the sort of recruit the services dreamt about. The training took longer than usual because at the end of each day I had to do the same thing all over again, only a lot quicker because 'Roggy' wanted to go home. It lasted four days and as the time flashed by our nerves were honed to perfection.

On the third day we lined up for what the RAF call the Outdoor Exit Trainer, cheerfully nicknamed the 'Knacker Cracker'. It was a tower that looked as if it had once been part of a prisoner-of-war camp. However, unlike a prison camp, there was a means of escape. Two long cables stretched from the tower to the ground and students would jump out of the tower to swing in a body harness connected by a pulley to one of the cables. It was supposed to simulate the sensation of an aircraft slipstream.

As a male you had to be careful to make sure the harness was correctly fitted. Janet was fine but when I leapt out to swing in the parachute harness I experienced exquisite pain in my groin. I later found out that I had ruptured myself and eventually I had to have a hernia repair. The Knacker Cracker had lived up to its name and I wondered how many others had fallen foul of it. The Knacker Cracker has now gone to the knacker's yard.

(Right): Sgt Nigel Rogoff makes final checks on Janet Ellis and Alex before their first static-line jump

7–8 September 1983
RAF Hullavington

The night before our static-line jump I don't think either of us slept very much. We were going to do a balloon jump (from a basket suspended beneath a balloon) and I had noticed that neither Ally nor Nigel were very keen on it. It wasn't hard to see why.

When you jumped you counted '1000, 2000, 3000' and then looked up and shouted 'Check canopy'. If the parachute hadn't opened you immediately pulled your reserve. The trouble was, the balloon was tethered at 800 feet and the canopy was unlikely to open until 600 feet above ground at the earliest. I reckoned this gave us a total of five or six seconds before we hit the deck. Assuming we did the emergency drill as fast as we could, the reserve canopy could take another three or four seconds to deploy. I did the maths and it didn't look good. I practised the drill in my sleep until dawn.

We motored to RAF Hullavington and saw the balloons. They were huge, ominous and Second World War vintage, and sagged with the lack of gas. It was overcast with a lively wind and there were about sixty worried-looking paras milling about.

In our balloon was a young officer who was fighting panic. It was comforting to know we were not alone. Janet and I did not have much to say to one another. I have a mortal fear of heights because I get an overwhelming desire to jump whenever I look down. This is very bad when you are not wearing a parachute. However, as I was about to find out, it is not so bad when you are.

We were slowly hoisted to height and at 800 feet the young officers jumped out. And then it was just the three of us left to go. Ally shouted 'Geronimo' and disappeared out the door. Nigel grabbed Janet and she moved into the door. She smiled nervously and turned a shade paler. I

(Left): The Knacker Cracker or Outdoor Exit Trainer at RAF Brize Norton

noticed on the film later that she had a sort of grey-green tinge to her, and it wasn't because of the film. She went out the door – eyes glazed – and made a perfect descent. Later in the cutting room I watched as, having landed safely, she couldn't stop talking. Her relief at being safe on the ground was obvious.

It was then my turn and, quite unexpectedly, I got a surge of excitement. I suppose I was about to do what I always instinctively wanted to do without a parachute. I leapt out with a surge of delight. I whooped all the way down at the top of my voice and then made an appalling landing. I was lucky not to break a leg.

That night I tried to hide a huge bruise on my bum. There was much manoeuvring at bedtime so my wife Lynn wouldn't notice. Very embarrassing because I had promised not to jump...

8–9 November 1983
RAF Weston-on-the-Green

Several weeks later our second jump loomed and this time it was from a C130 Hercules, renowned as one of the longest-serving military aircraft ever built.

We were joined by the 60 other paras who filed on board clutching their equipment. For me it couldn't have come at a worse time as I had just been offered the opportunity of a lifetime.

I had just heard that Biddy wanted me to produce the films for *Blue Peter*'s annual appeal in Peru and Bangladesh. If I broke anything I would have to stay at home and the job would go to someone else. I was determined that this would not happen.

We had a refresher with Roggy and then lined up with the paras. The RAF Falcons reluctantly agreed to jump with Janet to give her moral support. I explained to a very amused cameraman that I intended to direct the film in the aircraft and then parachute out before Janet so I could then direct what happened on the ground. I don't think he believed me – until he saw me strapping on a parachute. From then on there was no stopping him. I had been told that he could be a bit dour but not on this occasion. He whizzed about helpfully, chuckling all the time.

Come the moment, I stood in the side door of the Hercules and looked at the engines 'turning and burning' away. The ground was shimmering in the exhaust while we flew a wide circuit around RAF Weston-on-the-Green. After a full 15 minutes of circling I began to wonder if I had made a wise decision. I had done absolutely nothing in the directing role and I stood a chance of breaking a leg and losing the trip of a lifetime. We turned for the run in.

'Action stations.'

'Red on.'

'Green on.'

I braced myself to jump.

'Go!'

It took all my strength to get out of the door. I remember Roggy saying, 'Take a good jump because otherwise you'll do a rivet check down the outside of the aircraft.'

I had thought it funny at the time. In a second I was out and I saw the aircraft flying away through my boots which were locked at the heel at 45 degrees. I was in the second part of the swing as the wind caught the parachute and it deployed.

The ride down was fun but not as much fun as the first jump. This time I made no mistake and made a textbook landing. I had plenty of time to disentangle myself from the harness and get on with directing the crew on the ground. Janet and the Falcons were the last to jump.

The troops were jumping with heavy loads that they released at 200 feet and which swung beneath them on a rope so they would hit the ground first. Ally was by my side. In a matter-of-fact way he said, 'If they forget to release the load, the extra weight on a leg will snap it clean. You'll hear it all over the airfield.'

Janet jumped, the Falcons gathered around, and her relief was obvious again because she couldn't stop talking. Everything was fine but this was just the second in a sequence of hair-raising films. I was grateful we had both survived. Poor Janet was in for some truly awful experiences and nearly didn't. But as the daughter of a soldier, she turned out to be a real trouper in the best *Blue Peter* tradition. Looking back, she said:

> I was scared when I jumped but I also knew that if a camera was on me it didn't want to catch me looking fine and joking with the Falcons (which wasn't difficult, they were very funny). So Alex and I made a series of films where I looked frightened, then did things anyway, then looked relieved. True *BP* 'I'll have a go' style. A lot of it was a lot of fun.

(Left): The balloon and basket being winched to height

(Right): Janet Ellis and the RAF Falcons embark on a C130 Hercules for Janet's second static-line parachute jump

(Above): Janet Ellis seconds before leaving the aircraft

(Left): Janet immediately after the jump, chatting to Mike Milburn, the RAF Falcons' team leader

9

The dizzy heights of television

(Right): Simon Groom in Peru, reporting to a 'live' studio in London

28 November–9 December 1983
Peru

Getting to location with the crew can make a better story than the film itself. We were off to Lake Titicaca in Peru, where the level of the legendary tranquil water of the lake was falling because of drought. I was looking forward to seeing the famous reed boats but wary of the real reason for the trip – the potato famine that was wreaking havoc in the area.

It was all part of the *Blue Peter* Weatherbeater Appeal, which was the good cause for the year. We took off from Lima for Juliaca on the shore of the lake, which is at a dizzying altitude of 12,500 feet, and landed at Arequipa, a small town halfway up the Andes, at 7,500 feet. The drought had broken and torrential rain had made the airfield at Juliaca too soft for a safe landing. Between us and Lake Titicaca lay the mighty Andes.

Simon Groom was the presenter. We got off the aircraft in Arequipa feeling quite bullish because the weather was glorious. There were snow-capped mountains wherever we looked and the sky was a powder blue. I reckoned that all we had to do was hire a couple of vehicles and drive over the top of the Andes and down to the lake on the other side.

It was a journey of 151 miles and it was only one o'clock. Perhaps the thinning air was starting to affect my thought processes but I reckoned we had plenty of time. We adjourned for a leisurely lunch while our fixer, Pocho, rustled up some vehicles.

I was new to working at altitude. I didn't understand that the high level of oxygen at sea level is crucial for both humans and vehicles to operate normally. As we motored onwards and upwards in a small convoy of three vehicles, we gained thousands of feet. We began to feel light-headed and the engines began to sound rougher and rougher. We crossed shallow rivers and wound our way up dirt roads until we were completely and utterly alone. We had been on the road for about four hours and the mountains had shrunk to the edge of a vast plain. Anxiously, I asked where we could get some petrol. I was assured that there was a filling station up ahead.

I could see nothing but rocks and distant hills until we reached an even higher plateau at about 17,000 feet and, incredibly, there were a few drab single-storey iron-roofed houses. I scoured the landscape anxiously for the petrol station but couldn't see anything that looked remotely like one. Our little convoy halted beside a collection of half-empty 44-gallon oil drums, which resembled an unsuccessful scrapyard. Then I saw a hand pump on one of them. This was the promised filling station! Pumping furiously, the garage owner transferred precious fuel into our tanks while I pondered the risk we had taken. There was only half a drum of fuel left and we shared it out between the three vehicles.

Meanwhile, Simon, who always made an effort to make friends, decided to join in a game of football with the local children. Two minutes later he was staggering about with the lack of oxygen and we had to support him back to the car – he was laughing a lot about nothing – and I was concerned. This was oxygen starvation, and I hoped our Oxfam advisers knew what they were doing, because I didn't.

Simon recalls the journey vividly:

> The contrast between the laid-back feel of Lima and the stark, isolated Andes mountain range was extraordinary. As we progressed higher into the mountains I became light-headed with the lack of oxygen and I didn't really know how it would affect me.

We drove on and up over the barren, rock-strewn, high pass at 18,500 feet and down the other side to about 17,500 feet, where the equipment vehicle got its first puncture. By this time we were all off our heads with the lack of oxygen. Despite my feelings of intoxication, I still have a very clear image of the sound recordist putting the jack under the curved part of the rear spring and trying to take the wheel off. It was the sort of thing you only do if you're drunk, which in a way we all were. Fear kept me sober enough to point out that if it slipped off the jack, we would be stranded. For us a couple of days without enough air to breathe could have been fatal. For safety we repositioned it under the flat part of the axle.

It was snowing, getting dark, and a large herd of llamas gathered around to see what was going on. They had magically appeared out of the gloom and stood about curiously as white flakes settled on their coats. I walked about in small circles, kicking at loose stones to keep warm and appear calm. The wheel was changed and the nightmare continued. We drove all that evening out of the snow and into the night until four in the morning, when we arrived in the outskirts of Puno, a grim-looking place not far from our destination. The Land Rover carrying the equipment was on three flat tyres. We had been up to 18,500 feet and now we were back at 13,000 feet. Some sanity and hope had returned. None of us felt tired because of the thin air.

Our Oxfam contact, Pocho, said that he'd like a word in private. He told me to send the crew on to the hotel so they could rest, and that I should stay with him.

'No problem – good idea,' I replied, wondering why.

So, while the rest of the party set off in the pouring rain, he and I stayed with the vehicle, which we parked up, resting on its rims. With only dim yellow lighting overhead, we stood under a leaking tree next to a wall in a narrow street. I considered how best to feature torrential rain into a script that was all about drought. Time passed. Simon recalls the moment he got to the hotel:

I foolishly jumped out of the Land Rover and ran inside with some of the luggage … I virtually collapsed in reception (where I spotted you could hire oxygen masks) wheezing and gasping for breath … and obviously still had no concept of what filming at altitude involved.

Back in Puno I mused on what I was doing and why I was doing it. The plan was that the Land Rover was to be rescued by another Oxfam worker and I asked Pocho why he needed me to stay.

'If you not stay, they kill me for sure,' he replied.

'Who?' I asked, alarmed.

'The cocaine paste smugglers. They want the Land Rover for spares. They will come looking and when they do there will be two of us so they won't attack.'

And he was right because after half an hour or so a suspicious looking vehicle turned the corner and into our street. On his command we stood out from the shadows. The driver paused to look at us and then drove on. We performed the same ritual about five times. The smugglers were very eager to get those spares. It had been a particularly harrowing 24 hours and I was exhausted. Curiously, I wasn't sleepy, just soaking wet and freezing cold. If they had just stopped and asked for the vehicle, I probably would have given it to them.

The next day we woke up to an otherwise deserted hotel on the shores of Lake Titicaca, which stretched as far as the eye could see. Because of the lack of oxygen we were all very wide awake and ready to get started.

We visited a community that was starving because their potato crop had failed. Everything was a drab brown colour and not helped by the overcast sky, which was heavy with the returning rain.

We were on the high plateau at about 14,000 feet and Simon was in his element. He had been helping to plough a field to plant seed potatoes when we got some alarming news. A group of armed men had entered the far end of the village and we had to leave. They were the Shining Path guerrillas and they were terrorising the area. If they caught us we could look forward to being held hostage – or worse. We bundled into our vehicles and sped off.

However anxious we felt, our Oxfam fixers were old hands and not the kind of people to waste an opportunity. They stopped about five miles away so we could film a family making *chungyo*, a sort of porridge made out of freeze-dried potatoes that was only eaten in dire emergencies. I reckoned we had an hour before even the most determined guerrilla would catch up with us. It took almost that long to prepare the food. The family lived in a tiny mud and straw hut and, after much grinding and boiling over a small mud oven outside the front door, the resulting mess tasted vile. I could well believe it was eaten only as a last resort. We thanked them profusely.

I was humbled by their generosity and their gratitude when we gave them our empty plastic water bottles. It was only then that I truly realised just how poor they were. Money had no value for them

(Right): Lake Titicaca – the view from my hotel window

because there was nothing for them to spend it on. There was no sign of our Shining Path pursuers. Back at the hotel Simon celebrated a good day's filming with the local beverage, Pisco sour, and began to enjoy a drink or two. What none of us knew was that at altitude alcohol can be fiercesome stuff. Simon was wise after the event:

> I seem to recall reading a BBC handbook about the dos and don'ts of filming at altitude…one of the things I remember was the advice about wining and dining, which basically said, 'When filming at altitude, take care not to consume heavy meals and large amounts of alcohol.' So what did Groom do? Consumed a heavy meal and large amounts of alcohol!

When he didn't show for breakfast the following morning I banged on his door. After a long pause he opened it. He looked awful.

'I feel really rough, youth. Can't do anything. Got to stay in bed.' I headed for the kitchens to find someone who could help.

'No problem, sir. I give you something for him. He will be fine,' the waiter said.

He gave me a straw and a bowl of what looked like leaf-porridge floating on a whitish liquid. It was mate tea – an infusion of coca leaves and super-strength. I delivered it to Simon.

We went out filming without him and about three hours later I knocked on his door. He bounded over to answer it. He was enthusiastic about the tea, which had made him feel a lot better. He asked for some more. He'd had rather more of the cocaine-like mate tea than was usual or safe. I didn't tell him what it was and I didn't get him a second helping.

Back at the hotel and lying in my bed, that and every night, was hell, because coping with the altitude was an ordeal. I would doze off and re-awake every few minutes, gasping for breath. Yet every time I

(Left): Making *chungyo*, a vile-tasting porridge made from dried potato

(Left): Juliaca

lay down to sleep the room would spin around so much I felt dizzy. It was about as close as you can imagine to those uncontrollable room spinning experiences after an unwise drinking binge. Unknown to me, Simon shared my misery:

> I would awake in the middle of the night feeling extremely rough, and unable to breathe … and I'll never forget the nightmare sensation of opening my bedroom window, taking a huge gulp of air, and … nothing happened. The air was so thin and lacking in oxygen that I broke out into a cold sweat, still unable to breathe and feeling very panicky.

It was torture and we both counted the days. The glorious vista of the lake and the unusual reed boats were little compensation.

Getting back to the UK from Lake Titicaca was nearly as difficult as getting there. The weather had broken and rain had kept the airfield at Juliaca unserviceable.

We abandoned flying and moved into the nearby town of Puno to catch the overnight train. It meant waiting a full day in what looked like a film set from the Mexican wild west. And we might as well have strolled into town with dollar signs printed on our T-shirts. The Peruvians were allegedly light-fingered and we were a juicy target. The solution was to book a hotel room to secure the baggage.

Simon and I took a walk to look at the street markets and we saw a young boy aged about four or five lying in the gutter. He looked as if he had a high fever and was shaking. Sweat stood out on his face. There were lots of people nearby and they looked unconcerned. I was nonplussed because he was obviously ill and yet everyone ignored him. He could have been a victim of the drought and starving to death. Why didn't somebody do something? Puzzled, we walked on for a minute or two and then turned back to help – but when we got to the spot the child had disappeared. Had it been a con? Or had the child died and been taken away? I am not sure what we could have done, but we will

never know for certain what the reality was. Simon was concerned and I felt we had lost a valuable opportunity to answer a cry for help. The Peruvians were proud people and I am quite sure that once we were past, the child was removed.

That evening the train arrived and I briefed everyone to keep an eye on the kit while we escorted it on a trolley across the square to the railway station. While I fended off unsolicited porters, the others took the piles of boxes and suitcases and stowed them away on the train. I thought our system was foolproof. Even so, a briefcase went missing. Henry Farrar, the cameraman and owner, was not best pleased. All the important customs documents for the equipment were in it. We called the police.

A plain-clothes policeman appeared almost instantly and I showed him our letter from the Peruvian government stating that we were guests and should receive any help we required. He disappeared and 20 minutes later returned clutching the missing briefcase. To our surprise the only things missing were Henry's traveller's cheques.

We rumbled into the night in reclining seats and I dozed off with the gentle swaying of the carriage. About one o'clock I was rudely woken up. The gentle swaying had become a violent rocking and I thought the train was about to topple off the rails. There was an almost constant screaming of metal on metal as the brakes struggled to control our headlong progress. We were all awake. I asked the sound recordist, Bryan Showell, what was up. His reply was like a red rag to a bull.

'Whatever you do, don't look out of the window.'

Of course I did, and was horrified. The train was hurtling down the side of a mountain with a drop of thousands of feet inches from my face. The brakes screamed every time the train came to a sharp bend. Physics defied what was happening. It was all so terrifying I shut my eyes and forced myself to relax. I could imagine the news report and our mangled bodies lying under a tangle of twisted metal at the bottom of the ravine.

Back in London Biddy had been told that we had missed our flight back and had announced this on the programme in the style of 'breaking news', naming the entire production team almost as if we were goners. Maybe she knew more about Peruvian railways than I did.

Of course, we still had to survive the first leg of the long flight home. We flew back over the heart of the Amazon rainforest and the aircraft settled down to a low-level approach to our first destination, Manaus. Searchlights blazed from each wing because we were in the throes of a major tropical storm and the driving rain almost obliterated the beams. As an amateur pilot I knew something was wrong. I knew about radar-controlled approaches from my University Air Squadron days. It was how aircraft approached and landed guided only by flight instruments. But in my experience they never, ever, lasted as long as 45 minutes.

Eventually, we landed safely. We stayed on the tarmac drinking

(Below): A street scene in Puno

coffee and watching the rain pour down until the storm had cleared. The next day I heard on the news that several aircraft had gone missing worldwide in the most savage night for many years.

At Heathrow I apologised to Henry and promised I would make it up to him with some 'easy' trips to make up for the hell we'd just been through.

He smiled knowingly but said if I could fix something good it would suit him fine. For the next three overseas expeditions we had the same damn conversation as one hellish trip followed another. I'm not sure if I ever made it up to him even though I enjoyed working with him because he never seemed to mind too much. Perhaps the more fitting tribute was that we named our son Henry after him.

(Above): Simon shows the *Blue Peter* book to curious villagers

10

Real *Blue Peter* appeal

The first time Peter Duncan was offered the job of presenter he turned it down. He already had a successful career as an actor. He had appeared in feature films so had little to prove. He was used to the ways of the world and could turn his hand to almost anything. He once remarked to me that he preferred the uncertainty of being freelance to receiving a monthly salary.

Peter described these feelings vividly. He compared himself to primitive man who left his cave to gather firewood and food for his family. In the same spirit he would leave home for a day's work, never quite knowing where the next day's pay would come from. I wondered if it was this uncertainty that gave Pete his zest for life.

He was not a fan of large organisations because he preferred the flexibility of smaller ones. Put a barrier in his way and he would do his best to batter it down.

In short, Peter was a bit of a rebel and he revelled in it.

In my world of location filming in 1983 there was some flexibility but not nearly as much as there is today and certainly not enough for Peter at that time. For me the film script was an operational order agreed by the bosses and with clear aims. Being ex-army I understood this and like Peter I always fought to achieve my objective.

Peter was different from previous presenters because he actively sought spontaneity. And this didn't always fit either the script line or the programme duration. Everyone could see the benefits and there had been many spontaneous moments over the preceeding years between Peter Purves and John Noakes.

In live television it was risky. Too much ad-libbing led to the programme overrunning. Even a few seconds over the allotted programme time really mattered in a live transmission and could result in it being cut off before the presenters could say goodbye.

I asked Peter about how he felt when he first joined:

> I was always seeking some kind of spontaneity. As an actor
> you are always looking to appear (usually) spontaneous but

if you are playing yourself I saw no need to fake it, although I probably did a lot more pretending than you imagine. I never wanted to be a conventional presenter.

So here he was, an interesting and likeable chap whose mindset had been moulded by the theatre and who was poised to take on completely new challenges.

And his early days as a television presenter proved quite tricky just because of his theatre experience. He interpreted scripts as actors are trained to do. Quite often on location and referring to the script, he would ask, 'What is my motivation here?'

It was not a question that I, or any of the production team, was used to answering.

He was physically tough and still quite young so was given more action films to do than was usual. And that meant that he and I were thrust together. Me the ex-army officer and him the actor.

I soon discovered that beneath an affable exterior Peter had a steel core. On location he increasingly questioned his scripts and I wrestled to reconcile his ideas with *Blue Peter* custom and practice. As time went by I learnt to expect that every film with him would be a struggle. Meanwhile, Peter thought I was a bit of a bully, and he was right. Just over a year and a half had passed since the death of our beloved daughter Lauren. The experience had hardened me and I was not as sensitive to his needs as I might have been.

Even so, I knew that debate on location was good and I had learned not to be too forceful because it could be destructive and destroy the presenter's performance. After all, you cannot expect anyone to behave normally after a blazing row! And back in the cutting room all that mattered was a sparkling presenter because it would make or break the film.

Quite often I felt that I had to take more than I could dish out. In my bullish, calloused state of mind I had yet to soften to my normal self.

So Peter and I rubbed along for a year or two and I saw him as the irritating grit in the oyster that produced the pearl.

Meanwhile, Lynn was pregnant with our second child and was understandably anxious that the pregnancy should be trouble-free. And it was about this time that Peter and I set off to Valloire in France to film him learning how to slalom-ski.

5–6 January 1984

Valloire, France

It must have been a troublesome day and Peter must have done a good job of winding me up because at the end of the first day I retired in high dudgeon to my hotel room and phoned home. Lynn, my ever-patient

(Above): Peter Duncan learning to live off the land

(Right): Peter Duncan at the end of a day's skiing. Cameraman Henry Farrar shoots a few general views

and loving wife, listened to my rant and then told me about her worries for the child inside her. After the call I continued to talk aloud to myself to get the frustrations and anxieties out of my system.

While I was in mid-vitriolic outburst, and unknown to me, Peter had come looking for me. He cannot remember why. As he approached the door to my room he heard me effing and blinding away and it came as a bit of a shock to learn that the root of my problems ... was him! Rather than disturb me, he quietly returned to his room.

At breakfast the next day I braced myself for another day of conflict and was immediately puzzled. Peter was utterly charming and stayed that way all day long. We flew back to the UK, comfortable in each other's company, and I marvelled at the new Peter with huge relief.

'You seemed troubled and vulnerable,' he later told me. I was surprised and touched by his concern.

In truth, Peter was a team player and made great efforts to get on well with Sarah and Simon. He knew from his experience in the theatre how important this was. He was himself and over time came to a compromise with the traditional *Blue Peter* way of doing things. Spontaneity became more part of the programme mix than it had been in the past.

Peter was invited back for a second run of programmes after he had left. By then he was one of the most successful presenters we had ever had.

I have often wondered how I could have improved my dealings with him and the other presenters. But because we were worked so hard there was very little opportunity or time to do anything else but get

the job done. Deadlines were always looming and quite often it was just a question of putting your head down and getting on with it. This was probably why some things about the presenters' personalities were never really discussed.

During the writing of this book some thoughts have surfaced in my understanding of the show that might account for on-location 'strife', if strife is the right word for very minor disagreements.

Sarah Greene, who, in Biddy's own words, 'gets it', opened my eyes with some very interesting thoughts about her fellow presenters Peter and Simon and their prescribed roles before Janet Ellis joined the team:

> Biddy 'cast' us very carefully. I use this word advisedly in that we really were playing parts most of the time – and often not fully being ourselves. Biddy's genius was recognising the 'essence' of who we were, finding the part that fitted into the mix of characters best and then concentrating on that aspect. But this emphasis can be very one-dimensional and distort a *full* representation of who that person actually *is*. As characters delivering the lines in her scripts, we were playing 'versions' of ourselves – versions that fitted into a comfortable mix that worked well for the programme. I say that because I always felt Simon and Peter's real personalities were almost switched

for the programme. Simon was never the naive, wide-eyed, horny-handed son of the soil. He'd been a teacher, working in London and DJ-ing in nightclubs before going anywhere near the BBC. He knew his way around. Likewise, Peter was never really the street-wise cockney-sparrow cheeky chappy.

I think that they were – and still are – very good actors. My place between my two 'brothers' was as the theatrical princess sister ... a bit like the character I'd just played, before starting on *BP*, in *The Swish of the Curtain*. This wasn't who I actually was – but it was a great part I enjoyed playing. It helped – though I didn't realise at the time how lucky I was in this – that I genuinely adored these brothers of mine. It was only when I persuaded Biddy to let me rework her scripts for myself that I could start to learn how to be 'me' on screen and to learn how to present properly.

1–2 May 1984
Liverpool

(Left): On location on the river Treweryn near Bala. Cameraman Laurie Rush films as Peter Duncan prepares to set off down the rapids

Janet Ellis and I wrestled not with our respective roles but with the weather, which thwarted us at every turn. Her parachuting challenge became quite prolonged.

There was little else for it but to while away the hours, which ran into days, drinking coffee in the Falcons' crew room at RAF Brize Norton, waiting for the clouds to part. It was so costly that subsequent parachuting challenges with the Falcons (latterly involving presenters Stuart Miles, Simon Thomas and Andy Akinwolere) took place in the sunshine state of California, where good weather was guaranteed.

Janet's first freefall jump was at the time state of the art but, compared to modern training methods, about as primitive as surgery without anaesthetic.

After a quick refresher Janet rejoined the Falcons, who were preparing to jump at the opening of the Liverpool Garden Festival. We watched as the team jumped off the ramp at the back of the C130 with red 'smokes' that burned from each ankle. In seconds they were tiny dots that blended into the urban sprawl, and then we turned away to land at Liverpool airport and wait for their return.

Out of our sight it had been a dramatic display in more ways than one. Ally MacDonald's parachute malfunctioned and when he tried to release it the straps caught on his wristwatch. He had only just managed to slide the watch off his wrist and deploy his reserve in time. He was under the canopy for less than three seconds before he landed on a car roof. If his watch had had a leather strap and not an expanding metal one, he would have been in serious trouble. I found him looking very thoughtful, sitting on the aircraft ramp at the back.

'Makes you think, Alex. Makes you think,' he said in his rich Scottish accent, and then prepared for Janet's jump with perhaps a renewed sense of mortality.

Janet was quiet and thoughtful as the C130 Hercules climbed to altitude. I watched and prayed she would be all right. Like her I was new to freefall and there was a lot going on.

At 12,000 feet Janet jumped, facing towards the aircraft and held by Ally and Roggy, so she exited backwards. Within seconds both Ally and Roggy had lost their grips and she was on her own, tumbling out of control. Some primitive need to survive must have kicked in because she 'threw a delta', which is best described as what Superman does when he wants to go really fast. Her arms were straight back and swept out like the wings of a fast jet. In this position she immediately stabilised enough for Roggy to get back and grab her to get her into the right position and pull her main canopy. It had been a close call. If she had continued to tumble, at 4,000 feet her automatic opening device would have activated and she might have rolled herself up in her parachute as it deployed.

I knew nothing of this until I saw the helmet-camera footage when the whole horrifying drama was played out. Thereafter Ally and Roggy took a firmer grip. And so did I. However, our good intentions did not stop other disasters from happening. Janet was quite sanguine about it all:

> My dad had been in the army when I was little although he left to go into visual effects at the BBC and I ended up interviewing him on *Blue Peter* about *Dr Who*, but that's by the way – so I was used to the services, and you couldn't find a more relaxed bunch than the RAF. They always seemed to really care about me, too – although one of them revealed that they didn't want anything to happen to me as 'there'd be a ton of paperwork' if it did.

12 September 1984

RAF Weston-on-the-Green, Oxfordshire

Janet consolidated her freefall skills, which meant she spent much of her free time hanging about at RAF Weston-on-the-Green, waiting for gaps in the weather. She had to accumulate as many jumps as possible before going onto the next – high level – phase of her training.

I could not be with her all the time because I had other films to make. Luckily she had struck up a very good rapport with Roggy and the Falcons' team leader Flight Lieutenant Mike Milburn. Inevitably there were moments when she was bundled on to an aircraft to jump when the weather was at the limit for safety. They kept a close eye on her. Even so, one jump was rather more of an ordeal than either she or they could have anticipated:

(Bottom right): Janet Ellis exiting from the ramp of a C130 Hercules, the RAF Falcons' favourite display aircraft

(Top right): Janet in the freefall flight trainer at No. 1 Parachute Training School RAF Brize Norton

> It was just me and Nigel that day. We jumped from a Cessna and despite landing well on the DZ, I couldn't get up. It was an impact fracture probably caused by a rock hidden in the ground. The Falcons wanted to go to Brize Norton for a practice jump so I drove home!

Once home she couldn't get out of the car and an ambulance took her to hospital, where an X-ray showed she had a cracked pelvis.

And it was just as the programme was due to go back on the air after the summer break. To reassure *Blue Peter* viewers we filmed Janet sending a message to them from her hospital bed.

Biddy sent flowers and, understandably, Janet's confidence was shaken:

> Breaking my pelvis nearly finished it all. It set us back a long time and although I didn't want that accident to be my last jump – not a great way to finish – I wasn't sure about record-breaking attempts either. Biddy took me to lunch and suggested that if I had any parachuting courage left I should think of it like the sauce at the bottom of the bottle, and turn it round and give it a good thump. So thump I did and jump I did and for a nanosecond held the High Altitude (civilian)(female) record.

Her injury, and the onset of winter, put the challenge on hold for a long time. It wasn't until June the following year that we picked up the reins again.

Meanwhile, I was about to experience one of my biggest *Blue Peter* challenges to date.

28 November–6 December 1984
Ethiopia

The Ethiopian drought and famine were massive. The newscaster, Michael Buerk, had reported on the terrible drought for *BBC News* by holding a starving Ethiopian baby as he spoke. The impact of his report was profound and heart-wrenching. The effect was no different among staff in the *Blue Peter* office.

Blue Peter appeals are at the programme's core because they encourage children to think about other people apart from themselves. The key was to provide an achievable aim that could be exceeded. So every year we sought to mobilise the enormous strength of feeling that could be harnessed by setting a powerful, yet achievable, goal. And the determination of *Blue Peter* viewers ensured that every year this expectation was exceeded.

Biddy told me that the appeals began back in the early 1960s. The two programmes before Christmas had traditionally featured toys. It was all very materialistic and she and Edward thought that instead they should be remembering those children who would not be having a nice Christmas. They wanted to include even the poorest viewers so it was decided that no money should be requested. Only rubbish that could be converted into cash. They worked out a target so the maximum rubbish could be sent in for the minimum postage. And with huge audiences it really was a case of 'every little helps'. Our targets were met with a multiplicity of small donations.

And that was the point: to encourage children to feel responsible for something that they had in their power to put right.

Even though it was the turn of a UK cause, the need in starving Ethiopia was so overwhelming that Biddy reacted almost instantly. She devoted half of the annual *Blue Peter* appeal to it. Advised by Oxfam, we planned to provide water tanks and water supplies to the people in the north of the country with cash raised by donations of used postage stamps.

It wasn't the first time that the programme had been to Ethiopia. During a previous drought we had provided terraced gardens in the north of the country. Oxfam reported that the only green, seen from satellite photographs, was those gardens.

It was my first time back in the tropics since my year of teaching in the Solomon Islands as a VSO volunteer. When we landed at Addis Ababa airport the sight and damp smell of the spiky African grass was curiously nostalgic.

My old friend Simon Groom was the presenter, and as we left Addis we saw lorryloads of what looked like amorphous shapes hiding under sun-bleached colourless rags that fluttered in the wind. At first glance I couldn't believe that they were people. As they hurtled past we could see that there were indeed human beings, all travelling south as we headed north towards the disaster area.

Our Oxfam field worker and guide, Mikel Woldemariam, was upset. In Addis, life for him had gone on almost as normal and he was not fully aware of the real tragedy. The sight of the hundreds of refugees was a genuine shock to him.

Henry Farrar, my long-suffering friend from Peru the year before, was the cameraman, and George Cassidy was the sound recordist. Graham Banks was Henry's assistant and as it turned out he was a more important member of the team than being the film magazine loader.

We drove out of the plains around Addis and towards the hills. Soon we were wending our way through passes where troops of baboons scattered at our approach. There were gum trees on either side of the road and an occasional cluster of thatched buildings.

After a while, the oncoming flow of lorries stopped and in their place appeared groups of people walking down the road, carrying their possessions. We stopped to distribute some Oxfam high-energy biscuits. Immediately we were surrounded by needy families desperate for help. Simon remembers the moment well:

Mikel, my gentle and caring Ethiopian guide and translator, helped me…my lasting image is of gaunt, terribly care-worn faces, but how polite and dignified the travellers were as they waited patiently for their biscuits. One lady's gaunt face – most of her teeth were also missing – I still remember vividly…

(Above): Interpreter Mikel Woldemariam and Simon Groom before heading to the drought-ridden refugee camps of Ethiopia

The biscuits soon went but the real need was water and we had very little of that. Incredibly, the people had lined up to be 'served' and I asked why they didn't just help themselves to the food that was growing in the fields on either side of the road.

'They wouldn't, because it isn't theirs,' was the matter-of-fact reply from our Oxfam field worker.

'But they are starving to death,' I said, surprised.

'Even so.'

Simon also admired their self-control:

> As I write this, I feel a sort of revulsion towards our supermarket-obsessed culture here in Britain, and recall a lady who telephoned BBC Radio Derby last Christmas, saying that she had been shopping and experienced road rage (couldn't find a parking space), trolley rage (a real rugby scrum for trolleys) and bread rage (people fighting over the last few loaves) – no dignity here!

Like Simon, I marvelled at their moral code. I couldn't imagine there would be much restraint if the same situation happened in the UK. Likewise, later in our journey I saw – on more than one occasion – a mother hold out her hands in a plea for help, only to be reprimanded by the head of the household.

Further north we caught up with another convoy of trucks. It was the Red Cross, carrying supplies.

And then we got behind another convoy that was carrying supplies of a different kind. The Russians were helping the Ethiopian government to fight the Eritrean 'rebels'. It was a supply convoy carrying munitions for the fighting in the north. Quite coincidentally, that night we ended up in the same hotel as the Russian military.

Dinner was a strange affair with the Russian officers in one corner and us, a couple of table lengths away, in another. They were obviously uncomfortable with our presence and shunned all contact. We were curious and relaxed while they seemed tense. We laughed and joked and the Russians steadfastly ignored us. After dinner I tried to engage one of the younger officers in conversation in the hotel corridor. He looked startled and could not get away quickly enough. The next morning we set off before them, and we did not see them again.

Our little convoy had its own troubles. Graham, the assistant cameraman, was driving the equipment vehicle and he was concerned.

'The brakes are faulty,' he reported.

We stopped and made some immediate repairs. There was a fluid leak on one of the front brakes and with help he put a metal tack in the end of the offending pipe to seal the flow. From then on whenever he braked the vehicle lurched savagely to one side. It was very dangerous yet there was no other way until we could find a garage to repair it properly. Graham came into his own as he wrestled to keep control of the vehicle at every bend of the road.

Meanwhile Simon was preoccupied with other equally serious thoughts:

> We'd heard awful reports back home from Michael Buerk about the situation and I was worried about the sheer scale of the suffering that we would find. Also, from a somewhat selfish viewpoint, I wasn't sure if I knew, as a presenter, how to find the right words – and the right tone – to convey the reality of the situation.

Our first stop was a refugee camp at Bati. It was a shocking sight. Twenty thousand people had gathered together and many were dying. When we drove into the barren earth compound, which had baked rock hard in the sun, the refugees gathered around us. Barefooted, they looked on quietly. The children all had swollen stomachs and the adults were little more than walking skeletons. At first I didn't know what to do and then a Scandanvian lady from the Red Cross came out to greet us and she spoke in English.

'You are welcome but please understand you will not under any circumstances eat anything in sight of the people here. If you need to eat then go inside the tent and close the door.'

It was a stark reminder their survival was balanced on a knife edge and she indicated a small tent off to one side.

I introduced everyone and asked her if she would mind showing Simon around. Simon recalls:

> The nurse was called Elisa who I believe was Finnish… She told me that some people had been in the camp for two months, and that, the same morning, a woman had walked for four days to get there – and died on arrival. Elisa also said that 90 people had died the previous night. It was a sobering thought that we were filming people who would probably not survive the night.

They walked Pied Piper fashion, with a tail of children following. It was all so sad I didn't have the heart to ask them not to stare directly at the camera. The blank staring seemed part of the general hopelessness.

'How many people are here?

'Will they all recover?'

Simon took the initiative and asked all the questions that anyone who cared would have asked, and I left him to it.

'Last night we only had 90 deaths. When we first got here, the worst night we had over 280.' Simon was flabbergasted.

'Every night?'

'Yes, every night there are deaths. Mostly the very young die first and then the old.'

'What happens to them?'

'We have a mortuary and it's full of bodies.' And so it went on.

> I remember the flies…everywhere…and one boy, lying in the hot sun, his face covered with flies, and no shelter. Elisa said that at night the temperature dropped to almost freezing – hard to imagine. I was nervous about how to put things into words and I actually wondered if we should have been there at all. Were we being intrusive? However, a few minutes later, a woman with a very emaciated baby actually held her child up towards the camera as if to say, Please film this – please show people in the West our plight – and what is happening to us.

There were makeshift tents as far as the eye could see, hundreds of them no more than four feet high and made from a few sticks and a piece of tattered cloth. Many families had nothing and people lay unmoving on the ground as their lives ebbed away.

There should have been some noise yet it was eerily quiet. There was hardly any movement except the occasional swirl of dust.

I saw a funeral procession carrying a small child covered in a white cloth. An old man was weeping and the mother was beyond grief.

After the interview Henry came up to me and said quietly, 'Give me 40 minutes on my own. It's the only way to get the extra shots.'

I remember being initially much less affected than the others at first because of Lauren's death, which was still fresh in my mind. Terrible things happen. Deal with it, I thought. But later, when the horror had really sunk in, I too was in tears.

We didn't stay that night. Late into the afternoon we drove away in silence. Nobody spoke. We were all too preoccupied with our thoughts.

We drove into the night and we neared a village when it was pitch black. Our fixer told us to stop. We were on the edge of the war zone. I was told that each village was guarded. Very possibly the watchmen would be armed and they might shoot if they didn't know who we were. We got out and walked up the road, calling out to tell them we were coming. Eventually we reached them. The guards had one old .303 Lee-Enfield service rifle between them. It was an ancient Number 1 model dated 1908 and I suspect the ammunition was of the same vintage. I wondered if it would actually have fired but was glad we hadn't found out.

The next day we came to a remote refugee post where people literally walked out of the desert and collapsed. With Oxfam workers, led by the red-haired and energetic Paul Sherlock, we built a water tank and then Simon went inside the building to report.

Imagine a large corrugated-iron-roofed hut full of half-starved mothers and babies. They were desperate. It was agonising to watch those who could be helped being brought back to life. I have seldom seen Simon look so angry. He was still smarting from the shocking

(Above): Famine is a way of life in the Bati refugee camp. The crew (Alex, foreground, Henry Farrar and Graham Banks) film the plight of the starving thousands

(Right): Water taps

(Below): Simon talks to refugees in Bati

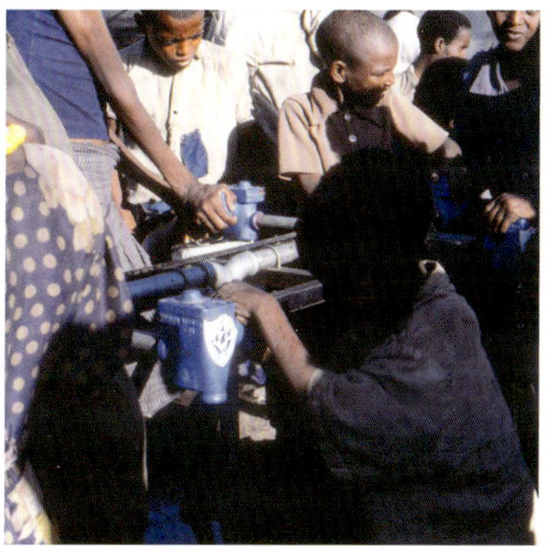

(Left): Simon recalls: 'Despite the appalling conditions at Bati, families at the camp did have a supply of clean, fresh water. This was thanks to water kits that had been supplied by *Blue Peter* viewers'

sights of the day before and he could not believe that human beings could be allowed to suffer so much. While he interviewed the mothers through our interpreter, his flushed face and glittering eyes showed how his anger simmered inside.

Much later, when we were back in the UK, I heard that in that hut the week after we left there was an outbreak of measles and every baby, all 60 of them, died.

There was worse to come at a feeding station another day's drive away. Very malnourished young children and babies were being weighed and measured by British nurses. They could only be helped if they were under a certain weight. Between filming I went back to the organiser's tent to reload my stills camera and there I found the matron in tears.

She had found herself in an impossible situation.

'I have to act as judge and jury and they all need help. I have to turn some away when tomorrow I can help them. But they don't come back. They don't understand.'

Ten minutes later she was back in charge, dealing with the hopelessness in the best way she knew how.

That night we all sat down together in a mud hut and someone produced a bottle of brandy. George, the sound recordist, was a caring Welshman and, depending on your point of view, either the best or the worst sort of man to have on this troubling shoot. He decided to quote from the play *Under Milk Wood*.

After the scenes we had seen, Dylan Thomas's words should have been profound. It was all too much. It struck Simon and me as absurdly funny. We struggled to conceal our hysterical mirth. In desperation I suggested we go for a walk. We went as far away as we could and then roared with uncontrollable laughter. Afterwards we both wondered why. Neither of us wanted to hurt George's feelings, which were sincerely meant; it was just that the awful stress of the past few days needed an outlet.

(Left): This one room held about sixty half-starved children and mothers. Simon chats to a British aid worker

That night we slept in our sleeping bags, camp beds touching, and listened to the low baying noise of people grieving about three hundred yards away. Rats scampered across us all night long and I remember that in the morning Simon woke with blood on his ear where one had taken a bite out of it.

We drove back to the airport at Addis Ababa brutalised by the experience. We passed families and village groups walking away from the drought area and heading south. We got ahead of them and on to a metalled road that led as straight as a die across a large, flat plain. Then we saw a young mum and two young children. One was wrapped in cloth on her back and the other strained to hold her hand as he tottered along beside her. My instinct was to stop. But our driver pointed out that if we did we might split the family if her husband was following behind. We hurtled past and I debated the issue in my mind. The road was empty and I couldn't see how this would matter in such desperate times. By the time we had argued about it the moment had passed and they were far behind.

From that point we began to find bodies lying at the side of the road.

The next village was 50 miles further on and there were more refugees huddled in groups. We filled a large basket with fresh bananas for them. Later I bought jewellery at inflated prices thinking to sell it to raise money for the appeal later. All the while the young family we had passed on the road played on my mind. I'd like to think that they survived, but I fear they did not. Simon, like me, was reflective:

> I was amazed at the dignity of the Ethiopian people: quiet, polite and restrained, despite the appalling conditions… and two huge ironies: Ethiopia is actually a very beautiful country…stunning landscapes (if, on this occasion parched), and fascinating flora and fauna; also many of the Ethiopian women had strikingly beautiful faces…I know that may seem a strange thing to say in a famine situation – but that's how I recall it.

Nearing Addis, we had problems of our own. The trip had been very last minute and there had been no money in the *Blue Peter* budget to pay for the flights. Very gratefully we had accepted a lift from ZAL Airlines of Egypt, which was based at Stansted. It was one of the many chartered airlines ferrying emergency freight to Addis Ababa. On the way out I had asked about the number of aircraft in the fleet and discovered there were just three, with one usually in maintenance. Clearly, the margin for error was slim. It didn't come as a huge surprise when the aircraft we were expecting didn't turn up.

At the airport we had already put our equipment through customs and it had been taken it away. With no aircraft to board we were left with just a few toiletries and wondering what to do. At huge expense to the programme I put Simon on a scheduled flight with the film rushes and then focused on what next. Henry, the cameraman, remarked that there were quite a lot of aircraft flying in and out and perhaps we could cadge a lift.

Even though the RAF was happy to fly us to Cyprus, we needed to get home. Then we spotted a Boeing 707 land and it had a great big Union Jack on the tail. It was from a company called Tradewinds and they agreed to carry three of us back. That meant that one of us would have to stay behind. I asked Graham whether he would mind drawing the short straw. He was surprisingly good about it. I told him to look out for the ZAL aircraft, which was on its way.

Our gear was stored somewhere on the airport and the Tradewinds crew wanted us there by 0530, half an hour before the nightly curfew came to an end. This didn't affect the crew because they could walk straight through without checking in. The question I faced that night was: could we?

At 0500 we found a cab to take us to the airport illegally and paid a heavy tip. Amazingly, the airport building was open and everyone was asleep. We literally walked across sleeping armed guards to go 'airside', and then split up to look for our equipment. To my surprise we found it quite quickly in one of the baggage buildings. It was on its own trolley and we trundled it across the tarmac to the silent aircraft. We opened the forward hatch door and piled it into the empty hold, then secured it with a cargo net. A couple of minutes later the flight crew turned up. Thirty minutes later we took off. We hadn't gone through passport control so as far as the Ethiopian authorities are concerned, we are still there.

I later heard that Simon fought tooth and nail to prevent the authorities from opening the cans of film to see what was inside. He refused even to let them X-ray them because it would have fogged the contents. Had he not won his battle the entire shoot would have been in vain.

Graham came back a day later on the ZAL flight. They had told him they were going to Holland. He was quite surprised when he got out and found that the aircraft had actually landed back at Stanstead.

Much later, Simon was given a tin mug by the crew in memory of the trip:

It still sits on my desk and the crew had written on the side 'Used in Ethiopia in 1984 – from the crew, to Simon – who dug deep to find the words'. What a generous tribute from my fellow professionals – a gift and a sentiment I will always treasure.

I was deeply affected by what I had seen, yet Ethiopia had stirred thoughts that were not entirely charitable. *Blue Peter* and Live Aid a year later had done the right thing and had saved lives – but to what purpose? I could not fault the compassion and generosity of *Blue Peter* viewers and I felt guilty having less than worthy thoughts. There would be other droughts and perhaps all we had done was to ensure there would be even more people left alive to suffer the next one. Life in sub-Saharan Africa was precarious. Maybe drought was nature's way of controlling the population. Maybe the kindest thing, in the long run, would be to encourage people to leave the danger zone.

Meanwhile, back home in the studio the famous *Blue Peter* 'Totaliser' swung into action like never before, showing how many envelopes of buttons and postcards had been sent in. The target of 800,000 envelopes was reached in just eight weeks. Perhaps more fittingly, long before Live Aid, it was *Blue Peter* appeal money through Oxfam that was actually helping to save lives.

By the end of the appeal viewers had sent in enough buttons and postcards to provide money for four irrigation schemes, 24 water tanks, six water pumps, a well-digging scheme, 330 latrines, a 10-ton truck, 30 tons of wheat and 220 tons of molasses.

Fast forward to 2011, and Simon was reunited with Oxfam water engineer Paul Sherlock to make a very special presentation. He was giving him the coveted gold *Blue Peter* badge for a lifetime of saving lives.

As he was leaving after the celebrations were over Simon was approached by a young Oxfam worker, whose words about the whole *Blue Peter* appeal struck a profound chord. Simon recalled: 'He obviously wasn't referring to me, personally – but to the whole *Blue Peter* ethos, demonstrated by those extraordinary fund-raising appeals, helping the World's poor and trying to reduce – and eliminate – suffering.

The Oxfam worker said, 'I just want to say – you're the reason I'm here.'

(Above): Simon Groom, Henry Farrar and George Cassidy waiting for take-off

(Right): Michael Sundin with the young winner of a design competition enjoying her prize visit to Sweden with her family

11

'Give us a kiss'

Within a week of returning from Ethiopia, I faced the surreal experience of leaving behind dying children in one land to film a supposedly lavish Christmas story in another. The location was Tomteland (Santa Land) at Mora in Sweden. This also meant going from the high 80s Fahrenheit (low 30s Celsius) to below freezing. But it wasn't the working conditions that got to me.

6–9 December 1984

Mora, Sweden

The programme had agreed to stage a competition to design part of a new theme park that was all about Father Christmas. The winner was going to visit the site, where their winning design would be re-created from recently reclaimed pine forest. It all seemed so trivial, and I wasn't sure what was in it for our viewers because Mora was quite a hike from the UK.

It didn't help that the presenter was Michael Sundin, who, stockily built with curly blond hair, was never really comfortable on screen. This was despite his repertoire as a successful trampolinist, television actor and star of West End shows such as *Cats*.

The crew had arrived the day before and had been taking shots of everything that had snow on it. Unfortunately, the one thing that hadn't been filmed was Tomteland, which remained an unsightly half-completed and snow-free building site. The cameraman had developed a warm relationship with the promoters so when I arrived I felt outnumbered. They had already decided what was to be done. To make matters worse, I had an acute attack of diarrhoea from something very dodgy I had eaten in Africa.

So here I was, filming conveyor belts pouring toys into Santa's sack, when I had just been with families who had been afforded not even a

shred of common decency. Absolutely nothing. Not even enough to eat or drink. My indignation only increased when, that evening, a local dignitary wanted to know if I wanted some 'nose candy' (cocaine).

I finished the film and it was transmitted. I instantly forgot about it.

And now for something completely different.

1–2 May 1985

Topsham, Devon

My home, Topsham on the river Exe, is just a mile or two upstream from the Commando Training Centre Royal Marines. They were always pleased to see us. On this occasion I had an idea for a race. It would involve crossing the river at low tide.

The estuary of the river Exe, opposite the Royal Marine camp, is about a mile wide and at low water the water occupies about a hundred yards of it. The rest is soft, oozing mud.

The idea was that Hunter Troop, recruits who had been 'back trooped' for fitness reasons, would race across it with the presenters Janet Ellis and Michael Sundin (who, remember, had once been an Olympic athlete). It was a mad idea and the Royal Marines loved it.

We placed sheets of plywood on the mud at strategic points for the cameramen to stand on while Royal Marines in assault craft stretched a rope across the water bit of the river for safety. It all had to be set up as soon as the tide was out, so urgency was everything.

Hunter Troop and the presenters lined up ready on the far side of the river. We watched anxiously for the lowest part of the tide. A Gazelle helicopter hovered with an observer gauging the depth, but low tide didn't come. At the appointed hour the current was still quite strong. To my consternation there was much more water in the river than there should have been. It had been raining on Exmoor in North Devon and the rain draining away was going to make the race more of a challenge than it should have been. I wondered what to do.

The Royal Marines didn't hesitate. They said go. Hunter Troop was cockily confident and Janet was allocated a tall and very strong NCO to look after her. Michael Sundin, who wasn't the tallest presenter we've ever had, had to take his chances with the recruits.

It proved quite a spectacle as a 150 young men and one woman streamed across the mudflats towards the torrent that was the river Exe in flood. I was airborne in the Gazelle and we filmed the race leaders as they slurped their way across half a mile of mudflat. Then they reached the channel and waded in.

I told the pilot, 'Go low – we need to get closer shots.'

The Gazelle swooped down and hovered about twenty feet above the contestants. Seconds later there wasn't a single swimmer to be seen. The downdraught had pushed them all under the water. The river was

(Right): Janet Ellis during the muddy river Exe challenge at the Commando Training Centre Royal Marines, Lympstone, Devon

only supposed to be a metre deep but the rain had doubled that. There was frantic waving from the safety boat.

'Up, up,' I yelled to the pilot.

I looked anxiously as they rounded up swimmers. I could see no casualties and the race continued.

At the finish on the far side of the river it was a very subdued and muddy Hunter Troop that emerged from the river. At the end Janet was virtually carried to the far bank by her corporal and Michael finished under his own steam. He finished in the top ten.

As he emerged from the mud there were cries of 'Give us a kiss, Michael' from the recruits. It was the first and only time that anyone openly remarked on his sexuality. It was never an issue on the programme.

Back on the river Exe I heaved a sigh of relief that no one had drowned. Meanwhile, a senior officer had joined us.

'Terrific. We should make this an annual event,' he said, full of enthusiasm.

June–July 1985

Australia

That summer the expedition was to Australia.

Michael had moved on to pastures new and it was only Simon and Janet who would go. I set off for Australia knowing that I would be away for nearly two months. I would miss my daughter Hannah's first birthday and this was a big disappointment. Like everyone who worked on the programme, keeping the show on the road was one of the downsides, and we all accepted that. We knew there were plenty of upsides.

Two of us set off for Sydney. I was joined by Sue Root, the production assistant, who would do the paperwork and sort out logistics. My job was to work out what stories to film and write the scripts before the presenters and crew arrived.

I was very keen to make a film about camel-trekking with Noel Fullerton, who lived about an hour and a half out of Alice Springs. He was a typical Australian and was a rakish figure with a long white beard. He regaled us with stories about camels and the Aborigines and took us out for a short camel trek to get the feel for it.

'How long can a camel live without water?' I asked as we lurched

our way through the bush. He replied in a burst of staccato Oz.

'Several months, and by that time its back will be as flat as a cow's.'

He then went on to tell us about how the early settlers had hunted down the Aborigines and, a bit of an eye-opener, there were stories that they played football with their heads.

I returned to the subject of the camel trek and how we would meet up. He was going to be away trekking with a small group so it wasn't going to be easy. He reckoned we could meet him and his group at a place called Cockys Creek. Even though I had absolutely no idea where it was, I promised that we would meet him there.

We needed a helicopter and at Alice Springs airport I found one – a Jet Ranger 7. It was the most modern helicopter in the region and the owner was very keen to know who would be flying it. So was I. With no pilots on tap he suggested I enquire in the bar at the Gap Hotel on the outskirts of town.

The bar at the Gap was full of lager-drinking cowboys, at least that's what they all looked like. Several wore riding chaps. They used both horses and helicopters to round up their charges. When I told them I was looking for the best helicopter pilot in the region they were very interested and insisted on buying me a drink.

'Justin's your man. He's the best.'

Justin appeared about an hour and two pints later. When I told him about the Jet Ranger 7 he was very interested.

'I've been trying to lay my hands on that one for a while now,' he said happily.

'Have you flown one before?' I asked uneasily.

'No, but I can fly any helicopter,' he replied. 'Leave it to me.'

By that time I was flying too – on lager. The deal was done.

A couple of weeks later we all met at the airport and I asked the owner about using Justin, bearing in mind he had never flown a Jet Ranger 7 before.

'If he breaks it, you pay for it,' he replied ominously.

I signed the contract with nervous misgivings and wondered if the BBC would ever cough up.

Our weight was an issue and we ditched everything that wasn't absolutely vital, and stowed several crates of water in its place. Justin was unrepentant. 'Could save your life, this stuff.'

We flew to Noel's ranch where we refuelled and took off again, heavily loaded, flying low and forward, dodging the trees until we were airborne. Justin the flying cowboy, who mustered cattle from a helicopter rather than a horse, weaved his way between the trees with ease. I imagine he would have done justice to any tactical flying unit fighting in the Middle East today. We settled at about a thousand feet altitude and cruised into the desert.

After about an hour we came to where he reckoned Cockys Creek was, and circled about. Over the intercom he warned, 'We've got five minutes to find them. Then we turn back.'

It was an anxious five minutes and we all scoured the ground below. Just when I feared I was one film and several thousand Australian dollars poorer, Justin spotted a camel and rider standing on top of a small hillock. We landed and began filming.

To me the outback was a revelation. The sky was an incredibly deep blue, almost violet because of the lack of pollution. It was like staring up directly into deep space and it smelt of ozone. The trees and shrubs were no more than fifteen feet high and the dried-out vegetation crackled underfoot. When we stopped moving it was unbelievably quiet. There was absolutely nothing to break the pure silence. It freaked the sound recordist, Chris King, who kept checking his dials. His normal job was to judge when the background noise got too intrusive. He stopped the filming at one point and asked if I could hear anything. I couldn't. Not a thing. Then about five minutes later I could. It was a motorbike and it was a long way off. We stopped filming because the noise was loud enough to register, and after about ten minutes the rider came into view. It was the farmer and landowner. He had seen us and wanted to know what we were doing on his land.

I was alarmed to discover that Noel had just had a run-in with the same farmer who had shot dead a camel calf that had come along with its mother as part of the trek. It was also very unfortunate that the calf also happened to be a pet that belonged to Noel's daughter. Even though it had been an honest mistake, the scene was set for a fierce exchange of views. We backed away and pretended not to listen. I reached for my wallet.

(Right): Simon Groom finding his 'seat'

(Below): Simon Groom and Janet Ellis getting ready to start a camel trek

We were lucky. The camel shooting and our unannounced visit cancelled each other out and there was no fee to pay. Within minutes he was on his way. I heaved a sigh of relief.

After a day re-creating a camel trek in less than half a mile, we said our goodbyes and prepared to leave.

We circled over the camp, waving, and then headed home. We flew at treetop height along valleys, inside steep-sided gorges, and chased families of kangaroos across the open plains. The sun was low in the sky and the dancing shadows of the darting animals were like shoals of startled fish. At dusk, with large black shadows turning blue in the setting sun, we landed back at Alice airport.

I thanked Justin. 'No worries, mate. She flew like a beaut.'

He told me to say hello to the lads at RAF Boscombe Down, who'd known him as Kiwi One when he'd been crop dusting in Hampshire a few years previously.

'I liked the UK,' he said, and cheerily departed.

The next day we were back at the airport and airborne again with the Royal Flying Doctor Service, which was based at Alice Springs.

Arriving at the Napperby station an hour or two outside Alice, we were warned not to film anything. Puzzled, we put away our equipment as the owner, Tony Chisholm, strode up and shook hands. There was something strangely familiar about him. Then the penny dropped. He was the spitting image of King Edward VIII who abdicated to marry Wallis Simpson, a story now even more famous thanks to the Oscar-winning *The King's Speech*.

We subsequently heard rumours – and that was all they were – that he was the Prince's illegitimate child. His mother was Mollee Little, a Sydney socialite, and she had made friends with the prince when he visited Australia in 1920. It seemed unlikely that this man was his son because the Prince had left three years before he was born. Even so, the resemblance was remarkable. He was shy and without the commanding confidence usually associated with royalty. Nevertheless, we were very British and minded our Ps and Qs. Just in case.

Years later I read in the newspaper that he had died and the rumour of his parentage died with him. He had been charming and very welcoming.

Napperby station played host to an Aboriginal settlement and our Flying Doctor representative showed us around. He explained the difficulties the indigenous people had had in adjusting to the twentieth century. It was the first time I'd heard the expression 'It's a two-dog night', a reference to the number of dogs you need in bed to keep you warm.

Finding the patients wasn't always easy, as Simon recalls:

> I have a very vivid image of us both literally chasing a patient through the bush – an elderly lady called 'Kitty' and she wore a bright orange hat. She was I believe suffering from cataracts. According to our flying doctor it was not uncommon for him to 'treat' some of his more unwilling patients in this fashion – if he could catch them first!

As we walked around the settlement treating new injuries and ones that hadn't healed properly, I thought that the Australian authorities had a conscience about the way the Aborigines were treated. There was a concrete block and corrugated-iron-roofed building for every family, but they didn't live in them. Instead they preferred to strip the iron off the roof and make their own lean-to shelters outside. The whole place was covered with litter.

'They don't see man-made things as any different to a broken branch. What looks like litter to us is to them no different to fallen leaves and part of nature,' our doctor told us.

We explored the Aboriginal concept of life at Ayers Rock and at Kakadu National Park. It seemed the more we found out, the more complicated it became. Towards the end I began to wonder if we were being told anything we wanted to hear because it was hard to come to any conclusions. The Aboriginal people were so very different and there was a huge gap between them and the so-called 'New Australians'.

While I was away I made sure I phoned home every couple of days to chat to the family. Admittedly, conversation was a bit one-sided with my 11-month-old daughter, Hannah, but I found a way to communicate as only besotted fathers can.

I would say 'Hannah say fork' or 'plate' or 'head' and Hannah would dutifully say 'ork', 'ate' or the nearest sound to it.

What intrigued me was her interpretation of the word 'spoon' because however hard I tried to get her to say 'spoon' she always said 'push'. I think it was because I always laughed when she said it, and that was what she really wanted to hear. From that moment, and for several years after, a spoon was always a 'push'.

Coming home after seven weeks away was traumatic. I knocked on the front door of our white-painted semi-detached in East Sheen and waited. Then Lynn and Hannah came to the door. Hannah had grown so much. She looked up at me and then at Lynn as if to say 'Is this who I think it is?' Lynn nodded several times and smiled and then Hannah was staggering forward, arms outstretched, and in my arms, where she held me in a vice-like grip for about twenty minutes. Eventually she let go and I realised how much of her young life I had missed.

The next morning was dreadful because she didn't want me to go to work. And there was no way of explaining to her that I would return that evening. For Hannah I could be gone for another lifetime and I could not make her understand. It was an uncomfortable day for both of us. Even so, by the end of the week things had almost got back to normal.

12

HALOs, hippos and hospitals

18 October 1985
Salisbury Plain

That autumn I renewed my efforts to get Janet Ellis's parachuting challenge back on track. We gathered on Salisbury Plain to join a group from special forces who were training for a certain type of jump called a HALO, or High Altitude Low Opening. It was a quiet afternoon and we watched as they landed on the open wild grassland and gathered up their parachutes. We talked about the possibility of doing a practice jump with them the following day. It was agreed that no one from the SAS would be filmed because secrecy of identity in this elite regiment is sacrosanct.

Very early the following morning I had a phone call from Mike Milburn, the Falcons' team leader. He had some terrible news to break.

'Alex, there has been a parachuting fatality. I don't want this to put Janet off but we cannot go ahead today because there will have to be an inquest and a board of inquiry. It's likely to put us on hold for a while.'

'For how long?' I asked, having expressed my shock at what had happened.

'Several months at least,' he replied reluctantly.

In fact, it was six months before we made another attempt. By the time we got back Mike's commanding officer had ordered him to take personal responsibility for Janet. Ally, Roggy and Mike had moved on from the Falcons but with Mike now in charge of high-altitude freefall, it was he and Sergeant Bill Jenkins who were to complete the record-breaking descent with Janet.

2 May 1986
RAF North Luffenham, Bedfordshire

The final part of Janet's parachuting challenge began in the decompression chamber at RAF North Luffenham, where she had to be trained to recognise oxygen starvation, as Mike remembers:

> Funny things happen when you are starved of oxygen. We were asked to count backwards in threes starting at 100 and writing down the answers. 'One hundred, 99, 98, er, 96, 94, 90' as the starvation befuddled our minds.

'OK, everyone, put your oxygen masks back on,' said the doctor, much to our relief.

It was a few days after the Chernobyl disaster when a Russian nuclear power station had blown up and the air above Lincolnshire was hazy with dust. We'd spent most of the day inside the large metal tube of the chamber, breathing pure oxygen. When at last we emerged to breathe the autumn air on that sunny and very hazy day, I wondered how much nuclear contamination was going into our lungs. Everyone was worried.

There were speculative reports later that Cumbrian lambs that had grazed on contaminated grass were unfit for human consumption.

8 October 1986
RAF Weston-on-the-Green and Salisbury Plain

By now Janet was ready for the challenge that had cast a shadow over her life for so long. It began with a practice descent at Weston-on-the-Green from 12,000 feet, breathing oxygen through a mask as she had been trained to do. She was confident as Mike launched out of the back of the Hercules C130 and the descent was completed without incident. It was time for 'the big one' – the record attempt from 20,000 feet over Salisbury Plain.

It wasn't just Janet who was bursting with anticipation. Mike, Bill and two freefalling RAF cameramen shared her anxieties as, with cautious trepidation, she boarded the Hercules C130. They took off and climbed to 20,000 feet. Meanwhile, I set up to film on the ground on Salisbury Plain. Everything was reported to be going well and I was unaware of a minor drama that was being played out nearly four miles above my head.

Much later, in the cutting room, it was revealed to me. About three minutes before she was due to go there was a minor panic as Mike Milburn and the other instructors fiddled about with her equipment. I rang Mike and asked him what had happened.

(Above): Safe landing:
Janet Ellis at RAF
Weston-on-the-Green

His reply was alarming. 'Her goggles weren't fitting properly and if a blast of cold air crept in from the side it would freeze her eyeball.'

She would have landed safely – and been blind for the rest of her life. Mike takes up the story:

> Janet was so nervous she tried at first to put on her helmet back to front. We reassured her, shouting over the noise of the aircraft, and she quickly got 'into the zone' as we approached the drop.
>
> 'P minus 4 [minutes]' came the order on a written board. 'Fit oxygen masks. 100 per cent oxygen.'
>
> P was the time of the parachute descent. No one could speak with their faces covered with oxygen masks.
>
> 'P minus 2.' We stood up and moved to the back of the Hercules.
>
> Janet, facing forward and looking out into the 20,000 foot void, steeled herself.
>
> 'Red on.' The red warning light came on above our heads.
>
> 'Green on, go!' And the despatcher waved for Janet to jump.
>
> I had hold of her right arm and leg and Bill had hold of her on the other side. We all rocked rhythmically forward then backward and then launched out of the Hercules. Janet made a textbook exit.
>
> She settled into nearly two minutes of freefall. We released her arms so she could experience the freedom of flying her own body. At 5,000 feet she looked for the ripcord handle that would deploy her parachute. She looked but missed the handle and grabbed the oxygen hose that connected her mask to the oxygen bottle instead. I spotted this and knocked her arm off the hose, rolled underneath her, to pull the handle for her. The canopy opened and Janet floated down to earth safely.

True to form Janet had been courageous to the end. Thinking of the loose goggles and using a terrible pun, she had 'blind' faith that the boys would look after her. They always did.

So, on that day and on the dropping zone, miles away from anywhere, Janet appeared from the heavens and made a textbook landing. Her relief was obvious and there was much celebration from the Falcons, and particularly Mike, who were relieved to be free of the burden of responsibility. Janet's parachuting project had been a white knuckle ride from start to finish and we were all glad it was finally over. She became the new record holder in *The Guinness Book of Records* as the female civilian who had made the longest freefall parachute jump.

> I'm a little proud and slightly astonished that I did one jump, let alone thirty-five. Alex and I were a good team. You don't get that sort of chance very often, and when it involves training with the best and really stretching yourself

to do something extraordinary, how lucky to be able to grab it. Although my motto since has always been: never again.

Janet's was the first of four similar challenges with the RAF Falcons that I would film, and I had learnt some useful lessons. We would never again attempt any freefall parachute training in the UK because of the weather. And we were never again allowed to attempt a HALO jump.

And, coincidentally, eyes were to be the focus of my next assignment.

12–21 November 1986
Malawi

The autumn Sightsaver Appeal was for mobile eye units in Africa. As part of the appeal, we followed a mobile eye unit in Malawi. After my experiences in Ethiopia I felt that Malawi was going to be a walk in the park. We landed at Lilonqwe and when we met Moses Chirambo, the country's chief eye surgeon, our spirits soared. He spoke excellent English, was cheerful, intelligent, modest and a good organiser whose presence was felt every time he entered a room. He was the ideal contributor and we liked him very much.

Mark Curry was the presenter and he and Moses got on very well indeed. Mark is a bit of a song-and-dance man. Tall with glasses, always cheerful and with a mop of reddish hair, he looked as if he might have been one of the original Milky Bar kids (he wasn't!). It wasn't long before he was trying to teach Moses a music hall song 'Moses supposes his toeses is roses but Moses supposes erroneously...' and so on.

They sang together in the back of the Land Rover as we bumped along dusty bush tracks between villages. I can't say that Moses was ever word perfect, but in idle moments their duet kept us all going.

We headed to Lake Malawi and joined a mobile eye unit team on their rounds. The unit comprised a Land Rover, a driver and two health workers who were trained to do simple cataract operations. We moved between villages and filmed as a cataract operation was performed. It was extraordinary to see the head of the patient sticking out over the tailboard of the Land Rover while the surgical team stood over it and cut into the surface of the eye to pull out the clouded lens. I am not sure I would have yielded to the knife in such circumstances but here there was no option. As Moses pointed out, there was no need to bring the patients to the eye hospital 200 miles away. It was all very impressive.

One evening we went sightseeing for hippos. We had been told there was a creek at the side of the lake where they lived, so we scouted excitedly, trying to find them. I stumbled upon an almost perfectly circular tunnel through the thick undergrowth and explored until Moses anxiously hissed at me to get out. He didn't shout in case the tunnel had more than one occupant. Alarmed by the tone of his voice, I got out – fast.

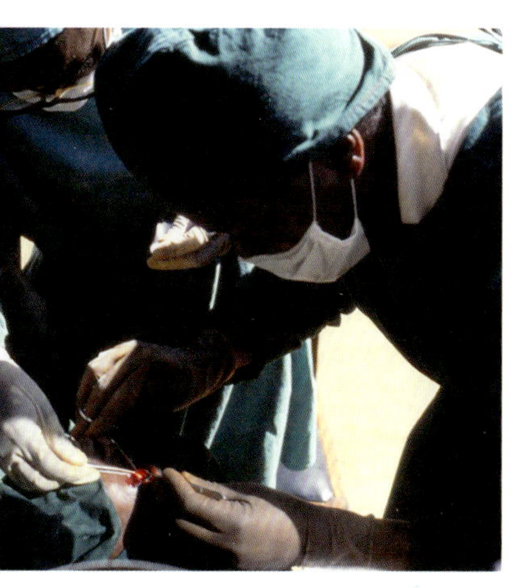

(Above): A cataract operation by a mobile eye unit in Malawi

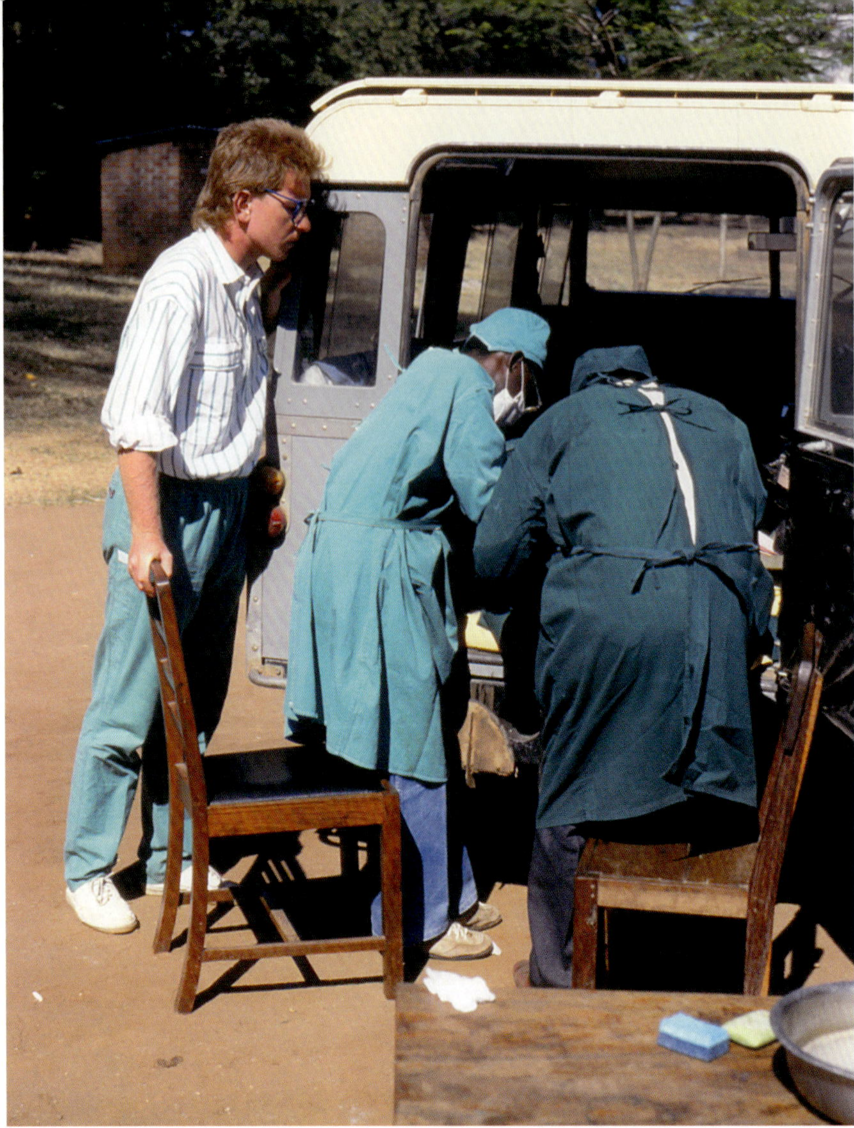

(Left): Mark Curry looks
on as local eye specialists
perform a simple but
life-changing cataract
operation

'What's the problem?' I asked nervously.

'You were in a hippo run. Very dangerous,' came the response of my anxious host. Eye surgery was one thing but putting me back together after a hippo attack was a far less attractive proposition.

The tunnels were the route hippopotami took from the land to the water. Hence the circular 'hippo' shape. If there had been a hippo in the tunnel, and we had frightened it, there would have been a ton or so of monstrous, iron-hard flesh thundering towards the water that would have literally flattened everything in its path.

With this sobering thought we settled down to wait. In a short while several hippos appeared with their young and they yawned and snorted at each other while we watched. Giant jaws agape and massive tusks displayed, they played in the water less than forty yards away as the large yellow African sun sank behind them.

Lake Malawi used to be known as Lake Nyasa when Malawi was Nyasaland. At ten years old I used to collect postage stamps and the ones from Nyasaland were among my favourites. They were illustrated with drawings of palm trees, thatched houses and dugout canoes and they all looked like scenes from paradise. Now I could compare fantasy with reality, and I wasn't disappointed.

And there was mystery too. In the heat of the day huge dark clouds grew out of the middle of the lake and then disappeared in the early evening. I later learnt that these 'clouds' were, in fact, flies. There were countless millions of them.

Another phenomenon was the daily movement of thousands of cormorants. They roosted on the island directly across from the beach hotel where we were staying, and on a given signal they would take off and fly down the lake, I assumed to rich fishing grounds. Then, on another cue, they would come back, hundreds of squadrons of them, circling to land back on the trees to roost for the night.

The reality of Malawi hit home several days later when I followed Moses into the eye hospital. There was a long queue of patients and he noticed one small boy in particular.

He was with his mother and after a look at the boy's eyes Moses had a brief word with her. At the end he walked off and would not respond when I asked him what was wrong. He was very angry.

Later he told me the reason. The mother lived with her family a long way from the city and the only medical help was at a mission station manned by some elderly nuns. The boy had what Moses thought was 'pink-eye', which would have cleared up by itself, but the mother had been concerned. She took him to the mission for the nuns to treat him. Unwittingly, they poured neat carbolic acid into each eye and blinded him for life.

'This is not the first time they have done this. They are too old to know what they are doing. I must go and see them before they blind any more children.'

I was appalled. 'Why do the people go to them if it's happened before?' I asked with an equal sense of anger.

'The local people think that because they are "God's chosen", what they do is right. They won't listen to me. I have to speak to the nuns and make them understand.'

Even today I think of that little boy growing up in darkness because of the well-meaning stupidity of those elderly ladies.

Malawi was also a wake-up call for me in another way. I had noticed that I often felt unwell in hot climates and Malawi was no exception. We had eaten a barbecue of buffalo and salad and that night I was very ill. I had constant vomiting, which did not relent for more than two days. Others had eaten it too and were unaffected so it wasn't food poisoning. Moses came to see me and diagnosed a different cause – dehydration. He brought some salt and sugar mix for me to take with water. With difficulty I swallowed some whenever I could. I persisted and soon the vomiting stopped, and I recovered enough to just have a blinding headache. After another day the headache went away.

It occurred to me that a problem that had troubled me on several occasions was because I sweated too much and probably drank too much water as well. Unwittingly I was flushing all the salts and sugars out of my body and this led to the feelings of nausea and headaches.

Nowadays I take one sachet of rehydration powder every morning and evening and dehydration is no longer a problem. I have smugly administered this miracle mix to others and watched their speedy recovery.

One evening we were sitting on the hotel balcony, waiting for the call to dinner, and Mark emerged to say that the BBC programme *The Late, Late Breakfast Show* had been taken off the air because a contributor had been killed during the making of it. We debated the causes and consequences. It was a terrible shock, which had an immediate impact on the BBC's approach to high-risk filming, for which, of course, *Blue Peter* was famous.

Michael Lush, a 25-year-old hod carrier from Southampton, had volunteered to take part in a death-defying stunt: bungee-jumping from a box suspended from a giant crane. After proper instruction he had practised unsupervised and on his final jump the other end of the bungee hadn't been attached to the top of the crane. How it happened was the subject of much investigation and many court appearances for the BBC Safety Officer and others. It was one hell of a mess. There were several different theories and the verdict was one of accidental death.

It had been an accident waiting to happen because producers constantly fought to attract more viewers by pushing the boundaries of safety. The incident changed the entire nature of location filming. Gone was the gung-ho 'let's do it' attitude and in its place came a sea of paperwork.

I don't think anyone could have foreseen the quagmire of risk assessment documentation that would sometimes take longer to fill in than the filming itself. Over time it became more streamlined, but for a period of years the restrictions got tighter and tighter and caused me much exasperation. Safety considerations are now a significant part of the director's job and they take up a lot of time.

9–18 January 1987
Lake Malawi

I returned to Malawi with Janet to do a follow-up report about a child, Emmanuelle, whose eyesight we had already filmed being corrected the previous November. We took her back to her home, travelling cross-country, bouncing across cassava fields and untamed bush to a remote village, but when we arrived there wasn't a soul in sight. It was a very strange experience and we hung about, waiting for someone to return. There we were, a film crew with a little girl, and no one to hand her over to. Yet Moses was unperturbed.

(Top right): Janet Ellis at a crowded village eye clinic with cameraman Henry Farrar and sound recordist Bryan Showell

(Bottom right): Janet Ellis chats to curious children who'd never seen a white person before

After about ten minutes the people started to appear and they were very curious and hospitable. We explained about the camera and they were a little wary. We filmed an interview with the dad and to begin with he was fine. As the interview went on and the camera changed position he began to look alarmed and we stopped the filming. As we left I asked Moses where the people had been when we arrived.

'Oh, they ran away because they hadn't seen white people before.'

I cursed myself. I just wish I had known that at the time and had made a feature of it.

Flights to and from Malawi at that time were infrequent and it was the only occasion I can remember when we had very little to do and, rather perversely, a huge amount of time to do it in. It was a pleasant 75°Fahrenheit (24°Celsius) on the shores of the lake, while at home there was a blanket of snow ten inches deep.

We had the agreeable prospect of topping up our tans and relaxing on the beach. Henry Farrar was the cameraman and I thought, *At last I have been able to repay him for Peru and Ethiopia*, both of which had been harrowing and uncomfortable shoots. Alas, it was not to be. Henry was very worried that all the pipes in his ancient country house near Reading would freeze. He had to get back. The only flight available had seats in first class and both he and Janet stumped up the extra cash and jetted back home.

Janet was very eager to get back to her family and her daughter Sophie, who was only six years old. (While still in her teens, Sophie Ellis Bextor took the charts by storm as the lead singer of the indie rock band Audience, and now enjoys a hugely successful solo singing career.)

I still remember that trip as the only one in my entire filming career when there was time to spare. Mostly, though, I will remember Moses

Chirambo, the hugely charismatic man who made us laugh and gave sight to many, leaving a legacy that remains internationally recognised after his death in 2010. *Blue Peter*'s success relies on inspirational people like Moses to shine a light into corners of a world normally hidden from view.

As it turned out, the programme influenced the charity with more than financial support. The term Sightsavers was the title we had given to the *Blue Peter* appeal, while the charity was called the Royal Commonwealth Society for the Blind. *Blue Peter*'s strong editorial instincts for a snappier and more memorable name caused the charity to adopt Sightsavers as its official name.

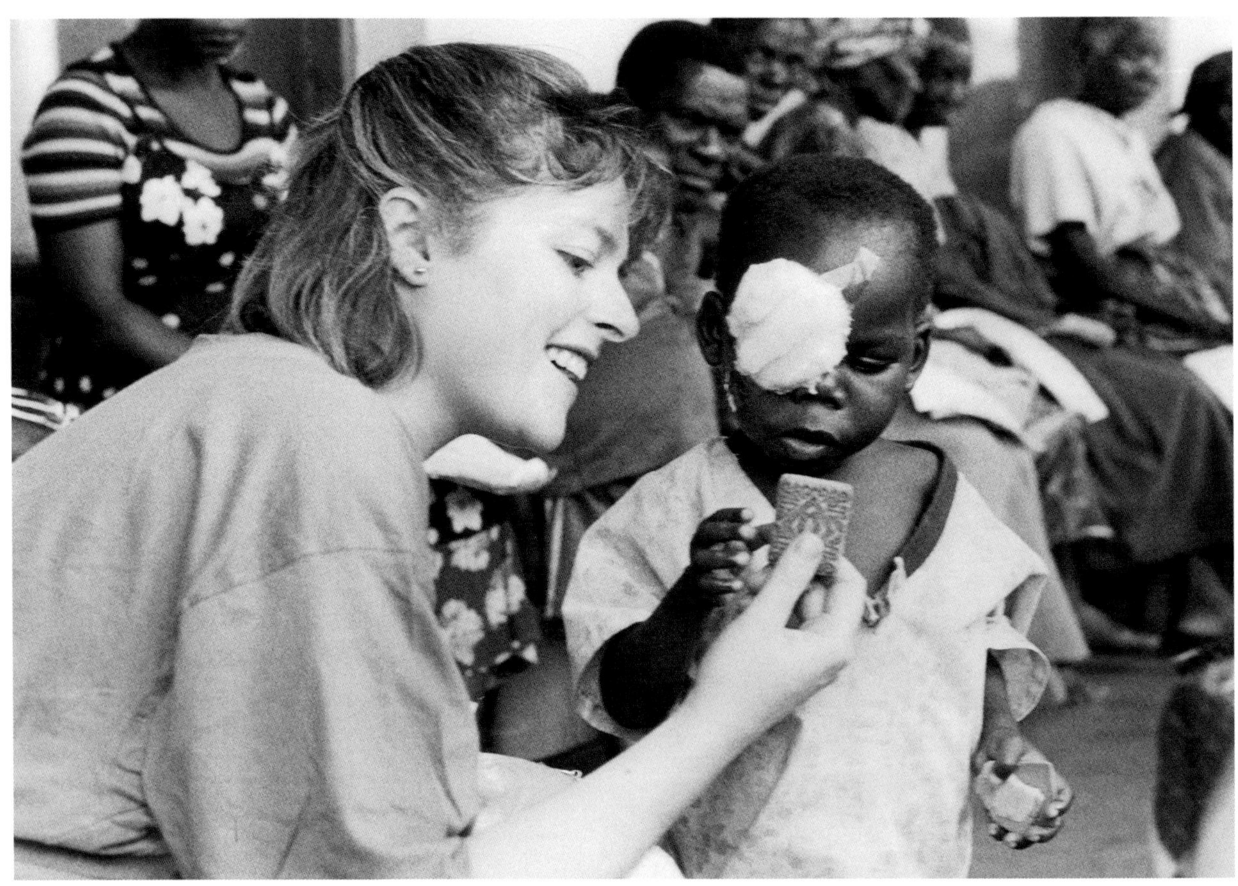

(Above): Janet Ellis rewards two-year-old Emmanuelle with a very British custard cream after his eye operation

13

Turbulent times

May 1987
London

Blue Peter wasn't just a favourite children's television programme. It was a British institution and as such also one of the favourite targets of the tabloid press. Biddy Baxter, our revered and fiercesomely protective leader, often warned us about being on our guard.

As the one who was constantly on the road, I was perhaps more susceptible to the press than most. My first brush with them had been while I was trying to do two jobs – producing *Duncan Dares* with Peter Duncan and working for *Blue Peter* at the same time.

Duncan Dares was a *Blue Peter* spin-off, with Peter Duncan tackling even bigger challenges. My projects took him into the wilderness of Wales and the Brecon Beacons to live off the land, aloft to become a hang-glider pilot, and with the Royal Marines to attempt their 30-mile green beret test. Finally we teamed up with the London Fire Brigade and Kentish Town Fire Station to make a feature about becoming a firefighter.

It was the last that caused trouble with the press. There was an industrial dispute brewing within the fire service and we unwittingly got caught up in the middle of it. We had discussed storylines with our Kentish Town colleagues for Peter's 'dare' and decided that he would help put out a fire in an abandoned building and rescue a body from the flames.

It would have meant taking a fire engine off station and therefore risking fire cover, so we had explored other possibilities. One was whether a reserve vehicle could be used. And because I had two jobs to do, I had a unit manager who was looking into this and he made the necessary enquiries.

It was quite a shock to discover, when I returned to the *Blue Peter* office after setting up another *Blue Peter* film, the world's press wanting to talk to me. A story had got out that the BBC were going to set fire to a house and one paper even reported that Peter Duncan was going to rescue not a dummy used by the fire brigade for this kind of exercise – but a living child. We were also going to use an improper vehicle on a location that might endanger life and limb of the general public.

Urgent meetings with the Controller of BBC1, Michael Grade, followed and we refuted the whole thing. Even so, the story was still printed in one of the tabloids. Only *The Times* printed the real story and reported underlying tensions within the fire service.

I found it astonishing how many seemingly sensible people actually believed we would deliberately put a child's life in danger. It was laughable and at the same time terribly damaging, and ever since that time I have been very wary of the press.

Early summer 1987

As I approached my 40th birthday I thought long and hard about my future. I recognised all too clearly that my work had an adverse effect on my family life. In truth, I enjoyed film-making and travelling to distant parts. However, *Blue Peter* was a hard taskmaster and I had to spend more and more of my time away from home. Like all producers, I wondered if I could make a living outside the BBC. Even though London was my base, my heart was in Topsham in Devon, where I had been brought up and where my mother and youngest brother lived.

In a very rash move I decided to relocate to Topsham. Anna Home, who was head of Children's Programmes at the time, agreed I could work part-time on a one-year renewable contract and continue with the programme. Thank goodness she did.

In September we moved back to Topsham and I realised that things were going to be even more complicated. It was quickly apparent that working for the programme would mean more work, not less. For the next three years I saw even less of my family because, even though I was now part-time, no one else thought I should work part-time. Yet I was home in every sense of the word, and no amount of work deterred me from making the arrangement work.

29 June 1987
Yvette Fielding joins the team

In 1987 a very young and sparky presenter joined the team. Her name was Yvette Fielding and she was curly haired, petite, quick to smile and make friends and just 17 years old. Looking back, I am astonished how well she did under the pressures put on her at such a young age. She was new to London and very vulnerable. Coupled with this were the usual

(Above): Biddy Baxter makes her traditional speech at the end-of-series party

(Right): Yvette Fielding makes friends with some orphaned and abandoned Romanian children

expectations from Biddy so she had a heavy load to carry on her young shoulders.

I liked Yvette because she empathised with the contributors and when out filming she was accomplished and fun to direct. I have known presenters to be difficult, inept or overconfident – no names, of course – and Yvette never was. We made sure that we always took an assistant with us who would act as a friend and look after her because her vulnerability was obvious.

I confess that by this time I had seen quite a few presenters come and go and was pretty single-minded myself. Looking back, I hope I didn't add to Yvette's burden. I am inclined to say I didn't – or I was forgiven – because we have always had a good time whenever we meet up. Back in 1987, Yvette and I didn't know it but we were about to share some pretty unpleasant filming locations over the next few years.

But that was all to come and it wasn't just the locations that were the trouble. It was the media again, turning up like a bad penny.

22–23 September 1987

Sibson airfield

Molly Sedgewick was the daughter of Dolly Shepherd who was a famous 'aerialist'. At just 17, Dolly had joined Buffalo Bill Cody's *Wild West Show*, and caught the imagination of the public by dropping, by parachute, from a hot-air balloon.

And while her grandmother did her parachuting as part of a novelty routine in the years before the First World War, Molly was going to celebrate the connection by doing a tandem jump at the tender age of 67 – and we thought it was our exclusive. The link to the programme was Janet's freefall parachuting exploits, and we turned up at Sibson airfield for day one of a two-day shoot.

From the moment I got out of the car I could see that the organisers had other ideas. There were at least two crews from ITV also hoping to cover the event. To make matters worse, they were news crews, which meant that the story would be transmitted later that day. By the time it was shown on *Blue Peter* it would be history.

Biddy was adamant. We would not cover it unless we could be guaranteed exclusivity, and I totally agreed with her. I was doubly fed up because, with so little time to film, I would have to abandon my script. We would have to skirmish in a press melee, and that was not at all what *Blue Peter* was all about.

The day progressed bitterly and I was very keen to ditch the whole thing and call it a day. The organisers were horrified. They had promised Molly that she would be on *Blue Peter*. Local news was good yet not as good as network television.

I was in a quandary. Like or lump it, we now had a responsibility to Molly and I had no doubt that the news crews would relish the bigger story: '*Blue Peter* renegades on pensioner's challenge'.

I decided that the only way was a 'go slow' and to hope that the weather would deteriorate and the jump be called off. I guessed that the independent television companies would be unlikely to come back for a second day. As the day progressed we all filmed our bits as best we could and tried not to get in each other's way. The weather was getting worse, yet not bad enough to end it. I was running out of reasons for not going ahead. One of the other reporters was an old hand and knew I was over a barrel. He also knew I would fight to the bitter end. As the hours ticked by so tensions rose, and by mid-afternoon feelings were very sore.

The BBC Safety Officer, Gavin Birkett, was there to keep an eye on the parachuting and I asked him to keep an eye on me as well. I felt very uneasy because the two crews were so irritated. I thought that if there was going to be any trouble it would be handy to have a witness.

By four o'clock there was only one crew left because the others had lost their deadlines. It was marginal that the remaining crew would make the news at six o'clock and I did a last-minute negotiation. If we went ahead now, could they guarantee that the story would not go national with ITN? I was assured that if they could have access to a few seconds of our air-to-air shots, this would not happen. I took a gamble and agreed.

Just minutes after four o'clock, Molly completed her jump.

The ITV crew managed to transmit its story because I did not know that they had an edit suite 20 minutes away. It did not run on ITN, even though the pictures of Molly in freefall were spectacular. But the whole episode left a bitter taste in my mouth and I vowed such a thing would never happen again.

Autumn 1978–spring 1988
From film to video

The BBC was going through a transition period from film to videotape. 16 mm negative film had wonderful qualities and lasted for decades but it had drawbacks. After each shot the film gate had to be checked by the camera assistant, who would remove the lens to check that the film gate was 'clear'. This was because the movement of film would rub against the gate and create a slight electrical charge that would attract fluff and dust. So, quite often, a great performance by the presenter would have to be repeated because there was a 'hair in the gate'.

There was another drawback and this was expense. Every ten minute roll of Eastman 7247 negative film stock cost (at that time) £150, including the first 'rush' print.

It all sounds a bit complicated and, heaven knows, it took me a while to get a grip on what film was all about, but basically the 'rushes' were used for editing. Next the film would be 'neg cut' and the negative would be cut to match the cutting copy (the edited film from the rushes). Then the 'negative' would be sent off for 'positive' answer and transmission prints made. The answer print was a trial and the transmission print was the corrected answer print. All this going backwards and forwards was very time-consuming. Meanwhile, the sound tracks would be laid against the cutting copy. There could be several magnetic sound tracks for music and speech, and they would be laid parallel to each other. At every stage of post-production there was a chance of error.

For the director, the strain of shooting film was all to do with the amount of film used. A shooting ratio of no more than 10:1 was universally agreed, and much less for drama. So a seven-minute film would be shot with no more than seven rolls of ten-minute film. This demanded discipline and judgement of a high order. The strain of getting it wrong was ever-present because nothing could be reviewed.

Even in the dubbing theatre there were problems. The film and magnetic sound tracks had to be kept 'in sync', which was easier said than done. Once the voice track or commentary was recorded, it would be layered into the overall mix and positioned by advancing or retarding the spools of film and magnetic track. A lack of concentration could mean hours of fiddling about as an assistant tried valiantly to get the whole thing 'back in sync'. On more than one occasion films were transmitted a frame 'out of sync' so the words didn't look absolutely natural with the moving picture.

However, the advent of videotape was not without its own problems. Non-linear editing had yet to come. The new style Betacam videotapes had to be transferred to VHS with 'burnt in' time code visible on the picture before editing could begin. VHS editing was slow and labour intensive, and with each transfer from one tape to another there was a loss of quality. After three or four 'generations' of edits the tape was almost unviewable because the quality was so poor. And before transmission the pictures had to be eye-matched with the original Betacam to 'conform' in order to restore their quality. Until technology caught up, a seven minute tape could take half a day to 'conform' to the original.

But there were huge advantages when using videotape. Gone was the cry of 'hair in the gate', and it was impossible to lose anything – including sync – although we all had our moments of anxiety. And shooting ratios went out the window because tape was cheap. Ratios of 25:1 or even 40:1 became common. The art of direction became the art of post-production.

June 1988
London

Change came suddenly. One minute Biddy was soldiering on, working harder than anyone, and then, out of the blue, she announced her intention to leave the programme. There was a very good reason. Her husband had been posted to Hong Kong and she needed to be able to be with him. She had also been offered consultancy work by the BBC Director General.

It was a shock because we'd all believed she was invincible. *Blue Peter* without her was unimaginable. For the first time in my life I felt sorry for her because my own departure was a nightmare I dreaded. She may have been difficult at times yet she was loyal and a powerful ally in times of trouble. Nothing rattled her except, it seemed, the prospect of moving on. I could not bear to see her moved to tears. It was after all a momentous time in *Blue Peter's* history and not surprisingly the occasion got to her. Believing she was about to weep, I announced we should all go to the BBC bar for a drink. The moment passed and, irrepressible as ever, she perked up.

I cannot say that the news of her departure came entirely out of the blue. We could all see that the pressure of writing two scripts a week was a growing strain, even though she has always denied that it was. And she never complained because she wouldn't have had it any other way.

Biddy's last programme was transmitted on 27 June 1988. She described being editor of *Blue Peter* as 'the best job in the world'.

Her departure marked the end of an era. Biddy Baxter MBE had shaped so many people's perception of life for the better and had become a television legend. From that moment the programme began to change and would never be the same again.

(Right and bottom far right): Biddy with Mark Curry, Caron Keating and Yvette Fielding just after Biddy's last programme as editor

(Bottom right): The *Blue Peter* end-of-series garden party. Philip Schofield talks to four-year-old Hannah Leger

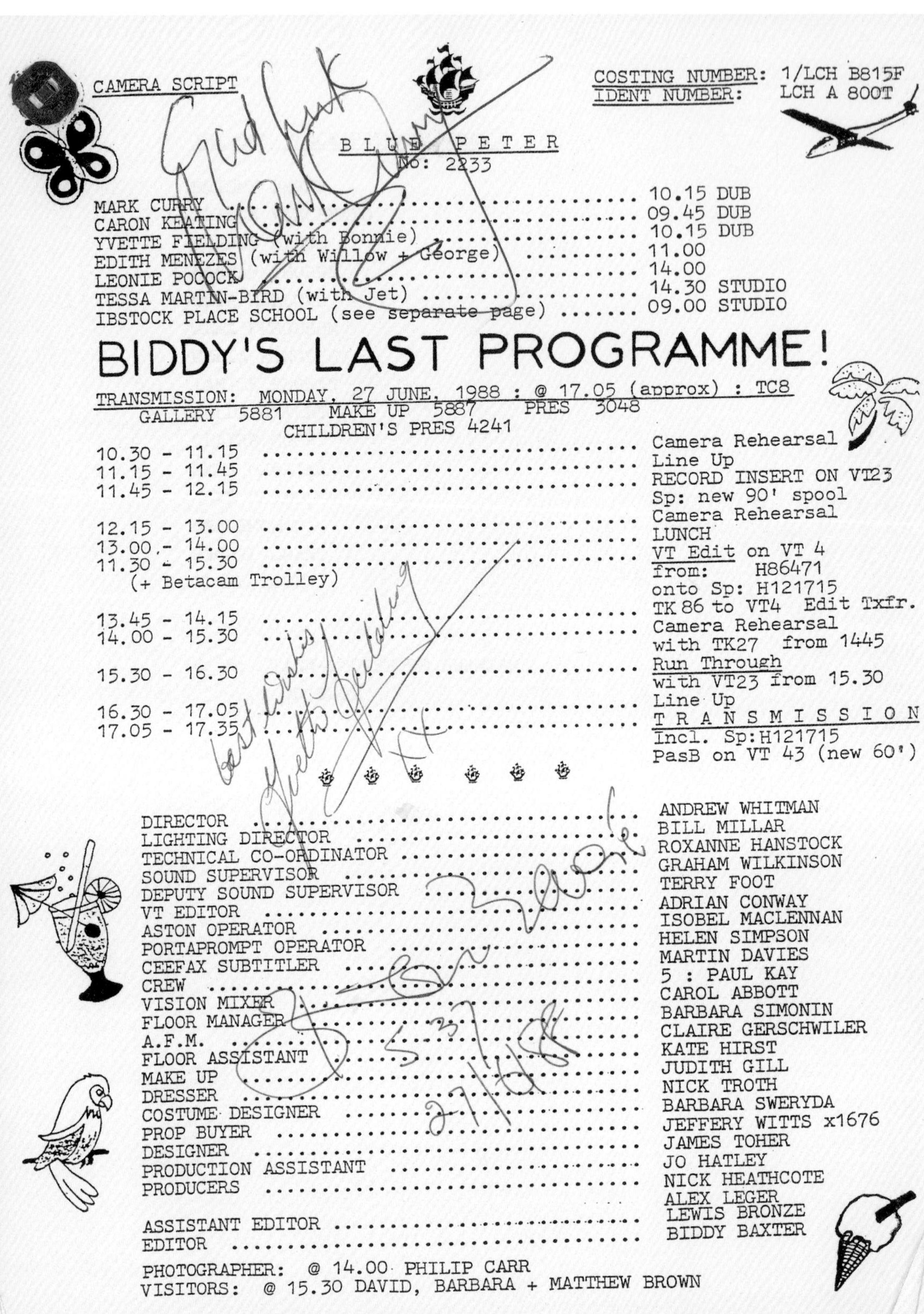

COSTING NUMBER: 1/LCH B815F
IDENT NUMBER: LCH A 800T

B L U E   P E T E R
No: 2233

MARK CURRY	10.15 DUB
CARON KEATING	09.45 DUB
YVETTE FIELDING (with Bonnie)	10.15 DUB
EDITH MENEZES (with Willow + George)	11.00
LEONIE POCOCK	14.00
TESSA MARTIN-BIRD (with Jet)	14.30 STUDIO
IBSTOCK PLACE SCHOOL (see separate page)	09.00 STUDIO

BIDDY'S LAST PROGRAMME!

TRANSMISSION: MONDAY, 27 JUNE, 1988 : @ 17.05 (approx) : TC8
GALLERY 5881   MAKE UP 5887   PRES 3048
CHILDREN'S PRES 4241

10.30 - 11.15	Camera Rehearsal
11.15 - 11.45	Line Up
11.45 - 12.15	RECORD INSERT ON VT23
	Sp: new 90' spool
12.15 - 13.00	Camera Rehearsal
13.00 - 14.00	LUNCH
11.30 - 15.30	VT Edit on VT 4
(+ Betacam Trolley)	from: H86471
	onto Sp: H121715
	TK 86 to VT4 Edit Txfr.
13.45 - 14.15	Camera Rehearsal
14.00 - 15.30	with TK27 from 1445
	Run Through
15.30 - 16.30	with VT23 from 15.30
	Line Up
16.30 - 17.05	T R A N S M I S S I O N
17.05 - 17.35	Incl. Sp:H121715
	PasB on VT 43 (new 60')

DIRECTOR	ANDREW WHITMAN
LIGHTING DIRECTOR	BILL MILLAR
TECHNICAL CO-ORDINATOR	ROXANNE HANSTOCK
SOUND SUPERVISOR	GRAHAM WILKINSON
DEPUTY SOUND SUPERVISOR	TERRY FOOT
VT EDITOR	ADRIAN CONWAY
ASTON OPERATOR	ISOBEL MACLENNAN
PORTAPROMPT OPERATOR	HELEN SIMPSON
CEEFAX SUBTITLER	MARTIN DAVIES
CREW	5 : PAUL KAY
VISION MIXER	CAROL ABBOTT
FLOOR MANAGER	BARBARA SIMONIN
A.F.M.	CLAIRE GERSCHWILER
FLOOR ASSISTANT	KATE HIRST
MAKE UP	JUDITH GILL
DRESSER	NICK TROTH
COSTUME DESIGNER	BARBARA SWERYDA
PROP BUYER	JEFFERY WITTS x1676
DESIGNER	JAMES TOHER
PRODUCTION ASSISTANT	JO HATLEY
PRODUCERS	NICK HEATHCOTE
	ALEX LEGER
	LEWIS BRONZE
ASSISTANT EDITOR	BIDDY BAXTER
EDITOR	

PHOTOGRAPHER: @ 14.00 PHILIP CARR
VISITORS: @ 15.30 DAVID, BARBARA + MATTHEW BROWN

14

The Iron Lady's koala

Lewis Bronze stepped into some pretty big shoes when he took on the role of *Blue Peter*'s new editor.

He was an old friend and had worked as Biddy's number two for five years. With brush moustache, twinkling eyes and an explosive laugh, he was a journalist and the ideal successor. He had a focused understanding of what the programme was all about.

One of his first big projects as the new boss was to sort out the *Blue Peter* autumn appeal. It had been nine years since Simon Groom's dramatic report as one of the first journalists into Phnom Penh, Cambodia's capital city, after the county's liberation, and Lewis decided to do a follow-up.

26 October–4 November 1988
Cambodia

I was excited at the prospect of going to Cambodia yet had doubts about the presenter, Caron Keating. She was mischievous, very pretty – and liked to get her own way. Living conditions were going to be primitive and, putting it bluntly, Caron was quite fussy about her hair, which was long and bouncy. Camping was not on her list of favourite pastimes. It was going to be a tough trip and I wondered how she would deal with it.

There was also the matter, no small one, of the 'Killing Fields' and the torture of civilians, which were all part of the background to Cambodia's difficulties. The Khmer Rouge, led by the evil communist dictator Pol Pot, had taken the country back to 'Year Zero' when Pol Pot had forced people to go back to living off the land.

His control had been absolute and his relentless campaign of murder had notoriously led to the mass killings of intellectuals, professionals and city folk. More than a million, some say more than two

(Left): Biddy Baxter's final programme script, signed exactly two minutes after coming off air

(Left): Caron Keating in between takes in Cambodia in 1988

(Below): Caron Keating and Bill Yates from Oxfam on location in Cambodia

million, were massacred in the Killing Fields.

Caron would have her work cut out to present this in a child-friendly way and avoid letters of complaint.

She was going to be accompanied by Bill Yates from Oxfam, who would act as her adviser, and I could not have wished for a better person. Tall, gregarious and lean, he was a great advertisement for the charity (he even looked underfed) and had a passionate concern for people who needed help. He had a comprehensive understanding of Cambodia's problems (and latterly his advice, when I was writing this chapter, has been invaluable).

In 1978 the Vietnamese army had pushed the Khmer Rouge out of the country and in the following year's *Blue Peter* appeal viewers had provided 50 Leyland lorries, several hundred thousand hoes, a vehicle ferry across the Mekong River, fishing lines and other essentials to enable Cambodians to survive and begin the huge task of rebuilding their country.

The aim, ten years later, was to rebuild the Mekong ferry, which was worn out, and to refurbish the city's water supply, which was still in a dire state of disrepair. There were also plans to provide workshops for repairing irrigation pumps used by farmers, and a technical school.

It was a trip that began with a few difficulties. Our departure from Heathrow coincided with an Air France strike. After an unplanned stopover in Ho Chi Min City and a night-time rickshaw ride, sightseeing darkened streets still scarred from the Vietnam War, we ended up half a day late in Phnom Penh. Ever anxious to nail the story, I had delayed our departure for our next location to complete some scene-setting filming around the city. Bill had expressed his concern but, head down, I would not be deflected.

Bill put it this way. 'I was angry with all of them because delay was dangerous. We were very late leaving Phnom Penh.'

With the sun low in the sky, we drove out of the city to a place called Takeo. Eager to find out more about the country, I shared a vehicle with Caron and Bill and listened in on their conversation.

Bill explained that the country was still not at peace because the Khmer Rouge leaders continued to hold the Cambodia seat at the United Nations, and there were still marauding bands of Khmer Rouge hiding in the hills. Cities and towns were still under curfew. At the end of each day workers from outlying areas would flock into the city. As we left the safety of the capital on our 40-mile journey, we saw a vehicle flying a huge Red Cross flag driving at full pelt in the opposite direction, trying to get back to Phnom Penh before it got dark.

Bill remained calm but he had recognised the warning signs. He said nothing and in tense silence, not helped by his frustration that we had not taken his advice, we battled along a heavily potholed road filled with mud and puddles. As we drove further and further away from the safety of Phnom Penh I could feel Bill's unease increase. His silence said it all. Then I saw that the driver was upset. Had he had a bereavement? Had his wife left him? Bill told me not to talk about it. Then I realised it was fear. Pure and simple. During the day the road was controlled by government forces, and during the night they left and the Khmer Rouge took over. And it was now dark. We passed deserted traffic control blocks and crossed bridges with deserted gun pits on either side. We couldn't go faster than about six or even seven miles per hour through the mud because the potholes were so deep. If this was a road controlled by the Khmer Rouge, we were sitting ducks.

Caron didn't miss a beat. If anything, she cheered up. I think she thrived on the uncertainty because, like many presenters, she got bored very easily. For hours we lurched from one giant pothole to another as the driver battled not only with the road but his very real fear of the Khmer Rouge. When we did arrive at Takeo, unharmed, we discovered that our hotel rooms had been cancelled because it had been assumed that no sane person would risk travelling after dark.

I wondered if the whole thing was a little overblown, but then the next day we were stopped from leaving. We hung about impatiently for a couple of hours before an armed escort from the Cambodian army joined us. With a couple of vehicles armed with machine guns and a lad with a rocket launcher, we got back on the road.

From that moment, wherever we went it was under an armed guard. I continued to think it was a bit over the top until we stopped in a small village for a coffee break. Our escort stood guard, keeping the locals away, and I wandered over to say hello. From the safety of a ring

(Top right): The challenges of getting about on location when the roads are almost non-existent

(Top left): Caron Keating and Bill Yates with our military escort

of soldiers I locked eyes with a man who stared back at me. His eyes were black with hate and I instinctively knew that he would have killed me if he could. I returned to the group slightly shaken. I asked Bill why they hated us so much.

'Oh, simple. They think we're Americans,' he said knowledgably.

At the time of the Vietnam War the American B52s had bombed Cambodia mercilessly. They had dropped a greater tonnage of bombs on Cambodia than was dropped by all sides in the Second World War. It was described at the time as an attempt to 'bomb Cambodia back to the Stone Age', and the ferocity of the Khmer Rouge against their own people was in some measure a reaction to it. It was clearly too soon to forgive or forget.

Caron, meanwhile, was warming to Cambodia and hanging on Bill's every word. My fears about whether she would be able to cope were completely unfounded. She didn't seem to care about her hair. She brushed it back knowing that, in her present circumstances, there were more important things to worry about. And there were some really grim days ahead.

We spent the next night in a town next to a large lake. The 'hotel' had been attacked by rockets and there was very little left except the floors, and there were lots of large jagged holes in the walls. There was one room that was habitable, even though there was barely three inches between the beds. We all piled inside.

Temperatures were in the high 80s Fahrenheit (low 30s Celsius). It was humid and getting dark. Someone spotted a light switch and flipped it on to see if it worked. It did. Within seconds the room was filled with a swarm of flying beetles. We switched the light off and the swarm settled like a carpet of creepy-crawlies smothering the entire room. We brushed them from our beds and on to the floor. From that moment on, wherever we went, it was like walking on gravel, crunching the beetles underfoot. It wasn't the sort of thing that bothered me but I was concerned for the film crew. Luckily for me, like many BBC Ealing film crews, they were made of stern stuff. Henry Farrar had already endured the previous expeditions to Peru and Ethiopia.

Johnny Austin, the assistant cameraman, escaped to have a shower. He was an ex-Royal Marine commando and I grabbed the chance to be next.

'You'll like the shower.' He smiled knowingly. 'Something special.'

It was pitch black and, using a torch, I could see the spray head was missing. I couldn't see the floor because it was covered with water, and because my torch was running low I switched it off. Doing everything by touch, I got wet enough to get thoroughly soaped up. Then the shower slowed from a steady trickle and stopped. About the same time I realised that the water was very slow to drain away and there were soft, squidgy things around my feet. I trod on one and it squeezed up between my toes. I became aware that something was in the shower with me. I grabbed the torch. A couple of rats had joined me and they were intent on eating the squidgy things around my toes... The sewers had backed up. I was stark naked, covered in soap, and ankle deep in excrement and gorging rats.

Not since the day I had an engine failure while flying solo in an RAF Chipmunk had I been quite so compromised. Thank goodness it was dark. I walked naked to the lake through more piles of human excrement and washed off. I returned to crunch my way to bed to warn the others and listen to Johnny laughing. It was a great morale booster. The ordeal that night continued for many hours because it was the hottest of my life.

I remember turning on my side and the pools of sweat that had gathered in my eye sockets poured down my face onto the pillow. I woke up knowing that life could only get better. As we drove to the next location I was glad to leave the memories of the night behind.

It hadn't been a night of hell for everyone. Caron took great delight in telling us that her room (which was somewhere upstairs at the other end of the building) had air-conditioning and a sink!

Cambodia was full of exciting sights and sounds. The low, rhythmical chanting of Buddhist monks in the early morning across a wide expanse of water; broadly smiling faces under wide-brimmed hats as they offered large platefuls of deep-fried tarantulas; whole families finding room on a single moped: these and many other things were the normality that hid a violence that was never far away.

A night or two later we were in a small town to meet up with two volunteer aid workers who were in charge of drilling wells in remote villages. One was a serious American who wanted to remain anonymous. He succeeded. I can hardly remember what he looked like and he said very little. His colleague was an affable, rotund red-headed man from Yorkshire. I thought they were an unlikely couple yet maybe the difference in their personalities made them a good combination. They were laid back about what they did, yet in reality they were risking their lives every day to provide people with clean drinking water. Conversation revealed that they had taken over from two Russian volunteers who had been killed by the Khmer Rouge and they now had a whole company of the Khmer army to protect them.

For every village they visited, one platoon of soldiers would protect their route in, while another secured the village itself. A third platoon would go ahead to the next village to secure their safety. At any time a determined assassin could slip through the defensive line of soldiers and kill them. I was puzzled by their lack of concern. I wouldn't have lasted a week.

That night we went to the theatre. It was a bizarre experience. The village hall was packed and not dissimilar to village halls the world over, except this one was ready to repel boarders. Soldiers lined the inside with their Kalashnikovs at the ready, some even sitting in the wings on the stage. We sat in the front rows as guests of honour and watched the play unfold. A grotesque figure in black appeared and reappeared and exerted his will on the terrified people. It was a play all about Pol Pot, and it went on for hours. The cigarette smoke was worse than in a night-club in the 1970s and it was very hot. At one point I went outside for some fresh air and noticed soldiers stationed around the village square. We were secure both inside and out and there was no chance of sneaking off.

As we travelled back to Phnom Penh we passed temples with neat piles of human skulls outside that had come to symbolise the aftermath of the Killing Fields. We stopped to film and I asked why the skulls were there.

Our interpreter explained, 'The Khmer Rouge used the temples as places to torture and kill. And when they had killed their victims they

(Left): Human skulls, the remains of tortured villagers, piled high outside a temple for all the world to see a decade after the notorious Killing Fields

threw the bodies in the moat surrounding the temple.'

He had been 16 at the time of Pol Pot and I asked him whether he would talk about that time on camera. We set up the interview.

'Tell me about the time of Pol Pot,' Caron asked curiously.

Our man tried to answer but nothing came out. Instead the tears rolled down his face and I stopped the filming. This was not for *Panorama*, it was for a children's programme and I had to make sure I didn't forget the reason we were there.

I felt like a bully and apologised, yet deep inside I knew it had been right to try.

Back in Phnom Penh we filmed the urgent need for an effective water-treatment works. Ten years after the departure of the Khmer Rouge the city was still without clean water. The effects of this were truly devastating, especially to the very young. We saw how drinking water and open sewers ran side by side, causing severe tummy upsets and diarrhoea that could kill. I suggested we go to the children's hospital where scores of children were being treated.

The ward was full of little wizened old people, except they were barely three or four years old. One was trembling as he tried to drink a milk mixture from a plastic mug. Henry, the cameraman, filmed another as she found the strength to reach out and take the biscuit that was being offered. Her hand was shaking and her outsize head was grotesque with the skin tight against her skull. The abnormally large eyes were pleading for help. Henry looked at me.

'Did you really want to film this?' he asked quietly.

Yes, I did. I felt angry and said that this was so shocking that people should see what dirty water actually meant.

I left Henry filming and went outside to find Bill Yates, our adviser from Oxfam.

'I feel sick,' I confessed.

'I feel sick too,' he agreed.

Caron was equally traumatised. 'I can't believe what's in there – unbelievably shameful – awful.'

A few minutes later Henry emerged with a sense of helpless resignation. 'You'll never use it.'

Henry's pictures were truly shocking and we agonised over whether to show them to an audience of five to six million children and their families. Hard as it was, the decision to show the shot of a dying child that Henry thought was too awful to broadcast was the right one.

It is an image as vivid in my mind today as it was then.

Caron didn't emerge from the shoot entirely unscathed. The day before our departure for the UK she went down with a tummy bug that reduced her to a miserable state. The hotel in Phnom Penh was little better than a concrete box with a bed in it. Sometimes the lavatory wouldn't flush and there would be random power cuts. She did not appear for the evening meal or breakfast the following day.

I went to check she was surviving and to remind her that it would soon be time to leave. I found her sitting, as if with tummy cramps, on

(Left): Cameraman Henry Farrar films as Caron Keating shows the magic of instant pictures to a crowd in Phnom Penh

her suitcase. Her hair was flat against her skull with sweat, and her face had an unhealthy green tinge. She had one eye constantly on the lavatory as if about to rush there.

'I am so sorry, but we have to leave in about half an hour,' I said apologetically.

Caron was, of course, a real trouper in the best *Blue Peter* tradition. 'Don't worry about me. I'll make it.'

The airport was crowded and under a corrugated-iron roof it was unbelievably hot. We kept an eye on her, fearing she might collapse in the lavatory and miss the flight. We needn't have worried. Absolutely nothing would have stopped Caron from getting on that plane.

I hardly saw her on the long haul back to London because she spent most of it in the confines of the loo.

After we landed and had got through customs she rushed into the arms of Russ Lindsay, Peter Powell's new business associate at the agency that represented her. This was Caron's new love and in Russ she found an attentive and caring person who adored her. They later married.

Bill and Lewis discussed the results of the filming, which were powerful. Both were very keen to highlight the plight of the Cambodian people. Lewis thought he could exploit the storylines more effectively with official comment. He asked for an interview with the Prime Minister, Margaret Thatcher.

16 December 1988
10 Downing Street

It was the same day that Edwina Currie had resigned over the salmonella issue and when we arrived (Lewis, myself, two film crews, two electricians, photographer and make-up designer) we were told to set up in an upstairs drawing room (I think it was the White Room). I knew the Prime Minister wouldn't suffer fools gladly so I was determined to be ready the moment she appeared.

As in sitting rooms the world over, everything was placed the way the owner wanted. I had been warned not to move anything. Unfortunately, the layout wasn't good for a two-camera shoot, and rather than compromise I shifted a few things about. I did it in such a way I hoped she wouldn't notice. I should have known better.

In her distinctive low, disciplined tone, Mrs Thatcher remarked, 'I see you've made yourselves at home.'

The Prime Minister came into the room with one of her advisers. She then quickly settled down, reminding herself, and us, that at that time Cambodia was referred to as 'Kampuchea'.

Caron was having a challenging day. In the morning she had been rehearsing for the *Blue Peter* pantomime, dressed as Carmen Miranda and practising a song-and-dance routine to 'There's an awful lot of coffee in Brazil' and, following a quick change into elegant businesslike attire, had come straight from the studio to join us for the interview.

Caron was well and truly on top of the questioning. With Bill and Lewis she had worked on practising the different directions in which the interview might go.

The interview was going well. Then Mrs Thatcher made the interesting

(Below): Prime Minister Margaret Thatcher presents a koala paperweight to Caron Keating to be sold for the appeal

remark that 'Not all the Khmer Rouge are all bad.'

Caron immediately picked up on that comment and quickly pressed home with her questioning. And in front of us the Iron Lady seemed suddenly a little less firm. You could see her thinking, *Isn't this a children's programme?* as Caron asked about the British Government's policy of recognising only the deposed and disgraced Khmer Rouge regime as Cambodia's legitimate government.

Given our recent experiences with so many frightened and traumatised Kampucheans, I didn't think any of them would have agreed with her. To them the Khmer Rouge were all sadistic killers.

When the interview was over I tackled the Prime Minister about her remark 'Not all the Khmer Rouge are all bad' and explained my reservations. I said that, judging by the way the Kampucheans lived in constant fear of them, there was no good side to their presence. She replied with some vigour that because of the troubles in Northern Ireland she was in constant danger herself – from the IRA. I didn't think she had answered my question but I was impressed that she was not afraid to respond to her critics, however lowly they may be. Just when I thought to pursue it, Lewis appeared and diplomatically suggested we have a group photograph. He told me later he was worried about the studio deadlines – he had to get Caron back to finish the song-and-dance routine. The timely distraction ended any further opportunities for informal questions, and Caron's remarkable day epitomised the strange life of a *Blue Peter* presenter.

Bill later remarked:

> Caron was great. Her *Blue Peter* exchange with the Prime Minister was one of the first cracks in the British government's ignoble diplomatic position of allowing the Khmer Rouge leaders to continue to represent Cambodia at the United Nations.

That position changed a year or so later, and today those same Khmer Rouge leaders have all been indicted for crimes against humanity.

The afternoon had been fruitful. Mrs Thatcher's comments on the Khmer Rouge made one prominent newspaper and I was left with more respect for the Prime Minister than I'd had previously.

And in the best of *Blue Peter* traditions, the Iron Lady herself donated an attractive koala paperweight to the appeal. When Caron presented the PM with a 'bring and buy' sticker she didn't hesitate to put it on her famous blue suit. All these years later, the interview is still widely viewed on YouTube, as are many other famous moments on the programme.

15

Whip crack-away, whip crack-away

8 July–7 August 1989
Zimbabwe

Under Biddy's leadership (and since) the programme was often accused of being middle class and too conventional. Whatever your view about what children liked or did not like, there was pressure to change. Lewis at his first office meeting had announced that 'glasnost' had arrived. Referring to President Gorbachov's programme for openness in the Soviet Union, it was Lewis's way of saying that we all now had a responsibility for the output. In a more than symbolic move, he had BBC maintenance men remove the automatic door-closing devices (breaking fire regulations) that sealed the *Blue Peter* offices away from the rest of the children's department. From then on there was literally an 'open-door' policy on *Blue Peter*.

We could question the output more and do things differently if we wanted to. We were encouraged to experiment.

The summer expedition was to Zimbabwe with John Leslie, a tall, good-looking, affable Scot who had just joined the programme, and Yvette Fielding.

Yvette, who had suffered anxiety attacks in the studio from the pressure of live television, was recovering her self-confidence and was returning to her bubbly self. Now she had another challenge.

Of all the animals we might face, Yvette's pathological fear of spiders was what gave her the most cause for concern.

Zimbabwe was tightening its grip on foreign reporting and we were allocated 'minders' from the Ministry of Information to watch what we did. I wondered why, because at no time did they tell us not to do anything.

We chose to cover the plight of the black rhinoceros, which was being poached to the point of extinction, so getting permission from the Director of National Parks and Wildlife proved tricky. I suggested to the director's office that we might be willing to film a subject that he wanted in exchange for permission to film the poaching issue.

At the last minute a compromise was reached. Two mature rhinos were being exported to zoos in America and flown out from Harare airport. It was going to happen during the night and because no one knew exactly when, it would cause havoc to our filming schedule. Yet it was a small price to pay for the bigger story.

We arrived at Harare Airport at ten o'clock at night and waited for the lorries carrying the rhinos to arrive. We continued to wait for three and a half hours. I didn't know what was going to happen so I told John to describe it all in his own words as the action unfolded. Today this would be the normal thing to do but in 1989 it was a big departure from the *Blue Peter* way of filming, which mostly stuck to a script.

At about two a.m. the lorries arrived and John leapt into action. He was fluent and accurate, and his participation made filming easy. It also gave the whole episode an immediate appeal and it felt much less staged. I knew this was the right way to go.

For me this was hugely significant because from that moment, whenever we worked together, I encouraged him to tell it in his own words. In my opinion John was the first presenter who was able to do this reliably and fluently and it suited his personality. Working first with him, and then with other presenters, I relied less on the written word and more on spontaneous reporting. It's a style that has taken over.

There was an unexpected edge to the poaching story. The head of anti-poaching was an ex-special forces soldier called Glen Tatham and on his advice we travelled to Fort Mana at Mana Pools to see what was happening on the ground.

The fort was literally that – a blockhouse heavily reinforced with sandbags. Inside there were grim reminders that the rangers were engaged in a shooting war. Loops of machine-gun link ammunition were draped over the stair rail, one red-tipped tracer for every few solid rounds. Mounted in a light plane, a general-purpose machine-gun was used to flush out poachers by firing bursts into the bush, where they might be hiding.

John chatted to one of the pursuit rangers.

His line of questioning was direct. 'What do you do when you catch up with the poachers?'

The ranger didn't hesitate. 'We shoot them before they shoot us.'

On a piece of land we saw about six hundred rhino skulls lying bleached on the grass.

'There are more skulls here than there are rhino left alive in Zimbabwe,' the ranger informed us.

One day on the river Zambezi we were making a film about the wildlife there. We were doing what the tourists do, sitting in a catamaran canoe, gently moving with the muddy flow of the river and watching nature at work, with our guide, Jeff Stutchbury. He was talking about the group of hippo when he suddenly stopped. He looked through his binoculars at something that had caught his eye in the distance. He then

(Right): Watching our plane depart from the airstrip at Mana Pools, Zimbabwe

(Below): Guide Jeff Stutchbury

picked up where he had left off as if nothing had happened, and we wondered what he had spotted.

A few hours later I was on a personal mission to deliver a note from him to Fort Mana. I have no doubt that much later their light aircraft took off on a 'flushing out' patrol to try and catch poachers on their way back across the river. The machine gun would have been back in business as a ranger sprayed the river bank with bursts of gunfire to make the poachers break cover.

In 1989 Zimbabwe had a thriving tourist industry yet that did not mean we could always find a comfortable bed for the night. The hotels were at the tourist venues and not necessarily where we were filming. The situation was made all the more difficult because the feature film *White Hunter, Black Heart*, based on Peter Viertel's novel about his experiences with John Huston as he directed *The African Queen*, was being shot. The locations were on the shores of Lake Kariba and around Victoria Falls, and all the available hotels were fully booked.

One evening we had to make do with a row of corrugated-iron huts in a coconut plantation on the edge of Lake Kariba. Our evening meal was a cardboard box full of huge raw steaks and next to the box was a pile of firewood, some newspaper, a frying pan and a box of matches.

Film crews are not used to cooking their own suppers and I had a near rebellion until I pointed out that they were welcome to book into any hotel they liked – if they could find one. Meanwhile, I lit the fire and produced my first half-bottle of whisky, brought especially for emergencies.

We had a truly great night. A second half-bottle of whisky later, a blazing fire and some truly wonderful steak, and we had the best night of the trip. All except Yvette, who had to share with the production assistant who snored loudly all night long. We all heard the snoring but we were too tired or drunk to care. I promised that thereafter the snoring assistant would have a room all to herself and as far as possible from the rest of us. It was amazing how far the snores of even the female gender of *Homo sapiens* resonated in an already cacophonous wilderness. By comparison the constant racket of the cicadas was no worse than distant traffic.

We got on pretty well as a production team – almost too well. We were staying at Chikwenya, a very exclusive resort for wild-life on the banks of the Zambezi. The resort provided a Land Rover with bench seats set high up so we could see over the driver's head and observe the wildlife. As the sun set, we settled down to watch a stretch of riverbank in the distance. The cicadas burst into life, and as the light dropped, the last rays of the setting sun hit the far side of the river Zambezi. We waited. Then a giant male elephant emerged from the bush and went down to the river to drink. He was followed by a fe-male and her calf. And then others followed. More and more elephants crowded the banks until we lost count. Calves played in the water while the adults drank and washed themselves. White egrets stood out against the grey and landed on their backs. No one said a word. Even presenter John Leslie was lost in thought.

Suddenly it was all over and the herd melted back into the undergrowth. Our veteran guide broke the silence.

'That was lucky. Haven't seen that for a long time,' he mused.

God bless Africa.

We were halfway through the trip and a mood for celebration gripped the team. John started singing the *Calamity Jane* favourite 'The Deadwood Stage' and within seconds everyone was singing. It was a very jovial party that returned to camp.

We sorted the gear out and assembled for the evening meal with half a dozen other camp guests. Unlike us, they were there just for one night as a special treat to relish the sights and sounds of the African bush. Dinner was laid out in the open under the shade of two enormous flame trees.

Unfortunately, we were put at separate tables. I was with the guests at one table and the rest of the team was at another so when the team relived the joys of 'The Deadwood Stage' at full volume, my heart sank. I hoped it would be just a brief reprise. No such luck. 'Whip crack-away, whip crack-away, whip crack-away!' shattered the magical sounds of the bush. It was fun the first time but surrounded by disapproving guests, as I was, it wasn't.

Being part of a film crew often made you feel special and it was easy to think you were the life and soul of the party. Thank goodness the food arrived and the singing stopped.

In the interests of reflecting all aspects of life in Zimbabwe, we

(Above): John Leslie and Yvette Fielding in a field of ripe mangetout

went on to a white farming family near Harare.

In 1989 the white farmers were still very much in business and the family lived in a large, beautifully thatched house with fabulous gardens. One morning we joined the workers in the fields as mangetouts were picked and packed for an overnight flight to London. By the afternoon of the following day, we were told, they would be on the shelves in supermarkets all over the UK.

We also filmed at the farm's own 'village', where the workers lived and grew their own crops. Their houses were much smaller and also thatched. They had health visitors and the farmer genuinely cared for them. He knew their names and was a regular visitor and stopped to chat with anyone who wanted to pass the time. It may not have been very equal or even politically correct, yet we saw no resentment or unhappiness.

When, less than ten years later, the land was confiscated in the interests of equality and returned to the local people, it wasn't just the white farmers who suffered. The workers lost their livelihoods too, and the country slid into bankruptcy.

And what of our minders from the Ministry of Information while all this was going on? Very unwisely I let one of them borrow one of our vehicles one Friday night to visit 'friends'. He promised that he would return the next day, which was our day off. He didn't. He eventually returned on the Monday morning with a young lady in tow. He was very sheepish and when I pointed out that we had lost a whole filming day, and therefore valuable publicity for Zimbabwe, he wanted to make amends. Fearing I would lodge a complaint, he got permission for us to film in and around the security-sensitive Kariba Dam.

We walked down a steep concrete slope into the heart of the construction. I was surprised to find that the generators had been made in Warrington and the whole place was painted in garishly bright colours reminiscent of the 1950s. Later, on the parapet of the dam wall, as we walked towards the middle, we were warned not to stray one foot across a painted line because we would then be in Zambia, and the guards would not let us return.

The dam had been an interesting interlude yet not critical to our plot. From that moment I never lent anything that would compromise the filming schedule. It was better to give a bit of money as 'goodwill' and think of it as an unexpected expense.

The most bizarre moment of our Zimbabwean saga was with an elderly gent, Joe Susman, who had first crossed the Zambezi at the age of four in an ox cart. It had been kept afloat with empty wooden barrels strapped to its sides. Now approaching 90, he had a thriving tourist business just upstream of Victoria Falls. We joined him in one of his 'canoes' to hear his story and see a giant crocodile that habitually sat on a sand bar on the far side of the river. It was a favourite with the tourists and on this occasion it had fed well. It remained, as still as a statue, mouth agape, to digest its food. Yvette recalled how she felt:

> I gripped the sides of the boat so hard that I lost feeling in both hands. I saw my life flash before me as I stared into the eyes of one enormous crocodile.

The canoe was like an outsize Cambridge punt and relatively stable. The river was fast flowing and about two hundred yards across. The distant roar of the falls, *Mosi oa tunya* or 'the smoke that thunders', was a reminder that certain death wasn't far away if the outboard failed.

We edged closer and closer. The cameraman indicated that he needed to be closer still. Meanwhile, our man chatted to Yvette.

'They are the kings of the river. Magnificent creatures – beautiful but deadly. They're so quick. Just one flick of their tail and they are gone,' he said with a degree of relish.

'How dangerous are they?' asked Yvette.

'They are so unpredictable. You never know what they are going to do.' He gave the impression of being a man who loved and respected nature.

By this time we were within a few feet of the creature and I wondered who was going to say it was time to back away. We were well within tail flicking distance. I looked at our man. Joe looked distinctly uneasy and I made the decision. As we sped back out into the river he went through a remarkable transformation. He was shaking as if he had just suffered a near-death experience.

'I hate those fu**ers. They give me the willies,' he said as he frantically tried to light a cigarette.

I left the party that night and flew back to London. Lunchtime the next day I was at a church barbecue at the Turf Hotel on the river Exe and telling the story to my friends. I suspect the sudden change of scenery was more remarkable to me than my story was for them.

(Above): John Leslie and
Yvette Fielding at Victoria
Falls, Zimbabwe

(Left): Victoria Falls,
Zimbabwe

18 May 1990
Folkestone

The 50th anniversary of the Dunkirk evacuation hit the media in a big
way. I had been working on a film to commemorate the event for over
a month and had found one of the rescued servicemen, one of the little
ships that had helped with the rescue, and a member of her crew. We
had already filmed on the beaches of Dunkirk and all I needed was the
story of the little ship, the *Sundowner*, setting off.

And that was when the rest of the media caught up.

I arrived in Folkestone harbour, where the *Sundowner* was based,
to be greeted by Kate Adie and a BBC news crew, who were keen to
do their bit before the evening deadline. It was a sunny morning and
infused with goodwill I was pleased to help. But there were also news
crews from ABC, NBC and heaven knows where else. There were six
crews altogether and they all wanted the same story.

It was one of the few occasions I didn't need to fight to keep our
exclusivity. Our transmission wasn't for another week and we had always
known that coverage of Dunkirk was inevitable. Our big story was the
beach evacuation and that was already in the can. The weather was good
and I was told that each news team needed about an hour with the
contributors. I told them to go ahead and we would wait.

We sat about biding our time and feeling virtuous. It was a far
from sensible move. By the time we got our chance to interview our
crew member, Gerald Ashcroft, he was very tired. He had told the same
story seven times and had lost much of his enthusiasm. And he was not
a well man. It dawned on me that I had been duped by my own largesse.
I vowed never to give in to peer pressure again.

16

The Great Bring-and-Buy Sale

The 1990 series began with a phone call from Lewis about the autumn appeal. The charity we had chosen was the Romanian Orphanage Trust. It was a small charity with a big idea.

After the fall of the dictator Nicolae Ceausescu of Romania, a dark secret had been revealed about the country's orphaned and abandoned children, and it filled the headlines.

During Ceausescu's time in power, people had been denied contraception and encouraged to have children to build up the workforce. Inevitably, large Romanian families were soon unable to feed themselves. Ceausescu told the people to give their children to the state and reassured them that they would be well cared for. But Romania's orphanages filled so rapidly that care workers were unable to look after them properly. Conditions deteriorated so badly that many children were forced to live in appalling conditions. They were often restrained, near naked, and smeared in their own excrement. It became a scandal of epic proportions.

The Romanian Orphanage Trust suggested a revolutionary idea. It was to build 12 houses in groups of three or four that would take children from the orphanages and prepare them for adoption. The houses would become small communities and a halfway house back to the community. It was a great idea because it had a tangible aim that the viewers could achieve through bring-and-buy sales.

8–11 October 1990

Romania

I joined Lewis on a reconnaissance mission to see the sites where the houses might be built and to make contact with the people who would build them. Our destination was Bacau, about five hours' drive north-east from Bucharest airport.

(Left): The first of the *Blue Peter* houses, Dragos Vota site, Bacau

Bacau was a rather depressing town in a heavily industrialised area of the country. We drove into the centre through tall, half-built blocks of flats, an ugly legacy of the Ceausescu era. We stayed in a small hotel and we could see from the start that this was going to be a serious challenge.

It began with breakfast. There wasn't much choice. It was either eggs or eggs, so we ordered boiled eggs and toast. After about half an hour, during which we observed the comings and goings of the chain-smoking locals, the boiled eggs arrived. They were of the three and-a-half-minute variety, out of their shells, and served in a wineglass. There was no spoon and I wondered whether to drink them or pour them onto the toast. Of all the things I had seen in Bacau, those eggs were the most disturbing. I had my suspicions and now I knew for certain – the Romanians were not like us.

However, you can get used to anything and after the second day boiled egg 'à la wineglass' seemed as normal as chain smoking, and we learned that a packet of cigarettes left on the table speeded up the service wonderfully.

There were power cuts and lavatories that worked for only a few hours a day, both signs that Romania was falling apart. Building our houses for the orphaned and abandoned children would mean a change in attitude to life and work and we had to find a way to get things moving.

Our chain-smoking interpreter, Dan Ciofu, was handsome and charming. He spoke English eloquently and was filled with a boundless enthusiasm for the houses project. Almost instantly we became good friends and he was very emotional about the meeting of East and West that was taking place in the hire car. At the end of the first day he turned to us and, moustache bristling and voice breaking with emotion (or it might have been the cigarettes), declared, 'A year ago you were my enemy. And now you are just like us. I can hardly believe it.'

We visited the factory where the houses would be built and Lewis had a long discussion with the owner, who listened with interest and, I thought, some disbelief.

(Below): Builder John Birkett from Wimpey International, interpreter Dan Coifu and an official at the Dragos Vota site

We called in at Bacau Leagan Number Two, the first orphanage that would be involved in our plan. The children were very excited to see us and milled about, arms outstretched, pleading to be picked up. They were well dressed, although the orphanage had the most primitive laundry on the planet. The overall effect was 'poor but coping'.

We returned to the UK and I set about a filming plan.

Yvette Fielding seemed the natural choice to do the reporting. She loved children and believed totally in the aims of the appeal. She was ideal for the job. After a testing first year on the programme living up to Biddy's expectations she was becoming more confident on location, even if she had been left with an irrational fear of live television. Occasionally she would still suffer from panic attacks and they were very debilitating. Even so, out of the studio she would cope well.

22–26 October 1990
Bacau, Romania

We returned to Romania just over a week later and flew up from Bucharest airport to Bacau for the unbelievably low return fare of 204 lei (about £2.38) each for the 50-minute flight. There were very few Westerners and the country had yet to become aware of business opportunities or the true value of anything.

Yvette had problems even before the filming began:

> I was the only one not to get my luggage so had to live in the
> same clothes for the duration. Most unpleasant and Caroline,
> the assistant, gave me half of her underwear.

We spent the first morning at a 'get to know you' event at Bacau Leagan Number Two. It was a concrete box of a building on two storeys and it had developed that ugly black stain so prevalent on ageing 1960s architecture. The windows were metal framed and modest in size. It was a singularly unattractive building in contrast to the hospitality we received. For lunch we were treated to a feast of Romanian dishes cooked especially for us by the staff. It was the first and only good meal we ate outside Bucharest during six separate filming visits over the next eight years.

In the afternoon we filmed well-dressed children playing in large spartan rooms filled with toys. I knew that things were not as they seemed and wondered how to get at the truth. I couldn't blame the workers for putting on a good show, yet it was hardly likely to encourage viewers to hold bring-and-buy sales.

That evening I decided what to do. I would call the crew and Yvette for 5.30 a.m. – about three hours before we were expected – and get shots of the children waking up.

We arrived on the doorstep of Bacau Two in the half-light of dawn and went inside. The smell of excrement and cries of the children were a warning of the production line of misery that greeted us. Children of two or three years old sat in rows, naked, waiting for their turn under a cold-water tap where they were scrubbed with a brush. Children were hauled about by one arm and dumped from one row of screaming bodies to another. The white coats of the sturdily built female workers stood out in the dark hell that was all around us.

The cameraman, John Goodyear, flew into action and I knew that these were the shots we needed. From that moment on, the staff did nothing to hide the true conditions from us. In truth, they were very understaffed and so the brisk no-nonsense handling was the only way to get the job done, however brutal it appeared. When the matron arrived two hours later she explained this to Yvette. She seemed relieved that the deception was over. Dan, our interpreter, was very helpful and explained that the truth was all that mattered. We were there to raise money to pay for things that would help make their lives easier.

I could see that there were kindly carers and brutal ones. I am certain that none were born unkind – it was just the sheer pressure of work that made them behave that way. Over the next few months several of the carers came up to me and, through Dan, explained that they did not agree with what was going on.

For Yvette the most shocking sights were in the AIDS wards. They were full of babies who were not expected to live for more than a few months. She cradled one small, emaciated baby we were filming as, with tears in her eyes, she explained to viewers that this little person was going to have a very short life.

'It's so unfair,' was all Yvette could muster while trying to maintain some semblance of composure on camera.

(Top right): Yvette Fielding with a Romanian orphan

(Bottom left): Cameraman John Goodyear films Yvette by cot in an AIDS ward

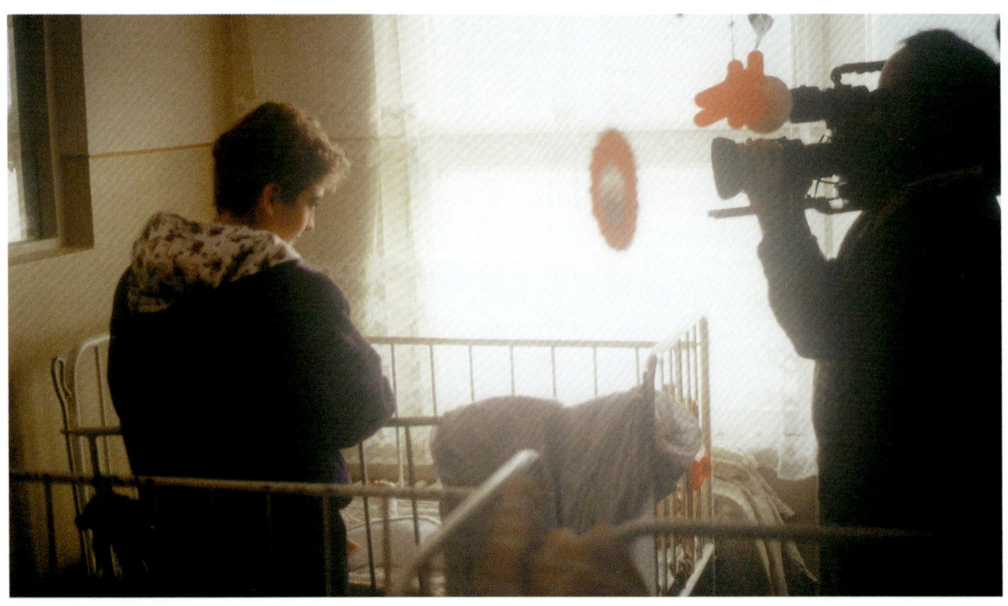

To the rest of us this was a massive understatement of an appalling tragedy.

Back in the UK, Yvette's reports were edited into a series of hard-hitting packages. Each delivered a separate message. The response from the viewers was instantaneous. The target set on the appeal launch programme was reached in three days and a second target was set. This, too, was reached within days. The breadth of the appeal was extended to include industrial washing machines to replace the ancient devices that were little better than a stick in a bathtub. Later, a mobile workshop was introduced to tour the orphanages and provide repair facilities. And as the money raised soared into the millions, nursery nurses, fostering schemes and a mother-and-baby unit became part of the aim.

We returned three times in the first year of the appeal and each time we noticed huge changes in the orphanages that we visited – and in

(Bottom right): All smiles as cameraman Keith Hopper films workers at Leagan Number One Bacau

the country as a whole. On one visit the coal miners went on strike and marched en masse into the capital, Bucharest.

Yvette recalls, 'Being stranded in Romania during an uprising, we had to stay in our hotel rooms as rioting had begun. I was terrified.'

I was awoken by the sound of tanks in the square below. We were in the same hotel as an ITN news crew and Julian Manion was the reporter. I linked up with their producer in the hotel foyer to work out how to get back to the UK. Julian noticed our concentration as we crouched over a large-scale map.

'I see the escape committee is in session,' he remarked with amusement. Luckily, our plans were unnecessary.

Work on the houses progressed and experts from the UK were hired to supervise the construction. John Birkett, on loan from Wimpey International, got a workforce together and prepared the sites. Our four sites in Bacau, now with 12 *Blue Peter* houses, were a tribute to his skilful handling of the workforce and the local authorities.

In Bacau Leagan Number One, another orphanage in Bacau, the question was raised as to whether or not the adoption of Romanian children by families outside the country was necessary or even desirable. The director was adamant that it was neither. The majority of children adopted this way had not adapted well to their new surroundings and many had been abandoned to the state because of the huge difficulties adopting families faced.

Meanwhile, the desperate plight of Romania's forgotten children continued to shock *Blue Peter* viewers.

10–14 December 1990

Bacau

For our second visit it was bitterly cold and we stayed at a plush-looking hotel. However, the facade concealed a hideous peril. We arrived late evening and settled down to an entrée of cold meats and salad, which made a very pleasant change from the usual menu of stringy, overcooked chicken and shrivelled chips. It was a terrible mistake. That night the sounds of vomiting echoed around the corridor and the next day, pale and very fragile, we struggled to film at all.

In between sequences we were running relay races back and forth to lavatories best described as stinking holes in the floors to be ill over again and again. It was a most unpleasant day.

Lewis was very keen for the Romanians to participate in the fundraising and it was decided that Dan, who was also an English teacher at a local school, would encourage his class to hold their own bring-and-buy sale.

I did not imagine that this would be a problem. But however hard I tried to explain, Dan and his pupils could not quite understand how it worked. A day or two before the sale I was rung up in the middle of the night by a very worried Dan.

'Explain to me, Alex, because I am not sure I understand. If I bring something, do I then buy something else?'

'Yes,' I reaffirmed, explaining in the simplest terms. 'The idea is that you bring something you don't want and then buy something that you do.'

Dan sounded relieved. 'I understand now. Thank you so much.'

His class, even though they were the cleverest students in the school, still had trouble getting their heads around it. More by luck the sale was a relative success and Yvette asked them what they thought of it.

'I think it would be easier just to give money,' one said frankly.

'Why?' asked Yvette.

'It seems silly to bring something just to buy it back again,' concluded a rather bemused young man whose life could not have been more different from that of a *Blue Peter* viewer.

The root of the problem was simple. In Romania they owned nothing that they did not need or want. In their case, after forty-odd years of communism, the idea of unwanted excess was a mystery. And that was just as much a mystery to us.

4–8 May 1991

Bacau

On our third visit Lewis joined me and, in contrast to the bitter winter, Romania was warm and welcoming. The first of the *Blue Peter* houses had been finished and we filmed the local priest as he blessed each one in turn. It was an amazing achievement in such a short space of time. There was an atmosphere of excitement and optimism. The care workers who had been chosen to look after the children were especially happy.

To think that just a few short months earlier the only alternative had been the hell of the orphanages.

I had never thought that religion had played much of a part in communist countries but this was not the case. In Bacau the Christian Orthodox Church was alive and well. Whenever we filmed in the little church close to the first group of houses, it was packed. The priest was very influential and we filmed interviews with him to get the local angle. To begin with I was not entirely convinced of his commitment, but on that sunny May afternoon, surrounded by his congregation, I was left with no doubt of it. He could see a winning formula and was all for it.

Experts from Barnardo's, led by Maggie Kelly, joined the project to set up a training course for nursery nurses and we filmed the course in action in Bucharest. Yvette continued to excel.

Then something happened in Bucharest to upset her. One of her

(Top left): Programme editor Lewis Bronze and Yvette Fielding review a 'take' by replaying it on the camera

dreaded panic attacks from her early days as a presenter struck while we were driving between locations. It was the middle of the rush-hour traffic and cars were flying past. Lewis stopped the taxi and I opened the rear door to help. She was hyperventilating and on the verge of passing out. I raised both her feet in the air and Lewis held a bag over her face to reduce over-oxygenation. After a minute or two she recovered and with my assistant I took her to the local hospital for a check-up.

The hospital was a very grim affair. There was virtually no furniture and the concrete walls were bare. It reminded me of what I imagined to be the worst kind of prison. It was hardly the atmosphere of reassurance and comfort that Yvette so desperately needed. The doctor was very sympathetic and gave her some kind of mineral cocktail to drink. She very nearly succumbed to a second attack soon after, yet found the strength to stagger to the exit supported by Wendy, the production assistant. Even though her body might have caved in, her spirit hadn't. She knew her best chance of survival lay elsewhere. And that was at the airport.

10–14 June 1992

Bucharest and Piatra Neamt

Over the next year or so the Romanian Orphanage Trust acquired storage facilities for all the supplies brought over from the UK. They were deep in the bowels of Ceausescu's palace of the people in the capital, Bucharest, known as 'Little Paris' in the 1920s and 1930s. The palace itself was a gigantic concrete box, because that's all it was in 1992, even though it was the second-largest building in the world

(Above): Yvette, Alex and charity workers outside Ceausescu's palace

(Left): Assistant Wendy Hutchinson comforts ailing Yvette Fielding in a Bucharest hospital

after the Pentagon. I wandered about inside, alternatively marvelling at the dimensions and recoiling at the appalling taste. From the outside it looked fine, built at the end of a majestic avenue with exotic-looking streetlamps. Yet inside it was utterly soulless. Just bare concrete walls with no plaster. It was extravagant nonsense that was more about one man's opinion of himself than anything else. I looked up at the concrete ceilings towering above me and thought of all the wasted money, the delusions of grandeur and the misery of a hundred thousand abandoned children.

In the basement there were rules that were only broken at your peril. The Trust had space on the second level and there were more levels below, and these were occupied by troglodyte communities that emerged to scour the city's streets for sustenance. The Trust's storage was heavily fenced in and no one ventured to the lower levels. The 'main roads' for these hidden inhabitants were the underground heating ducts that criss-crossed the city. If you watched carefully you would see people emerge or disappear down the manholes. In winter I saw people walking barefoot in the freezing weather, scampering from one manhole to another.

As the organisation of the Romanian Orphanage Trust developed, the *Blue Peter* appeal also began supplying washing machines to orphanages in the towns surrounding Bacau. We travelled to Piatra Neamt, about an hour or so to the north, to see how the newly-installed machines were working. The matron was an interesting woman, greying and in her fifties, and she had a kindly heart. She was also an ardent admirer of Sir Winston Churchill. As in all the other orphanages we had visited, she did not have enough staff to look after the children properly.

In one ward there were the usual cots filled with children who rocked to and fro and banged their heads on the cot frames. There must have been thirty or forty of them, all being driven mad with boredom. The incessant rocking was the only way they could get any stimulus. There was no running about. It was like a battery farm for children, each in their own cage.

I spotted a three-year-old boy lying beside an open window in the sunlight, crying feebly as he lay on his back. I went over to see what the matter was and found nothing obvious. On closer inspection I saw that his skin under the woollen clothing was red and inflamed. In horror I realised that the child was wearing about five layers of clothes and he had severe heat rash. I called to the carer and demanded that some layers be taken off. I was told that in the night it was very cold and that he was the farthest away from the heater. They didn't always have time to take off layers of clothing during the day. While I watched, he lay in misery in the full glare of the hot sun. I wondered what to do because I did not want him to freeze at night either.

Before I could do anything, Yvette lost her temper. It was all too much for her. The conditions in that room were positively cruel and she said so, demanding that something should be done about it at once.

I calmed her enough for her to deliver an important piece of the

(Above): Anthea Turner with happy residents of the *Blue Peter* houses

script to camera while the carer did some urgent changing of clothes. We then moved on rapidly to the next location to keep pace with our busy filming timetable.

I so regret that with the pressure of directing the film the plight of that little boy, literally roasting to death in the hot summer sun underneath that window, went clean out of my mind. I remembered him, too late, as we drove back with the sun setting behind the hills. If he had not gone mad with his day of torture, at least the temperature was dropping to something that he would find tolerable. A moment of respite perhaps before the whole ghastly thing began again the next day.

It was an unspeakable situation. I wondered about carers who were being driven mad by the constant demands from hordes of children while at the same time having to bring up their own large families. I thought about how they might be tempted to wreak revenge on their small charges.

We followed the construction and blessing of more of the *Blue Peter* houses and filmed the first inhabitants as they enjoyed life as it should be lived. I do not know exactly how many of the children were adopted back into Romanian society but I do know that for several hundred children, at least, life was bearable once again. They played in sandpits and on lawns with flowerbeds and lived in small groups of about eight. They were very well looked after by loving carers who were chosen to be the vanguard of the new system of childcare.

In 1996 the Romanian Orphanage Trust established Pentru Copii Nostri (PCN) in Romania, to be run by Romanians who did much of their own fundraising. In Britain the organisation became the European Children's Trust and subsequently Every Child, and they released funds as and when necessary.

Pentru Copii Nostri copied the way they worked from what they had learnt from the West. They raised money for themselves in a variety of ways. One was by voluntary deductions at source from pay packets and they were very successful

It is hardly surprising that not all the systems that were put in place survived. Ten years after the crisis was first revealed, BBC's *Newsnight* programme did a report about what had happened to the money raised as the result of the *Blue Peter* appeal and from the whole of the UK. They visited the mother-and-baby unit in Bacau that I had filmed shortly after its completion in 1998.

I was galled to see the *Newsnight* reporter cataloguing everything that no longer worked or had broken.

She walked up the very same flight of stairs as our presenter had done, commentating, 'Taking one step further than my BBC colleagues,' as if we had turned a blind eye to it all.

What the Great *Blue Peter* Bring-and-Buy Sale for Orphaned and Abandoned Children had set out to do was what we always did. We had set a challenge to the viewers that could be realistically achieved by a collective effort. And that's what the viewers did, tenfold, in Romania.

(Right): The plaque fixed to each *Blue Peter* house

(Above): An RAF
Phantom jet acts as escort
into the Falkland Islands

17

Lovesick in the Falklands

27 January–7 February 1992
The Falkland Islands

It was the tenth anniversary of the Falklands War and we joined a procession of programme-makers and journalists heading for the once-troubled waters of the South Atlantic. It was January in Britain and cold and miserable, while in the Falklands it was the height of summer.

Getting there was simple. There was a twice-weekly Tri-Star military flight from RAF Brize Norton and it was almost like a normal airline. However, any sense of normality evaporated when, as we approached Port Stanley, a pair of Phantom jet fighters intercepted us and flew as our escort, one on each wing.

I loved the Falklands on sight. They were all the more appealing because they weren't a tourist destination. The presenter, John Leslie, hated them. The love of his life was Catherine Zeta-Jones, an actress whose star was rapidly rising, and he would be away from her for the best part of two weeks. John went very quiet, probably thinking of missed opportunities, while I pondered on the ones that we must not lose.

I had been told that the biggest snag, apart from unexploded bombs, was the wind because, reputedly, it blew a gale all day long. I had also been warned that the islands were under a large hole in the ozone layer and severe sunburn could be added to the list of hazards, even if the sun was behind a cloud.

A couple of weeks before we set off I was interviewed by BBC External Services in Bush House for *Calling the Falklands*, the islanders' own programme. I explained at length how we were going to overcome the wind buffet on our microphones. It was an easy story to tell because Graham 'Ace' Bedwell, the sound recordist – tall, thin, bespectacled and wearing a flat cap – was a bit of a character. He had been practising with various microphone covers and a hairdryer. I had elaborated on this theme, thinking it would only be heard by half a dozen islanders, and had waxed lyrical about our practical if eccentric team member. Imagine my horror when, on the coach from Mount Pleasant airport to Port Stanley filled with journalists, the public address system crackled into life and my edition of *Calling the Falklands* was broadcast.

I don't know how long it went on for but my voice droned on and on for the entire programme about Ace and his hairdryer. I shrank into my seat and tried not to speak in case the rest of passengers guessed it was me. Ace was very kind. I think he was even flattered. Fortunately John was listening to his Walkman or I would never have heard the last of it.

As it happened, the Falklands didn't turn out to be terribly windy, although I did notice that almost everyone had a purplish complexion through too much exposure to the sun.

Port Stanley was charming and not particularly memorable. The timber and corrugated-iron-roofed buildings were brightly coloured and scattered higgledy-piggledy along the shoreline of a wide bay. Motoring by boat across the anchorage, we could see Mount Tumbledown, the Three Sisters and Mount Longden in the distance. They were a stunning backdrop to so many horrors of the Falklands conflict. We filmed in and around the settlement as John told the story of the war.

The governor joined us one evening and I think he was grateful for some new people to talk to. We got to know the schoolchildren, who were all on holiday. One day there was a children's party, and after a riotous round of musical chairs for about seventy, John did a question and answer session about *Blue Peter*. At the end he asked them what they thought of the programme and the presenters. I thought he might have been fishing for compliments.

One girl put her hand up and John listened eagerly.

'I think you are all a bit silly,' she said innocently.

John roared with laughter.

(Left): Cameraman Keith Hopper and sound recordist Graham Bedwell film John Leslie making friends with local schoolchildren

We flew, very bumpily, from Port Stanley to Pebble Island and, while we craned our necks to look at the battlefields of San Carlos, poor John craned his head into a sick bag.

There were about twenty inhabitants of Pebble Island and the day before we arrived one of them had committed suicide. After an hour on the island and a quick look about, we began to understand why. It was a very isolated settlement with only half a dozen houses and the sheep station for company. Tactlessly, I enquired what might have caused such a tragedy and was told that people on Pebble Island had 'too much time to think'.

With hardly a tree in sight, and only the small rectangular timber and corrugated-iron houses in the open shallow rolling hills, we were marooned in endless miles of sea.

Because there wasn't anywhere to stay, we had to pitch in with a couple of families. John and I stayed with Susan and Tony Hirtle and we shared a room. It was all quite amicable, even though John was not used to sharing with someone of the same sex. He confided to me that he was not enjoying himself. I told him that I quite understood and we chatted about Catherine, whom he sorely missed. We always got on well and I found him good company. Fortunately, he didn't snore and while I probably did he was kind enough not to mention it.

All the food was home grown and every meal was a variation of lamb, potatoes and carrots. The lamb was cooked a dozen different ways yet it was always lamb in the end. John was not very fond of lamb and I suspect he likes it even less now.

We did a bit of sheep shearing and met some professional shearers who came from somewhere near Coventry. In fact, you could not get much farther from Coventry!

They 'followed the wool', moving from New Zealand to Argentina, and heaven knows where else, before finally arriving in the Falklands. They told us a horrifying tale of a shearer gang who fell out with a farmer and they literally sheared the teats off all his ewes in revenge. The farmer didn't find out until they had gone and the entire flock had to be destroyed.

The reason we had decided to visit Pebble Island was the sheep, the wildlife and, of course, the war.

I had been told not to mention the war to the children because 'they'd been traumatised by it'.

In fact, I found the reverse to be true. They couldn't stop talking about it. Quite obviously it was the most exciting thing that had ever happened to them. I remember a story about a young lad called Russell Evans who, while he'd been out on horseback, checking the sheep, had found an Argentine jet that had been shot down and searched it for maps. The nine-year-old went back and reported the find to the family.

'Was the pilot there?' he was asked.

To which he replied, 'Yes, but his head wasn't.'

Russell had probably been butchering and decapitating sheep since he was strong enough to hold a saw so a headless body was no big deal.

(Below): John Leslie catching up with the new love in his life from a remote schoolroom in the Falklands

(Top left): John Leslie in the wreckage of a crashed Argentine jet on Pebble Island

To the soldiers who had to drag the headless corpse from the wreck and bury it, I am sure it was.

I learned that family life in the Falklands was complicated to say the least. With so little choice of a life partner it was hardly surprising that so many marriages foundered. I was told that it was quite usual to get married several times and the offspring belonged to the wider community. A child might have many 'aunts and uncles' and lots of cousins.

I talked to teenagers about their expectations and found very mixed ambitions. Some desperately wanted to leave the islands and work in Britain, while others had no such plans. With fewer than a hundred other beings to choose a spouse from, the idea of pairing for life must have been quite a challenge.

Pebble Island was home to thousands of sheep and even more penguins. There were tiny rockhoppers and Magellanics in their thousands, and they were unbelievably tame. They were completely unafraid of us and lived in nests on the ground or in burrows. Over a lamb sandwich, the crew and I took it in turns to pose in the middle of the flock and take photographs. John, meanwhile, had disappeared and it was some minutes before I found him comfortably sheltered behind a rock and deeply ensconced in his GameBoy.

We moved on, to the small port settlements of Darwin and Goose Green, location of one of the famous battles of the Falklands and made all the more notorious because a BBC reporter had broadcasted the imminent assault. However angry the British military may have been, the Argentines assumed such a gaffe had to be a piece of deliberate propaganda. It proved a crucial turning point of the war.

(Bottom right): John with John McCloud and Anna Robson, revisiting the Goose Green village hall where they had been held prisoner by Argentine troops

(Top right): John with a
colony of unconcerned
rockhopper penguins,
Pebble Island

Here we were confronted by a collection of weatherboard buildings mostly painted white or green. The harbour and dock area was built partly from the hulks of old square-rigged sailing ships. Nothing seemed to rot in the Falklands and these hulks must have been a couple of hundred years old. On one of the warehouse doors I found 'HMS *Exeter*' painted in bright red letters and I assumed it was as the result of a visit from the ship during the conflict. I subsequently found out it was a different HMS *Exeter* – the one that had fought the German pocket battleship the *Graf Spee* at the Battle of the River Plate in 1939. The paint looked incredibly fresh and it was hard to believe it was over fifty years old.

John told the story of the Battle of Goose Green, fought by the Second Battalion of the Parachute Regiment, from the point of view of two children who were sheltering with their families in the town hall. John McCloud, who was now 26, had glimpsed the start of the battle as the paras skirmished around the gorse that was on fire on the skyline. Together with Anna Robson, who had been three at the time, we relived the discomfort and fears of the 114 villagers as they came to the end of a month of imprisonment.

During the battle they were told to lie between the brick pillars that supported the hall floor to protect themselves from the bullets and bombs. They showed us the outline of the trapdoor that had been cut in the floor to gain access to the cavity beneath.

The hall doubled up as a bar and all the while we were filming, the landlord and a couple of others were enjoying a drink or two in the room next door. A family was leaving to resettle in Port Stanley, so the population would be dropping from 21 to 17, which was quite a blow to those remaining. I could see that the lack of work and other people to talk to could be a real test of one's sanity.

I had a particular interest in the Battle of Goose Green because I was at school with Charles 'Dair' Farrar-Hockley, who was company commander of 'A' company with the Second Battalion of the Parachute Regiment. It was reported that it was because 'A' Company's advance had faltered that his commanding officer, Colonel H. Jones, went up to the front. He then led a charge on the Argentine positions and was killed.

We made a pilgrimage to the spot where Colonel Jones had died and found the place marked with white stones on the side of a hill. It was a tragic sight and very moving. The grass was barely ankle deep and there was hardly any cover from the well dug-in Argentine troops. It did not take any imagination to see that Colonel H's charge and subsequent attacks in which Dair took part were acts of incredible bravery. They earned Colonel Jones the Victoria Cross. The 450 men of Two Para defeated a force three times their size. The Falklands campaign earned Dair the Military Cross.

The battle for the Falklands lasted 74 days until at 9 p.m. on 14 June 1982 in the capital, Stanley, the Argentines surrendered. More than two thousand servicemen had been killed or wounded, more than the entire population of the Falklands.

We found that the islanders were unanimous in their gratitude for being rescued from the Argentines, and British to the core. The whole place looked a bit like 'Dartmoor-by-the-sea' and it was growing on me. After a week I was sold on it. It was clean, uncluttered and unspoilt. I could well understand why people moved from Britain to live there.

Meanwhile, while Graham, our sound recordist, had coped with the wind, he had found unexpected challenges. The noise of barking sea lions, as it echoed up the cliffs, was so loud it drowned out John and a wildlife expert talking on the cliff top. And the last thing he expected to

(Bottom left): John Leslie relaxes between takes

(Below): Preparing to leave Pebble Island

(Top left): Alex at the spot where British hero Colonel H. Jones was killed

deal with was teenage vanity. It transpired that the young lady we were interviewing had improved her outward womanliness by padding her bra. Her voice was unaccountably muffled because the tiny microphone that had been pinned inside was fighting a losing battle, muffled as it was by a layer of cotton wool. The quality of the sound was the last thing on John's mind as he cast admiring glances!

There is one dark cloud, however. There are natural energy resources beneath the waves and exploration companies have begun drilling. I do hope that it doesn't turn into one huge oil and gas terminal because, in 2012, with oil discovered, this is a distinct possibility.

While I was sad to leave, John was noticeably happier as we boarded the Tri-Star for the flight back. We climbed up to cruising height and craned our necks for one last look at this tiny group of islands in a vast expanse of sea that for a few gruelling months in 1982 had been the scene for the remotest of British wars.

All flights had to refuel at Ascension Island, and when we disembarked for a short stopover we were told that the aircraft had developed a fault and we were going to be stuck there. The news was greeted with a universal cheer from the military passengers, who were very 'pleased' to be away from Mount Pleasant. John remembers it well:

(Bottom right): John stranded on Ascension Island

> There was a loud bang and when the plane taxied back we could all see the problem: a piece of the ageing Tri-Star wing had fallen to the tarmac. To my horror, despair and disbelief, we were confined to the island for three days while we waited for the wing part to be sent out!

I rang Lewis and told him the news and while everyone was excitedly preparing to go to the beach he asked, 'Can you make another film while you're there?'

It's the sort of thing you generally don't want to hear. However, as I'm not a great fan of lying about on beaches, it would give me a reason to snoop about. I knew that the BBC had a presence on the island because there was a transmitter relay station. After a ten-minute conversation with the senior BBC representative I realised that there was masses of good stuff to film. He told me about a research worker who, every night, tagged the turtles that arrived to lay their eggs on the beach.

We were given a BBC car and I needed a driving licence. It was surprisingly simple to fix because all I had to do was go to the post office and get one. I then had to break the news to John, who was relaxing on the beach and no doubt thinking of Catherine as he topped up his tan. John saw it rather differently:

> This [disaster] was compounded by the sheer joy of Mr Leger, who, after having corresponding with the office back home to explain our plight, was then given permission to make another film!!!

That night we filmed a giant green turtle, all of five feet long, clambering up the beach and digging a hole into which she proceeded to lay her eggs. Her huge shell gleamed brown and green under our single light. Curiously, she didn't seem to mind us being there. She took absolutely no notice and concentrated on despatching her load of eggs. The whole process lasted less than an hour and made a great sequence. John sort of forgave me:

> So there I was, at two in the morning, on the beach, watching the biggest turtles you've ever seen in your life, come ashore to lay their eggs. Of course sometimes you do not realise what a truly amazing experience you are in the middle of at the time. Looking back, I would not swap it for anything.

The next day my BBC contact took us on a tour of 'Green Mountain', a man-made phenomenon at the top of the island.

Ascension Island has been described as the 'biggest ashtray in the world'. It's a collection of about forty extinct volcanoes and lava fields that criss-cross the island. Centuries of bird droppings meant that the top of the island had once been covered with a thick layer of guano, and square-rigged sailing ships had arrived from all over the world to collect it. Back in the 19th century it was an important source of fertiliser. Today all the guano is gone and in its place is a miniature rainforest.

The ships that once took away the guano arrived empty but brought ballast to keep them upright and stable in the heavy seas during the long voyage. This ballast was good old topsoil, and the sailors carried the barrels of earth to the top of the island and emptied them before refilling them with bird droppings. Over time the soil built up, the guano went down, and tropical plants took hold. Green Mountain was born. Groups of tall Norfolk pines were planted to provide replacement masts and spars. They still stand like sentinels on Green Mountain and enjoy very different weather conditions to the rest of the island.

Like so many locations, Ascension Island had revealed her secrets and only *Blue Peter* could have enabled me to discover them.

Over the years, tight budgets have restricted curiosity, and while it's good for cost control, it's not good for the programme.

The programme had a universal curiosity about 'life', and I grieve the passing of the time when I could just go and look on the off chance of finding the sorts of televisual jewels that have been its lifeblood.

(Right): The envy of most British children, Sammy Lee enjoyed riding her motorbike around Pebble Island, despite being only nine

(Above): Kayapo mother and child in the Gorotire village, Brazil

18

Dressed to kill

11–29 April 1992
Brazil and the Amazon

Two months after I had returned from the Falklands I was off again, this time with the new *Blue Peter* gardener, Clare Bradley.

Clare was a force to be reckoned with. She knew her stuff and what she did not, she soon found out. Petite, and with a huge mass of red hair, she bounced with enthusiasm and energy.

We seized the opportunity to film in remote overseas locations using 'the environment' as the hook. The regular presenters could not be released from the programme for more than about a week unless there was a very good reason. Clare, on the other hand, could travel and report at will. Over the next few years Clare and I travelled the world, reporting environmental disasters and initiatives.

It was the year of the Earth Summit in Rio de Janeiro, and we set off to the Amazon rainforest for what would prove to be a challenging three weeks.

Clare had never actually delivered a speech directly to camera before. In television, this is called a 'piece to camera' or PTC, the stock-in-trade of the seasoned presenter.

She had expressed doubts but I brushed them aside because I was so keen to get going. I told her not to worry.

'We'll sort it out when the time comes,' I had advised her confidently.

It was a risky move because it is not something that anyone can do. As it turned out, apart from the occasional slight stammer, she was very good at it. It was just as well. The first time she tried it we were ten thousand miles away on the other side of the world.

Clare lived in Kew Gardens because her husband worked there. She had talked to the director of Kew, Ghillian Prance, about our ideas. He was very helpful and it was his contacts and ideas that became the substance of the shoot. However, even though dates and schedules had

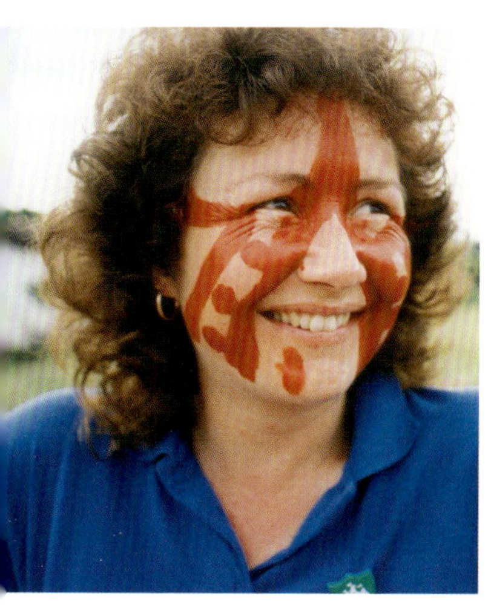

(Below): *Blue Peter* gardener Clare Bradley with Kayapo face decoration

been agreed and flights booked, it very nearly didn't happen.

We were booked on Varig Airlines, the national carrier for Brazil, because they were prepared to offer us cheap tickets. The flight was due to take off at 6 p.m., with check-in at 5.

It was long before the threat of terrorism so there were no lengthy check-in procedures. Thinking ahead, I decided to spend the morning packing and leave home in Devon at midday to allow plenty of time.

Unknown to me, Varig was then having financial difficulties. First thing in the morning, and even though it was Saturday and the Varig offices were shut, I thought I would double-check the departure time, just in case. Imagine my alarm when I was told that the flight had been moved forward to one o'clock.

Fighting panic, I asked them for a late check-in, promising to be there by 12.15, which left me 30 minutes to pack. I arrived at 12.25, the old Ford Granada estate smoking after the 180-mile dash up the motorway, met Clare, and we were rushed through to Departures. Half an hour later we were accelerating down Heathrow's main runway.

It was my first taste of Brazil and I thought that if things could change so radically with something as stable as flight times, the shoot would be full of surprises.

Not all of them were unpleasant. Rio was an exciting place and spectacular in so many ways. Sweeping views of beaches were everywhere and made my own local beach at Exmouth, in Devon, look less than impressive.

We stayed in a hotel overlooking the world-famous Copacabana beach and Clare, full of enthusiasm as usual, declared as darkness fell that she was going for a walk down by the water's edge. The bay was 180 degrees of apparently unspoilt sand where during the day both rich and poor topped up their tans and played games. In the evening it was totally deserted and I wondered why. Remembering Peru and Ethiopia, I was inclined to be suspicious and play safe. Any unforeseen incident could jeopardise the shoot so I reluctantly put my foot down and said no. Clare was not easily put off. It took all my powers of persuasion to divert her from the beach.

The next morning the crew turned up and after the usual greetings the cameraman, Brian Sewell, confirmed my instincts.

'Word of warning. Don't go on the beach at night. Looks peaceful but you'll get mugged.'

Clare was astonished and, remembering the fight we'd had the previous night, I resisted the 'I told you so' speech.

According to Brian, and his sound recordist Mark Van der Willigen (who had been especially hired by the BBC because they both worked as freelancers in South America), assailants would dig a pit in the beach to hide in and then cover themselves with a plastic sheet and sand and wait. They could then ambush a passerby and disappear again so quickly the police wouldn't be able to find them.

We spent the day travelling and filming in the Mata Atlantica, the Atlantic rainforest south of Rio, and then the next day flew north to

Belem on the mouth of the river Amazon.

Belem airport was a sign of things to come. It was hot, humid and falling down. Our fixer, David Hassett, who in real life ran a botanical garden, had recommended that we hire a twin-engine aircraft for our next flight to the Gorotire village, deep in the heart of the Amazon rainforest. When I queried the expense he reassured me that single engine planes had a reputation for disappearing with engine failure, so two engines were better than one.

David, bespectacled, engaging with twinkling eyes, had arranged through Funai, the Department of Indian Affairs, for us to spend six days with the Kayapo Indians, who were reputed to be some of the fiercest people in the Amazon. We had been lucky because it had not been an easy thing to do. His friendship with Ghillian Prance had helped, but it was his own curiosity that drove him. A visit to the warlike Kayapo was a rare opportunity to see an ancient culture before it disappeared for ever. Clare was curious too. She was madly keen to see how they managed their gardens because she had heard about their incredible gardening skills. I thought it a very strange mix – extreme violence and gardening – and to Clare the combination was irresistible.

Unlike the other presenters, and because of her specialist gardening knowledge, Clare (like the legendary Percy Thrower before her) set the agenda, and she had a very good eye for what would make an interesting subject. She was driven by a passion for all things green; the more unusual it was, the better. In this case the Kayapo had a particular interest in compost heaps, which was one of her interests too. On the surface it may not seem to be the most riveting of subjects, and I wondered why a tribe of bloodthirsty Amazonian Indians were so concerned. Her interest was enough to make even the most indifferent gardener sit up.

There were six of us in the party. Besides Clare, Brian, Mark, David and myself, there was our interpreter-cum-cook, Sandra, who was heavily pregnant. Her day job was as a research student who worked with the famous anthropologist Darrell Posey, and she understood the Kayapo language. We brought boxes of food for us and presents for the Kayapo. They had asked for medical supplies and our visit was conditional on bringing a wide variety of antibiotics, malaria treatments and eye ointments. I had also spent a fair bit of money in my home town, Exeter, shopping for fishing hooks, penknives and – the ultimate gift – solar torches.

Standing on the edge of the pitted tarmac, holes filled with water after a recent downpour, I looked dubiously at the charter flight company in Belem and wondered if they would bother to fly back and collect us on time. We had agreed to pay half up front and the rest when we got back. Even so, I wasn't convinced they would turn up. I could imagine them getting a better offer and leaving us with the Kayapo until it was convenient to return. I wondered how I could guarantee they wouldn't let us down. Then, suddenly, the problem was easily solved. When we loaded up the aircraft, the pilot spotted one of the solar torches and his eyes gleamed. I promised it to him – only if he stuck to our schedule.

Our happy band flew off deep into the mysterious Amazon basin to land at a place with the unlikely name of Redenção or, in English, 'Redemption'. What sins, I wondered, warranted such a name? The flight crew knew more about Redenção than we did, and refused to go into the town. Ominously, they said they needed to guard the aircraft. We hitched a lift to fetch the chief of Gorotire, who had developed a taste for town living. Perhaps he was in need of redemption, if only for the mod cons. As we bumped along dirt roads we passed men wearing pistols on their belts and carrying rifles. It was just like the Wild West, and we were told not to film.

The chief seemed perfectly used to aircraft and our half-hour flight to Gorotire was swift and uneventful. And then we landed and were nearly engulfed by huge plumes of water thrown up from the landing gear. Our hearts stopped in momentary panic. There had been a recent downpour and it had yet to drain away. Then the aircraft jerked to a halt and all was quiet again. Suddenly there were Kayapo women and children everywhere and they helped us unload and transfer our equipment to a pick-up truck. I noticed that there wasn't a man to be seen.

It wasn't long before the mystery was resolved.

The truck went ahead and we followed curiously and timorously on foot. The village was strangely deserted and it was getting dark. Ahead of us was a large open-sided building with a tin roof and I thought I saw feathers and sticks flickering in the half-light. As we got closer we saw and heard the low murmur of a village meeting. All the men were there, packed in orderly rows, bristling with weapons and

(Above): Living the exotic lifestyle of a TV film crew; four of us were cramped into a single room with all our kit for a week

(Left): Clare Bradley after landing at the Gorotire village

dressed to kill, in more ways than one.

Unknown to me, we had timed our visit well. It was the start of a week of celebration and all the warriors of the village were wearing full ceremonial regalia. With exotic headdresses, bodies covered in intricate black and red patterns, clubs, spears and bows and arrows in their hands, they sat packed together as we walked past. I wondered what to do. Should I perhaps say hello?

There was no need. They hardly noticed us. They were totally enthralled as they were addressed by the chief. They emanated a proud arrogance, which was both impressive and frightening.

While Clare and Sandra made camp in the village surgery, the rest of us unloaded into a small room about 15 feet by 8. It was just the right width to sling our four hammocks. We sat down and looked at ourselves. This was going to be our home for the next five nights and while Mark removed the last vestiges of dog poo, Brian produced a bottle of pisco, a product of Chilean origin similar to brandy but far more lethal. He and Mark had just returned from a challenging shoot in Peru with the Shining Path guerillas. The challenge had been to evade government forces that were looking for them.

'I find this is just what we need at times like this,' he mused.

Not far away, Clare was settling in with even less comfort:

> The walls were covered in slime and there was spit every-where. No one seemed to see the dirt even though we were making our home in the village surgery. There was a toilet in the next room and even though it wasn't plumbed in, people still used it. The whole building stank to high heaven.

The village meeting must have ended because we got a visitor. A huge, muscular young warrior covered in scars, black patterns and feathers strode into the room and sat down beside me on one of the equipment boxes. Brian and Mark were old hands here and had filmed at Gorotire before.

'Don't give him more than one small one,' Brian warned, as I offered the warrior a drink. It was all nodding and smiling for a few minutes and then the apparition of primitive violence said thank you in Portuguese and left. He reappeared moments later with the most stunning feather headdress that he wanted to sell. It was so colourful and intricately woven that my first thought was, *How much?*

Mark, however, had other thoughts.

'Don't buy it. It's illegal. If you do, you'll endanger the birds. Hundreds were killed to produce that. You buy it and he'll produce ten more.' He was right, of course.

Gorotire was like a theme park for the Amazon Indians. They danced for several hours each day and the whole community sat around to watch. Our presents had been accepted, and the fish hooks and solar torches (minus one) had gone down well. We made contact with the local medicine man, Beptopoop, who was also the Kayapo gardening expert, and Clare started to scout about for compost heaps.

The village was built around a wide avenue of corrugated-iron and breeze-block bungalows with the meeting hall at one end. Traditionally-built leaf houses were scattered about, protected by huge unsightly sheets of black plastic. The overall impression was that no one cared. Litter was everywhere and all the taps leaked. Even so, the people were friendly, happy, and they made us feel welcome.

As we ventured into the bush gardens, communication became a problem. For Clare to ask Beptopoop a question, David had to ask Sandra in Portuguese, and then she would ask Beptopoop in Kayapo. The reply, when it came, had to go back up the chain to David, who would translate back again into English. Meanwhile, Beptopoop, who was a dear old man, did very little in the way of gardening and sat in the shade while his wife did all the work.

We discovered that the Kayapo gardening methods were ahead of their time. They used generations of experience to mix together plants that attracted pests that would destroy each other: ingenious bioengineering in its infancy. They also planted manioc and other plants for use in future years. The idea was to stick them in the ground and forget them until there was a dire need. It might be years before they cleared the bush and dug them up. I wondered how they knew they weren't digging up their neighbours' secret supply.

Weeding was somewhat neglected. These and what was left of harvested plants were allowed to rot naturally and provide nutrients for the new crop. It's a technique now being adopted by environmentalists

(Above): Cameraman Brian Sewell and sound recordist Mark Van der Willigen film Kayapo ceremonial dancing

(Left): Fixer David Hassett, interpreter Sandra Machade, Clare Bradley and Kayapo medicine man Beptopoop in the bush garden

in the UK. It wasn't all good news. The compost heaps were a touch mythical and even Clare had to admit that she was not impressed.

Every day from about two o'clock in the afternoon there were celebrations when everyone turned out to watch the dancing. One of the dances was a strange affair when a young woman led a huge conga of men around the village square. She carried a very new baby on her shoulders. Immediately behind her came three or four stern-faced women. Behind them followed most of the men of the village, who alternatively whooped and sighed as they danced. Unlike the women, they looked as if they were really enjoying themselves as they laughed and joked. I asked why the women looked so stern and was surprised by the reply.

'The child is being introduced to the village and the four ladies behind the mother are the aunties. When a man joins in the dance he has shown that he accepts the child into the village and in return he has the right to have sex with each of the aunties until the next full moon.'

The children of the Kayapo used their mothers' second names because no one really knew who the fathers were. I was told that sex was a favour given freely. For example, if one man agreed to repair another family's roof then he was repaid by having sex with the man's wife. It was a currency as much as any other. There was little evidence of the paper variety.

Life in Gorotire got better as we became used to it. Every evening we would go en masse and join the entire village to wash in the river. The women would use one part of the river and the men another. At about six o'clock there would be a murmur of 'Malaria time' and everyone would go back their homes and sit beside smoky fires to keep the mosquitoes away. Then the evening would settle down and the only sounds, apart from the cicadas, would be the dogs barking and the constant sounds of a population with a head cold. However far I travelled, the common cold always got there first. Dreadful stomach-churning sounds of sniffing and coughing constantly assaulted our ears.

It was very hot and humid and there was scarcely a breeze to take the edge off it. All our clothes were sweaty, dirty and damp, and no amount of hanging out to dry made any difference. The grime of the village, the litter and ubiquitous dog mess began to wear on my nerves. By the sixth day I was looking forward to leaving.

When the last day came we all scanned the sky for our aircraft. Without it we were stranded, unless we fancied a week of trekking to get to the nearest village with a radio. That was too awful to contemplate. Our eyes searched the horizon and we listened carefully for the familiar buzz of the engine. Had the lure of a solar torch been enough?

It came without warning as the pilot flew low over the village and did a wingover to land out of sight. We threw our gear into the pick-up and headed down to the airstrip with more urgency than was polite, even though we had already said our goodbyes.

Climbing gratefully into the twin-engine Beech Air, the air conditioning hit us like a sledgehammer. Nothing had ever felt so good. The pilot smiled as he pressed cans of ice-cold beer into our hands. Within seconds all sweat had dried and we took off. I craned my neck to have

(Left): A typically colourful Kayapo family

(Right): Rainforest timber splitting in the baking sun

one last look at our Kayapo Indian friends in Gorotire. Even though they had been very kind to us the relief to be gone was overwhelming. I counted my lucky stars I had been born into Western society and not part of their community.

Clare was equally relieved and she was transfixed as we flew across the Amazon basin:

> The flight across the Amazon rainforest was fabulous. The trees stretched to the horizon and you could see the flood water glinting under the forest canopy.

After an hour's flight we landed at Porto Trombetas, a tributary of the Amazon, where there was a bauxite mine partly owned by Shell. The miners had stripped off the rainforest to scoop out the valuable ore. It would have been an environmental disaster if it were not for the activities of one Harry Knowles.

Harry had warmed the hearts of conservationists worldwide by spending a lot of Shell's money, and his own time, replanting the rainforest.

We settled into some refreshingly clean accommodation built on stilts about half a metre off the ground. Glancing down, I noticed that the shade under the bungalows had attracted the snake population, which slithered about unmolested. I wondered if they ever tried to climb up. Even so, snakes or no snakes, we were in heaven.

The mining had stripped the ground bare of vegetation and at first sight the situation seemed hopeless. I thought it would take decades for the rainforest to return. But Harry was a pioneer and he proudly showed us how branches and scrap timber had been buried and the topsoil returned and replanted. I was amazed at how little topsoil was needed to fuel rampant growth. Harry showed us a spot where a small pile of topsoil had been left and a 30-foot tree grew in the middle of it. A few yards away there was very little topsoil and the same variety of tree stood less than half my height. The knack was to replace the right amount of topsoil and Harry had made a study of it.

Sadly, we saw acres of timber waiting for collection and splitting in the sun. It was like a graveyard for the lungs of the world and a very dispiriting sight. Sadder still, in untouched rainforest nearby and waiting for the chainsaws, Clare saw a mature Brazil-nut tree for the first time in her life and demonstrated its girth by trying to wrap her arms about it. A few days later no doubt it, too, was cut down.

We were all recovering from our Kayapo ordeal and Mark was limping badly after an insect bite on his ankle. Clare had been bitten in another, very unfortunate place. I noticed that they were the only two people who had worn shorts, and it confirmed the importance of being suitably covered up, especially when there were insects about. Harry proved dexterous with a magnifying glass and confirmed that Clare's bite, although uncomfortable, wasn't serious. Then we boarded a river boat and headed back down the Trombetas River to rejoin the mighty Amazon.

All our clothes had been washed and pressed and it was in the late afternoon when we set off. We cruised down the river, 100 metres wide as it undulated down the flood plain. Tall tropical rainforest overhung the banks and, as we followed the channel, we alternately closed with one bank and then the other, and then swung away again.

We pitched camp in the bow and watched the sun go down and listened to the gurgle and splash of water against the hull. With cans of cold beer in our hands, we knew the worst of the trip was over.

Darkness fell and the boat turned on its powerful floodlight and caught myriad flying creatures in its beam. The trees on the nearest bank, picked out by the light, looked as if they had been arranged by experts in a well-tended garden. We floated by, every yard revealing more wonder and surprise. I marvelled that during the day I hadn't even noticed.

We awoke at dawn to find the wide expanse of the Amazon stretched out before us. There was a large brown stain that showed where the waters of our tributary and the main river met, and as we crossed over the line I could make out the buildings of Santarem on the far bank, our next destination.

For the next few days we filmed how different people made a living out of the rainforest without cutting it down. There were the rubber tappers who made rubber gloves, cocao-bean farmers, and people who collected acai. The purple acai berries were ground up to make a vile drink that was considered a local delicacy and very good for you. Annatto, used in ice cream, was another fruit of the rainforest, and we saw how a variety of produce was harvested and sold in the riverside markets. This activity was sustainable and brought no harm to the rainforest.

In Belem we had booked into a riverside hotel with a swimming pool and because there was some building work in progress, there was a large pile of timber stacked at the end nearest the river and around the corner from the pool. Clare saw the opportunity for a final piece to camera and on a table next to the pile of wood she stacked all the local produce we had featured. She then delivered her final thought to camera.

'You can either have this ...' indicating the timber '... from the rainforest or all of these wonderful things ...' and she listed them '... for ever.'

It was a good piece but not perfect and I said so. Mark was not happy. He put down his headphones and sound mixer and stormed off around the corner and out of sight.

It is fair to say that Mark was not having a good time because apart from his foot, which was giving him constant pain, he was going through a divorce and he was worried about his mother, who had just had a serious eye operation. Up until then he had concealed all this from us. But that afternoon while we were filming something in him snapped. There was a family in the pool and Mark had already asked them to be quiet for a few minutes even though they had a perfect right to make as much noise as they liked. They had taken little notice and the father, a great bull of a man, was shouting at his children for some reason. Mark was all out of patience and there was a violent altercation.

We were blissfully unprepared for what happened next.

Mark returned, tight-lipped and white-faced with anger, to resume his sound-recording duties.

'Take two,' I said automatically. Clare looked very unsettled because she could see the raging father – blood frothing from his mouth – rushing towards us. He shouted something unprintable at us, seized the camera and threw it down onto the concrete surface. I tried to apologise for whatever it was that had upset him, but to no avail. He then raged some more, turned over Clare's table and stormed off. Many years later Mark explained what had happened:

> I was not in a good place. That day was the blackest day in my life as a sound recordist. I lost control. I am sure he was after me but got to the camera first. I was lucky.

Meanwhile David Hassett, our fixer, was very concerned.

'He is very well connected socially and he has said he will get his men to kill Mark. He has gone to ring the police.'

David then explained that there were two types of police in Belem: the civil police who were 'negotiable' and the criminal police who were not. We fervently hoped that it would be the civil police who answered the call. My main concern was to protect the rushes because if the criminal police turned up they would imprison Mark and impound all our equipment. David knew of a contact in the city and I loaded all the videotapes into a bag and grabbed a taxi. I gave David what money I had in case he needed it. As we drove off, the raging man rushed out, indicating to the taxi driver that he should ring him.

David had written down his contact's address and I hoped that the taxi driver wouldn't give me away. Ten minutes later we arrived at a heavily fortified house with imposing metal-spiked railings topped with an electric fence. The wrought-iron gates opened automatically as we approached. The owner of the house greeted me warmly and we put the tapes in his safe. He then gave me a cup of tea and I sat down to reflect.

Like most of the houses in Belem, every window had metal bars. I was caged up, protected from the outside world. I wondered what sort of society it was that meant people had to live like this. Time passed.

About three hours later a very relieved party arrived without Mark, who remained at the hotel. David recounted what had happened. Fortunately, the civil police had taken the case. He had pretended not to understand Portuguese so he could work out how best to handle the situation to Mark's benefit. At the right moment he had suggested that some justly deserved reparation might be paid to the angry man to pay for his injury and damaged pride.

They accepted David's offer and the incident ended.

Mark had a very restless night and we caught the next plane back to Rio at six o'clock the next morning. The airport was quiet and empty and he looked about nervously. The victim of the previous day had threatened to kill him and, compensation or no compensation, he did not look like a man who would go back on his word. Only when we took off did Mark return to his old self, chastened by his experience. He later told me:

> I was very worried that my passport would be confiscated because I was due to fly back to Holland to visit my mother. It was a close shave and I vowed never to lose my temper ever again.

And what about the licence-payers' money? I hear you ask. I had already agreed with Brian to pay him US$1500 overtime because of the very long hours we had spent on location. The compensation David had paid was from that money. Brian wasn't best pleased but knew it was his man who had been at fault. The camera needed repair and Mark had other bills to pay. Our shoot was over, or 'wrapped'.

The excitement, however, was not. As we drove from Rio airport back into town a police car overtook us, lights flashing. It cut up a van about half a mile ahead of us and screeched to a halt. Three policemen jumped out, their submachine guns at the ready, and aimed at the occupants.

Brian was very sanguine about it all. To my surprise he remarked dryly: 'I just hope they don't open fire until we get past.'

Much later, at his home and protected by a 24-hour guard, Brian explained what I now knew about Brazil and the impact it had on his daily life.

'It's a very violent country. I came home one day and the house was being ransacked. The intruders were armed with pistols and high on drugs. They tied me to a chair and I was waiting for them to shoot me as they left, but they didn't. I was lucky – and now I have the guards.'

The Amazon had been a *Blue Peter* adventure and a half. I couldn't wait to leave Rio. I didn't feel comfortable in a place where guns ruled. Maybe it's all changed now. I haven't been back to find out.

(Above): A typical village scene that belies the harsh realities of the remote parts of South America

19

The Zeta-Jones effect

I first met archaeologist Margaret Rule in 1977 when a bronze cannon was being auctioned in Penzance. It had been found by a young lad out diving near Teignmouth and it made about £7,000, a huge sum in those days. She exploded with fun and enthusiasm and her love of life was infectious. As we chatted she hinted at a project that would rock the archaeological world.

In 1982 the secret was out. Her team had discovered the *Mary Rose*, King Henry VIII's flagship. The raising of the *Mary Rose* on 11 October was a national triumph and today it has pride of place in the Royal Navy Dockyard in Portsmouth. Ten years after it was rescued from the Solent, I had to update the reports that Sarah Greene had made during the excavation. (Sarah, a native of Hampshire, had dived on the wreck site and had watched as the timbers had been lifted dramatically to the surface.)

29–30 September 1992

The Mary Rose

Before the filming day I went down to Portsmouth to have a look. Margaret was as animated as ever. She asked me whether I fancied a ride in the crane bucket that they used to inspect the ship. By now the *Mary Rose* was upright and held in place by scaffolding while water and wax was sprayed onto her ancient timbers.

We swooped down over the main deck and hovered about six inches above it. Then she got out and walked along the deck to check something. To my delight, she invited me to join her. My imagination went into overtime. One step and I was actually walking where the crew of the *Mary Rose* had walked in 1545. I felt so privileged. The deck was faintly springy underfoot and the wood was soft yet still firm after the water spray. The whole structure was amazing. I looked along the deck

(Left): Cameraman Mike Radford films artefacts from the *Mary Rose* with Margaret Rule and Diane Louise Jordan

to the bow, trying to imagine the deck crammed with sailors.

And then it was all over and we were back in the hoist and flying back to the gantry. Margaret turned to me and stated proudly, 'You are one of only nine or so people to have walked the deck since she was recovered. Prince Charles was the eighth.' (Or he might have been the seventh.)

After that the filming was a 'mere bagatelle', as Biddy used to say, and there were no more perambulations along the decks of 16th century flagships.

27 September 1992

Rallycross

In the autumn of 1992, I had an unexpected surprise. John Leslie and Catherine Zeta-Jones were still an item and I had to make a film about John racing a Formula Ford in a rallycross meeting at the Croft circuit near Scotch Corner. John asked if I minded if Catherine came along and because I had spoken to her on the phone I was curious to meet her.

She was stunning and obviously very fond of John. At the time she was in her early twenties and had recently signed up for a film (I think it was her first) in America. Her minder was never far away. John was happy she was around and I suggested we film her cheering him on during his race. To my surprise, the answer was 'no', on two counts: the first because she was in an exclusive contract with the film company; and the second because she would not be allowed anywhere near where there was the slightest chance of an accident. The perimeter fence was just too much of a risk. Welcome to the world of Hollywood A-listers-to-be.

(Above): John Leslie lines up before a race

(Top right): John Leslie and girlfriend Catherine Zeta-Jones

So she had to stay in and around the caravan that was the Formula Ford base. And that's why I found myself trying to get John to do a piece to camera by his car before the race, surrounded by hundreds of well-wishers who would not stop talking. Even though John was flattered by the attention, it was all too noisy. The growing crowd was out of sight behind the camera, so there was no visible reason for the distracting sounds. I wondered what to do. Then I had a flash of inspiration. I asked Catherine if she would mind taking a walk around the site with her minder. As she left, the whole crowd followed her as if she were the Pied Piper. John was quite taken aback. He had yet to get used to Catherine's growing fame.

13 November 1992

Diss, Norfolk

Presenter Diane Louise Jordan's eyes always sparkled with pleasure. Don't get me wrong, she did have her moments, but her genuine love for people and an interest in their lives more than made up for any hiccups.

Diane was and still is a vegetarian and she took her convictions very seriously. It led to some interesting moments because the programme often featured animals and animal-related stories. One of these was near Diss, in Norfolk. It was all about a brand-new 'biomass power plant' that had just been commissioned. It made electricity by burning all kinds of waste (like mushroom compost) at very high temperatures.

The power station at Eye was an innovation and at that time it was mostly fired not with vegetarian mushroom compost but with turkey litter. Key to the story was a direct link between Sir Bernard Matthews' turkeys and the lighting up of a light bulb. Needless to say, it fired powerful emotions in Diane.

She was up for doing the story but wary of her feelings towards Sir Bernard. I was wary too and approached the great man with some trepidation because I imagined him to be someone who would expect straight talking and efficiency. Any 'fannying about', to quote a popular sitcom, would not be tolerated.

As it happened, I found Sir Bernard to be a likeable man and he found time in his busy schedule to be interviewed not just once but twice. The first was with a group of local schoolchildren who had inspired the use of turkey droppings as fuel. They had written to him suggesting that turkey poo should be burnt in the new power station nearby rather than be used as a fertiliser. They had concluded that the nitrogen run-off from fields constantly spread with turkey droppings would pollute the river system. Sir Bernard agreed with them and he congratulated them on their findings. The interview went well.

Then it was Diane's turn. She was surprisingly good-natured given her misgivings, and we lined up camera positions for the interview outside the mansion that was now his headquarters and which had once housed the turkeys.

Diane launched into her questions and then something very unusual happened. Sir Bernard became unexpectedly camera shy. He became quite tongue-tied, and after several false starts we decided to write the outline of his replies on giant crib boards to remind him of what he intended to say. They would be out of sight behind the cameras.

Diane was now deeply sympathetic to Sir Bernard's plight. Gone were all the adverse thoughts about the living conditions of millions of turkeys. In its place was anxiety to put Sir Bernard at his ease. She was so distracted she found it hard to remember her questions! Now one problem had become two, and a second giant crib board was marked up. The situation had become interestingly ludicrous and as the filming took its uncertain course I took refuge out of earshot for a quiet chuckle. To this day, I wish I had taken a photograph.

Back at the power station my only overriding memory was the overwhelming stench of ammonia in the hall where the lorries arrived to tip out ton after ton of turkey droppings. The cameraman, Godfrey Johnson, good-natured as always, ventured into this hellish environment to take the necessary shots.

15–21 March 1993

Namibia

Clare Bradley was always full of ideas and she would send them to me almost on a weekly basis. As I sifted through one pile, a particular

(Above): Clare Bradley bears witness to desertification. The Oshakati region once teemed with wildlife that roamed in thick bush

environmental problem caught my eye. It was based in Namibia and was about how large parts of the world had been abused by human occupation so that fertile land had been turned into deserts, a problem called 'desertification'.

Unlike what we'd done in Brazil, we decided to do a recce because desertification was a tricky issue to explain and would need careful scripting. We joined our fixer, John Hines, an ex-parks warden, and he took us off on safari to visit the afflicted areas.

We drove north from Swakopmund along a modern road built by the South Africans; its beautiful tarmac surface had been part of a military strategy. They had waged war against SWAPO, who had fought a guerrilla war from across the Angolan border, and the road had been a supply line for the soldiers. The tarmac was in itself a protection for the South African army because there was nowhere to conceal landmines. The days of massive roadside bombs were yet to come.

Namibia was stunning in parts. Towards the coast, the deserts were filled with giant dunes hundreds of feet high. Other parts were lush with thick rainforest. But the picturesque journey dissipated as we headed farther north. Gradually the tree life faded into an ever more barren wilderness until eventually there was not a tree in sight. This was desertification, the subject of the film we planned to make, and it had a huge impact on Clare:

> It was so very shocking, animal carcasses lying about. The soil was salty because the natural goodness had been washed out of it. There was virtually no hope – and there was no organic matter to put back into it.

In a nutshell, the road we were driving along had caused the disaster. Built up above the surrounding plain, it had diverted the flow of seasonal flood water that made the grass and trees grow. The South African army had compounded the problem by creating a huge supply base in the Oshakati region. This caused previously nomadic people to stop their wandering and settle down outside the camp gates because the base needed workers. And then they cut down the trees for fire-wood. Clare and I saw people digging up the tree roots in a last-ditch effort to get firewood. Yet many of them remembered when the bush had been so thick they hadn't walked alone for fear of attack by lions and other creatures.

I filmed everything in sight with my newly acquired SVHS video camera so I would have something to refer to when I wrote the script back home. Our guide plied us with bottles of ice-cold beer, which was very pleasant and thirst-quenching. It was, however, also lethal in such a climate. After three days I collapsed with dehydration. The taste of the cold liquid was beguiling and deadly, and my body rebelled. I swallowed gallons of water and rehydration salts but nature had its way and it was 36 hours before I could face so much as a boiled egg.

We headed to Gobabeb in the South Namib Desert and marvelled at the giant sand dunes that marched to the horizon. We stayed at the research institute and awoke the next morning to the sound of thunder. Yet this was one of the driest places on earth. Curious, I set up the camera and waited. Lightning flashed and we waited expectantly for rain. The sky got darker and darker until it felt like late evening. Just when I was beginning to wonder whether we were wasting our time, it started: a huge deluge that lasted for about an hour. We had stumbled upon an event that happened once in a blue moon, or this case every seven years. Within hours the desert began to show signs of green. As we motored in the direction from which rain had come, we saw that the sand was alive with yellow flowers.

We stopped at one point and Clare picked a stem from a plant she had spotted at the side of the road. It was the resurrection plant. It could 'die' and all its leaves and stem would turn brown and brittle. Yet stand it in water for half an hour and green leaves would appear. I took some home with me in a tin. Sure enough, months later in a jar of water, it came back to life.

Regrettably, my SVHS footage looked too primitive when shown against the Betacam, the broadcast standard at the time, and could not be shown. The age of 'anything goes' began about ten years later.

(Above): Cameraman John Adderley gets the impossible 'point of view' shot over Anthea Turner's shoulder

(Far left): The desert two or three days after heavy rain

(Left): The desert springs to life

12 May 1993
Crystal Palace swimming pool

A few days after it was announced that Anthea Turner would be joining the programme, she and her husband Peter Powell came to visit the office to meet us all. Everyone in the office felt welcome into both their lives.

Anthea was bubbly and inherently kind. She identified with the ideals of the programme and wanted to be involved as much as possible. Despite a near miss when presenting an outside broadcast in 1989, when a visual effect had detonated prematurely, she was eager to take on any challenge we could throw at her.

But her biggest challenge she kept a secret from us. She suffers from a mild form of dyslexia that could have been a huge handicap because of the last-minute script changes that are the lifeblood of live television.

Every *Blue Peter* live transmission was the result of a day of rehearsals followed by a 'run through', or the dress rehearsal about an hour before its 5.05 p.m. deadline. In the short time between the end of the final rehearsal and transmission, Lewis would give his last-minute script changes in the form of 'notes'.

Coping with these notes must have been a terrific test of Anthea's resolve.

Unaware of her struggle, I wondered at the time why she was so unwilling to indulge in any small talk in the 20 minutes that led up to transmission. Instead she would find a secluded spot away from us all, way upstage on the studio floor. She would pace backwards and forwards only a metre or two from the huge studio cyclorama backdrop as she fought to memorise her new words. Unlike the other presenters, John and Diane, she could not depend on reading the teleprompter.

I later asked her about it:

> Yes, it's true but I kept it quiet then as I thought I'd not get the job or get the sack!
>
> My dyslexia isn't severe but it does mean that I have to concentrate more than the next guy. To be truthful it probably helped; it made me diligent, learn the nuts and bolts of the item and not have to be a slave to the teleprompter.
>
> I work now for Dyslexia Action, raising awareness and funds. It's something that cannot be cured but can be coped with if at an early age you get the right help. We raise money to send specialist teachers into schools.

She had also decided to keep quiet about another important fact. She couldn't swim! Ignorant of this as well, I blithely suggested a high-diving challenge. I then marvelled at her determination and professionalism as she slogged away with her coach, former World, European and Commonwealth diving champion Chris Snoad, at the pool at Crystal Palace.

She disappeared for several sessions under cover of 'getting up to speed' for the filming. In reality she had confessed all to him and had thrown herself on his mercy and pleaded with him to teach her to swim. Chris had told her that the quickest way to learn was to dive in head first. So that is what she did, and with the filming deadline looming ever nearer, she accomplished her task.

On the day of the shoot I noticed nothing except a stubborn streak of determination, and someone who fitted her swimming costume rather well.

22–23 May 1993

Topsham, Devon

(Above): Anthea Turner after a successful dive

Ideas for films come from all over, and one came from an old friend who had a daughter who was doing a couple of years with Voluntary Service Overseas in Africa. She had reported that the school where she worked did not have electricity so in the evenings study had to be done with paraffin lamps. And there was not enough paraffin to go round. My friend intended to raise some money to pay for solar panels and asked if I could I help.

Normally we wouldn't have considered this because it would have conflicted with the *Blue Peter* annual appeal. But then I thought that if we did a sponsored clean-up of the river Exe near Topsham, it would fit our fashionable 'green' objectives. The idea slipped under the editorial net and the filming was on.

Diane Louise Jordan was the presenter and she was quite keen on cleanliness. She would even take her own bed linen on location rather than risk the hotels', so I watched with some interest as she joined girls of the Maynard School in Exeter to pull debris from the glutinous river mud.

To my delight she revelled in it and emerged completely covered in the stuff. She even put up with the high-pressure hose of the Topsham fire brigade fire engine, which was the only way of getting the mud off. Meanwhile, my wife Lynn, eager to play her part, had organised a mug of mushroom soup and a roll for all the volunteers.

To make it visual I had bought an old wartime soup kitchen from a local bric-a-brac dealer and into this vast metal contraption she poured the fresh ingredients ready for heating. Then something horrible happened: the fresh cream reacted with the tin-plated insides and promptly curdled. The soup, while hot, was undrinkable.

Suddenly the Lighter Inn on Topsham Quay was besieged with a request for sixty-odd ham and cheese rolls and endless cups of tea. At that time 20 rolls would have been a busy day.

The next day we weighed all the rubbish that had been collected at the council weighbridge in the Marsh Barton Industrial Estate. While

(Right): Diane Louise Jordan with the girls of the Maynard School, Exeter, getting hosed down after removing rubbish from the river Exe

we did not manage to raise the full amount, the fundraisers were more than halfway there; and today the school in Africa has its own electricity supply.

Diane still rings me when she's down in Exeter, and while she no longer brings her own bed linen, I suspect she keeps well away from the river at low tide.

21 September–5 October 1993
Namibia

It was the day after we had arrived for the shoot and we had flown to the research station in the middle of the Namib Desert to get scene-setting shots for the desertification story. All around were giant 600-foot-high sand dunes like yellow hillsides, immaculately smooth and curved in their slow march with the prevailing wind. The sky was a powder blue and it was cool, with hardly a breeze. We filmed as Clare Bradley climbed up the shifting sand towards us, the only disturbance in a vista of razor-sharp dune ridges that stretched to the horizon.

As the sun began to set we reluctantly retraced our steps to our simple accommodation at the research institute. Arthur Chesterman, a veteran sound recordist, who had seen more of the world than most, was overawed by the experience.

'Thank you for that,' he said. 'Quite remarkable and very special.'

I wondered if his kind remarks might have had something to do with the fact that he had left his all-important radio microphones behind in London. It was a ghastly mistake and I resigned myself to making do. We improvised with a woollen sock over a hand-held microphone until the proper wind shield and other equipment arrived!

(Left): Cameraman John
Adderley and sound
recordist Arthur
Chesterman film Clare
Bradley in the dunes near
the Gobabeb Training and
Research Centre, Namibia

(Below): Wildlife
cameraman Des Bartlett
prepares to take off with
Clare in a microlight
to look for rare desert
elephants

As well as the depressing desertification story we filmed the
wildlife producer and cameraman Des Bartlett at work deep in the
Skeleton Coast. He had pitched camp about twenty miles inland and
used microlights to go elephant spotting. Both Clare and I flew with
him low over the dunes, looking for tracks. The microlights, open at
the sides, gave an unobstructed, if alarming, 180-degree view. It was
exhilarating to skim along at a height of 50 feet or even lower. Groups
of ostrich belted off in surprise almost as fast as we were flying.

I had spent many hours flying enclosed by a cockpit as a private
pilot. Now, with the hot wind blasting from all sides, it was as different
as riding a motorbike was from driving a car. And as Des climbed to
7,000 feet to get a better view, all the fun turned to fear. It was one of
those times when a better view didn't make you feel better. I felt very
vulnerable, and sadly we found no elephants.

I marvelled at how Des and his family lived, for years at a time,
while he waited patiently for the elephants to appear.

Leaving Des, we set up camp in the evening on the flat shoreline of
the Skeleton Coast near Move Bay and lit a campfire, which flared in the

wind. We watched the everlasting breakers thundering onto the beach as night fell and revelled in our isolation. There were wrecks of ships that had been battered to pieces and I wondered about their crews. How could they have survived? There was no sign of life for hundreds of miles. Even if they'd had water, lions roamed the desert, and they would not have stood much of a chance.

Here history stood still. Even the constant wind could not delete the past. Cart tracks, made two centuries earlier, were as clear as the day they had first cut a groove in the shale sand surface. There were strict rules about not leaving the roads and I mused that without them this little piece of unspoilt nature would soon resemble a motorcycle dirt track that would never go away.

One plant that liked the desert was the welwitschia, which grew to several feet across. It was the ugliest plant I had ever seen and would not have looked out of place on a *Dr Who* set. It was a real survivor: the sun was so fierce it actually burnt its flowers and leaves, yet the welwitschia lived for hundreds of years.

Finally we returned to the Oshakati region, where rainforest had given way to a horrible man-made desert. We filmed as some communities tried to create gardens in the arid soil and noted that many hours were spent carrying water to irrigate their cabbages and other vegetables. There was also a scheme to plant a species of tree that thrived in these dry conditions.

It all seemed too little and far too late. My overriding memory is of long lines of women waiting patiently for their weekly ration of wheat or rice sent by a benevolent USA. And while the free handouts continued I doubted that much effort would be made to find a long-term solution. Certainly the farmers could not compete in a market place where everything was free.

(Right): Clare and the bizarre welwitschia plant which can live for centuries

19 November 1993
Empire Test Pilots' School, Boscombe Down

I had suggested to Lewis that we revisit the Empire Test Pilots' School on Boscombe Down, the scene of Simon Groom's spectacular inverted spin in the Hunter T8 ten years previously. Simon had celebrated the school's 30th anniversary and Anthea would mark the 40th. Being as keen on aircraft as I was, Lewis agreed.

I expected some difficulty making the arrangements because the test pilots' school was not totally controlled by the RAF, but I did not anticipate that my problems would be less about Ministry approval and more to do with Anthea's body weight.

She was half a stone too light for the ejector seat. The seat contained a powerful gun that would, in an emergency, blast the seat through the Perspex canopy to safety. Unfortunately, with her being too light, it would create such a force on her bottom it could compact her spine.

So Anthea became a little bit more shapely, and managed to gain the necessary pounds. Even so, it was decided that her experience of stalling and spinning would take place in the Tucano turbo-prop trainer and not the mighty Hunter jet.

Her problems were not over. Despite a very careful face-mask fitting by an RAF equipment specialist on the ground, in the air things did not quite go according to plan.

Much later and looking at the tapes from the fixed cockpit camera, I thought she seemed rather light-headed. At 20,000 feet her remarks and reactions made me wonder what she was on. No drugs, of course, and certainly not alcohol, just a spot of finger trouble. Having loosened her face-mask for some reason, she had not quite got the knack of tightening it back up again. A lack of oxygen from a leaky face seal had done the rest. She probably enjoyed the stalling and spinning more than she should have.

Of course, for safety, Anthea had already been taught to recognise the effects of oxygen starvation in the base's decompression chamber the previous day. She was asked to write 'the cat sat on the mat' and draw the face of a clock several times as she was steadily deprived of oxygen. I kept the piece of paper with her handiwork on it for posterity.

Because we had filmed the test pilots' school ten years before, I did my best to find something we hadn't filmed previously so long-term viewers would not feel short-changed. I decided that she should inspect the coldest place on the base, the environmental test chamber.

Imagine an aircraft hangar converted into a giant fridge where all the air had been sucked out and replaced with a nitrogen mixture lethal to all human life. Wrapped up in a huge parka to keep out the cold, Anthea was again asked to wear an oxygen mask and breathe clean air. Inside the chamber she joined a Sea Harrier jump jet (now sadly a thing of the past in the Royal Navy) for a very chilling experience. The jet was white with hoar frost as it was cooled to a temperature somewhere below minus 50 degrees Celsius (minus 58 degrees Fahrenheit).

Like many other odd and unusual moments, this stuck in Anthea's mind – as did the troublesome ejector seat.

Much later she confessed to having had 'devil thoughts' as she sat in it at 20,000 feet. Her hands had itched to pull the black and yellow striped handles that would have sent her skywards and crushed her with a force 12 to15 times the force of gravity. It was a memory that tormented her for many years. In 2003 she saw an ejector seat for sale at an auction, bought it, and now keeps it in her front room, where she can indulge her fantasy without the inconvenience of any spine-compressing explosions.

After only two years Anthea was poached by GMTV to join Eamonn Holmes on *Breakfast Time*. It was too good an opportunity for her to miss and we were very sorry to see her leave.

(Above): Cameraman Paul Dobson and sound recordist Keith Potts film Tim Vincent as he straps into an Aermacchi MB-339A/PAN of the Frecce Tricolori display team

(Left): Tim ready for take-off

20

Marry me, Tim, you hear?

14–18 June 1994

Rivolto Airbase, Northern Italy

Blue Peter had always had a good relationship with the Ministry of Defence, yet in 1994 there was still one part of the Royal Air Force that would not cooperate. It was the RAF's jewel in its public relations crown – the Red Arrows. Apart from John Noakes's early foray into the Reds in 1973 (when a special programme was made about them at RAF Kemble) and a film that I directed in 1984 that featured Michael Sundin, I had had no luck in 'lifting the lid' on what made them tick. It was this that made me feel all the more determined to make it happen.

I had learnt that there was no point in trying to make a film with the Reds in less than two or three days because of the time it took to install the cameras on the aircraft, the distinctive BAE Hawk jets for which the RAF paid around £18 million each. Another issue was the weather, which had to be just right. Given this was rarely possible in the UK, my idea was to join them in Cyprus during the build-up to 'red suit day' when they were inspected and passed fit for role by a very senior officer of flag rank.

And year after year my proposal was turned down.

Getting frustrated, I wondered what to do about it. Then I came up with the idea of stirring up a frisson of rivalry by filming the Italian Air Force aerobatic display team instead, the Frecce Tricolori. I thought that if I could make the Reds realise that they were not the only aerobatic team in the world, they might change their minds.

After several phone calls and a letter to the Frecce's home at the Rivolto Airbase in Udine in Northern Italy, they agreed.

In 1994 the Frecce were everything the Red Arrows weren't. They were visitor- and filming-friendly. Every time they practised, which they did twice a day, the general public was invited to watch. The team leader, T. Col. Luigi Zanovello, conducted the display by radio from the ground, standing in front of the crowd. Publicity was like meat and drink to them, and when I told them about the difficulty I was having trying to get permission to film the Reds, they were astonished.

The presenter, Tim Vincent, with his dashing good looks and clean-cut appearance, was just the image they liked. He flew with the Colonel, 'The Boss', and when a camera jammed after the second flight, they didn't hesitate to go up again. It was all going well. We were three days into the shoot and our relationship with the Frecce was everything we could have hoped for. Tim remembers the occasion rather differently:

> I survived various life-changing moments with the extremely gregarious and charming Frecce, including the 'Lomcevak', which is a continuous tumbling after a vertical stall.
>
> To make the buttock-clenching manoeuvre happen, the pilot and passenger, me, would fly as high as we could when the engine was cut and the plane would fall any way it wanted downwards, trailing coloured smoke. At a couple of thousand feet Luigi would regain control and fly the plane out of a potential nosedive into the ground.
>
> If that wasn't bad enough, it was some surprise then when having finally finished filming for the day my real brush with death was when Alex drove us back to the hotel in the hire car. As we left the airfield he tried to cross over two lanes of traffic to turn left onto a dual carriageway and stalled the car in mid-lane.
>
> Rather than calmly restarting the car, he repeatedly turned the ignition, jabbed at the pedals, and gave me a quick potted history of the Italian car industry in a lecture along the lines of: 'This is typical of cheap Italian jobs, piece of tin pot crap car, I'd never buy one of these rust buckets.'
>
> All whilst several mad Italian drivers were hurtling towards me at speed!

I blush with shame, and he might have a point.

Back on the base the next day and out of the blue, a Red Arrows Hawk jetted into the Italian airbase with two senior members of the Red Arrows command team on board. They had stopped off to refuel on their way back from their training in Cyprus to their base at RAF Scampton in the UK. The Italians, thinking we would be pleased to meet them, introduced us. It would have been a pleasant meeting except that I knew that the senior officer had been instrumental in turning down my repeated requests. It was an uncomfortable moment and I wondered if I had provoked the Reds too far. My aim had been to twist their arms a bit. Not put them off for good.

To the astonishment of the Frecce, the squadron leader left with a parting shot aimed at us.

'Don't let them mess you about,' he advised our hosts.

I explained my ongoing difficulty with the Reds, and they reassured me that we were no trouble to them at all: we were always welcome.

I thought that it was the end of any chance of working with the Reds. Yet the reverse was true. Tim's film with the Frecce was shown several times on BBC1 and when Simon Meade took over as Red One in 1997, the mood of the Red Arrows changed from 'do it our way or nothing' to a friendly 'how can we help?'

My tactics had paid off and since then we have made several films with the Red Arrows, the best of which was an entire programme that was filmed in Cyprus in May 1998. The presenter, Katy Hill, warm and outgoing, loved it. She was a vicar's daughter, and strikingly glamorous with a dazzling smile that would do justice to a toothpaste advert (and subsequently did).

I wasn't surprised that the Reds took to her. But we were all surprised to discover that she thrived on aerobatics.

The Red Arrows could not have been more helpful because they were confident that they would be treated fairly on screen. We have always been 'in for the long haul' on *Blue Peter*, as it's the only way to sustain a programme hungry for items. If you do your best for your contributors, they will come back to you with more ideas. The Reds were no exception. Several years of filming followed.

Blue Peter needs to be a well-oiled machine to keep the programmes action-packed. And it's just as important for directors to nurture their relationship with presenters. A director may 'call the shots', but so often it isn't just the shot that's being called. Often it's a very fine judgement about how the presenters will appear to the viewers. Sometimes what may appear good to the director can cause a rift with the presenter. Trust is a huge issue, and can take years to win back once you've lost it.

In June 1995 I took Tim Vincent waterskiing at the National Watersports Centre at Holme Pierrepont near Nottingham. What started as a perfectly normal *Blue Peter* film turned into something neither of us recognised at the time. Tim did very well at learning how to waterski. He did so well that his skiing appeared almost effortless and I was left wondering how to increase the sense of danger and excitement. I suggested that he try ski-jumping, even though it was not part of the original plan. He readily agreed, as he always did.

In no time at all he was hurtling towards the ski ramp and soaring skywards and down again to end in a huge ungainly splash as he failed to recover his balance after the jump. Doggedly he went round and round and every time he got closer and closer to achieving his aim. Eventually, after the fourteenth attempt, he succeeded and it was a moment of genuine triumph. And because it was such a hard-won victory, when I came to edit the film I put the struggle in at length, using each attempt to build up the story.

When the film was dubbed I felt quite proud because it showed Tim overcoming a difficult challenge. Yet after transmission I was surprised because Tim was upset. He had been teased by his friends. What to me had looked like a battle to succeed looked to his friends like a series of entertaining falls – not helped by what Tim called the Benny Hill music – and he was not pleased. We both believed in our

(Below): Tim Vincent learning how to ski-jump at Holme Pierrepont

points of view and we talked about it at length, though neither of us gave much ground. Thankfully, Tim's generous nature won the day and I was forgiven. I can see his concern now, even if I did not at the time. It was a lesson for both of us and a warning that there are hidden traps to snare unwary director and presenter alike.

6-15 October 1995
Florida

Cypress Gardens, Florida, and Tim and I were afloat again. This time it was to take part in a pyramid of waterskiers.

Imagine a three-storey pyramid of young people dressed in violet and pink and being towed behind a powerboat. Tim joined the colourfully dressed men who formed the base of the pyramid to support a beautiful array of scantily clad girls. There were no complaints from Tim this time, even though he detested the pink outfit. The girls had to sit on the men's shoulders before standing up to make the pyramid. Tim remarked that it was disconcerting to have naked thighs so close to his face.

I asked the commentator to announce him to the audience and reluctantly he agreed.

Tentatively he said into the microphone, 'Ladies and gentlemen, we have a visitor to our display, Tim Vincent from the BBC and a programme called *Blue Peter*.'

Instantly the public stand erupted into wild screaming and cheering from the large British contingent in the audience and the Americans joined in as only they knew how. We filmed the display several times and, fortified by this unexpected success, the commentator built Tim's role. At the fourth show, a day later, he screamed Tim's name as if he was the highlight of the show. It was met with deafening silence. There was not a single British visitor in the stand.

I asked how they managed to keep the girls in shape. They showed me a double metal hoop.

'If they can fit through this then they keep their jobs,' I was told. The men did not have to jump through hoops to keep theirs.

All through the filming, Tim and I were the centre of attention. The girls in particular were very attentive and for a few precious, deluded moments I thought it might be me. Looking back, I realise that I was only the centre of attention when Tim was with me. Oh, well – it was good while it lasted!

He looked like a male model and the Americans loved his English accent. The magic continued when we moved on to film manatees at Homosassa Springs Wildlife State Park. One evening we went out to a restaurant on the other side of the creek from the park and the waitress was very taken by Tim. She attempted to chat him up but without success.

(Right): Tim Vincent (second from the left) joins the base of the garishly dressed pyramid of skiers during rehearsals at Cypress Gardens, Florida

As we left, she could contain herself no longer.

'Come back and marry me, you hear?' she cried out as we headed hastily for the door.

We bought some souvenirs in an antique shop and in an unthinking moment I bought a practice US Army Second World War hand grenade for three dollars. It was made of iron and was hollow so it was completely harmless. I thought it would go well with my eclectic collection of army memorabilia which sat on a shelf in my office. When we arrived at the airport and we checked in our luggage I thought maybe I should mention my unusual purchase. Tim remembers the whole episode in all its embarrassing detail:

> On the way to the airport I nagged him to tell the check-in staff that he had packed *a grenade*. Initially he was relaxed if not irritated by my nagging. But he obviously had second thoughts when we checked in. Of course it was in the bag we had put all our recent purchases of new clothes and presents for the family and he had smothered it with sticky duct tape to make sure it didn't burst open on the conveyor belts.

Alarm bells sounded and the conveyor belt slammed to a halt. I was the focus of angry looks. My bag was retrieved and, feeling very embarrassed, I produced the dummy hand grenade.

> There was much sweating and cursing as all the duct tape was ripped off and the offending article removed. I was shoulder to shoulder and busy signing autographs for the hordes of British children who, alongside their families, were catching flights home.

Eventually I was allowed to put the 'offending article' on board in a special container. The previous week a similar device had not been declared and the whole airport had been shut down for two hours. It made Tim's day and the incident still follows me to this day as one of his favourite moments. He picks up the story:

> As I continued towards the departure gate along one of those incredibly long travelators I remember spotting a familiar figure coming towards us. It was Steve Hocking [another producer and later editor of the programme] with Katy Hill, who had just landed to continue with more filming for the programme.
>
> We had twenty seconds or so of dialogue before we passed each other. It went something like this:
> 'Steve! How are you – good flight?'
> 'Tim! Yes, thanks. How did the filming go – where's Alex?'
> 'It was great fun. Alex has been delayed. He tried to bring a hand grenade through customs.'
> 'Of course.'
> Steve's face, as we passed, was not one of shock, just bemused and amused acceptance.

17–20 February 1996

Norway

Even though the armed forces have always played a part in *Blue Peter's* voracious output, they are not everyone's cup of tea. The presenters often find the military ethos rather strange and alien. Maybe it's the blind obedience that they always expect, or the way they talk and joke about serious risk and trauma, or maybe it's the massive understatement about what they have to do. It's an undeniably different outlook on life from the way we see things in civvy street.

Tim told me his experiences with the paras were a real eye-opener.

We were in Norway in the depths of winter. We were all being kitted out with everything we needed to join the paras, who were planning to camp on top of a mountain. There was a huge mound of

(Above): The BV206
all-terrain vehicle

(Bottom right): Ice-cold
with Alex, Tim Vincent (in
sleeping bag) and
instructor inside a snow
hole

special clothing to keep us warm and some other items that we had not expected. The major in charge identified each item as we removed it from the Bergen haversack.

'You will notice that you have two chapsticks. One is for your lips and the other is for your bum... I advise you to mark the one for your bum with a large cross,' he told us in all seriousness.

We drove in a convoy of tracked vehicles (BV206s) up the mountainside until we emerged on to a vast white plain. It was a freezing hell and the wind blew viciously. To survive the night we had to dig out a shelter. As we settled down for a miserable night in a 'snow hole' dug into the side of a snowdrift, the cameraman, Rick Manzanero, produced a bottle of brandy, which we swigged happily between filming the preparations of the evening meal. The meal was simplicity itself. Everything from apple flakes to mashed potato powder and biscuits was mixed up with snow and heated together. To save on washing up there were no knives or forks and we all shared the one spoon.

After the filming was over, I listened in to a conversation between Tim and our guide, Corporal Jones. Tim was privately appalled by the unpleasant living conditions. Their conversation went something like this:

'Why did you join up? Why do you do this?'

'Oh,' came the reply. 'It's not all bad. There's fantastic times as well as bad. You've just got to get through the bad and then you have some really good times.'

Tim was curious. 'When are the good times?' he asked.

'Now is one of the good times.'

The corporal's reply spoke volumes about the military mindset.

It was so cold we were advised to sleep with our boots inside our

sleeping bags or we would never get them on in the morning, and a thick hoar frost settled on the icy interior. Outside it was minus 40° and lavatory stops were all but impossible.

We had been warned that the roof of our chilly abode might sink lower during the night, so to make sure we didn't suffocate we had to take it in turns to watch a candle flame in an alcove. If it went out the person on watch had to punch a ski pole through the sinking roof to let more air in. The roof was only two feet or so above our sleeping ledge and we were packed like sardines in a tin.

Sleep did not come easily because we knew too much. Even if we weren't crushed under the weight of snow, we could all suffocate if the candle watcher didn't stay awake. I did not sleep a wink.

The next day we went down the mountain 'skijoaring' or towed in long lines on skis behind a BV206. It was a lot of fun until we came to a lake back down in the valley, when all the jollity stopped. The instructors had used a chainsaw to cut a rectangular hole, about fifteen feet by eight, in the ice. Then the entire company of paras lined up to ski into the water, each carrying a heavy Bergen haversack. It was what they endearingly called 'ice-breaking' drills, and it was the nadir of Tim's adventures in the snow. It was also the most memorable.

Once in the freezing water it was very difficult to think, breathe or even talk. I was asked whether I was going to take part but when I told them my age they wouldn't let me. I was too old and might have had a heart attack in the cold water. I feigned regret.

Tim reluctantly moved up the line until his turn came and in he went. The moment is indelibly etched on his mind:

> A minute or so before I was due to jump into that obscenely cold water with my 60-pound backpack, having seen battle-hardened soldiers floundering about in the depths and even watching as they chainsawed the ice open again as it refroze, Alex asked for a final piece to camera, *possibly the final piece to camera,* about how I felt.
>
> He rather dryly didn't accept my version as I was, in retrospect, a little insensitive and off colour as I focused on how to cross the menace without drowning under the weight of my equipment.
>
> 'Tim, just say what you are thinking. Good luck, by the way.'
>
> 'OK, Alex.'
>
> I turned to camera.
>
> 'I will be the first person since Jesus Christ to walk on water.'

I knew Tim was a bit stressed so said nothing.

All things considered, everything went well until he was asked to give his name and date of birth. He had to do this before he was allowed to 'dagger' his way out, using his ski poles. While he remembered the correct actions he could not say anything intelligible. And the more he

(Above): Tim skijoaring

(Below): Tim puts on a brave face ahead of taking the deathly cold plunge

(Right): Tim practising ice-breaking drills in water cold enough to numb every fibre in the body

tried the more incomprehensible he became. It was very amusing yet there was absolutely nothing funny about it. And he couldn't remain in the water for very long because of the risk of hypothermia. To my relief the instructor conceded that he was doing his best and gave the order to proceed. Gratefully he used the points of his ski poles to gain a grip on the ice and pulled himself out.

Despite its funny side, Tim has never minded this clip being shown because it looks so appalling.

There was a large paratrooper who, once he had given his name, rank and number, could not physically get out of the water. After about a minute the instructors went to help him.

'Leave me!' he shouted aggressively, and redoubled his efforts. Several times they tried to pull him out and each time he refused. The seconds and then minutes ticked by and we began to fear for his safety. Then, to the relief of all of us, he made it. I asked why he had been so adamant about doing it on his own.

'If he'd got help he'd never hear the end of it and he would have had to leave the regiment.' It was that important to him.

It was good to know that honour in our armed forces was alive and well. What we had seen was so nearly death without dishonour in futile circumstances. Yet come the real battle I would choose to have that man at my side.

Back at base there was a general celebration of many bowel movements, all part of the real-life *Blue Peter* experience, but, as they say, 'What happens on the shoot stays on the shoot.'

'I've just had the dump from hell' was a universal cry as, heavily booted, the paras happily stamped their way on bare floorboards to more baked beans at breakfast. Not for the first time I marvelled at the military's colourful use of English, which so aptly described one's private thoughts.

COSTING NUMBER: 1/LCK T228S
IDENT NUMBER: LCK D346R

B L U E   P E T E R
No: 2631

JOHN LESLIE	1000 STUIDO
DIANE-LOUISE JORDAN	1000 STUDIO
ANTHEA TURNER	0940 DUB/1000 STUDIO
EDITH MENEZES (with Kari, Oke & George)	1530
LEONIE POCOCK (with Bonnie)	1530
MISS CARON KEATING	1330
MR MARK CURRY	1345
MR JOHN NOAKES	1400
MISS VALERIE SINGLETON AND MISS LEILA WILLIAMS	1430
MISS LESLEY JUDD/MISS TINA HEATH & JEMMA/	1500
MISS SARAH GREENE	1500
MR SIMON GROOM	1500
MR PETER DUNCAN	1515
MIKE HASLAM + DRAGON BOAT	0800
BOOTLEG BEATLES	1045
BRENTWOOD BUGLERS	1100

TRANSMISSION: THURSDAY 14TH OCTOBER 1993 IN TC6

GALLERY: 60261   MAKE-UP: 60267 NC1: 63047   SOUND GALLERY: 60265
SUBTITLING: 65415   CBBC OFFICE: 64241   DUBBING THEATRE Y: 65506
PRODUCTION STORE: 68638   VT2 60402   VT5 60405

0845 - 1000	Camera Line-up
1000 - 1230	Camera Rehearsal
1230 - 1330	LUNCH
0900 - 1545	VT2 EDIT onto D114510
1400 - 1530	Camera Rehearsal
1530 - 1635	RUN THROUGH WITH VT5
1635 - 1705	Line Up
1705 - 1735	T R A N S M I S S I O N
	Inc. Sp: D114510
	PasB on VT5 D729702
1735 - 1800	REH/RECORD OMNIBUS LINK

****

DIRECTOR	PHIL CHILVERS
PRODUCER	CATHY DERRICK
PRODUCTION ASSISTANT	JACKIE CARTLIDGE
RESOURCES CO-ORDINATOR	NICK MOORE
LIGHTING DIRECTOR	TERRY BRETT
SOUND SUPERVISOR	KEITH BOWDEN
DEPUTY SOUND SUPERVISOR	ANDY HEWITT
VISION MIXERS	SUE COLLINS/ALISON BARTROP
FLOOR MANAGER	CARMELLA MILNE
A.F.M.	CRISPIN AVON
FLOOR ASSISTANTS	JULIAN STEEL/MARTIN WELSH
CAMERA SUPERVISOR	PETER WOODLEY
DESIGNER	DINAH WALKER
COSTUME DESIGNER	DENNIS BRACK
DRESSER	SUE BURROWS
PROP BUYER	LEE CRAIG
MAKE-UP	LARA COPLEY-SMITH/JENNY EADES
ASTON OPERATOR	MELISSA BADDELEY
SUBTITLER	CAROLINE WIGGINS
PORTAPROMPT OPERATOR	HELEN McLEAN
VT EDITOR (VT2)	DAVID HAMBLETON (KEN SOUTHERN)
VT OPERATOR (VT5)	RICHARD BAINBRIDGE
EDITOR	LEWIS BRONZE

21

Blood, sweat and tears

(Right): Digital television comes of age; the Sony VX1000E camera became a workhorse of documentary film-makers

(Left): A treasured souvenir of *Blue Peter*: the 35th anniversary programme script signed by the presenters

16–24 May 1996
Cameroon, West Africa

The year 1996 was a milestone in the way I worked. The unions had lost much of their power and programme-makers were being allowed, if not encouraged, to try their hand at camerawork and recording sound. It was all to do with saving money as budgets were reduced. I already owned an SVHS camera and *Blue Peter* had bought its very own Sony VX1000E, the first of a new generation of small hand-held digital cameras. It was all very exciting. The picture quality of the Sony camera, in bright sunlight, was probably as good at first glance as that of the Betacam – the professional video standard at the time. It was a technological breakthrough with profound consequences that even Sony could not have foreseen.

I hired Godfrey Johnson, a jovial ex-BBC cameraman and old friend, to teach me how to use it. Henry Farrar had retired by this time.

With *Blue Peter* gardener Clare Bradley, who came up with the idea, we set off to explore Mount Cameroon in West Africa. Godfrey was tall, slightly built and a delightful man, always smiling and pleased to help in any way. I knew he would be very patient with me and, more importantly, he would not resent my intrusion into his role as a cameraman (or at least he would be tactful enough not to let me see it).

Even then, in the mid-1990s, it was difficult to predict just how important multi-skilling would be in changing the way television was made. Significantly it broke down all sorts of demarcation taboos.

The Mount Cameroon Project was linked to the Royal Botanic Gardens in Kew and unknown species were being found every week. Clare was very excited and the scene was set for a new way of working. The 'director/cameraman' had arrived and I have been told more than once that I was the first.

There was another innovation that was no less important. It affected us in an unexpected way. Lariam was a new antimalarial drug and it was very effective against malaria. It was a potent concoction developed by the US Defence Department in response to the high numbers of troops contracting malaria during the Vietnam War.

But users could pay a high price for combating malaria. There was a list of potential side effects as long as your arm. Some people could go a little bit crazy and behave strangely. A junior manager at the Overseas Development Agency had once joked to me that they sent more people home with Lariam poisoning than with malaria.

Unknown to me, and on the advice of her doctor, Clare was taking it and, when we arrived at the Atlantic Beach Hotel, overlooking the beach in Limbe, she began to question everything we planned in a persistent, irritating way. She began with the script I had written in the UK under her advice. I was dead tired because we had not slept for 24 hours but I began to change it where I could. Clare's alterations went on and on. However much I altered the script, Clare wanted even more changes. Getting frustrated, I pointed out that it would have been helpful to have done this before we had set off, but to no avail. Clare got more and more argumentative and the script alterations became more and more ludicrous. After about half an hour my temper was wearing thin. I asked her if she was taking any unusual medication because she was behaving very strangely indeed. And that's when we realised she was on Lariam. I suggested she stop taking it and share my antibiotic instead. Whether the-out-of character behaviour was due to the drug or just fatigue, in a couple of days Clare returned to normal.

In colonial times the Cameroons were part British and part French, and we were in the bit that used to be French. I thought that the people were far more aggressive in East Cameroon (which used to be a French

(Above): Cameraman Godfrey Johnson with Mount Cameroon as an impressive backdrop

colony) than in West Cameroon (which used to be British); and they weren't even taking Lariam.

We spotted some unusual residents in the hotel. They were shaven headed and a tough-looking lot and they kept themselves apart. Not tourists, but French legionnaires. There were about a dozen of them and their helicopter was parked incongruously on the hotel lawn. It begged the question, 'Why?'

It turned out that Cameroon was in dispute with Nigeria because of the offshore oilfields that we could just see flaring away on the horizon at night. We learned that there were gun battles being fought only 50 miles away from the hotel, on the Nigerian border. Every morning the legionnaires would depart in their helicopter to act as advisers to the Cameroon army, and most evenings, if the fighting had died down, they would come back. It was all very strange and it got stranger when I asked one of the legionnaires about it.

'Yes, we tell them how to fight and there is another group from the Legion doing the same thing on the other side.'

One night during the week I awoke to the sounds of lorries revving their engines as a military convoy rolled into town. At breakfast we were told that the fighting had been particularly fierce and they were bringing back the bodies.

Luckily the only 'war' we had to fight was against mosquitoes as we forayed out into the rainforest in search of rare plants.

Cameroon wasn't called the Mosquito Coast for nothing. On the second day of filming, one of the helpers didn't turn up for work. He had malaria. We learned that the local hospital had a whole ward equipped with drips so sufferers could 'mainline' on the right drugs for a near-instant recovery. Our man was back on duty the next day. From then on almost every day someone would go down with the disease.

Because the locals did not take precautions the symptoms were easy to recognise and do something about. Antimalarial drugs suppressed the symptoms and this could be dangerous. It was possible to have the parasites in your blood without knowing it, and if the course of treatment wasn't carried out to the letter, full-blown malaria could result. Worse still, it often manifested itself weeks later. The BBC lost a cameraman to malaria he had caught overseas because treatment back in the UK had been too late to have any effect.

On location in the bush and grappling with the new digital camera, Godfrey taught me the basics of photography and was extremely good-natured about it. Nothing could go wrong, I thought.

I was forgetting the vagaries of the rainforest.

We had decided to do a Land Rover 'passing shot' (when the vehicle drives past the camera), and having found a suitable bend in the road we asked Clare and her driver to reverse out of sight and wait for our signal.

To get the shot we had to get off the track. We found a place where we could frame some leaves in the foreground and give the shot more inter-est. We stood in the drainage ditch at the side of the road and debated the perfect position. We stood still too long and the attack, when it came, was sudden. We felt vicious bites on our lower legs. Single nips were closely followed by a major and very painful attack all over our legs and thighs. We looked down to find that we were standing in an ants' nest. Within seconds we were back on the track, ripping our clothes off in desperation to remove the agony. Stark naked, we frantically searched for the little blighters. At the same time we constantly glanced anxiously down the track for the advancing vehicle and Clare. Luckily for us, and free of my direction, she was enjoying a botanical gossip with her colleagues.

Filming in the town of Limbe wasn't easy. As soon as the camera appeared, so did people, asking for money. To film a wide shot of the whole street was well-nigh impossible. We learnt to set up the camera as if we were about to film a single person – making furniture or whatever – and made a show of paying that person accordingly. We would then appear to be checking the camera while at the same time recording the shot we needed. It was the only way, and it didn't always work.

On one occasion we set up to get a panoramic view of Mount Cameroon across the bay. There was no one in shot, only fishing boats, so we thought there would be no problems. Not so. Some youths who had been lounging around a solitary tree 25 yards away near the water's edge spotted us and came over. The demands for money began. Each youth, and there were about 15 of them, wanted US$10. As they persisted, more youths arrived and joined in. Godfrey saw that the situation was getting nasty and told me, smiling all the time, to take the camera and get back into the car. We retreated in a tight group to the car and all the while the mood was getting uglier and uglier. Despite threats, Godfrey smiled and talked to them and pretended not to understand. At the last moment he jumped into the car and we sped away, listening to the stones that they hurled at us bouncing off the taxi roof.

I asked Godfrey why he had kept smiling.

'It's very hard to attack someone who is being friendly to you,' replied the voice of experience.

It's a lesson I have never forgotten and I had reason to remember it much later when filming in another part of Africa.

We filmed in more affable surroundings when we ventured out to the remote villages on the slopes of Mount Cameroon. Clare joined a small botanical team who sold important plants to the villagers hoping to encourage them to plant more varieties in their bush gardens.

We would park in the centre of groups of corrugated-iron-roofed huts and wait for customers. You would think it was a bit like taking coals to Newcastle yet apparently not. Some plants were very popular. There was one plant called *eru*, an obscure vine that tasted not dissimilar to spinach and was a national dish. Villagers queued up to buy *eru* plants at knock-down prices.

Despite nightmare battles with mosquitoes, Clare was in gardening heaven.

One man was more aware of the importance of biodiversity than most and had encouraged the planting of the African cherry because of its medicinal properties. The bark of the African cherry tree is used to treat prostate cancer and yet its numbers were dwindling through excessive bark stripping. Despite living cut off from the rest of the world, our contact understood the importance of these trees and why they should be replaced. He knew that the African cherry had to be preserved and had begun a one-man conservation project.

Just outside the village were several orchards of these valuable trees.

While we filmed, a man staggered past, carrying a load of thick bark on his back. The red sap dripped like a mortal wound and our contact said it was the bark of a whole cherry tree. 'Yes,' our contact explained, 'the bark will be used to treat cancer, but by stripping off the whole bark from the tree it guarantees it will die.'

The orchard, on the other hand, would be harvested in a renewable way so the trees would continue to grow bark for many years to come. That villager, with his extraordinary ability to influence others, was a rare breed.

And how did my cameraman classes go while all this was going on? I learnt a lot, and my intention to be multi-skilled was resolute – but the new digital camera did not fare so well. It eventually came to grief under Godfrey's armpit. During an afternoon expedition through some particularly sweaty rainforest to film the waterfall that had featured in the film *Greystoke*, Godfrey's perspiration had unexpected consequences. The lethal liquid became a second waterfall and dribbled onto the camera slung over his shoulder. During the three-hour walk his sweat seeped inside the camera and by the time we got back to the hotel the damage was done. It never worked again.

Blue Peter features were often the result of blood, sweat and tears. But on this occasion it was quite literally the case.

(Above): Wing Commander Jon Fynes, son Peter and Katy Hill at RAF Cranwell

22

Flying solo in the digital age

In the summer of 1996 *Blue Peter* lost its editor of eight years, Lewis Bronze. Being the boss of the programme was very hard work and demanding in many ways. I believe that Lewis needed new challenges. His enthusiasm, though impressive, was nearly exhausted and he had made many changes.

Children were now included more frequently, and their appearances were less rehearsed, giving the programme a more relaxed and naturalistic feeling. More humour was injected, even if it didn't always work. 'Green' environmental issues had been addressed in an impressive way and there had been the publication of the best-selling *Blue Peter Green Book* as well as the *Blue Peter* annual. His boldest move of all was to take the programme to three broadcasts a week. It took nerve and, while I saw a dilution in programme content, it worked.

Lewis gambled that his talent would allow him to succeed away from the comfort of 'Auntie', a supposedly affectionate term for the BBC, derived from the yesteryear saying 'Auntie knows best.'

So he now took his incredible courage and became an independent producer for the newly formed Channel 5. He has since admitted it was not his happiest time and he simultaneously pursued another idea with extreme tenacity – to provide dynamic education for UK primary schools through the internet. Despite courting failure on several occasions he was successful. By 2012 Espresso Education was suppling educational content over the internet to over half the schools in the UK, and further afield as well. Espresso Education is one of the leading companies in its field and their work has been showered with accolades. An interesting related fact worth throwing in here is that, thanks to Lewis, *Blue Peter* was the first regular children's television programme to have its own website, way back in 1994, when most people hadn't even heard of the internet.

Oliver Macfarlane, who had been Lewis's deputy, took on the mantle and became the new editor. Described as a 'safe pair of hands', he was not driven in quite the same way because his first love was classical music. He had joined the programme during Biddy's reign and understood the programme's subtleties, a real bonus at a time when all programme budgets were under the microscope. Thanks to Oliver the daunting task of cost-cutting, which had begun in earnest, was carried out successfully and the programme survived these early skirmishes. But these were warning shots in the budget battles that were to come.

6–7 November 1996
RAF Cranwell

We received a letter with a challenge that we simply could not turn down. Eight-year-old Peter Fynes challenged Katy Hill to fly five different aircraft in a single day. Peter had a slight advantage because his dad was the highly respected Wing Commander Jon Fynes, the boss of the RAF Standardisation Flight, the unit that checks the flying abilities of all the RAF's pilots. He was based at RAF Cranwell where, under his influence, the five aircraft were – the Hawk, Turcano, Bulldog, Viking and Jetstream.

Katy loved the idea. She liked nothing better than flying and did not care which way up she was. I was faced with the daunting task of working out how to rig each aircraft with cockpit cameras in time for each flight to take place. It was a risky shoot because so much could go wrong.

On the appointed day, the sun shone brightly one moment and went behind a cloud the next, a nightmare for camerawork. On the first flight of the day, in the little Bulldog trainer, the cockpit cameras were set up for sunshine and just after Katy and Jon took off the sun vanished behind a cloud. The shot of Jon and Katy in the cockpit was so dark it was unusable – until, that is, Jon Fynes suddenly leaned forward, looked at the camera, and opened the exposure on the side of the camera body.

It was the sort of multi-skilling of which 'Auntie' would have been proud.

Instantly the picture lightened and we were saved from an embarrassing and time-consuming reshoot. I asked Jon why he had done it.

'The sun had gone in and I thought the stop needed changing,' he said matter-of-factly, as if it was no big deal.

'So you know about cameras, then?' I asked.

'I don't, but I watched your guys set the camera up and thought that the stop was in the wrong place.'

I cannot think of anyone, apart from Jon, who would have taken the initiative. I certainly wouldn't have. Jon thought what he did was logical and unremarkable. I beg to disagree.

Much later in the day and on our third plane, I was in a black Hawk trainer to get air-to-air shots while Katy was in another. We were flying at about 500 feet in formation so that I could get close pictures of her. We had already flown in the Bulldog and Tucano, and another aircraft, the Jetstream, was yet to come.

The two British Aerospace Hawks moved in comfortable unison and I was hypnotised by the gentle undulation of Katy's aircraft, which was no more than 30 feet away. This was my fourth flight in a Hawk and by now it felt familiar. On the ground the North York Moors floated beneath us and I strained to spot Grosmont at one end of the North Yorkshire Moors Railway. How often, I thought, had I travelled that line, following the progress of the 60532 *Blue Peter* steam engine?

It was by now well past four o'clock and the hillsides were yellow in the sun's oblique rays.

'Like a go?' came the voice of the pilot over the intercom.

'Yes, please,' I replied eagerly. As an amateur pilot I never gave up the chance to take control.

'Follow the other aircraft,' came the order.

Katy's aircraft banked and I followed the turn 60 feet away. For the next five or ten minutes we flew, turning left and right back down the route of the railway. Then I noticed that Katy's pilot had raised his hands above his head – and to my surprise so had mine. It was a clear sign that, at that minute, Katy and I were in charge in both aircraft. It was a bizarre moment. We were in control at the same moment, flying in loose formation, and I wondered why it amused me so much.

If anything had gone wrong, the headline would have been worth reading.

(Right): Post-flight smiles for Katy Hill and Alex, armed with one of the new cameras

(Left): Richard Bacon with canoeist Tom Paterson at Holme Pierrepont. A 'gun' camera is being fitted to the helmet to get action shots racing down the raging white-water course

22–23 February 1997

Holme Pierrepont, Nottingham

When the resident 'hunk', Tim Vincent, left after three years, the programme gained a new presenter in the form of Richard Bacon, an affable Nottinghamshire lad.

Richard was quirky, good looking, and with a sense of humour straight out of the Alan Partridge school of entertainment. He was a born television presenter and it was obvious from the start that he would fit into the programme like a hand into a glove. He made a feature of his naivety, which meant that he was very easy to work with – there was nothing that didn't inspire his curiosity. He always left the audience, and us, quietly chuckling away.

My first film with Richard – and it might have been his first film on the programme – was white-water canoeing at the Nottingham National Watersports Centre at Holme Pierrepont, just a stone's throw from where he grew up.

Faced with the raging waters of the artificial course, he had noticed that there was a sign advising canoeists to drink Coca-Cola. The river Trent had an unfortunate reputation for causing vomiting and diarrhoea and the fizzy stuff was a good way of preventing it. Richard was more interested in the efficacious properties of Coke (and I mean the drink, not the powdery white stuff) than the challenge ahead, especially when I told him it was so powerful that dull copper coins would sparkle if immersed in it. He wasn't happy until he'd had some.

He hurtled off down the raging waters of the canoe slalom course with a good-natured smile on his face, until the inevitable happened and he capsized. It was a promising start to what I thought would be a glittering *Blue Peter* career.

It was not to be. It was very regrettable that it was exactly his strengths (curiosity, adventure and a degree of naivety) that made him such a natural presenter and which eventually led to his downfall on the night of the programme's 40th birthday celebrations in October 1998, 18 months away. More on that later.

5–10 April 1997
Turkey

I was gaining confidence with the new digital VX1000E camera and it was time for me to take full responsibility. It wasn't an easy decision but I knew I couldn't put off the moment for ever. I asked Clare, the *Blue Peter* gardener, to be the subject of my experiment.

It didn't take long for Clare to come up with a suitable idea. She had a particular gripe about non-cultivated bulbs that were being imported from Turkey, and she wanted to do something about it.

All our snowdrops, winter aconites, cyclamen, even tulips were brought to the UK by the pioneers of gardening like Sir Joseph Paxton. When the fashion caught on, in the first part of the 19th century, the hillsides where the flowers grew wild were literally stripped bare of wild bulbs. Nowadays there is a campaign to stop the harvesting of wild bulbs and cultivate them instead.

We teamed up with Flora and Fauna International, who arranged for us to visit Cimi, a small Turkish village high in the mountains, to see how this domestic cultivation was progressing. And because snowdrops are early bloomers, we arrived just as the last snows were melting, or should have been.

We were met at the airport by two men with their dilapidated blue minibus. We had our fingers firmly crossed as they drove us into the hills. It was snowing steadily and after a while it was several inches deep. We drove for hours on end with pine forests on either side. Just when I thought we were doomed to slide off the hillside we stopped to fix on tyre chains – and our journey got more and more precarious. One look down the precipitous slopes was enough to make me wonder if this filming was at all wise.

When we arrived at Cimi it was nearly dark and we were ushered into the bulb farmer's home and set up camp. They were very welcoming but there was very little space for us all. Clare and Abigail Entwhistle from Flora and Fauna International were given some privacy in a separate room. Jonathan Watts, the sound recordist (lean, eccentric, with a brush moustache) and I settled down to sleep on the living-room floor. We were exhausted.

When we awoke the next day we saw the huge sacrifice that the

(Left): Clare Bradley (right) with Dr Abigail Entwhistle (centre) as tyre chains are fitted to our vehicle

family had made for us. All four of them had retreated into a very small single room and no filming could happen until we had got up and cleared our equipment away. We washed under a single tap and ate breakfast – and all subsequent meals – cross-legged on the kitchen/ dining-room floor. We used our fingers as knives and forks. The family were friendly and it all felt very natural. We had been catapulted into a completely different way of life and, like so many times with *Blue Peter*, we had crossed a barrier in a way that no tourist would ever be able to do. I felt like I was in a time warp, living life as one might have done a century ago. Clare felt the same way:

> I had never been anywhere like that before. Cimi was magical and so cold. It was like being in a time warp, so remote, peaceful and rural. Everyone had their own thing going on and they were so generous and hospitable.

By now I had sussed the secrets of the new digital camera (the office had bought another one to replace the one destroyed by Godfrey's sweat in Cameroon). I was consumed with perfecting shot composition and spent every spare moment capturing all aspects of village life. I spooled away, hungry to get it all. Mud houses with flat roofs perched on the hillsides, smoking chimneys, old men wielding ancient axes as they chopped wood, children playing – it was a feast to my eye and, I hoped, to the camera too.

As a director, I had had to stand about, bored and impatient, while the cameraman fiddled about, eye glued to his viewfinder. Now boredom was a thing of the past. Time flashed by as I tried one angle after another. Hungry for lots of different shots, I began to develop an 'eye' for a picture – and this was important because no schedule allowed enough time for each shot to be covered 15 different ways.

I had always admired the skill of BBC cameraman Henry Farrar. His shots were always beautifully composed, pin sharp and rock steady. Those images, which had been the backbone of my film-making to date, were etched in my mind. I tried to emulate what he might have done, and because zooms and pans were hard to control, I concentrated on single-sized shots, moving the camera rather than the zoom bar. I was in the vanguard of a new way of working and I knew my camerawork would come under intense scrutiny by the non-believers when the film was transmitted.

It dawned on me that the success of the shoot was all down to me. I had crossed a huge divide and there was no going back. My ability – or lack of it – would be on display for all to see. I tried to put my unease to the back of my mind even though I knew that child critics were amongst the toughest to please.

In those early years of 'self-operation' I believe it was a fear of failure that deterred many would-be directors from following my example.

As it turned out, Turkey was a real 'turkey shoot'. Everywhere I looked there was something worth filming and Clare was in good form. And, as a bonus, every night high in the heavens the comet Hale Bop was there, like an omen of good fortune, its tail like the wake of a ship in the ocean and closer than ever in the clear, crisp night air.

15–20 May 1997
Zanzibar

I pressed Clare for more ideas. They were not long in coming. Her cousin had married an environmentalist, Andrew Cooke, and he was fighting to preserve the coral reefs of Zanzibar, a tropical island just east of the African coast. It was agreed to make the plight of the world's coral reefs the subject of a whole programme.

The environment had been Lewis's big initiative for several years, which was why Clare and I had made films in Brazil, Namibia, Cameroon, Turkey and now, it seemed, the Spice Islands, or, as they are called today, the Zanzibar Archipelago. I did not know it at the time but the other presenters had become quite envious of Clare's exploits (even though they did not have her expert knowledge) and Zanzibar was to be her last overseas assignment. It was the beginning of a new culture, so prevalent these days, of sharing around what were recognised as 'perks' – regardless of individual ability to deliver the best product.

Even though Turkey had been a relative success, I was still not 100 per cent certain that I could 'deliver' as a cameraman, and Zanzibar was a long way from home. In a crisis of confidence I asked Godfrey Johnson (of the sweaty armpit in Cameroon) to come to my aid once again, as my sound recordist this time – and keep an eye on my camerawork just in case. It was to be the very last time I had an expert to guide me.

It was hotter and sweatier than anything I could remember and Zanzibar was full of the curious and the unexpected. It wasn't quite as exotic as I had imagined from my stamp-collecting days when the rich images of dhows and tall palm trees had burned a longing into my soul, yet the large bronze elephant spikes on the ancient doors (which were intended to stop the elephants from leaning against them, even though there were no elephants on the island), still fired the imagination. A futile search for Freddie Mercury's birthplace and a roof terrace restaurant, where we sat cross-legged in the open air as the orange rays of the setting sun brought to life the vivid colours of the hand-woven carpets, added to a happy week in the sun. It was a fitting end to the last overseas shoot that Clare and I would do together.

For Clare the matter didn't rest there. She became godmother to the first child of her cousin and Andrew Cooke. At the christening she met Andrew's younger brother Henry, and they found they had a lot in common. By this time Clare had split up from her husband. To cut a long story short, they fell in love and married in 2000 and Clare retired from being the *Blue Peter* gardener.

They had an extraordinary wedding with the biggest bonfire I have ever seen, created from the vegetation cleared from the ground for their new garden. They had chosen to settle in a ruin next to the main railway line from the West Country to London and they have subsequently restored it to near perfection. Even now, when I pass on the train going up to London from Exeter, I still give her a wave. Just in case.

(Left): Godfrey Johnson moves Clare Bradley into position for a 'piece to camera' overlooking Stone Town, Zanzibar

23

All steamed up

In December 1997 a young Bangladeshi beauty with long dark hair and large brown eyes joined the programme. She was Konnie Huq and she was a Cambridge graduate with a degree in economics. She told me that while most of her fellow students had gone into the City and were making fortunes in banking, she had decided on a career in television. She was the youngest in her family and had already made an appearance on *Blue Peter* as a teenager with the National Youth Music Theatre in their production of *Captain Stirrick* in 1989.

Konnie was quite different in personality and outlook from Katy Hill.

Katy had been on the show for three years and was incredibly hard working. She was also very attractive and the audience loved her. She threw herself fearlessly into everything. There was something very British about Katy and she had a strong sense of what was right and wrong. This was perhaps from her dad, who was a vicar. She was fun to work with and had a knack of getting the best out of nervous contributors with her infectious humour. She had no truck with anyone who did not pull their weight.

Konnie was glamorous too but her appeal was with the younger viewers. I thought I detected an element of competition as the new girl made her mark. This notion has been rejected by both of them but even so for a while the new dynamic in the presentation team was unsettling.

For Katy, *Blue Peter* was the dream job, but she had seen how it was possible to stay too long and get jaded. It was a dilemma for her and we talked about it on more than one occasion. She adored the show, and said she wanted to leave on a high when she still felt she had more to give. That time came in 2000 when she left for Saturday morning television. She certainly got her wish of leaving on a high. I have been told that more people phoned to vote for their favourite Katy film on her leaving the show than at any other point in the programme's history.

She was awarded a BAFTA Best Presenter award in recognition of her achievements on the show. But all that was to come.

(Bottom left): The 60532
Blue Peter locomotive
renaming ceremony at ICI
Wilton in 1991

18–19 April 1998
The 60532 Blue Peter locomotive

Every so often the editor of *Blue Peter* would come to me with a challenge. And it was always the same.

'We've got a slot that needs filling. Any ideas?'

And on this occasion it was for a whole programme.

My imagination went into overtime. I have always maintained that if I could think it, then I could do it. It was a very motivating thought.

I had a list of emergency ideas that had been rejected over and over again. They did, however, stay on my list. Some ideas remained on the list for years.

This time it was 160 tons of dark green steel that filled the gap. It was a monster that moved with grace and power and captured the hearts of thousands of well-wishers. It was the 60532 Peppercorn Class A2 Locomotive, 'Blue Peter'.

In a nutshell, my idea was to make a whole programme about the 532 steaming down the East Coast line from Waverley Station in Edinburgh to King's Cross Station in London.

The organisers had overcome myriad difficulties to implement the steam journey of a lifetime. The big breakthrough came in 1998, when once again the romance of steam travel was about to make a truly historic return. At a meeting in the *Blue Peter* office with some of the most self-willed enthusiasts of steam, we planned how to film it. I knew it would make a cracking programme. All I had to do was get in some jaw-dropping sequences that the viewers would never forget.

Such is the heady atmosphere in which many projects begin, and while the imagination may run riot, reality is less flamboyant. Luck plays a bigger part than one cares to admit.

There was a special significance to this particular steam run because it celebrated the 60532's 50 years in steam, *Blue Peter*'s 40 years as a programme, and 30 years since the last steam run on the East Coast mainline.

It was like planning a military operation. Come the day, while Stuart Miles and Konnie Huq rode on the train, Katy Hill prepared to join at York with a quick tour of the Steam Museum, and Richard Bacon prepared to ambush the train with a helicam (a camera mounted on a model helicopter). All four would ride the rest of the way in the dining car and cook for the passengers.

Stuart, boyish with an impish sense of humour, would work on the footplate and hopefully shovel enough coal to get the 532 to 75 mph on a predetermined stretch of line. Konnie, meanwhile, would sing the journey away with The Likely Lads barbershop quartet. At the end of the line at King's Cross, John Noakes and Valerie Singleton would be part of a nostalgic welcoming committee with the Pandemonium Steel Band.

(Top left): The imposing 60532 Blue Peter locomotive in the early morning mist

There would be ten film crews and two helicopters spread out over 500 miles of track. I asked for volunteers from the *Blue Peter* office and 17 people stepped forward.

And that's when the production assistants got their hands on it. The PAs are a tidy lot and, unlike me, they actually like paperwork so my thumbnail schedule did not measure up to their high standards. After much tut-tutting and typing on their parts, led by the redoubtable Lucy Morris, honour was satisfied. I pretended to be chastened but they knew what I really felt. I was very fond of Lucy and she read me like a book. I think it gave them all pleasure to be able to point out their usefulness to me; it was a sore point since I'd said in an unguarded moment that I didn't need them on location because 'I was perfectly able to get my own coffee'.

(In 2012, with the mushroomed health and safety issues – and regulations for working with children – their workload has increased dramatically. Someone has to pick up the pieces and make sure the paperwork is in order and, uncomplaining, they do a great job.)

There had been just one major problem and that was the number of people allowed on the footplate of the 532. The maximum permissible was three and there were already three essential personnel – the engine driver, the fireman and the footplate inspector. That meant sacrificing one of them for a presenter to make the programme work in the best *Blue Peter* tradition. Stuart Miles was lined up for the job but it was by no means a done deal. Stuart would have to work, and work hard, for his passage. Whether or not this would happen was left hanging as the 532 sounded her whistle and began her journey.

We had rigged several fixed cameras on the footplate and more to the outside of the engine. The engineers had set up their recorders and monitoring equipment in the first carriage.

The success of the programme hinged on one moment. I desperately

(Top right): A stopover at York to refuel. Camera crew plus Stuart Miles and Paul Hutchinson from the North Eastern Locomotive Preservation Society, pose for my camera

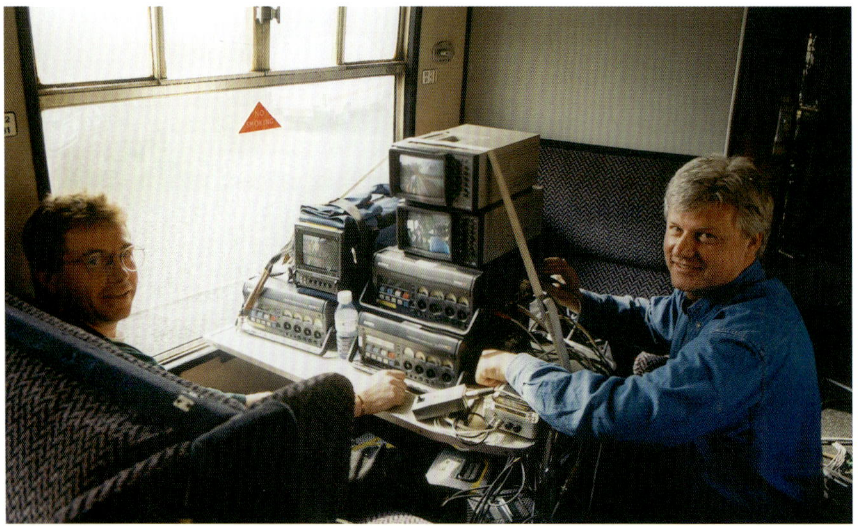

(Left): BBC engineers and their equipment in the first carriage

(Bottom right): Katy Hill and Stuart Miles in good spirits during the journey

wanted Stuart to be on the footplate when the 532 attempted 75 mph – the top speed allowed at the time. He would need to do an awful lot of shovelling. There were two big questions: Would he be up to it? And would the footplate inspector allow it?

The footplate inspector was Peter Kirk, an uncompromising man who followed regulations to the letter. I knew that to try and persuade Peter one way or another would be a waste of time. He was a man who would make his own decisions.

As the 532 steamed out of Waverley Station I had everything crossed and prayed for a minor miracle.

To my great surprise, Stuart and Peter got on rather well, even though Stuart made light-hearted remarks about the quality of his coffee. 'I don't give him long,' Stuart quipped after tasting it for the first time. Peter accepted all this with good humour and proved to be a very good contributor. Watching on the monitoring equipment, I could see he was beginning to buy into the whole idea. On his instructions Stuart shovelled coal like a demon and left the footplate exhausted yet happy at York to let the regular fireman take over:

> Shovelling coal was back-breaking work and something I suspected Peter thought I would give up on but I was determined to prove him wrong. I knew what I had to do and was determined not to be proved weak. Unlike some other *Blue Peter* presenters I was not physically strong in stature but tried to make up for it in sheer determination.

I was certain that what we had achieved would probably have been enough, even though being on the footplate for the speed attempt would be very special. Peter made no comment and I didn't ask. Had Stuart done enough to impress him? We would have to wait to find out.

The stretch where the record attempt would take place was between Essendine and Bytham. The sense of anticipation was palpable.

It was about four o'clock in the afternoon when we approached Grantham, the last stop and opportunity for Stuart to rejoin the footplate. We drew into the station and came to a halt. I had resigned myself to making do with what we'd got. Then Stuart was summoned to the footplate and told to get shovelling. It was quite a shock. He needed no encouragement and rushed to the front of the train. Seconds later we pulled out of Grantham for the 75 mph attempt.

My heart was racing with doubt about whether Stuart had the strength to shovel enough coal to build up the necessary head of steam. It would mean an hour of back-breaking work and even then there was no guarantee of success. Minutes passed and Stuart shovelled furiously.

The speed mounted very slowly. Too slowly for me. Fifty, 60, 65 mph. It was agonising. However hard Stuart shovelled, the speed remained painfully off the pace. And then I saw Peter take the shovel. Coal fairly flew into the fire box and the speed slowly picked up. Stuart and Peter took it in turns. With the veteran steam enthusiast as fired up as the old locomotive herself, Stuart summoned every ounce of his strength and

shovelled like mad to try to match his unrelenting effort.

Their combined effort was verging on the heroic. With five miles to go, the 532 was steaming at well over 70 mph.

The last few miles were very exciting indeed.

Stuart strained his voice. 'Are we going to do it?'

Peter was resolute. 'Not if you don't keep shovelling.'

The 532 reached 75 mph and beyond. I am not at liberty to reveal what the top speed was, except that the driver was later reminded of the legal limit.

As we steamed into King's Cross 12 hours after leaving Waverley Station in Edinburgh, even the presence of John Noakes and Valerie Singleton with the Pandemonium Steel Band couldn't top that glorious moment. I believe it was the pinnacle of the 532's steaming career.

30 May–4 June 1998
Romania

In late spring 1998 I made my last visit to Romania with Konnie, and it was with some nostalgia that I landed at Bucharest airport. I had been to Romania five times before, following the progress of our appeal for Orphaned and Abandoned Children, which had begun in 1990. I had seen Bucharest airport change from a wreck with jagged holes in the concrete floors and cracks in the solid concrete ceilings to a modern, functioning building.

That was not all. The currency had changed from a conversion rate of 40 lei to the US dollar to more than two hundred, and the bullet holes in the square opposite the Intercontinental Hotel, evidence of the revolution, had been filled in. Gone were the lines of tinned tomatoes and instead the shops were bulging with the bounty of Western capitalism. Even the road to Bacau had been rebuilt, and what had been little better than a wide cart track was fresh tarmac. Even more impressive, and a wonder to behold, was the appearance of cat's-eyes.

Romania had become the focus for overseas investors who had a greedy eye on her fertile plains and the treasure trove of minerals beneath – and of course her oil. Flights were packed with businessmen trying to get in on the act, and with so little regulation they rushed to take advantage. However, as Romania's fortunes had changed, so had industrial pollution, and chemical plants belched out poisonous fumes. It was a worrying and growing threat, although it would be a very long time before it matched the problems that other countries, like China, have today.

We drove north to Bacau, as we had done so many times in the past, and Konnie reported on the success of the houses we had built. Several hundred children had been moved out of the orphanages and back to family life.

(Right): Cameraman Peter Loring, sound recordist Phil Clayton and Konnie Huq on Baia Mare Station en route to Bucharest

She was quite taken by what she saw and made friends with the children, who wanted to play with her. She learnt her script quickly and delivered it in her own quirky way.

The first morning went well until I realised that she had not been wearing a *Blue Peter* badge. I had asked her to put one on at the start and asked her why she hadn't done it.

'I decided not to and wondered how long it would be before you noticed,' she joked mischievously.

I fell for it hook, line and sinker. She had, in fact, forgotten to put the badge on but thought it would be more fun to wind me up. I was easily conned because I had noticed a rebellious streak in Konnie that I secretly quite liked.

We had to reshoot the sequence the following morning and lost time as a result.

Konnie was coquettish, willing to please, and fun to film with. She made friends with everybody. As with all new presenters, I wondered how long it would last.

As we left Bacau and headed into the hills for the proposed site for more *Blue Peter* houses, it wasn't long before the Romanian way of life around us changed. Fields were peppered with mini-haystacks and we saw lines of workers turning hay with wooden pitchforks. At one point we slowed to a stop to allow flocks of snow-white geese to be herded along the main road. The road verges were a mass of colour with wildflowers. No weedkillers here. I was reminded with some sadness of my childhood when the hedgerows in Devon, too, had been all the colours of the rainbow. I wondered how long it would be before the north of Romania followed the same fate.

The city of Baia Mare was unremarkable and at the hotel we saw another aspect of the Romanian way of life. As we lined up to sign in and get our room keys, we noticed half a dozen women who had appeared as we arrived. It turned out that as well as rooms, a swimming pool and a restaurant, the hotel offered sex as part of their services. The concierge thought this was all quite normal. Whether or not this was legal I never found out, and the incident served as reminder that however much we may think we may understand our East European neighbours, we don't.

I was sad to see the last of Romania because it is a beautiful country. While the people had been brutalised by the Ceausescu regime and, in my opinion, had very little artistic taste, they were keen to change. There was a ruthlessly logical side to them, the side that thought it was all right to have too many children because they could give them to the state to look after – and I found this hard to understand. Whenever I brought up the subject there were some who professed regret at the orphanages along the lines of 'we had no choice'. I wondered whether, deep down, they thought it was the government's fault and therefore no fault of theirs. I certainly found it hard to find women who would express any deep emotion on the subject.

Looking back and reading reports today about Romanian gangs illegally applying for social benefits in Britain, I can see how they would not see this as a crime. During communism in Romania, their main activity was to seek as much financial help as they could from the state, and it was perfectly acceptable for them to do so. Whether it was morally right or wrong would not have been an issue, and I suspect that our largesse is just viewed as a business opportunity.

I am left with a dread that, 21 years since the human disaster was revealed, Romania has unleashed some hundred thousand maltreated children who may feel that they do not owe the world very much. If you link a brutalising childhood with a tendency for logic rather than compassion, you have an unpleasant cocktail of influences in a whole generation that I hope will never be in a position to get its own back.

Konnie remembers Romania as the place with the worst hotel she has ever stayed in. It was a million miles from her glamorous lifestyle – but right on the doorstep of a crisis in need of the generosity of *Blue Peter* viewers. In the end, we made a difference and it was a big one.

24

The danger of pointing fingers

May 1998
Cyprus

In May the same year I set off with Katy Hill and Stuart Miles to make another programme based on the Red Arrows in Cyprus. While Katy experienced the thrill of formation aerobatics, Stuart discovered an island that was deeply divided into a northern part, which was Turkish, and a southern part, which was Greek. The border between the two was the 'green line' – a strip of no man's land – and where it divided the city of Nicosia it was sometimes no more than a few metres wide.

The Royal Tank Regiment was part of the United Nations force overseeing the ceasefire agreement that had ended the fighting in 1974. We filmed as Stuart and Lieutenant James Grimshaw walked down the alleyway that was the green line. We passed a house where a lady called Annie had lived until she'd died, her only entrance a door into no man's land. Every time she'd wanted to go shopping she'd had to have a military escort, which must have been a nuisance all round, yet she resolutely stuck it out to the end. Otto's Café was another spooky reminder of the past, with its tables and glasses left exactly as they had been when the fighting had ended. They were all covered in a thick layer of dust.

The green line crossed rooftops, went through buildings and we exited its tortuous route at a UN post after about a mile. We were told a horrifying story of two Londoners, one Greek, the other Turkish, who were lifelong friends from Camden Town. Each was required to do military service, and by an amazing coincidence ended up on opposite sides of the green line. The Greek boy took a chance and moved across the line to speak to his friend. All went well until a Turkish officer approached, and the Greek boy had to retreat. He wasn't quick enough. His Turkish friend was ordered to shoot him. In fear of being shot himself, he picked up his rifle and, although he aimed to miss, the

(Top left): Stuart Miles and Lieutenant James Grimshaw in the green line that separates the northern part of Nicosia from the south

(Top right): Katy Hill with Red Arrows team leader Squadron Leader Simon Meade

bullet hit his friend's head and he was killed outright.

Relations between Turks and Greeks have eased today; in 1998 there were many signs that the hatred was just beneath the surface. To move from the south and into the north we had to be accompanied by UN observers so our passports would not be stamped. A passport stamped by the Turks would make it very difficult, if not impossible, to re-enter the south. And we were warned not to talk about our visit when we got back, except amongst ourselves, because it could cause a great deal of ill-feeling.

Nicosia airport was a massive no-go area in the middle of the green line, and we joined Greek children who walked stray dogs along their side of the airfield. An airliner had been unable to take off during the fighting and was stranded on the tarmac, wrecked and abandoned and

(Bottom left): Stuart Miles by the abandoned airliner stranded in no man's land

(Bottom right): Cameraman Rob Llewellyn and sound recordist Darren Tate film Katy Hill with the team

devoid of life, as if left over from a nuclear war.

Walking between abandoned houses high on either side, hearing the stories, hurrying past danger points in the hot sun, I was inclined to think the green line should be preserved, if only to remind ourselves of the fallibility of man.

Meanwhile, Katy, on the coast at RAF Akrotiri, was a big hit with the Red Arrows. Simon Meade, the leader, was welcoming and helpful at every turn, and allowed us to witness red-suit day when Air Chief Marshall Sir David Cousins adjudicated whether or not the team was fit to carry out their task. As the formation looped and rolled in front of them, Katy flirted outrageously with Sir David and I could see that not all his concentration was on the boys in red.

'It's all looking good, isn't it? Come on, you have to admit it.' Katy was the master of leading questions and Sir David was forced to agree.

In a packed crew room Sir David solemnly announced that they were the finest team he had ever seen and they had passed.

Much later that day Sir David asked me about the filming and how it had gone. I told him that Simon Meade had enabled us to film behind the scenes in a way that had not been possible for years. He had transformed relations between the Reds and the BBC. It was a lead that was followed by other team leaders like Andy Offer and Dicky Patounas.

23 August–2 September 1998
Uganda

Later that year I teamed up with Bill Locke, who had once worked on *Blue Peter*. I asked him to help me make a programme about the legendary mountain gorillas in Uganda. At the time Bill was, like me, doing his best to become a cameraman as well as a director. I hired him as a second camera because it would double my chances of getting shots of the gorillas when we met them.

He knew Stuart Miles and, a happy band, we set off northwestwards from Entebbe in two Land Rovers towards the town of Kabale. My old friend Colin Bowes was the sound recordist and we had fixers from the International Gorilla Programme to help us.

All went well to begin with and Bill, who had just spent three years in Ethiopia, reminded us of the dangers of driving after dark. At this stage of the trip he alone really knew the risks we were taking.

After about three hours of fairly rough motoring, alternately speeding up when we came to a flat stretch of road and then slowing down almost to a stop for the massive potholes, we saw a commotion up ahead. There were police everywhere and to avoid awkward questions I put my camera down and tried to look like we weren't from the BBC.

The commotion turned out to be a bus or, should I say, what was left of a bus. The top half was missing and it had been on fire. I noticed several bodies lying at the roadside covered up with ground sheets with just their feet showing. It didn't look like the scene of an accident and we drove past wondering if there had been a bomb – or something like a bomb. There were soldiers everywhere.

Later that night, we heard on the news that two buses had been the target of terrorist bombs that had been concealed in paint tins. Eleven people had been killed and many more injured.

Stuart was quiet and he confided to me that perhaps we ought to listen to Bill. When we later stopped to film our vehicle passing by, Bill reminded me, 'It's going to be dark in an hour or two. We can't travel at night. Let's get on and no more stopping.'

We drove on, ruminating on the possibilities of ambush and terrorism, and reached our first destination as dusk fell. We decided not to investigate the bright lights and to get an early night.

The next day we drove for hours up into the hills as we headed for Kisoro, not far from the border with the Congo. The camera scarcely left my hands as I shot endless views out of the car window as we passed crowded markets and herds of cattle. Every new turn of the road presented another shot I just had to take – something I would later regret in the edit suite as, with hours of material, I spent far too long looking for the best bits. The regular beat of the motor and lurch of the vehicle were too much for Stuart. He went to sleep and I could not resist filming his recumbent form.

We arrived at our destination in torrential rain in time to hear a Dutch journalist loudly filing his report. A young couple, recently married, had been on their honeymoon and had strayed across the border into the Congo and disappeared. It was a big story in Holland and he had been in the hotel for some weeks, reporting developments. He confided that the couple had almost certainly been captured by Congolese rebels, and because no ransom message had been received, the man was probably dead and the young woman was probably being treated very badly. It did not bear thinking about and our hearts went out to them. I confess that being taken hostage in Africa is one of my worst nightmares, so the incident focused my mind wonderfully.

The hotel, which was little better than a corrugated-iron hut with a single tap and a hole in the ground for the loo, did not have enough rooms for all of us and I had to sleep in a tent outside the entrance with our driver. Stuart wisely opted for a room inside. I remember thinking, as I tried to get to sleep, that a tent flap was not much protection if we were visited during the night.

The journey to Bwindi (the impenetrable forest) took us through some of the most spectacular scenery in Africa. As we neared the Congo and Rwandan border there were breathtaking views of the volcanic hills at every turn of the track – a very pleasant change from the flat plains surrounding Lake Victoria. We ventured into the impenetrable forest and spotted black and white long-tailed colobus monkeys and other creatures high in the treetops. We drove for hours, bumping along a narrow dirt road through thick bush, and arrived at our destination well after dark.

(Left): Alex, Stuart Miles, sound recordist Colin Bowes with Bill Locke (seated) on the Equator

(Right): Final interviews ahead of the trek to find gorillas

We awoke the next day, in our relatively posh circular mud and thatched huts, to find that we were on the side of a valley with steep hills on three sides with a view down the valley itself. Breakfast was boiled or fried eggs and bread, and we assessed the situation.

We had to register our intention to visit the gorillas by applying for a permit.

Gorilla tourism was big business, so it was of little surprise to find fifty or sixty visitors queuing for the privilege of a close encounter with these gentle giants. Visits were strictly limited to one a day and there were only two groups of gorillas in the vicinity. With a maximum of two groups of eight to ten visitors setting off each day, it was not unusual to have to wait a day or two.

We spent the first day with our gorilla guide, who took us on a two-mile nature walk that ended up by a stunning waterfall. We talked about the dos and don'ts of gorilla watching, and filmed giant butterflies drinking from large puddles of rainwater in the sunlight. There were giant snails, spiders and ferns. Stuart was curious and asked probing questions.

'Can you tell when they are going to charge?' he asked with a strong sense of self-preservation, additionally enquiring, 'And what should we do if they do?'

He liked to be prepared.

Thankfully attacks on humans are extremely rare. If anything, gorillas are shy and strongly communal animals and our guide simply advised us in the event of any aggressive behaviour to 'Stay still and look down at the ground. Call their bluff.'

Oddly, they don't like being pointed at either.

Bill and I spent the rest of the walk competing to find the best shots. It was good to be out of the vehicles and getting some exercise.

The following day we met with the community officer, Ross, a lean likeable man who had called a meeting with the villagers to discuss the problems and benefits of having several large groups of gorillas on their doorstep. The main problem was damage to crops because the gorillas were very fond of bananas, and from the evidence we filmed it was difficult to see who was winning: the gorillas or humans. There were benefits to having the gorillas around. The money that tourism brought in was essential for building schools and hospitals, so the compensation system worked, even if there were fewer bananas to eat.

The following morning we set off to see the gorillas. We trekked through uneven bush and needed both hands on occasions to steady ourselves as we jumped from one branch to another a couple of feet above the ground along a route cut by our guides through the thick vegetation. I carried my camera on my chest in a small haversack worn back to front so I could grab it quickly if something happened.

We were a little group of seven, including a couple who were in their mid-fifties and who very kindly did not object to being filmed. We took it steadily because we had been told it was quite possible that we could be walking (if that's the right word for tripping up over every tree root) for up

to 12 hours before we found them. Even then there were no guarantees.

It was spongy underfoot and damp with decaying leaves, the air rich with the peaty smells of the tropical jungle. All we could hear were the sounds of our guides hacking away at the undergrowth and the murmur of conversation. It was hot and humid and the sweat poured off us. Every puff of wind was pure ecstasy. The clouds gathered and then parted, but under the thick jungle canopy we hardly noticed. As the hours went by we began to tire and care less and less about anything, except getting back.

Then our guide stopped by an unpromising pile of something that was the same colour as the jungle floor.

'Gorilla been here. This where he stopped.'

He had found a pile of gorilla poo. As we had seen precious little else of consequence, I struggled to get a close-up shot of it; most children are quite interested in poo.

'Over there they sleep in a nest in the trees,' he said, pointing to some broken branches and leaves. I had heard that gorillas slept in nests and had only half believed it. Yet here was the evidence. It made an equally unpromising shot.

'How far are they?' Stuart asked, and we all waited eagerly for his reply. 'Not far. Maybe a few hours, not more.'

We struggled noisily up hill and down dale for over an hour, more concerned with keeping going than not disturbing our elusive friends. I began to wonder when we would have to turn back. And then our guide stopped and turned to us, finger to his lips. We immediately froze in silence.

'Gorillas very close now. Must be very quiet.'

Our hearts pounded with excitement as we emerged on to a track to hear a deep coughing noise not far away. It was the unmistakable sound of an adult gorilla feeding, and we could just catch the occasional swishing noise as it broke a branch and ate the leaves.

Then there was a sudden thudding through the bushes and a dark shape moved briskly about fifteen yards away and parallel to the path.

'Silverback,' our guide whispered.

One by one the whole family group emerged and began to settle in the open. After seven or eight hours of searching we had a grandstand view of the extended family group. For Stuart Miles, it was the kind of unforgettable encounter that made the job of *Blue Peter* presenter the envy of everyone who grew up watching the programme:

> I was in awe of this gorilla's size and strength. At that moment you become extremely aware of your own physical weaknesses and vulnerability but in no way did I feel terrified despite the fact it could have killed me with one hand. All I felt was a huge sense of excitement knowing I was experiencing a once-in-a-lifetime moment.

They settled in a patch of sunlight at the base of a gigantic tree. Bill and I filmed away while Stuart told the viewers what was going on and how he felt. The big silverback regarded us with contempt. He turned

his back and lay down and appeared to go to sleep. There were several babies and they created mayhem amongst the sleeping adults. It was very reminiscent of my own family on the beach at Exmouth when my children, Hannah and Henry, had been toddlers. The youngsters played and screamed with pleasure and the adults lifted them when they needed help and groomed them when they sat still for a few seconds.

There was so much understanding between the two groups, humans and gorillas, it was uncanny. Neither group was afraid of the other because to be afraid you needed uncertainty.

Stuart was entranced by them. 'I didn't know what to expect. They are just like us,' he whispered to camera. These little asides were vital to communicate how he felt. Then there was a sudden movement as the silverback ran three or four paces towards us, puffing up his chest. Someone had taken a flash photograph. Stuart looked shaken. 'Whew! I thought we were for it. Just shows that anything can change in a moment.'

Their immense strength was awe-inspiring and we knew that if they had charged we wouldn't have stood a chance. Yet an attack seemed inconceivable. It was hard to think of them as wild animals because they seemed to know who we were and what we were doing.

Unlike David Attenborough, who famously enchanted a nation with his very personal interaction with mountain gorillas in 1979, we were not allowed to go near them. Much as I would have liked Stuart to join in and rub shoulders, the rules had long since changed for the sake of the animals and such encounters were forbidden. We had to keep our distance.

(Left): This moody silverback adult seemed camera-shy while others in the group played happily

And as we were vulnerable, so were they, and I had the uneasy feeling that encounters like ours would not be possible for ever. Yet the idea of this happy family group coming to harm was as outrageous as something similar happening to anyone I knew.

We watched and filmed for about an hour and then we had to leave so they would not get too used to us. There were traces of tears in Stuart's eyes as he turned to camera for the final time.

'I hope they have a very happy future. It's been such a privilege even just to watch them.'

We returned the next day to find another group because I needed as many shots as we could get. I filmed an adult female and her offspring who were no more than thirty feet away in thick bush. There were other babies playing in the lower branches and I was completely absorbed in my work. Someone whispered something to me that I could not quite hear and almost instantly I was nudged to one side by muscle that was as hard as iron. A young male had just emerged out of the bush on my immediate left and had walked past me. It was as if he had pushed me out of the way to put me in my place. It was not aggressive.

People say that an encounter with the gorillas is profoundly moving and some, like Stuart, were genuinely moved. I was intrigued by the way they had accepted us. I found the experience rather more thought-provoking than moving. I thought that if I had to come back as an animal, let it be as something as majestic as a gorilla.

There was a terrible aftermath to our visit. About six months later there was a ghastly catastrophe.

A band of Congolese rebels had moved from the border near Kabale and crossed into Uganda at Bwindi. They lined up the waiting tourists and asked for their passports. They then divided them into two groups and took them into the hills. At the border all nationalities except the British were allowed to return. What the authorities subsequently found on the track on the way back was dreadful. The six British tourists who had been separated from the main group had been murdered.

In Bwindi village the rebels had burnt the tourist lodges and had singled out the local leaders, including our gorilla guides. While most escaped, one didn't. He was the one person who was most concerned about the gorillas. I read the newspaper report with horror. They took him and locked him inside a vehicle and then set fire to it. He was an honourable man who worked tirelessly on behalf of the gorillas and the local community, and his murder was a terrible crime. I heard later that the Ugandan army had set off in pursuit. I did not hear whether they had caught up with the rebels. I very much hope that they did.

The incident was on the BBC news for a week and, because there was very little video footage of the region, I rang up the duty news editor to explain that I had some shots that might be useful. He was fairly sceptical because he knew I was a producer and not a cameraman, yet he gave me the benefit of the doubt. I edited a tape together and went to the BBC in Exeter to send the footage up the line to London. He had only asked for a couple of minutes and I had put together about half an hour of various shots. He watched the first minute or so and said with gratifying candour, 'I think we'd better have all of this.'

The shots were precious because it would take too long for a crew to get to the scene. They were used on every bulletin for four days, even on *Newsnight*, the last place you'd expect to see *Blue Peter* footage.

16 October 1998
The Natural History Museum, London

The summer of 1998 was a milestone for *Blue Peter* because it marked 40 years of programme-making. A celebration was held in the awe-inspiring cavern of the Natural History Museum and I wondered if the dinner might mark the end of an era.

Like all reunions, it was both happy and sad at the same time. I could not believe that I had been on the programme for 24 years, and seeing all the people I had worked with and hearing what they had been up to was disconcerting. Should I have left and tried my hand elsewhere? It's a question I have asked myself time and again. And yet...every face there reminded me of a kaleidoscope of indelible

(Right): Team photo: Romana D'Annunzio, Richard Bacon, Katy Hill and Stuart Miles

memories. Only a few professions, or television programmes, can boast such a rich cocktail of life.

The dinner was a great success and when we emerged on to the pavement outside there were photographers waiting. They weren't interested in John Noakes or Valerie Singleton. Instead, they were hoping to get shots of our newest presenter, Richard Bacon.

A story had broken that Richard had taken cocaine and the press was baying for blood. He had been betrayed by a friend who'd wanted to make money by selling the story to the newspapers. Richard had taken the drug at a nightclub when he was drunk and his friend had then reported it to the *News of the World*. Having been told to get evidence, the friend recorded the telephone conversation with Richard when he got him to talk about it. On this occasion, his friend pointing the finger was far less brave than in the face of a mountain gorilla; I heard that this particular cheap gesture netted £20,000 as the price of friendship.

All credit to Richard; he did the honest thing and confessed all, steadfastly refusing to accept lucrative offers to bare all in a national newspaper.

He became the first *Blue Peter* presenter to be publicly sacked. His spectacular departure even prompted an on-air apology by Lorraine Heggessey, then head of BBC Children's Programmes.

Richard's career was in ruins but his personality and presenting skills, combined with considerable humility, would eventually earn him a place back at the BBC.

His great mistake had been to believe that he could live his life like any other person. What he had not realised was that his life, as a presenter of a national institution, was no longer his to lead.

We were very upset to lose him because he made an excellent presenter and we all liked him. I think he behaved bravely and honourably and it paid off in the end. Richard Bacon, television and radio presenter, is now much admired and respected.

(Above): Konnie Huq
takes to the skies, training
to become an air
stewardess

25

Blue Peter in first class

A shuffle in the presenting team started 1999. With Richard Bacon gone, we needed a replacement. Simon Thomas, who had been working as a runner for Children's BBC, had applied for the job twice before. So it was a case of third time lucky when he became presenter number 28.

He was like a favourite elder brother, good looking and with a quick wit. On screen he had a powerful presence. Like Katy Hill's, his dad was a vicar, and he empathised with the aims of the programme. Over the next six years Simon and I would share as many adventures as I did with the other *Blue Peter* Simon, Simon Groom.

Meanwhile, I was challenged to produce, direct and shoot a whole programme myself for the first time as a producer/cameraman.

30 March–5 April 1999
Bangladesh

Konnie, in common with many TV personalities, loved to entertain. Unlike her fellow presenters, she would happily repeat her speeches to camera as many times as the director wanted. For me, looking for slight nuances in delivery and being ever the perfectionist, this was a delight. I had to restrain an unbridled quest for the perfect piece to camera because I would inadvertently use up a disproportionate amount of the working day.

I found her to be very 'upfront' and her feelings were clear to everyone around her. For me this had both its pluses and minuses. I like plain speaking and while she could be kind and attentive with people she liked, she didn't suffer fools. She is blessed with a very good brain and gained nine GCSEs and A-Levels in physics, maths and chemistry, followed by an economics degree from Cambridge. I was puzzled why she took great pains to conceal her intelligence, almost as if it wasn't cool to be overtly bright.

I planned – at her suggestion – to make a programme about where she had spent her childhood in Bangladesh. The idea was the result of a conversation we'd had after a day making a film about Dogs for the Disabled in Cornwall.

It had all started back in 1997. Passing through Launceston, Konnie surprised me. 'I haven't told you this before but you know my uncle.'

'Do I?' I couldn't imagine where I could have met him.

'He's one of my favourite uncles and you filmed with him when you went to Bangladesh with Janet Ellis. He was the field director for Oxfam and he met you during filming. I call him Rockoo.'

I recalled a previous expedition, part of the Weatherbeater Appeal in October 1983, when we had also visited the British Airways-sponsored orphanage in Dhaka. The penny dropped, not because I recognised his name but because I remembered the trip so well. The Oxfam field director, Saidur Rahman, had made a big impression on me because he had been the best fixer I had ever worked with. I was intrigued.

'If your uncle can fix it, we should think of something to film in Bangladesh.' I immediately sensed a film that would work easily.

Ten minutes later we had formed a plan and the following day I got the go-ahead to film in Bangladesh on the back of short series of films about Konnie learning how to become an air stewardess with British Airways. She would work as a stewardess on the flight out to Dhaka just as I had filmed Janet Ellis doing 16 years earlier.

By the time I had persuaded British Airways and got the necessary permits, over a year had passed.

Rockoo, who now owned a clothing factory and had a very enlightened approach to employment, was a very busy man and he tried to keep out of the filming, without success.

Konnie's dad was so pleased at the idea that Rockoo was recruited to help whether he liked it or not. Messages flew back and forth and I knew that everything in Bangladesh would be as well organised as the flight out. Meanwhile, we filmed at the British Airways Training Centre at Heathrow as Konnie trained to become an air stewardess. Every time I hear the phrase 'Doors to manual and cross-check' it all comes flooding back. I just hope I never have to hear the words 'Wait, wait, slide inflating' at the emergency exit.

The trip was a huge thing for Konnie because it was about being Bangladeshi but also, since she had dual nationality, about being British. The film would be huge for me, too, because I had to come to terms with being on my own as the cameraman. Only the sound recordist, Colin Bowes, could help me if things went wrong. Konnie was a bit on edge too:

> I was very excited to be going back to Bangladesh and a bit sad that I hadn't been for so long. It was very strange to be going back with a camera crew, especially because going to see family, and family that you don't see very often in particular, is such a personal thing.

The shoot began in a crew briefing room for the fourteen or so crew members of flight number BA145 departing London Heathrow 21.50 hours – destination Dhaka, Bangladesh.

As Konnie was being introduced to the team and allocated her duties, my hands shook with nerves. This was truly 'it', and 'it' was more of a challenge than I had bargained for. To my relief my trembling steadied and the doubts disappeared. I was so absorbed in getting the best angles, I forgot about everything else.

Konnie pulled her weight, 'sponging' bread rolls and piping-hot dishes of food in first class with a pair of oddly shaped tongs or 'spongs'. Night turned into dawn, and then into day, and it was a very tired team that landed in Dhaka, some ten hours-plus later. We were sweaty and desperately in need of a shower and sleep.

We spent the next day filming at the British Airways-sponsored orphanage as I had done 16 years before with Janet Ellis and I marvelled at what had been achieved since that time. The orphanage had moved to more spacious surroundings outside the city. Its main supporter then and now, air stewardess Pat Kerr, was dressed traditionally in a flowing sari, and had lost none of her enthusiasm for the project. The children were overjoyed to see her and gave us all a noisy greeting, which seemed more normal than the human wave that had overwhelmed us when we filmed before.

(Left): Janet Ellis with Saidur Rahman (Konnie's uncle Rockoo) while filming in Bangladesh in 1983

Dhaka, the capital, was a feast for the film-maker. I had fond memories of the harbour from my earlier visit and I wasn't disappointed. It was just as magical as I had remembered. Looking up to the upper storeys in the narrow streets, we saw electric cables festooned chaotically where several hundred wires all met at a single point. How any electrician could fix anything when it went wrong was a mystery. Convoys of rickshaws clashed with street traders and yet there were no accidents. Ladies in brightly coloured saris gathered around a single tap to fill large dome-shaped metal water pots. It was exotic, intoxicating, and I was mesmerised. There was continual movement and an unrelenting noise of bells and hooters. The harbour teemed with activity as boats arrived, horns blaring, and piles upon piles of sacks were unloaded and carried ashore by hand.

The impact on Konnie was no less:

> I remember thinking on my last visit how colourful Bangladesh was and that struck me again on this visit. Compared to many other countries, especially developed countries, it's an array of smells, colours and noises, especially in the city, and this had not changed.

(Top left): Konnie Huq
and Pat Kerr at the
British Airways-sponsored
orphanage

Konnie was thrilled to see Rockoo and it was obvious that the chemistry between them would make for a very exciting shoot.

Rockoo was as delightful as I had remembered him. Distinguished, good looking, he had an air of authority that swept away the difficulties before us. Remembering his Oxfam days, he took us to visit the very poorest families in Dhaka who lived beside the railway line in the centre of the city. They lived in leaf houses built on stilts above open sewers, and within feet of the passing trains. People pressed around, curious to see who the beautiful lady was. In the crush I lost my wallet. I wrote it off to experience but I wasn't reckoning with Rockoo's contacts. Six months later it was returned to me and nothing was missing. He was a much-loved and respected figure. Konnie was deeply affected by what she saw:

> It was really sad to go to the shanty town but what really struck me was how happy everyone was there, despite the fact they live on a few pence a week. Unlike a lot of poor people, there was no complaining or resentment when I spoke to them – only happiness that we had come to see them. I felt really guilty in those overcrowded conditions in the downtrodden shacks with our gleaming, expensive camera equipment, and quite hypocritical. When the lady invited us to join her to eat I could have cried.

(Bottom left): The old port
of Dhaka

(Bottom right): Konnie
with her uncle Rockoo in
1999

One morning we got up very early to film in the fish market. As soon as I took out the camera a crowd formed. When I tracked back to film as Konnie and Rockoo walked towards me, I was conscious of the onlookers staring straight into the lens as they followed them. There was nothing I could do so I made a feature of it. Pressed from every side, we slipped between wooden tables where huge fish were being chopped bloodily into steaks. We moved on past piles of shrimp and octopus to find tables of vegetables and a veritable rainbow of herbs and spices.

I noticed that Rockoo was laughing and we paused in the melee.

'What's happened?' I asked worriedly.

He replied with a beaming smile, 'It is nothing. I have just heard two young men behind me talking. They both want to marry Konnie and were wondering how much she would cost to keep. One said about ten or even twenty dollars a day and the other thought as much as fifty, to which his friend said, "No woman on earth could cost as much as that." '

Local earnings were less than eight dollars a day.

The object of their affections didn't quite know how take this and we carried on filming in the crush of bodies.

Konnie was taking her time coming to terms with being back in Bangladesh, and I thought she did not seem entirely comfortable. She got more and more 'uptight' as we neared her old home.

Then she was in tears as she embraced her grandmother and proudly showed us around. I was very impressed by her family home, which was built around a courtyard with rooms for the extended family:

> I used to speak to my granny on the phone a bit, and even though we didn't see each other loads we really got on. She was a really lovely person and very jokey. I was a bit worried that I might cry on camera when I saw her again, and I did get a lump in my throat but managed with determination not to let my eyes water.
>
> Even though I hadn't been back for nine years I remembered it vividly. I was really interested to see whether it had changed lots or not. Because the village is so different to life in England I would not have been surprised if it was totally the same in its own little world – almost like time stood still. I was unsure what to expect but at the back of my mind I was really sure that it would be just as I remembered – and it was.

At one point she asked me what I thought of it, because I believed she thought it wasn't posh enough. I said that it was a wonderful building full of character and a perfect centre for three or four families and their collective activities. I think it is a shame we cannot live more like that in Britain. Living separately as we do, family support is not always possible.

It seemed to me that Konnie, like so many children of immigrants, had made a choice between being Bangladeshi and being British, and she found it difficult to be both. There are very big differences between

(Right): The Huq
family reunion at Pabna

life in London and life in Pabna. And showing how different cultures go about their daily lives was bread and butter for *Blue Peter*. How do you compare a modern kitchen in London with an outside fire and a mud oven in Pabna? Used effectively, they both cook food equally well.

There was a huge meal for the extended family to welcome us and afterwards there were games. 'Smash the pot' was one the girls played. Earthen pots that were cracked or past their prime were laid out in a row about forty feet away from the players, who were blindfolded. On a given signal they advanced towards the pots, banging the ground randomly with large sticks. The winner was the girl who managed to smash the most number of pots. I tried to get Konnie to join in but to no avail. She suggested a game of catch with a tennis ball:

> Being a Bangladeshi living in Britain makes me part of two cultures. Home is Britain but having strong roots, family and friends in Bangladesh is very important to me. When I have my own children I want to make sure they also know about Bangladesh. Together we'll celebrate this timeless place – so different to life in Britain.

(Left): Konnie Huq with
her father

By the end of the trip Konnie seemed to have readjusted as old memories had flooded back. She turned from being the visitor from Britain to being one of the family again. When we returned to Dhaka she made a great deal of effort to meet relatives in her time off, and she looked all the happier for it:

> It was a relief in many ways that everyone was as friendly and welcoming as I remembered them. It really was as though I hadn't been away.

Konnie was talented but she was by no means the easiest presenter to work with because she very easily got bored. Television people often refer to difficult and high-maintenance presenters as prima donnas.

I wouldn't put Konnie in that category, and, unlike some of my colleagues, I used her nature to my advantage. Richard Marson, who was to become editor in 2003, remembers that some directors were reluctant to work with her because of her intense dislike of having to follow a structured script and learn somebody else's lines. He told me that this was one reason why she was often assigned to me. I tended to shoot stories where the presenter had to rely on their wits and comment using their intelligence as the situation unfolded around them. I tried not to put precise words into Konnie's mouth and made her articulate her own thoughts. As time went by, she created a popular fan base with her unique style of presentation.

Behind the scenes she never had the filming workload of her co-presenters Simon and later Matt Baker because she wasn't athletic. Many film inserts at the time were action-orientated, which tested the presenter's fitness and co-ordination. Konnie was not the natural choice for action films and it was something that did not escape their notice.

She became a much more rounded human being as a result of her time on *Blue Peter* and her trip to Bangladesh perhaps made her appreciate even more the chances afforded to her in the UK:

> In a way, life's a bit of a lottery. Where you're born is a lottery and the fact that my parents even came out to the UK makes me think a lot about how things have turned out.

Konnie was also pleased to learn that perceptions in her parents' homeland had changed. They 'no longer believed that all British Bangladeshis worked in Indian restaurants'.

(Above): Konnie with her grandmother and great-aunties

(Above): Vincent Ndekezi
and fellow porters on the
slopes of Kilimanjaro

26

Breathless in Africa

In 1999, Oliver Macfarlane, the editor who had taken over from Lewis Bronze, left in February to pursue his first love – music. I had known, ever since I had supported Biddy with his recruitment, his ambition lay in classical music. A vacancy for an executive producer role in the TV Classical Music department opened and he got his chance. He went on to produce the *BBC Proms, BBC Young Musician of the Year* and other music programmes.

It was, again, a time of cost-cutting in *Blue Peter* and the new editor had to be a politician as well as a leader. The programme was under pressure to save money. Luckily for me, Steve Hocking was the right man at the right time and he needed multi-skilled producers around him. All my struggles with the new digital camera had paid off and it wasn't long before I was asked to prove my worth again.

25 August–7 September 1999
Kilimanjaro

Before he left, Oliver had agreed to make a whole programme with Sightsavers about six British and six African children with little or no sight climbing Mount Kilimanjaro, the highest mountain in Africa. It was a huge project and the film crew and participants all met and trained together over several weekends before the big event.

Every child had an adult guide to look after them and when we met up at the airport I was asked, 'What would you do, as the director/cameraman, if you couldn't make the summit?' I was by far the oldest adult on the expedition, so I suppose they thought I was a likely casualty. I said I would give the camera to the sound recordist, Colin, and he and the presenter, Simon Thomas, would carry on without me.

'And what if Colin dropped out as well?' I was asked rather pointedly.

I replied that he would give all the equipment to Simon and he would do what he could. They persisted. 'And if Simon had to give up?'

Determined not to be outdone, I replied, 'Then he'd have to film his own failure.'

What they were driving at was the real danger about climbing any mountain, and that is altitude sickness. The secret is to do it slowly because otherwise there's a good chance you'll get it. Altitude sickness means a blinding headache followed by vomiting and lethargy and then, if you don't get down quickly, possible death. There was a drug called Diamox, which alleviated the effects. As the challenge was not about me, I had no hesitation about taking it. Neither did Colin. But in the interests of fair play Simon did not take the drug. And we did not dare tell him that we had.

None of the children were allowed Diamox for medical reasons so, several days into the trek and above 13,000 feet, the expedition became a very miserable affair. Cups were, metaphorically, more than half-empty as deep pessimism pervaded the whole expedition.

We had set off from the Outward Bound centre at Loitokitok as a straggling column of about thirty. Another column of about sixty porters had gone on ahead of us and carried all the food and kitchen equipment. We carried our personal clothing, sleeping bags and tents. At 6,000 feet it was a pleasant walk and our spirits were high. We were so far from the mountain that we could only get the odd glimpse of it as we trekked through the tall African bush.

(Below): The expedition on the lower slopes at the start of their long ascent

(Above): Simon's 'buddy', Charles Ronayne

(Right): The campsite at dawn with Kilimanjaro

Slowly the vegetation began to change. As we climbed higher so the growth became more stunted and ropes of thick moss festooned the trees. Occasionally mists descended and it grew cold. It was a bit eerie and rather forbidding. As we made camp at 9,000 feet the children talked about altitude sickness because it worried them. Simon was just catching on to this peril and, true to form, put it to the back of his mind. Each adult was 'buddy' to a child, and Simon was paired with Charles Ronayne. He reassured him that there was nothing to worry about.

Charles turned out to be a real character with a great sense of humour. Simon liked him and they teased each other. When they were on potato-peeling duty Charles peeled away, but because he could not see what he was doing, a huge spud ended up the size of a walnut and caused much merriment.

As the days went by, the stunted trees turned into bushes and then eventually they disappeared. Over 12,000 feet the only plants that grew were grass and heather and we had an unobstructed view of the mountain covered in snow at its summit. We gazed thoughtfully up at the roof of Africa.

We had walked up to 13,000 feet in four days and had had time to acclimatise to the altitude, and on the morning of the fifth day we set off to assault the summit. There was a mammoth amount of walking to do. And that was when we had our first casualty.

Stuart Davis was from Wales and had been training hard, yet altitude sickness does not respect fitness. You can be an Olympic athlete and still get it. At one stop he sat down and could not get up. He was lethargic and unable to stand unaided. We all watched as he was taken down the

mountain and we couldn't help wondering who would be next.

Simon was becoming increasingly puzzled:

> I spent most of the time while we were climbing completely bemused by the seemingly boundless energy of Alex and Colin. While most of us felt lethargic with headaches almost permanently raging, they appeared to be unaffected. They were both a fair few years older than me so to see them at times looking like spring chickens while I felt I was suffering a slow death was more than a little perplexing and irritating.

Simon staggered on with a constant and blinding headache. He and Charles suffered together. While Colin and I sympathised, we worried even more about him learning our terrible secret – exactly why we were not so afflicted. It was clear that the perils of altitude sickness were preying on everyone's minds. The adults were particularly worried. Young minds were carefree and dealt with problems as they happened while older ones battled internally with imagined horrors. We continued the trek uphill across rock-strewn mountainside for about ten miles and by the time we reached base camp the adults had all but given up.

Kibu Hut was a very bleak place. The whole area was shrouded in mist and so cold and dry that the dirt was a fine powdery dust that got everywhere. We pitched camp on rock and were told to get a few hours' sleep. We lay shivering in our sleeping bags and thought about all the people who had nearly died until it was time to go. In the interests of getting the job done, I relented and gave Simon a Diamox tablet. He later told me he was dumbfounded. At last he knew how Colin and I had been immune to the headaches and had had so much more energy than he'd had.

(Left): Simon Thomas at Kibu Hut, the last stop before the summit

(Right): Members of the British team at Gilman's Point

At the appointed hour, less all but one of the adult buddies from Britain, we shuffled in single file, zigzagging up what I remember as a huge slag heap. Simon remembers it well:

> Getting to the top that night was the longest night I've ever encountered. No matter how many steps forward we took, the top never seemed to get any closer.

I had been told that as the loose shale froze during the night it would be easier to walk over. I can't say I noticed. It was minus 20° Celsius (minus 4° Fahrenheit) and getting colder by the minute. We had to walk at the pace of the slowest, which meant we never got warmer than very cold. And all the while other climbers, who had set out just before us and had gone up too quickly, were carried down past us, vomiting with altitude sickness.

After eight hours of freezing cold we scrambled the last 100 feet to Gilman's Point at about 18,600 feet. I found it very hard going and my slow pace was noticed.

I remember someone shouting to me, 'Be sick, Alex, you'll feel a lot better!'

I am glad to say that, loaded up as I was with Diamox, I felt fine, apart from being completely out of breath. I was managing about half a dozen steps before I had to pause to suck in more air. It was an interesting moment because my porter, Vincent, who was helping me carry my filming gear, vomited over his boots and I sent him down.

We paused in a confused heap at Gilman's Point and as the sun came up we posed for photographs. The entire African contingent was intact. Three of the five children from the British contingent made it and just the one adult guide.

As I had done throughout the whole journey, I filmed what I could and then sat down with exhaustion and relief. Wonder drug or no wonder drug, it had been a struggle. I had no feelings of victory or anything much else. I just enjoyed the amazing view, ruminating that I had seen it all before from the warmth and comfort of a 747.

My limbs ached unbearably, and slightly light-headed I looked at everything in a detached way. The mind-blowing view, the other climbers, my boots, they were all interesting to my befuddled mind. I dreaded the moment I would have to stand up again.

I shared Simon's reaction:

> The view from the top was everything I had hoped for as the plains of Africa stretched out below, a view that will stay with me for ever. The only disappointment (as when I climbed Mont Blanc a few years later) is that you feel so utterly exhausted that all you want to do is go straight back down. Altitude gives but a brief moment to savour the view and achievement.

And that moment arrived all too soon. It was too dangerous to stay at altitude for long and we had to go down. The expedition immediately splintered into ones and twos. Gone was the cohesion and unity of purpose. It was every man for himself.

We stumbled 3,000 feet back down the mountain, sliding ankle deep in loose shale, legs trembling as different muscles were brought into play. It was a different sort of pain to endure but with every step we could feel our bodies gratefully sucking in the thicker air. We struck the tents we had set up less than 12 hours earlier and trekked another 15 miles to yet another camp that was below 12,000 feet. In 36 hours we had trekked about 30 miles in sub-zero temperatures and had had virtually no sleep.

In celebration I paid a huge sum of money to local guides for some properly cooked food and the chance to sit at a table rather than on the ground. The table and bench were worth it but the food was a big disappointment. I know that both Simon and Colin appreciated the thought and, too tired to care, we joked about all the other suckers they must have seen coming. I was completely exhausted and in total admiration at the resilience of the 15-year-olds, who were happily playing football.

It had been fun, if that's the right word. But never again. I firmly crossed mountain climbing off my to-do list and vowed never to repeat such a punishing assignment as long as I lived, even in the name of *Blue Peter*.

27

Pilgrim's progress

(Top left): The British contingent back at 12,000 feet, relieved the worst is over

(Right): An artificial island in the Langa Langa lagoon, Solomon Islands

(Bottom left): Simon Thomas relaxing after his arduous climb

17 November–7 December 2001
The Solomon Islands

Sometimes it takes many years for an idea to come to fruition.

In 1966, when I was 19, I had left home and travelled 12,000 miles to the Solomon Islands in the Pacific Ocean to work as a VSO volunteer, living in a leaf house and teaching in an Anglican mission school on a remote island called Ugi.

Ugi was about four miles long and two across and shaped like a kidney, with a shallow range of hills in the middle. Palm trees lined the long white sand beaches and the reef was a treasure trove of colour and life. I taught, I explored, I snorkelled – I loved it. I learnt to fish with a spear, rub fire, and eat everything from flying foxes to coconut crabs. There was almost no contact with the outside world and I had to learn to be self-sufficient. My experiences in the Solomons were indelible, and for years I used to dream about returning to that amazing place that had been my home for a while. So when the programme's editor, Steve Hocking, gave me the green light to go back, it was like a dream come true.

As the VSO volunteer at the school, I had struck up a friendship with Willie Pwaisiho, who was about my own age and one of the students. Much later we got back in touch because I heard he had joined the priesthood and, surprisingly, was working in the UK as the rector of Gawsworth, near Macclesfield. I went to see him and together we planned to make two programmes about the Solomons. By this time Willie was also a bishop in the Church of Melanesia in the Solomons.

It was necessary to visit the islands before the shoot to sort out what we were going to do. The Solomons were just coming through what could best be described as a civil war between two of the largest islands, Malaita and Guadalcanal. They were neighbours across the sea and had fought each other for centuries.

Back in 1966 I had heard about a Malaita man and a Guadalcanal man who'd had a duel in the high street of the capital, Honiara, and the weapons of choice had been bows and arrows. At the time I had thought it was a great laugh. In 2001 the weapons of choice were the AK47 and the machine gun, and it wasn't funny at all.

The Solomons have a complex past. Their roots are in tribal tradition and, subsequently, in the church. The people are very religious, and the 'Melanesian Brotherhood', a religious order, was a result of their belief. There are about six hundred brothers and novices in a total population of about a hundred thousand and they are much respected because of their devout behaviour and unstinting help to others.

I was told that if I stayed with the brothers then I would be safe because 'they' wouldn't dare shoot at them in fear of the 'wrath of the Almighty'. Much later and lying in my bed in the brothers' rest house, with only an inch of planking between me and the main street, I listened to bursts of incredibly loud machine-gun fire about three hundred metres away. My belief in God was put to the test. It was all very unnerving and not conducive to a good night's sleep. I kept wondering how many planks it would take to stop a bullet. In the morning we heard the dreadful news that the house they had raided had been empty and an innocent woman and child had been killed in the house behind.

Honiara, the capital, where I was staying, was on Guadalcanal, one of the six huge islands that make up the major land mass of the Solomons. There were hundreds of other smaller islands in the group and these were scattered over a 100,000 square miles of sea. Much had changed since I had last been there. In contrast to the blaze of colour I had seen 35 years before, the main street was rather dull. Modern buildings

(Right): Setting off from Point Cruz, Honiara

were interspersed with the vestiges of the early wooden structures with corrugated-iron roofs. Worst of all, they had cut down the avenue of beautiful flame trees that used to give some respite to the hot sun. I was told it was to provide extra parking spaces. What madness! Fifty years of charm and shade had been destroyed in one go.

Surrounding the main street were suburbs of small wooden and corrugated-iron buildings that sprawled in every direction, and that was where the violence had taken place.

Undaunted, I continued with my recce. It was a fine day and the sea was flat and calm. It was a perfect day for exploring the nearest islands, clearly visible on the horizon. I set off with two of the brothers in a fibreglass canoe at 30 knots to cross twenty-odd miles of ocean. We headed for Tulagi on Gela, where the old capital used to be, skimming effortlessly over deep blue water. It was so all deceptively easy. We cruised around the island group, partly looking for things to film and partly sightseeing.

The hours ticked by very happily and it suddenly occurred to me that it must be time to go back.

It was four o'clock and there were a few clouds, and one on the horizon was ominously very black. The senior brother pointed it out and suggested tactfully that we should go back the following day and avoid the storm. I did not relish a night without a mosquito net, lying on a hard wooden veranda, so, on the spur of the moment, I suggested that if we went for it we should get back before the bad weather reached us. The brothers were too polite to disagree.

So we raced, throttle wide open, for 10 to 15 miles. And then the storm hit us like a sledgehammer. Waves broke all around and above us

and the rain was so fierce we couldn't see for more than 25 to 30 yards in any direction. The brothers navigated by the roll of the waves and a lifetime of experience; at least I hoped that was what they were doing. Rainwater built up in the bottom of the canoe so fast I took my hat off and started bailing. Lightning hit the wave tops with massive thunderclaps. Just as frighteningly, every time it happened, the outboard motor missed a beat.

And then the motor stopped altogether. The crew looked very concerned.

'Big problem, Alex.'

The senior brother looked worried. The fuel line had a blockage or something and they furiously started to fix it. The canoe was rolling dangerously and shipping water from the waves. My Melanesian friends had gone from jet black to a shade of grey. Then it dawned on me that we were drifting at speed down the length of Guadalcanal towards the open Pacific. The water was brown and angry as it boiled with white waves. I had heard that sharks sometimes came to the surface in a storm because they got disorientated in the poor visibility. I wondered if any had spotted our drifting craft.

I stopped bailing, thinking that by tomorrow we might need the rainwater to drink. There would be absolutely no hope of a rescue. I could imagine our desiccated bodies being discovered by the crew of a passing Japanese freighter in many months' time.

All in all it was a grim 20 minutes and my imagination worked on all the uncomfortable possibilities. I had plenty of time to reconsider their sensible offer of a nice safe wooden floor back on dry land. I wondered if they blamed me.

I anxiously watched them work on the repairs and debated if I should lend a hand. I had a huge urge to do something to save my life. To my eternal relief, the brothers got the outboard restarted. As they looked up I saw them calm down. I turned and saw the lights of the Point Cruz Yacht Club in Honiara, much further away and off to one side than they had been. They were a beacon of hope in the deepening gloom.

Half an hour at full speed and we hit the yacht club beach. I stepped ashore. Ten minutes later the heavens opened and it poured with torrential rain until daybreak. And then all the lights went out and the whole town was plunged into darkness. I walked off the beach clutching my lifejacket. I felt sick. Without the lights we wouldn't have stood a chance.

The rest of the recce was much less hazardous yet no less demanding. Everything had to be meticulously arranged for the shoot and I made contact with some of my old pupils, including Sir Ellison Pogo, recently appointed as the Archbishop of Melanesia. He helped me to set up the means to take Willie on a journey back to his village.

Sir Ellison and I also discussed a second programme about why the Solomons are known as the 'Happy Isles', the first in a genre of 'the meaning of life' that now seems to be catching on. Even though it wasn't a classic *Blue Peter* subject, it was one that was dear to my heart.

As with all trips to the back of beyond, you have to have people on the ground to arrange it for you. I was very fortunate to have so many old friends to call on. Even so, it took longer than I expected to arrange because the fighting flared up again. A year would pass before the violence subsided enough for the Solomons to be safe to visit once more.

24 August–12 September 2002
Honiara airport, Solomons

The islanders were fond of welcomes and the moment we stepped off the plane we were surrounded by dancers in traditional dress. The next day, when we met the brothers, it was a greeting of a very different kind. We were ambushed by spear- and club-waving warriors and Willie revelled in the impact it had on our presenter, Simon Thomas.

Simon is a devout Christian and perhaps more used to Western ways, so the apparent screaming hatred that filled the faces of the 'warrior welcome' was the last thing he'd expected.

Finally, when the brothers thought they had extracted as much

(Right): The traditional noisy warrior welcome to the Solomon Islands (taken by Simon Thomas)

fear as they could, they reverted to type and were all smiles. We joined a bamboo pipe band for the walk into Tabalia, where they were based.

The evening before we set off on the voyage back to Willie's village, our boat, the *Kopuria*, had berthed against the jetty in the harbour at Honiara. Unknown to me, as soon as it had moored, about a hundred people promptly camped on board to grab any chance to get a free trip home. None of the hopeful passengers actually knew where we were going; they just knew we were likely to be going somewhere nearer to where they wanted to be. Unfortunately, the ship was so crowded you could hardly move. And our party and the crew would be about another fifty so there was no choice. After a lot of explanation and apologies from my contact in the brotherhood, they left. The boat then moved away from the jetty and stayed anchored offshore until we were ready to load up the following day.

Our first stop was Savo Island, which was everything that Honiara wasn't. It was quiet, clean and peaceful, and we landed on a dirty yellow sand beach very close to our first port of call, the megapode fields.

Megapodes are Melanesian scrub fowl, large birds that lay their eggs deep in the hot sand to incubate. Being volcanic, the sand is hotter than normal and, even though they were extremely shy creatures, the birds always came back to the same place, time and again, to lay their eggs. Not surprisingly, ten years after our visit the location has become something of a treat for bird watchers from all over the world. For us, the tantalising prospect of eggs twice as large as chickens' eggs and twice as tasty was far more appealing.

For Simon it was an unforgettable experience for other reasons:

> I have filmed in some very hot places in my time on *Blue Peter* but the heat that morning digging for megapode eggs on Savo Island was something else. Alex had turned into a human shower and I had so much sweat pouring into my eyes that I could barely keep them open. It was one of those moments where you have to quietly remind yourself this is your dream job!

So the first hour was a real trial. The sun was so bright I could not think straight. With the help of the local farmer we dug up a number of eggs and took them to an open space under a large tree. In the relatively cool shade and surrounded by curious villagers, we prepared eggs 'à la bamboo' over an open fire.

It was a very simple dish. A section of green bamboo was cut so that one end was blocked by the join, and the other cut below the next join so that it was like an open container. Eggs were cracked and poured into the bamboo and then the open end was sealed with a twist of leaves. The bamboo segment was then covered by hot embers in the fire and the whole left to cook. After about ten minutes the bamboo was split open and the contents were ready to eat. The eggs had a wonderful smoky-cum-woody flavour and Simon's surprise and greediness caused much merriment.

(Above): Our home for the next ten days, the inter-island trading vessel the *Kopuria*

(Right): Willie Pwaisiho conducts evensong for the brothers on board the *Kopuria*

(Above): Bishop Willie Pwaisiho stands on the domed football pitch, which was perfectly flat when it was built. Now volcanic forces push up from below

The Solomons are on a geological fault and earthquakes are common. At Taroniara School I had been shown a football pitch that 10 years before had been perfectly flat. It now had a dome shape, with the centre of the pitch at the highest point about a metre higher than the edges. The headmaster explained it was the work of the Almighty and was a good sign. I wished that I could have agreed with him.

We cruised in the late afternoon sun across to Gela and entered the Sandfly Passage as the sun began to set. We motored through small hillock-type islands in a half-mile-wide channel. Groups of small thatched houses framed with tall palms faced on to white sand beaches. Willie held evensong for the brothers and novices and they sang in four-part harmony at the tops of their voices, almost drowning out the steady rhythm of the diesel engines. The last rays of the sun glinted on our wash as the islands and distant villages slipped astern.

Over the next few days we filmed the Solomons' last pagan priest on Laulasi Island, and he talked about his beliefs. We ventured into a corner of the island that was eerily scattered with human bones that were green with algae. Empty eye sockets in skulls sitting on piles of rocks were witness to our visit. Willie interpreted as Simon asked question after question, trying to understand what made the priest tick. He explained to Simon how his ancestors would come to him in the form of sharks and other creatures, even though their remains lay all around where they stood. The priest was sincere and this bothered Simon; he could not see how any normal person could indulge in what he saw as 'devil worship'. He later confided to me that it was the most extraordinary moment of his *Blue Peter* career:

(Left): Simon Thomas with a human skull from a pagan shrine on Laulasi island, Langa Langa lagoon

To walk into that wooded corner of the island and see bones and skulls scattered everywhere is an image I'll never forget. I had to keep reminding myself these weren't fake bones and skulls, they were the remains of this priest's ancestors. Bizarre as it sounds, the more we talked to him the more normal it felt and so I eventually asked Bishop Willie to ask him if I could have a picture with one of his ancestors. He said yes and the picture I have at home of me holding the skull of one of his ancestors is easily the most surreal photo I have.

We cruised down the length of the Langa Langa lagoon in South Malaita. The sun shone and there was a cool breeze and the villages of leaf houses were so close at times I felt I could almost touch them. We coasted majestically past tiny shipyards where similar vessels to ours were taking shape using building methods from the 19th century. Children in dugout canoes waved as we passed. Tiny artificial islands built by hand with lumps of coral rock from the reef slipped by, some with only a hut or two for their inhabitants. The people looked happy and I believed they were. And their happiness was infectious. I thrilled to the joy of the moment and, with nothing to worry about until our next port of call, I marvelled at the beauty of it all. Sadly, in less than four hours we had to leave the still-clear-blue waters of that little piece of heaven and head out back into the uncertain waters of the Coral Sea.

The *Kopuria* was built for inter-island travel and she took the waves with ease. In the stern, where our cabins were, they crashed across the deck, leaving traces of seaweed that caught on splinters in the wooden deck.

We anchored after dark off Fanalei village at Port Adam, where Willie's wife Kate had been born and had spent her childhood. I knew one or two of the inhabitants, including Walter Doraadi from my VSO days, and I wondered if he would remember me. Early the next morning I went ashore to film general views of the boat and the village. I saw Walter hiding in a doorway. He looked at me in a suspicious way and was far from pleased, as if resenting our intrusion. He had not recognised me and I decided to let time heal the effect of our sudden appearance and approach him later. I remembered him as an intelligent, good-looking boy who was always well turned out. Thirty-six years later he was a wild-looking man who looked as if he had never been to school. He had once worked as a nurse and was now the village's finest fisherman and could always find fish while others starved. He could dive to incredible depths and was a legend in the islands. Towards the end of our brief visit he began to look at me with renewed interest, and I believe he did recognise me, yet he maintained his distance.

We visited another community. Walande was built on an artificial island made from rocks piled together in the Port Adam Lagoon. We were privileged to be allowed to call because visitors were strictly by invitation only. The island was under threat from climate change and rising sea levels.

I had visited Walande before, in 1966, and I remembered that none of the houses had been on stilts, and now, 36 years later, they were. The people were originally from Papua New Guinea, then the Lau lagoon, and they had migrated south, building artificial islands, like this one, in the shallow water. As immigrants they had no legal right to live on the mainland and the locals were not welcoming. At the time it hadn't mattered to them because if they built their own islands away from the mainland, there would be fewer mosquitoes, so less chance of dying of malaria. In 1966 the highest tides were two to three feet below the islands' surface.

We had the most magical welcome. Giant war canoes, and paddlers sitting side by side dipped their paddles and screamed in unison as they drove their canoes through the still waters of the lagoon. Nearer the island

(Right): The people of Walande greet us in giant canoes

we joined them, and Simon and Bishop Willie were once more treated to a warrior welcome and a 20-strong bamboo band. This time Simon knew what to expect.

We witnessed a thriving community at work and play and Simon helped build up a section of the island that was susceptible to being flooded at high tide. As I filmed, men, women and children unloaded dugout canoes stacked to the gunwales with volcanic rocks from the lagoon. It seemed so little effort against so mighty an adversary. It had taken centuries to create the island, and climate change was happening in decades.

Walande was remote, beautiful and intriguing. Willie held Holy Communion to a packed congregation and ten minutes into the service half a dozen dancers traditionally dressed in frond skirts and headdresses approached up the centre aisle. They waved dancing sticks, rhythmically stamped their feet and chanted the traditional religious responses. It was raw, magical, and went to the core of belief. The hairs on the back of my neck prickled with the excitement. Human spirits from both cultures bonded with the joy of being alive.

It was so sad to know that this charming, unique, community would not survive for much longer. All the artificial islands in the Pacific are under threat from climate change and until we are likewise affected I do not suppose very much will be done about it. We left

(Left): Building up the sea defences on Walande island

(Top right): Alex and sound recordist Colin Bowes film a bride-price ceremony on Walande

Walande knowing that they were fighting a losing battle and indeed, in March 2009, Walande was finally abandoned as the rising sea levels made life there untenable. It was very sad news indeed.

The next day we achieved the aim of the first programme when we walked the last few miles on foot to Willie's village at Kalona. Bishop William Pwaisiho the village chief was home at last.

The celebrations were long and grand. Willie was the most senior chief of six other villages and a huge feast was held in his honour. Preparations went on all day as coconuts were grated clean and all

(Bottom right): Simon Thomas helps with the preparations for the feast at Kalona village

kinds of vegetable peeled and washed. Cooking fires were prepared and allowed to burn down to glowing embers before the dishes were steamed over them in leaf parcels.

The following day the sound of a conch announced that families from the other villages had arrived. It was a long procession in which large circular casava 'puddings' were carried, balanced on backs and supported by headbands. At the head of the procession a raft of timbers was carried on the shoulders of the fittest and a spear-waving warrior stood lookout. A single voice sang a song of welcome and at the end of each line there was a thunderclap of noise as everyone joined in. The procession wound its way into the centre of the community.

Ceremonial dancing entertained the watchers as people and food divided into family groups which, surprisingly, then separated into mini-picnics that took place at the far corners of the village. I had wondered about the islanders' unsociability at mealtimes before, in the 1960s, when I had noticed that they always ate in a circle facing outwards. The reason was simple. Before Christianity had come to the islands, the infamous head-hunting parties would strike when their enemies were least prepared, such as when they were eating. Keeping a good lookout was all part of staying alive.

Celebrations over, we could relax and enjoy being part of the community. I asked Willie to show us what life had been like for him

(Left): Villagers bringing large circular green parcels containing cassava puddings to the feast

growing up at Kalona. He began with how he was brought into the world.

Willie's mum was very elderly and during a quiet moment he asked her to show us where he was born. The old lady indicated the bush and down a steep slope.

'She says that I was born over there under a bush.' Then he added, 'She went into the bush with a friend and she cut my cord with a bamboo slit.'

It was the sort of information that is very hard to forget.

All but a couple of buildings were made of sago palm leaf, and inside a modest building that was built exactly on the same spot as his house had been, Willie reminisced about his childhood. At six he had been able to run about bare skinned and carefree and sleep on the earthen floor close to the fire in the centre of the building. There was, and still is, no electricity, and when he was young all fresh water had come from the stream at the bottom of the hill. And there had been no knives and forks, of course, but coconut shells fashioned into food scoops. A giant carved blackened wooden bowl would be used to contain all the food for the family meal. Everyone would dip in to eat their fill.

Everywhere we went little faces peeped out from open doorways and from behind coconut palms. There was innocence and curiosity in equal measure.

On a hillside a short walk from the centre of the village, Willie showed us the spot where he intended to build his house when he retired from the church. It was a beautiful site and it was not hard to imagine the thatch and wide veranda that he had planned in his mind. I asked him when he thought this might be possible and he replied, as all Solomon Islanders do, with optimism. Unfortunately, since the filming, his wife Kate has developed kidney problems, and without dialysis machines the dream of being able to gaze down at his domain and benefit from the cool evening breeze will remain just a dream.

We thought we were on the edge of the civilised world. Simon was amazed to hear that some youngsters had never seen a white person before, so it was with almost comical disbelief that the youngsters surprised him with a question about what they liked to do best.

'Football,' was the universal reply.

'What is your favourite team?'

'Man U,' came the reply.

'Who's the best player?' he asked, thinking to stump them.

'David Beckham!' they chorused.

The time came for us to leave and we set off early because it was an important day for me. Amid much waving and whooping we steamed out of the lagoon and crashed into the ocean rollers again, heading east into the Pacific.

We motored across a 100 miles of sea to Pamua on San Cristobal, another of the large islands that make up the Solomons. And en route we were going to call in at my old school where I had taught 36 years before.

Alangaula School, on Ugi Island, was the place that had filled my dreams for so many years. I had often dreamt about going back and, with the passage of time, Ugi had become, in my mind, an idyllic place that had contributed in no small way to the person I now was. It was where I had learnt how to treasure nature and also how to deal with solitude.

Four hours later, as we motored into Selwyn Bay, I searched for the white sand beach that was a feature of the school. It wasn't there. We dropped anchor, guessing at a safe spot since there were no familiar landmarks. Going ashore, there was a small gap in the vegetation that went down to the water's edge and we went through it. The school, with its neat coral paths and miniature hedges that had been so carefully trimmed, had been overwhelmed by the rainforest. There was no sign of the classrooms. The only building left standing was the school chapel, its corrugated-iron roof curled up at the edges and planks of timber cladding had slipped where nails had rusted through. It was a very sad sight.

Almost covered by vegetation, the large circular water tanks that had been built out of concrete remained like monoliths of an ancient civilisation, covered in a layer of green algae. They gave us a datum to work out where everything else had once been. There was something very familiar about the giant spider-like trees that grew randomly in one part. After a while I realised what it was – 36 years ago they had been two-foot-high ornamental bushes contained in flowerbeds. Over time nature had flexed its muscles in a spectacular way and they now towered above us. Alangaula now belonged to nature, and not to us.

Willie and I were crushed. There could be no nostalgic memories because of the devastation. I remembered, too late, that several years previously I had been told not to go back. I didn't regret it because it was something I had to do. And only *Blue Peter* would have enabled me to combine such a nostalgic pilgrimage with my career.

Venturing down the path to the neighbouring village of Hakanapua, we came to a coconut log bridge over the stream at the entrance to the village. In triumph we saw it was exactly as we remembered, although the logs must have been replaced more than once.

I thought of one last chance to rediscover the past. I had spent many hours swimming over the coral reef and I tried one last dive. I retraced one of my favourite routes through the coral and was amazed to find that absolutely nothing had changed. The coral was unspoilt and the huge brain corals were still there. Even the odd puffer fish appeared in exactly the same place as they used to. It was exciting and emotional. I could have been back in 1966 and my dream of revisiting the island, which had been shattered for a while, was once more everything I could have hoped for. I clambered back on board the *Kopuria* with peace in my soul, and I have never dreamed of Ugi since. As we steamed out of Selwyn Bay I watched my island, so important to my early understanding of life, fade into the horizon.

The Solomons had changed so much since my teenage days as a VSO volunteer school teacher and the present caught up with us.

Towards the end of the filming we heard that a local priest, about twenty miles from a Guadalcanal village we planned to visit, had been beheaded. Some temporary unrest in the islands had flared up and there was general disquiet that was shared by Bishop Willie. He advised, wisely, that we should avoid the region.

The tantalising story we had planned to film about the Moro Movement, who rejected Western influences and lived virtually naked as if in the Stone Age (and featured by Sir David Attenborough in the series *Tribal Eye*), had to change. To this day it is one of my great regrets. Yet the risk was just too great. Twenty miles wasn't far for a terrorist and we were a juicy target.

So our journey came to a disappointing end, even if the journey itself was a true voyage of discovery in the best traditions of the programme. It was another example of how the presenters experience more in their four years or so than most of us do in a lifetime. Both Solomons programmes were the result of meeting interesting people and remembering places I had visited. And in the television business the more you meet people and the more places you go to, the more ideas you have.

I took an unexpected and unpleasant souvenir back with me, courtesy of the pork I had eaten during our feast in Willie's village. About a year later I was in America to film Simon's comeback at freefall parachuting, and I was having what are best described as unexpected and explosive bowel movements. It was a week later back home in the UK that the uninvited guest finally reared its ugly head in the form of a foot-long tapeworm. The doctor said it was a very fine specimen and gave me some pills to get rid of its offspring.

(Right): Alex and Bishop Willie Pwaisiho on the coconut-log bridge to Hakanapua village, unchanged after 36 years

28

Blue Peter's very own right stuff

23–24 May 2000
Derbyshire

Every so often something happened on location that was so dangerous it would leave my heart pounding, my mouth dry and my mind racing to think up excuses in case disaster struck. Presenter Matt Baker gave me one of those moments. He reminded me of John Noakes because he sounded like him. And he was just as fearless.

It all began when I suggested he make an attempt at the world height record for a dual hang-glider.

Matt was unnervingly good at everything. He was a quick learner and his co-ordination was instinctive. Not surprising perhaps, considering his background as a junior gymnast. He recalls:

> One of the first things I learnt from Alex was to do something while I was chatting and this made me feel less exposed. It was the key to what became my presenting style. I would throw myself into a situation so I could react to how it felt.

Judy Leden and Chris Dawes were the world's leading hang-gliding experts. Judy was factual, focused and a very good communicator. With luxuriant black hair she looked younger than her age, and over the years she never looked any older. Her husband and business partner, Chris Dawes, was curly haired, had a gleam in his eye and watched over her daredevil exploits with concern. He shared her zest for taking on any challenge that life threw at them.

I had first filmed with Judy for the series *Duncan Dares* (1987) so I knew she was a safe, reliable pair of hands. Whenever the subject of hang-gliding came up, she and Chris came to mind. And they still do. They are a 'can-do' couple and a joy to work with.

I thought that if Matt learnt to fly a hang-glider solo it would

(Top left): Filming the ceremonial dancing

(Bottom left): The Brothers wave goodbye. For them life is a constant celebration

(Top left): Chris Dawes, Judy Leden and Matt Baker waiting for a gap in the clouds

(Bottom left): A final interview before the hang-glider record attempt. Matt's dog, Meg, sneaks into shot, bottom left

increase the jeopardy of the challenge and give him more of a role. Judy would be in control of the dual hang-glider for the height record and Matt could take over on occasions to give her a rest. Judy agreed and, needless to say, Matt was all for it.

We began lessons in a field near where Judy and Chris lived in Derbyshire. Chris went through the basics with Matt and saw that he was a fast learner. After only two days Matt could control a short flight with Chris and Judy running along beside him using long lines attached to each wing tip to stop him from crashing.

14–18 June 2000
Derbyshire

A couple of weeks later we continued with the lessons at Darley Moor airfield near Asbourne. The weather was glorious and there was a slight breeze.

Instead of running with the hang-glider to get lift, there was a winch that could drag Matt into the air for longer flights. We spent the first day going back over what he had already learnt and launched him for some short 'hops'. Then, on the following day, only the fourth full day of instruction, Matt progressed to longer flights. The aim was to go up to 100 feet in altitude. It was hot yet not uncomfortably so under the cloudless, powder-blue sky. Chris continued to be impressed with Matt's progress. In the afternoon it was obvious that he was ready for the next stage – to fly at up to 300 feet. Chris told Matt to let him know when he wanted to give it a try. For this important step, it was crucial for Matt to have the final say when he felt confident.

After three or four more flights at the lower height, Matt was nevertheless pensive. We recorded his concerns, with Matt talking to camera. His decision was to give it a go. He and Chris seemed to understand one another and I had the utmost confidence in Chris. Matt recalls, 'I remember feeling massively responsible for the decision because the film couldn't go any further unless I was prepared to push myself.'

We set up for what I thought would be the first of several more flights. I left the film crew to cover the take-off while I set up my camera at the other end of the field to capture the moment he got airborne. I noticed that the wind had freshened but thought no more about it. Matt got into the harness and picked up the hang-glider. He was ready to take off but recalls doubts:

> I had a really odd relationship with hang-gliding because I felt I really shouldn't be there. It felt so wrong to be hanging there in the air without a motor. Unnatural and unsettling to be in a bird's world, I was really afraid of the consequences – especially when you are the only one in control.

The winch whirred into action and Matt ran forward as it tugged at him. In seconds he was airborne and I could hear the high-pitched whine of the winch as it pulled him into a steep ascent. I filmed as 300 feet became 400 and then 500. To my horror, Matt was disappearing into the deep blue sky and it was hard to keep him in shot. He was at a chilling 800 feet before he eventually released the tow line. And then he was flying solo. My mouth was dry with fright. If he lost his nerve at that height, the consequences did not bear thinking about. I couldn't hear what was being said, which was probably just as well. It was much later that I listened to Matt's commentary and Chris' instruction.

'Very nice, Matt. Now turn right.'

Matt was high on adrenalin and turned left.

'Never mind, we can do a figure of eight,' Chris calmly reassured Matt as he turned somewhere high above me.

'Turn left, Matt, turn left.' Chris' voice again was measured and controlled, as if Matt's flight was the most ordinary thing in the world.

I noticed that the wind was still increasing. Matt continued to talk to camera, telling us how he felt. 'Bit bumpy but it's wonderful up here,' he enthused. He was confident and enjoying himself:

> Even though Alex thought he could hear both of us clearly, Chris was breaking up badly and I only got every other word.

'Turn left, Matt, turn left,' repeated Chris calmly, if with a little more sense of urgency.

Matt continued to turn and Chris told him to turn right to bring him back over the airfield. By this time Matt was at 500 feet or lower and it was time to set up for a landing. Matt, like the true professional broadcaster, continued to give a running commentary.

'Stop talking, Matt, and turn right,' came the instruction from Chris, by now with an edge of anxiety in his voice.

The wind was noticeably stronger. 'Turn right, Matt, turn right.' And then almost immediately, 'Turn left, Matt, turn left.'

Matt was now getting quite low and because of the wind he had strayed to the edge of the airfield, where there was a high barbed-wire fence looming into view.

'Turn left, Matt, turn left. I said turn left, Matt.'

Chris' voice was now filled with concern because Matt was still not over the airfield:

> By this time I couldn't hear a word of what Chris said and I was drifting towards the main road.

Chris was now pleading with Matt, albeit with measured authority, 'Turn left, Matt. Turn left.'

Chris would never shout yet there was no mistaking his anxiety. Matt hauled manfully on the A-frame, shifting his body to the left to bank the hang-glider to the left. Momentarily he crossed back over the fence to the field and I could sense Chris' relief. Matt turned into wind to land and crossed back over the fence again. Chris had seconds to turn a dodgy situation into a safe landing.

'Prepare to land, Matt.'

Matt pulled himself out of his bag and I saw his feet appear. I was transfixed. From where I was filming it looked as if he was going to land directly on the barbed wire. 'Get ready to push, Matt,' came the final approach instruction from Chris, while I followed the final few seconds glued to the viewfinder, hands shaking from fright.

(Right): Judy Leden and Matt Baker training over Derbyshire

Matt didn't land on the wire, just parallel to it and about twenty feet or so away and on the other side of the fence. As he touched down he plunged head first into a large bush. Luckily for him, the nose of the hang-glider hit the bush first and he stopped short of the branches. He had narrowly escaped being skewered. The radio crackled into life. 'A whole field to land in and he has to land in a tree.' I could hear the relief in Chris' voice. That was the last flight we did that day.

You would think Matt would have been shocked yet he wasn't. He was much more concerned that he had let Chris down and he took pains to apologise. His appetite for the record-breaking challenge with Judy had been well and truly whetted. I just remember Matt's girlfriend, Nicola, who, unusually for a *Blue Peter* partner, had been able to keep him company. Her sense of angst was palpable. She stood as if in a trauma, white-faced. She looked as bad as I felt.

By comparison the actual height record proved a doddle. Chris flew a microlight and towed Matt and Judy in the dual hang-glider to a height of 11,500 feet before they released to set a new world record for *The Guiness Book of Records*. Matt described the record as 'pretty cool' and one of the highlights of his *Blue Peter* career.

2–13 July 2001
North Vietnam

It was decided that the summer expedition, the highlight of the *Blue Peter* calendar, would be to Vietnam. The films producer, Kez Margrie, who had more faith in my camera ability than I deserved, was in charge of the project. To save money she needed to complete the filming in half the usual time and she asked me to go as a second director/cameraman. I was to produce and shoot a short film about monkey conservation and a programme about the hill people who lived in the north of the country, about two miles from the Chinese border. I asked Colin Bowes to join me on sound because he enjoyed camping, and where we were going there was going to be quite a lot of that.

Our fixer was a cheerful Vietnamese called Chuck, and he turned out to be ex-Vietcong. I have often wondered what the Vietcong really thought of the Vietnam War and Chuck let slip he was a veteran of the Tet Offensive. Tet was considered one of the major turning points of the Vietnam crisis when North Vietnam troops launched a ferocious attack on the South, taking the Americans by surprise.

As I got to know him better, I posed some questions.

'How did you live in the bush?'

'Did you kill any American soldiers?'

Chuck always replied guardedly, as if he did not know how to answer without giving offence. I persisted, explaining that I was curious to learn what really happened.

'What do you think of the Americans now?' I asked casually one lunchtime in Hanoi. Chuck had his back to me and he did not turn immediately. When he did, his mouth smiled but his eyes did not.

'Period of reconciliation' was the limit of his response. He refused to be drawn further. What he did admit was that he could not understand why the Americans had given up after the Tet Offensive.

'We had no one left to fight. They could have won,' he announced.

We boarded the train in Hanoi for Sa Pa, which was the furthest you could go by train without crossing into China. After a blazing row between the guard and some passengers (which I filmed with interest but remained none the wiser about), the train lurched off northwards. The presenter was Liz Barker – slender, mischievous, and, I thought, an amazing actress.

It was a wonderful journey. The coach was jam-packed with young and old alike. A rich cocktail with wizened old men who feigned sleep, their long drooping moustaches sometimes just appearing under their large circular straw hats. Young children peered at us as Liz did several speeches to camera about what it was like. Ladies carrying huge trays of snacks – everything from bread rolls to pots of tea – slalomed their way down the central aisle, tempting us to buy. We found a young lady who was selling ice creams from a basket and Liz explained to camera that

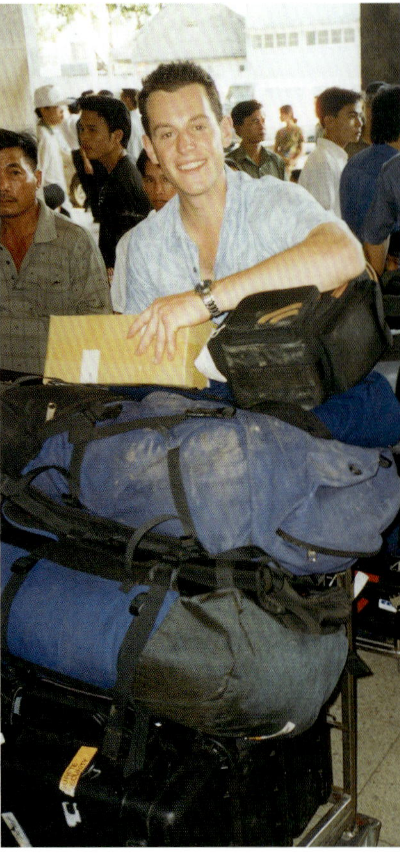

(Above): Matt Baker laden with luggage at Hanoi airport

the ice creams didn't melt because they were swathed in layers of cloth to keep them cool. Incredibly, the system worked.

All the carriage windows were covered in strong wire netting and I wondered why. 'Regret that some people throw stones at the train so wire mesh for safety,' Chuck informed me.

At lunchtime we moved to the restaurant car, which had a fully fledged kitchen. Not a microwave in sight. It was decked out with wooden chairs and tables at which we dined on hot spicy soup with noodles. Everything was cooked over wood-fired stoves in full view of the passengers. An entire meal cost us less than fifty pence each.

With Chuck's help I managed to get a ride in the engine cab. The train barely exceeded 40 mph and we trundled along happily, mesmerised by the sleepers as they flickered beneath us. Much later, with the sun past its hottest, I paused to get shots where the carriages were linked together and where there was no mesh over the windows to spoil the view. A guard saw what I was doing and offered me a drink. It turned out to be rice whisky and very strong, and I sat down with him. We polished off several glasses in peaceful companionship. I was quite mellow when at last we drew into Sa Pa at the end of the line.

From Sa Pa we drove to the banks of the Yellow River because I wanted a glimpse of the Chinese border. My mother had been brought up in Peking (now Beijing) in the 1930s, and I had harboured an interest in going to China one day. I would have to wait a further four years for my wish to be granted. Meanwhile, the sight of the border and the giant Chinese writing and banners fluttering in the wind had to do.

We drove up into the hills and wound our way up steep tracks to leave the plains far behind. That night we stayed in a very smart hotel, the last bit of civilisation we would experience for over a week.

The next morning we bought provisions at the local market and set off again. Our destination was about half a day's walk off the main road and Chuck had arranged for porters to help us carry our equipment. One young man really earned his money, carrying a heavy generator and a can of fuel on a pole across his shoulders. When at last we arrived he was near collapse. I like to think that Chuck rewarded him proportionately for his efforts yet I doubt it. I could do nothing. We were under strict instructions not to part with money because it would create a precedent that others might not be able to afford. Chuck was adamant that all payment should go through him and I did not feel comfortable about it even though it was the right thing to do.

As we entered the village I thought Liz looked visibly shaken by the primitive surroundings. Not even the children who gathered around her, playing with her hair comb, could raise her spirits. They were dressed in traditional clothes, colourful reds, greens and orange on black. She must have felt a million miles from home and looked anxious about this strange and alien environment. I tried to reassure her that in a day or two she would think it all perfectly normal, yet I fear I was no help at all.

The village nestled between steep hills covered with thick tropical rainforest and I had been told that there was plenty of space to pitch camp.

I noticed that all the buildings were on two-foot-high rock platforms. The ground was rock hard and smooth, which meant only one thing. When it rained, as it surely did, the water ran off straight through the village and took all before it. It was not a good place to pitch a tent. Colin had an idea. He had been chatting to the children (through Chuck) and had found out that it was the school holidays. That could only mean one thing – the classroom would not be in use. We could pitch our tents inside the classroom and stay dry if it rained.

Liz, who I sensed was close to tears, was not going to share our accommodation. She was going to sleep in the chief's bed while the chief was away. We filmed her misgivings as she settled in and prepared for the night. She was closely watched by a dozen children.

Later that night all the men in the village gathered in the chief's hut with her because that was where they always met in the evenings. They chatted, watched a black and white television, and smoked home-grown tobacco around the fire at the foot of her bed. She assured us, after a day or two, that she enjoyed their company.

Nothing in the village was secret, and because the classroom did not have solid walls we were all under constant surveillance. It had been built more with ventilation than privacy in mind, and we had many admirers who observed us through the gaps in the bamboo as we went about our business.

Worse still, there was no loo. The first night I needed to get up and find a bush. As I left the building in the cover of darkness, hoping for a rare private moment, every dog in the village started to bark.

The village was a strange mixture of the primitive and the innovative. We never did discover where the villagers went to the lavatory, but we did discover a series of rice mills that were driven by water. These were giant see-saws with the hammer bit on one end and a scooped bit, for the water, on the other. When the water filled the scoop, the weight

(Top left): Camera-shy children play under a table

(Top right): Like most villages here, they are built around running water

lifted up the hammer. As it did so, it changed the angle of the scoop and caused the water to spill out, making it lighter and allowing the hammer to crash back onto the rice. There must have been half a dozen of these machines and while the water flowed they continued to pound rice 24 hours a day.

There were small electrical generators too. Several were old and battered and all had been salvaged from cars and lorries. They were mounted vertically above the tiny streams and the rushing water spun a paddle wheel attached to each and generated the electricity. Bare wires then carried the power to light up homes. On one or two occasions I caught my hat on these overhead wires. There was a violent crackling and sparks would fly in all directions. Incredibly, there was still enough energy to light a bulb in every home and make the black and white television work in the chief's hut.

On the third day it rained and we awoke to a deluge. Water poured off the thatch into huge puddles. The morning light was grey, with the spray bouncing off the roofs. We watched from our secure and dry classroom refuge, thinking of what might have been.

Liz joined in village life, helping a local girl, Li, feed the pigs, dig the gardens and gather crops and firewood. She learnt a local dance and taught the children how to sing 'London Bridge is Falling Down', with all the actions. She even managed to persuade one of the women to take off her ornate hairpiece, which was secured by a single silver spike. Liz tried it on, much to everyone's amusement.

On the last full day she helped Li prepare a celebration dinner and that night we all sang and ate, and drank far too much rice whisky. I rendered my party piece, 'Where be yon blackbird to.'

The chief, who had returned, sang a beautiful song that put my crude efforts to shame. At midnight we staggered off into the night and stumbled into the stream that ran through the middle of the village. Squelching, we eventually found our sleeping bags.

The next morning we packed and said our goodbyes. Liz had grown quite fond of the chief's mother, who had fussed over her for the past week, and there were more tears as we left.

In the end Liz had coped well with a very challenging week. However, I thought she had missed the company of a female friend and confidante, and it had put a strain on her.

Yet she always delivered and often in spectacular style. She had a real talent as an actress and in the Christmas bonanzas *Christmas at the Club Blue Peter* and *Totally Blue Peter* she was a dazzling star showing talent that I thought she could have taken further.

In Vietnam, and a long way out of her comfort zone, it was obvious to us that she also missed her family and friends.

When Liz left *Blue Peter* in 2006, she looked back with huge affection. '*Blue Peter* is brilliant but it leaves no room for anything else and there's loads more I'd still love to achieve.'

(Above): Liz Barker puts her chopstick skills to good use during a farewell feast

(Left): Konnie and Liz on the long flight home

29

Dogged determination

I have been asked numerous times, 'What did Biddy do when she was short of an item?'

My answer is always the same. 'She would give the dog a bath.'

John Noakes and Shep were the most famous dog/man duo in the history of television. John's cry of 'Get down, Shep' became the title of a song by the Wurzels, an unlikely but charming farming band from Somerset whose novelty hit 'Combine Harvester' made the number-one spot in the sweltering summer of 1976. John used to have prolonged conversations with Shep in the series *Go With Noakes.*

It was hardly surprising that the programme's pets become the viewers' pets.

I have seen a great deal of Britain as a result of making dozens of guide-dog training films (Prince, Honey and Magic) and pet-dog walking films (Goldie and Meg). They are easy films to make yet difficult to make well. Some directors saw making such films as a chore. I never did because they attracted viewers. Occasionally what happened could become the stuff of legend.

19 April 2002
London

Meg was a Border collie and Matt Baker's dog. She was similar to Shep in the way that Matt himself was similar to John Noakes. Being young she was lively and unpredictable and I was tasked with making a film about her getting out and about in London.

It was a bit like a guided tour of London from the dog's point of view. But there was a snag. Meg, being a puppy, did not have an inexhaustible amount of energy, so we would not have a full day's filming.

The plan was to start early in the morning in Piccadilly Circus then go by Tube to Waterloo, have a trip on the London Eye, catch a ride on an open-topped bus to Tower Bridge and then finish on a boat trip back up the Thames.

Everything went well as we began filming in Piccadilly Circus, despite a skirmish with the turnstiles in the Underground. We set up on the platform and waited for the train to arrive. Meg was alive with curiosity, having sniffed her way past piles of human vomit and dirty abandoned train tickets. For her, life couldn't get much better. The staff of the Underground knew of our intentions and saw no need to give us a guide. After all, this wasn't the first time special dispensation had been given for a *Blue Peter* dog to travel on the Tube, and this was my fourth time of filming it.

The train rumbled in and we waited for the passengers to get off. We got the shots of Meg jumping on to the train from outside the carriage, and again from the inside to see her settling down. It all went very well. The journey was brief and we did not have time to discuss how to film getting off. This was a big mistake.

The train arrived at Waterloo and we filmed Meg getting off from inside the carriage. I then had an idea. I thought it would be good to get Meg leaving the train from the outside, with me on the platform. I leapt nimbly out of the train, leaving Colin Bowes, the sound recordist, inside to get clean sound close to the action. Yet no sooner was Meg out and on to the platform than the doors closed. Colin was inside the carriage and I was outside on the platform. The train started to move yet we were still connected by the umbilical cable, which now was protruding through the carriage door. I tried frantically to disconnect it while being dragged along the platform as the train moved off. A simple film sequence had turned into a nightmare in the space of two seconds. Just when I thought I would have to let the camera go, the train stopped and the doors opened. Disaster had been averted. I was brought back from the abyss. While the rest of the team couldn't stop laughing, my heart was pounding. It took several cups of coffee to restore me.

Matt told me later:

> I loved the way we would start a story and then see where it went and follow it. Scenes would develop that neither of us could predict. Hence the unexpected cock-up in the Tube.

4 October 2006

Trafalgar Square

Four years later I volunteered to film our new guide-dog puppy, Magic, and part of her training, too, was a walk around the London metropolis. It turned out to be no less eventful. Guide-dog puppies have to be introduced to all aspects of life, like traffic, crossing busy roads, trains, taxis, buses and meeting other dogs. One of my favourite puppy encounters involved a flock of birds. The pigeons in Trafalgar Square had always been a hit with the viewers and I planned an eventful route that began with a feathery episode with what I hoped would be thousands of London pigeons. Fired with the prospect, I rang Westminster Council to get permission.

They were dismissive. I was told that Trafalgar Square was no longer the place where pigeons flocked to sit on tourists' heads. Appalled, I went down to the square to see for myself.

They were right. It was pouring with rain and there wasn't a pigeon in sight. Questioning the wardens, I found out that although they were banned from the square, Save the Trafalgar Square Pigeons were allowed to feed the survivors twice a day on the North Terrace. I went up to the terrace and spotted a few half-starved pigeons huddled in a corner. I was assured that at feeding time lots would turn up so all was not lost. I paid the filming fee to Westminster City Council, several hundred pounds for an hour or two, and kept my fingers crossed.

A week later we arrived in Trafalgar Square to discover that we had missed the early morning feeding and, horror of all horrors, there was a man with a hawk on his wrist patrolling both the square and the North Terrace. All the pigeons had disappeared and desperate measures were needed if I was to get that iconic shot of a small golden retriever puppy walking through a flock of birds.

The hawk man agreed to turn a blind eye and ignoring the public signs that told me that feeding the pigeons was expressly forbidden I produced my bag of emergency bird food. I scattered a few handfuls of the grain, hoping to entice the pigeons back. One or two flew high overhead, looking warily as though they couldn't believe their good luck. It was a full ten minutes before the first took the chance for an extra meal.

Ten minutes after that, and with ten minutes left on our filming permit, hunger overcame fear and the pigeons swooped. Magic then walked through them, straining on her lead, and I filmed her reaction as the flock took off in her path. With the shot 'in the can' I began to pack up the camera and became aware of the sound of horses' hooves nearby. Two mounted police arrived.

'We have a report of someone feeding the pigeons outside the permitted times,' came the voice from one of the saddled officers.

I decided to avoid the issue. 'Are you from Great Scotland Yard?'

'Yes,' came the reply.

'Then we are due to be with you shortly to film our guide-dog puppy meeting the horses,' I said, hoping to distract him.

'Are you *Blue Peter*?' the other enquired.

'Yes,' I replied. 'Oh, that's all right, then.' And they continued with their patrol. Such was the power of the programme. Later, Magic was a big hit with the police horses.

Magic was a lovely dog but sadly, at the tender age of six months, she developed the symptoms of epilepsy. It was with great regret that, unable to continue her training, she would be retired to see out her days with her new owner in Herefordshire.

(Above): Matthew Bottomley from Guide Dogs for the Blind and Andy Akinwolere walk Magic through a flock of pigeons in Trafalgar Square

3–6 January 2003
RAF Brize Norton

Simon Thomas was ready for a real challenge – so in the best *Blue Peter* tradition and following in the slipstream of John Noakes, Janet Ellis and Stuart Miles, it was decided that he would attempt, as Stuart had done, to take part in an RAF Falcons freefall parachute display.

The RAF Falcons were, as I had anticipated, as welcoming as ever, and I felt as if I was coming home when I arrived at RAF Brize Norton to begin the filming.

Simon completed the four-day ground training course with his instructor, Sergeant Jim Dick, and at the end of the week made his first parachute jump. It was a static-line jump from the side door of the giant C130 Hercules with 60 other students. He enjoyed the jump and we progressed to the next stage, which was freefall. I knew from experience with Janet Ellis and Stuart Miles that the only way to be certain of getting enough parachute jumps was to train in the US, where fine weather was guaranteed. So we joined the Falcons for the last week of their regular training attachment at Otay Lakes just outside San Diego.

11–26 January 2003
San Diego, Otay Lakes, California

Sky Dive San Diego was set among the hills at the north end of a large lake about forty-minutes' drive from the city centre. The coaches, Roger Huskinson and assistant Toby Goodchild, planned to take over the day-to-day instruction from Jim. As we sat out in the sun on the drop zone the afternoon of the arrival day I thought, Why don't we do a tandem jump just to get him in the mood?

On the face of it, all Simon had to do was fall out of the aircraft strapped to the instructor and enjoy himself. But he didn't.

The tandem was fun for everyone, except Simon. I detected a slight hesitation in his voice when Roger asked him if he had enjoyed himself. He said he had, but I could tell he had reservations.

The next day his ground training began in earnest and in the afternoon Simon experienced his first freefall under instruction. This time his reaction was cautious yet still optimistic. Later he explained how the challenge was affecting him, and there was no doubt that freefall parachuting was going to be more of a test than he'd first thought. Simon had a great ability to communicate his feelings and part of his great charm was telling the viewers exactly how he felt. I knew this would be a personal journey, and the viewers would be

able to share every last moment of it.

The next few jumps were unsettling for Simon and I remembered how Stuart Miles had found difficulties at the sixth or seventh jump. I wondered how Simon would cope. Anxieties were not unusual and I knew of other parachutists who had felt the same way. Beyond the seventh jump it got a little easier.

Unfortunately for Simon, jump four did not go according to plan.

The parachute did not deploy the instant he pulled the ripcord. It stayed in its bag while the drogue flapped about behind his head. For a second or two Toby and Roger punched at the bag to dislodge it. Then, suddenly, the drogue caught the wind and pulled the main canopy out as it should have done. Simon landed safely and he watched a video playback of what had happened. It did not make easy watching. I could tell that the whole incident played heavily on his mind. He remembers the moment all too well:

> The freefall only lasted 45 seconds or so, so you don't have much time to fully appreciate what's going on. All I was aware of was that, having pulled the ripcord, there didn't appear to be a parachute above my head and Toby and Roger seemed to be punching the sides of the bag. Panic set in momentarily but before I knew it the canopy was safely above my head and all was well again. To this day I wish they had never shown me the video of the jump in the debrief after we were all safely down. I looked on in horror as I watched the footage of Roger and Toby punching the bag as we fell to earth at 120 mph. Later they privately admitted they shouldn't have shown it to me, but the damage was done. My bottle had gone.

Later that day we had a meeting about how to boost Simon's confidence and it was decided to send him with a small party to the freefall simulator – a vertical wind tunnel – in Las Vegas, to give him some experience of lying on the airflow without the fear of height. It was a good way to learn the freefall technique because two minutes in the wind tunnel was the equivalent of three jumps from 12,000 feet. We hoped that half an hour in freefall would reassure him and he would return reinvigorated and determined to complete his challenge.

But it was a chastened Simon who rejoined us in the hotel the following night, and his instructors were sombre too. The very communication skills that made Simon such a good presenter were working against him. He was talking out his anxieties and it wasn't doing him any good.

The next day, after the fifth jump, he was in a contemplative mood because, again, it had unnerved him. And then on an end-of-day recreational jump team member Toby Goodchild had a full-blown malfunction. His canopy started to split and he cut it away to go back into freefall for a few seconds before he deployed his reserve. The whole episode was caught on video. Watching the playback, the Falcons whooped with delight while Simon was horrified. We went back to the hotel that night knowing that the following day could make or break him.

The next day Simon boarded the aircraft and I set up on the ground to film the exit and descent while the cameraman, Stephen Wagstaff, filmed what happened aloft. Simon went into crisis mode and the whole drama was captured by Steve. Simon battled with his fears and the rest of the team knew this could be the end. Much later, during the edit, I realised that the storyline was red hot. But I was unaware of this as I waited on the drop zone.

Despite the crisis, Simon summoned up enough courage to jump and when he landed he was reflective. He spoke to camera in a way that made me wonder what had happened. He ended by saying, 'But I did it. Just.'

That night he decided he could not go on. My mind raced through possible ways of wrapping up the storyline. We went back to the airfield and took shots of him looking worried and thoughtful, looking up to the sky, and so on. I also took a number of shots of the empty spaces where we had filmed the ground training. When it came to the edit, these shots set the mood for his final speech to camera. In front of the parked aircraft Simon delivered a meaningful farewell: 'Parachuting is not for me but I will be back – I promise.'

It might not have been the story I had planned; it was a better one. It had a real human touch, the sort to which *Blue Peter* viewers could relate.

After transmission weeks later, Simon was inundated with sympathetic messages, proving that the viewers had liked what they had seen and empathised with him. His profile rocketed.

Meanwhile, back in America, I had a problem. It was only day five of a ten-day shoot, and the programme could not afford to waste valuable filming time. I had to make another film in San Diego. The big question was: what?

I toyed with Simon being a bell boy at the Del Coronado Hotel, the largest wooden structure in America, and where they had filmed the all-time classic Marilyn Monroe film *Some Like It Hot*. And following another lead, I enquired whether we could see how the military-trained dolphins were taught to lay mines to blow up ships. Both ideas came to nought. Instead I settled for a couple of days 'on call' at Pump Station Number Four in the gaslight area of the city with the San Diego Fire Brigade.

I had no idea that fire trucks (as they are called in America) also acted as ambulances and that each fire crew had a paramedic. If there was a callout it was a race to see which crew got to the scene first, the fire truck or the ambulance. There were other surprises. Part of the fire crew's day was a compulsory one hour of jogging and a shopping trip to buy food. Then there were cleaning and washing-up duties. It all felt quite laid back and we ate well and it felt more part of a club than a death-defying firefighting unit.

We were regaled with stories. Like the one about the 80-stone giant of a man who had to be extricated from his bedroom by taking out the bedroom window and sliding him into the ambulance on a makeshift ramp.

That night, as we waited hopefully, there were several callouts, and it made a rewarding film, which, under the circumstances, was more than I could have expected.

A year later Simon returned to join the Falcons and he faced his fears. He completed another 12 jumps, revealing yet again a stubborn streak that had seen him through many such trials.

(Above): Simon with
instructor in freefall over
southern California

30

Forgotten skills of the ancient world

Good programme ideas could come from anywhere and the knack was to recognise them. I spent a lot of time meeting and listening to people who were determined to tell you why their ideas were just right for *Blue Peter*. It was a struggle sometimes to explain for the umpteenth time why they weren't. However, sometimes they were and then it was a question of persuading my boss, the programme editor, to accept them. Sometimes good ideas happened on my own doorstep.

Claude Belanger was a builder in my home town of Topsham in Devon. Like my father, he was French Canadian so I felt we had a bond. He was tall and slightly built, a chain smoker and a man who loved a good pint. He was sometimes hard to understand because of his accent. Yet the most extraordinary thing about Claude wasn't the fact that he was French Canadian and a builder but that he had very close links with Belize and was an expert on the ancient civilisation of the Maya.

In a previous life he had been a full-time archaeologist and it was his discoveries at Lamanai that had helped to fuel a tourist industry that Belize so desperately needed. He had kept his links with the country and told me about the work of restoring the Mayan temples. He also told me about other interesting aspects of life in Belize. The country seemed jam-packed with interesting stories – from diving with sharks, to the Garifuna people, the Mennonites, butterfly farms, as well as the bloodthirsty history of the Mayan empire.

A new programme editor had just been appointed. Steve Hocking had left and Richard Marson had taken over. Richard was a risk-taker and *Blue Peter* was in his blood. He had already spent several years on the programme as a producer and instantly recognised the potential interest that our young viewers would have in a bloodthirsty ancient civilisation like the Maya. It was the first of several bold decisions that he would make and, like Lewis Bronze, he wasn't afraid to make them.

Claude had lots of useful contacts and I persuaded him to act as fixer for a shoot in Belize. After a week's recce we came back with a rich cocktail of items to fuel two whole programmes.

11–18 July 2003

Belize

To get there we had to fly via the United States. For those of you acquainted with Miami airport at that time I need say no more. Suffice it to say that it was a great place to get ulcers. For one of the most sophisticated countries in the world, the airport had to be an aberration – huge bottle necks of passengers in transit and customs officials who sent you to the back of the queue if they thought your handwriting wasn't neat enough. It was enough to send a normally sane person into a bloodthirsty rage and was made all the worse by the knowledge that the customs officials did not have English as their first language. With only a few minutes to spare we made our connecting flight to Belize.

We stayed at the Lamanai Lodge, the hotel for the newly excavated Mayan temples, and in the bar I spotted some everyday objects mounted on the wall. I took a closer look. There was a shaving brush and mirror and a few hand tools that had been used during the excavation. A small plaque caught my eye. 'These belonged to Claude Belanger, who worked as an archaeologist and discovered the temples at Lamanai.'

To the people of Lamanai, Claude was living history. He laughed when I pointed this out. Later he showed me where he had spent six years of his life. It was a small and dilapidated leaf house built on stilts a few yards from the lake. It seemed a very long way from the cosy town where we both now lived.

It was unbelievably hot in the Belize rainforest, and there was very little wind. It was a relief to climb the hundred-odd steps up the High Temple to get out of the heat. At the top, where human hearts had been ripped from the victims' bodies, we could see for miles and hear the howler monkeys. Their barking echoed around the surrounding rainforest that stretched to the horizon. It was hard to believe that the Mayan civilisation had partly failed through deforestation, which had turned the whole area into a desert.

It had been farming, whereby one man could produce enough food to feed ten, that had enabled the massive building programme that had created their empire. But it had backfired when too many trees had been cut down, creating a man-made disaster, and the people had starved.

Belize is now home to several nationalities. As well as the indigenous people, there are the Chinese, who began settling in the late 19th century, the Garifuna people, who came from Africa to the West Indies as slaves, and the Mennonites.

The Mennonites took their name from a Dutch priest, Menno Simons, who travelled and preached in Holland in the 16th century. Menno followed the teachings of Jesus as described in the Bible, and he disagreed with some of the practices of the Catholic Church. These were the payment of money for the atonement for sins, taxes to the Catholic Church, and waging war. The followers of Menno Simons broke away from the established church, and were persecuted and forced to leave Europe. Over the centuries the Mennonites formed communities in many countries all over the world and, since 1958, in Belize.

The more I found out about the Mennonites the more I was determined to film with them. It wasn't just the fact that they travelled by pony and trap, didn't wear leather and used oil lamps rather than electricity. Neither was it the fact that unmarried females would turn their backs and children hide if a camera was pointed in their direction. For me it was their incredible ingenuity, and ability to repair or mend almost anything that was broken.

'Waste not, want not' is one of my mottos, and in the Mennonites I found soulmates. They never ever threw anything away and odd pieces of scrap metal were treasured to be reworked or melted down and made into something else.

In our world, when a car or any vehicle broke down, the garage ordered a new part. In Belize, the Mennonites either repaired the part or made a new one. I was told that they could make a new car engine from scratch. They could build furnaces, make the moulds into which they could pour molten metal, and machine the castings to perfection. And it was all self-taught. Mennonite engineers learnt from an early age, using skills acquired over generations. These were the skills that we have forgotten – the skills that once put the great into Great Britain.

They were excellent carpenters too, cutting wood from the rainforest with antiquated circular saws and making delicate and beautifully designed cabinets and wardrobes. And like the ancient Maya, the land that they had cleared was used to grow food. Belize needed all these skills and they were highly valued.

26 August–11 September 2003
On location in Belize

Returning a month later, we filmed Mennonite Abraham Neufield as he showed us a tractor. Simon Thomas tapped on one of the huge rear tyres. Surprisingly, it was made of metal and was hollow. Abraham explained that they did not use rubber because metal lasted much longer and the 'tyre' could be filled with water to give it more weight and grip in boggy conditions.

We ate with another Mennonite family. George Penner had nine children and they provided one of the best meals of the trip, all ingredients locally produced. Simon was curious about their beliefs as Anabaptists, or 'again baptisers', because, as a Christian, he was impressed by their commitment. He was shown around the house, which had separate bedrooms and no corridor. Entry to one bedroom meant passing through another. Colourful boxes that once contained Christmas decorations were carefully stored on high shelves and every curtain was hemmed with lace. No electricity, of course, so no television or telephone, only several religious pictures. The house was spotlessly clean and simple.

Tackling a delicate issue, he asked about how young people met up. Courtship, he was told, was a cautious art, which was carried out after dark. A young man might shine his torch (torches were allowed) at the bedroom window of a girl he liked, and the girl, if willing, would ask her parents' permission to meet the boy. Only when permission was given would they be able to meet.

Simon learnt how to drive a pony and trap and we passed other traps coming in the opposite direction. Like most things associated with the Mennonites, it was peaceful and functional, and he waved cheerily to the other drivers.

I greatly admired the Mennonites' self-sufficiency and it made me wonder whether we, in the UK, have been caught in an information gap between the sophisticated and the elementary. We can no longer fix the things on which our lives depend, like computers and cars. We have also lost the day-to-day skills of growing our own food, like potatoes. If civilisation collapsed tomorrow, it would be the Mennonites – and not us – who would survive. We left the Mennonites with a feeling that they were on to a good thing. They were happy, and their self-sufficiency was reassuring in a world that could easily turn into chaos.

(Right): Simon Thomas, Liz Barker, Louise Belanger, Alex and Claude Belanger as we headed off to film Shark-Ray Alley

(Left): Simon Thomas with Mennonite George Penner and family. The unmarried daughters were visibly reluctant to be photographed

Belize is renowned for its cays and the coral reefs. On San Pedro, one of the largest island cays, Liz went lobster fishing and then both Liz and Simon took a dip in Shark-Ray Alley, where reef sharks and stingrays gathered to be fed by boatloads of tourists. In theory these creatures were friendly and Simon and Liz had nothing to fear. After a bit of a shaky start, Liz joined Simon in the water and the sharks and rays obliged by rubbing shoulders with them both. After the filming I took a swim too, and enjoyed touching the rough skin of the sharks and even grabbed at their tails. The water was warm and silky and the sun shone out of a cloudless sky as we swam around the stern of the yacht, twisting and turning with our new friends. It was one of the highlights of the whole trip.

Much later I looked at the underwater footage. I'd had no idea that sharks' heads looked so utterly evil. In close-up their little piggy eyes and rows of pin-sharp teeth were utterly terrifying. Even though I had been told that they were harmless, I would think twice about repeating the experience.

We had been told that the British army would be helpful to us, and would expect nothing in return. I telephoned the colonel in charge of the base. I asked if there was any chance we could hitch a helicopter ride to get shots of Mayan temples from the air and, if possible, the world-famous Blue Hole far out on the reef. The colonel was kind and co-operative. He agreed that if Simon would spend an hour at the school and meet the children then anything was possible. And that's how I found myself, camera in hand, in a Huey American helicopter of Vietnam War fame, facing outwards on a double bench seat, watching the jaw-dropping vista of the cays and reefs unfold as we gained height over the deep blue-green sea. We headed for one of the most exciting dive sites in the world, the Blue Hole, a gigantic underground cavern.

Our little band was about to expand. It would be the most expensive part of the trip, with filming fees and extra divers for safety, and I had suggested to Richard (the programme editor) that the programmes would survive without it. Having lived through long periods of austerity when programme budgets had simply not been large enough, I was cautious. Richard, however, had been adamant. It was one of those moments when I wondered whether the financial risk would pay off. Bad weather could scupper it all.

Back in the UK, Simon had been learning how to scuba-dive and now he made several qualifying dives over the shallow reef. The fine weather held. We had already seen him do his mask drills and swim through gaps in the fan coral and scatter clouds of yellow and black striped fish. He loved this new underwater world and was completely confident in it.

John McIntyre, our diving cameraman, had joined us from the UK. John had been a news reporter for the six and nine o'clock news but had abandoned his prominent journalistic role in favour of his first love, underwater photography.

The Blue Hole was Simon's first deep dive and the dark blue chasm in the reef was a mind-ripping place in which to do it. The 'hole' had formed when the roof of a huge cave below the sea bed had caved in. The sea had poured into the cave and giant stalactites, formed in the dry cave, now hung from its ceiling in the gloomy depths. Simon's first dive was to be only to 100 feet, not the full 130 foot depth of these extraordinary limestone structures. So Simon would have only a distant view, looking down on this wonder of nature.

The dive boat stationed itself on the edge of the Blue Hole and Simon and his instructor disappeared into the depths, followed by John, camera in hand. They were gone a long time.

When they reappeared about an hour later they were in a state of jubilation and we gathered to look at the tape on John's camera. The pictures were fantastic and we were instantly gripped by the magnificence of the underwater cave. Then I realised that I was looking at Simon swimming between the giant stalactites and not above them. Barracuda and shark curiously nudged between him and the camera. He wasn't looking down at the cave but swimming in it, at a depth near to 140 feet and much deeper than I had expected.

It was one of those moments when it was too late to be angry. Simon's deep dive was over and there were no more risks to take. He had qualified for his open-water certificate. I was reassured that because of his confidence he had indicated to go deeper, and his instructor had thought he was competent. Simon's adventurous qualities had taken over against my advice. I had to remind myself that it was because of his thirst for adventure that we had recruited him to become a presenter. He was safe and had been well supervised and the pictures were incredible. After making my point, I let the matter drop, yet it made me mindful for the future.

(Above): Simon Thomas
with diving instructor

Richard had been right. Back in London, the moments we spent underwater lifted both programmes. I was forced to admit I had been wrong. He told me later that he had negotiated extra funding to do it and if I had failed to deliver it would have caused him much embarrassment.

Back in Belize, and not far from the Blue Hole, John suggested a drift dive, allowing the currents to take the divers along the reef at a depth of no more than 20 feet. It was about five o'clock and they would be back within the hour.

At six o'clock all were back except John, and there was no sign of him. We were in a flat expanse of ocean and miles away from land. The water was getting choppy and the light was fading. The surface of the sea was becoming a threatening grey colour. It was impossible to spot a swimmer more than a hundred yards away. I felt panic rising. He should be out of air. Where was he?

At twenty minutes past six and just when I had given up all hope, he came to the surface and inflated his marker buoy. He was about a quarter of a mile away and it took the keen eyes of the crew to spot him. He came aboard, as laid back as ever, and said, 'Sorry to alarm you. Forgot to mention that I breathe very slowly underwater. Can make an hour's tank last another 20 minutes or more.'

Bloody hell, I thought. I was too emotionally exhausted to reply.

I found Belize good in parts and excellent in others, yet, apart from the cays, not a place I felt instantly drawn to. The American influence was inevitable and growing and, because of the mix of cultures, there was no real sense of nationality. My army friends have, without exception, raved about the place and, with Catterick or Aldershot as the alternative, I can understand why.

What perhaps was more extraordinary was how what had started as a chat over a few pints in a bar back home in Topsham had eventually turned into *Blue Peter* gold, representing in the two programmes all the things that make the programme what it is.

(Above): The Parachute
Regiment's infamous
stretcher race

31

Blue Peter presenters: it's in the genes

2–4 March 2004
Catterick Garrison

Perhaps the most gruelling challenge ever attempted on *Blue Peter* by two presenters at the same time was given to Matt Baker and Simon Thomas. It took place on the military training area for the Catterick Garrison, and the test is legendary within the British army. Like the Royal Marines, the Parachute Regiment have a unique way of selecting their own. They call it 'P company' (Pegasus Company), which is code for two weeks of pure hell.

The first week is to prepare for the tests that would take place in the second week. Out of every ten who are selected to attempt P Company, only four are expected to pass. Most candidates spend torturous months of road running, carrying heavy weights and circuit training. The most 'gruelling' thing Matt and Simon had done had been to present *Blue Peter* three times a week. They were supposed to have had time off to get fit. However, life in television is unpredictable and neither had got all the time off for the training they'd so desperately needed.

As Matt so aptly put it, 'We knew it was going to be hell.'

They had been entered for four of the seven tests, with nothing but willpower to keep them going. Company Sergeant Major Billy Dryden wasn't going to let them fail without a fight.

The magic ingredient to this inhuman cocktail of pain was competition. Matt and Simon were the best of friends but Simon could never resist trying to get the upper hand. And Matt was intent on beating Simon because that's what past members of the England gymnastics team always did. They had to win. It was in their genes.

The insanity of P Company has always intrigued me. Ten years previously I had taken Tim Vincent up to Catterick (2 February 1994) to attempt one of its toughest tests – the log race. Chatting to the officer commanding in his office, I had glanced up and noticed a macabre display in a case on the wall above the major's head. It contained a pair of knee caps, a painful reminder of what could happen with too much running while carrying a heavy pack.

The instructors looked for candidates who would run until they dropped. Physical fitness could be acquired; the grim determination to never give up is in the soul. You either have it or you don't. I have often wondered why Sir Ranulph Fiennes continues to punish himself with ever more daring exploits, despite his age. I asked him once and he told me quite simply that it was what he did. It was what he knew and understood. However, he doesn't have to do it, so why carry on? I can only assume that the 'never give up' part of his personality dominates his life, and is his reason for being. And you would expect such a person to be difficult and unpleasant company. Yet Ran is probably the most affable person I have ever met.

P Company was going to be a test for me in another way. In the past the armed forces had thought *Blue Peter* to be good publicity and had offered their facilities free of charge. Now that had changed. The Ministry of Defence had announced that it was going to change the policy of a lifetime and charge filming fees. I argued vehemently against this proposal and the Parachute Regiment, outraged at the idea, said we could film anyway. They wouldn't stop us. Apart from uniforms and some transport, we would not be using any extra MOD resources. The battle raged up until the deadline and with permission, even though the cost issue was unresolved, we began filming.

Four days into the shoot we were faced with a bill from the Ministry of Defence for £4,000. Unable to back out, we were held to ransom. Fuming with indignation, we paid out. What followed was the only film about the services to be shown on *Blue Peter* for the next year or so. The Ministry of Defence had priced itself out of the market.

Unaware of the wider battle that was taking place, Simon and Matt were issued their kit, which included a helmet that was hideously uncomfortable. They joined in some circuit training and then set out, with 40 others, on a 12-mile speed march, carrying full packs. Simon put his head down and got on with it, as did Matt.

I was unaware that Matt was suffering from a chest infection. The halfway point was a series of hills, and the group were told to run up and down them. Simon coped well and, having no experience of the military way of doing things, became progressively resentful of the instructors who shouted at him. Matt had suffered the England gymnastics team training sessions, so to him this was not new, yet he was struggling. At the top of the last hill his breathing was in overdrive and he was in danger of collapse. Despite his protestations, they pulled him out. He recalled:

> It was so frustrating because I knew I could do it but I was knackered that I couldn't. It was the worst moment for me on the programme because I felt I was letting myself down.

(Right): Simon and Matt before the P Company tests began

Within minutes his breathing was back to normal and he was fretful because Simon was still going strong. The competitive genes were frothing away and he would not be outdone. He rejoined the group and ran the last four miles back to camp. Company Sergeant Major Billy Dryden was impressed.

Simon and Matt returned to London to reflect on the tests to come and present two editions of the programme. Four days later they returned to attempt the tests in the second week of P Company. Matt was feeling better and Simon was raring to go.

17–18 March 2004

Catterick

The first test was the 'Tarzan course' or trainasium, which was a confidence test. Built of scaffolding poles, it resembled a building site without a building. They had to leap gaps, swing on ropes and finally climb up on to a parallel set of poles some 60 feet up and a couple of feet apart. In their own time they had to stand up straight, look straight ahead and give their name, rank and number. Matt and Simon simply had to shout their names and who they were.

Encouragement from those waiting to go helped; I underwent a similar test when I was in the army at Sandhurst and it was only the knowledge that others would suffer if I didn't get on with it that kept me going. It wasn't a race, and that was the only sane aspect to the whole exercise.

Matt and Simon took the challenge head on, and to my delight did well while some others did not. Their morale soared but they were blissfully unaware of what was to come.

The next test was the steeplechase. It was a mile and a half of jumping across logs, wading through muddy pools and crawling through water-filled tunnels (not to be confused with the sheep dip, a legendary underwater tunnel that is part of the Royal Marines Endurance Course).

(Left): Matt Baker, pauses to reflect, having given his all

It looked like fun and they set off at full speed, at one-minute intervals, and they came in ... joint last. They were astonished that they had been beaten by everyone in the group and, united in defeat, it made them think again. The really hard tests were yet to come.

The log race, of Tim Vincent fame, was just that. The 'log' was a wooden telegraph pole and attached to it were six short lengths of rope, each with a hand loop. CSM Dryden demonstrated the method for the race.

'You will put your hand through the loop and when given the order you will pick up the log and run with it. The rope must be at least at right angles to the log or angled forward. If the rope is angled backwards it means that you are pulling back on the log and you will be no longer pulling your weight. You will be told to run forward. If you refuse or are unable to do this, you will be taken off the log.'

It was hard to watch, let alone take part. Their tortured faces said it all. On a downward slope Simon fell and was taken off the log and joined the other failures in the back of the lorry. Matt carried on grimly, determined to succeed. Then, with just 400 yards to go, he, too, was taken off the log, as Matt recalls:

> Just after I fell down Billy said, 'You've just sacked yourself – you could have done it.' I was lying there in pain and I knew he was right. It was worse than all the aches and pains I was feeling. It was a life-changing moment for me and I have never sacked myself since. His voice echoes in my mind whenever things get really tough.

Simon was fed up. He had been put off by all the shouting, which had got on his nerves. He reckoned he would have done better without what he saw as aggravation:

The problem with doing these kind of films was that although I was desperate to do well and prove I could hack some of the armed forces' toughest tests, the reality was we were doing it to make a film, but for the guys we were doing it with, this was their career and for them failure wasn't an option. Because of this, when some instructor was bellowing in my lug holes to go faster or do even more press-ups, the temptation to tell him to just shut up, or words to that effect, was never far away. This wasn't me having a problem with authority, I had nothing but respect for the instructors, I was trying my utmost to make it a good film and not begin a career in the Parachute Regiment. The last thing I needed was someone telling me to push harder.

The CSM had noticed this rejection of the military way and remarked on it. We left Catterick for a couple of days, to return in time for the final test – the stretcher race.

There was one test that I wouldn't allow Matt and Simon to take. 'Milling' is a polite term for beating the hell out of each other, and it was designed to test the candidates' aggression, an important part of the Paras' ethos. With stretchers and doctors standing by, the major watched and adjudicated each three-minute bout. Boxing gloves were worn and no defensive manoeuvres were allowed. The aim was to land as many punches on your opponent as fast as you could. Prolonged circling to gain an advantage was strictly taboo. It was straight in and beat your opponent to the ground with your fists as if your life depended on it. And bearing in mind that these men were at the peak of condition, the punches had real power behind them.

So, with Matt and Simon safely away back to London, the test began and I watched with fascination. Blood soon flowed freely and then splattered with every punch. It was obvious that 'milling' came a lot easier to recruits from rougher backgrounds. A public-school education was no longer a good place for boxing, or any organised violence off the rugby pitch. Consequently, a bout between two young officers seemed a pathetic affair. They didn't know how to fight and, I suspect, had never been in one.

23 March 2004

Catterick

The day of the stretcher race arrived and the boys were quiet because they knew it would be a grim affair. The 'stretcher' was several lengths of heavy metal plate welded together. The plates were designed to be placed under the wheels of heavy vehicles to give them enough grip to get out of mud. Each team comprised four stretcher-bearers and four reserves, and every so often the positions changed. Everyone would get

(Left): The gruelling log race

a short rest from carrying the stretcher. The race was four miles long and it was up and down hills, in and out of streams, and a dash on flat ground before a final dip and a climb to the finish.

To film the mob of screaming desperation as it passed, camera crews leapfrogged each other from one vantage point to another. The plan worked a treat. Simon got shouted at. He shouted back. Matt frothed at the mouth with the effort and kept schtum. They both made it to the finish. Both passed. I noticed that the CSM was fuller with his praise for Matt than he was for Simon whose resentment of military authority had again been noted. Simon brooded on this for a while and then, ever the professional and never one to bear a grudge, he promptly forgot about it. Matt:

> It was great doing it with my mate Simon. We were in it together in more ways than one. I felt grateful for the opportunity to take part.

They had both done amazingly well considering their lack of preparation, and while both Simon and Matt complained about the lack of time to get properly fit, they had refused to give up. Matt again:

> The pain of that metal pole banging on my shoulder is a vivid memory for me as is the noise of panting in unison around the stretcher, the vibrations of the helmet, and the constant 'Stand by ... go!' urging us to dig deep and drive forward. The memory continues to haunt me and I get flashbacks.

Their effort had been magnificent and I knew it was the last time we would be able to film this test unless we recruited some serious athletes as presenters.

Perhaps the most extraordinary part of the whole of P Company was the drinking at the end. All the candidates, bar half a dozen, had been awarded their maroon berets and it was the celebration of the exhausted. The best candidate, who had been initially 'failed' on the parade to boost the morale of the real failures, had to drink everything and anything poured into a pint glass. This fine specimen of fitness and human determination (destined no doubt for high rank) drank the pint down in one. What madness, I thought, to poison the best candidate just when he had succeeded. I saw him trying to vomit soon after, and I hope, for the nation's benefit, that he did.

Simon was equally incredulous:

> I remember vividly Matt and I looking on with our mouths open as the best officer on P Company was forced, by tradition, to celebrate being top of the class by downing a pint of port! It disappeared in seconds and his face barely betrayed what had just been launched into his steel-like stomach. In some ways we'd have loved to stay on and join in the celebrations deep

(Right): The stretcher race, when the team took it in turns to help carry a heavy metal stretcher

into the night. But based on the opening few minutes it was probably a wise move to make a polite but sharp exit.

So we retired from the celebrations early to drive the 300 miles back to London. This was an ordeal in itself and one that we were all well trained for.

On reflection I could see that P Company was necessary and in some ways did not go far enough. I would have included killing a chicken or something real as part of the psychological testing. So often in the past recruits have joined up because the services were portrayed as a kind of adventure exercise rather than what they are – mercenaries of the Queen. When the programme was transmitted the general verdict was that it was too brutal for an easy watch. I was pleased because that was exactly what it was like in real life.

25 March 2004

Commando Training Centre Royal Marines, Devon

In direct contrast to Simon and Matt's experience, Liz and Konnie took on some challenges at the Commando Training Centre Royal Marines at Lympstone in Devon. To my consternation they displayed an extraordinary lack of fitness. The death slide should have been a jolly slide down a rope but I wasn't reckoning on Konnie's lack of upper-arm strength. True, her hands are small and the rope strop (a loop) big. Even so, she did not have the strength to hang on for more than a few seconds. She fell off at about 20 feet up, bounced on the safety rope and was caught by the instructor at the bottom of the slide. It was a terrible shock and I wondered if I should wrap the filming, but after a minute or two and a few tears she carried on.

I watched with more than a bit of anxiety, knowing that neither Konnie nor Liz was really strong enough, or fit enough, for the tasks. The rope regain in the pouring rain was another moment for the viewers to relish, and it was two very wet and bedraggled presenters that joined a troop of recruits who were about to do their exercises in the mud of the river Exe.

Almost unable to move because of the glutinous quality of the river's finest gunge, they were dragged and bullied until they were completely covered in the brown slime. It was obvious that they had both reached the end of their tethers. A fire hose got the worst of it off. I vowed not to attempt anything similar until they both were a lot fitter. It just wasn't safe.

For Konnie, the 'death slide' experience was compounded by the fact that her embarrassing fall was repeated for all to see as part of the training video. She remembers it as 'A terrifying, humiliating experience I will never forget.'

(Above left): Matt Baker and Simon Thomas bonded in adversity

(Above right): Konnie Huq and Liz Barker after exercising in the mud of the river Exe

32

The champagne lifestyle

It was an unusually busy year in 2005. *Blue Peter* had been instructed to produce five programmes a week and it was all hands to the pumps. As well as an adventure in Angola, I made a programme in Vermont, New Hampshire and Canada and a short film about the Red Arrows in Cyprus. Then there were two more programmes in Egypt and another in Australia. I also made a programme to celebrate Trafalgar Day and a memorable film about Gethin Jones attempting the Royal Marines Green Beret final test.

14–23 January 2005
Angola

This was Konnie Huq's second trip to Angola, having filmed there several months before to launch the *Blue Peter* Welcome Home Appeal, which was to reunite children (separated through civil war) with their families. It was my first, and I marvelled how she took the initiative as the experienced hand. She was quite a contrast to the Konnie who I remembered could sometimes be tiresome and on occasions keep us waiting. It became a daily joke that she would be ready to leave base before I was.

Safety was the watchword because Angola had spent the last 40 years in civil war. It was one of the most dangerous places in the peaceful world. We were to make a programme about children who had been successfully reunited. One of the families was at a village called Mavinga. It was notorious as the most heavily landmined place on earth. We would have to fly to Mavinga because it was the only way to get there safely.

Most of the roads in Angola had been mined by the Cuban army, which had supported the government forces during the fighting. Getting rid of the landmines was a slow and crude process. The de-miners did it by driving very slowly along a road with a heavy machine that impacted the road surface to detonate the mines. They would get most but not all of them. If you drove close to the side of the road, to avoid potholes, you were in danger of getting blown up because the de-miners did not bother with the edges.

We stopped for a break and I took the chance to answer the call of nature. Even though I was barely a foot off the road (to conceal my ablutions) I was hauled back on to the road by our fixer and warned not to try that again. His concern was alarming.

Landmines had effectively marooned communities and I thought that we should show the de-mining process, because without it the means of reuniting families would have been impossible. For our first encounter with landmines we joined de-mining supervisor Valdermar in Huambo, which had been the scene of fierce fighting. Close to the airport we were kitted up with incredibly uncomfortable body armour and a helmet. I found operating the camera almost impossible because I couldn't get my eye to the viewfinder.

We were taken to an area where the de-miners were locating and revealing landmines in a very slow and methodical way. They would dig a small trench and then scrape away the earth along the side of the trench. They would then move slowly forward along a one-metre-wide front. It was painstakingly slow and every so often they would encounter a solid object. Sometimes it was a stone and sometimes it wasn't. Sometimes it was a landmine. It was safe to touch the side of a landmine but not the top. I had learnt this when I had filmed this procedure before in Mozambique, where there had been an area just like this one for de-mining practice.

It got hotter and hotter and I took off my helmet and then my body armour in my efforts to get the really close shots with the camera. As the black circular disc of the anti-personnel landmine was revealed, the

de-miner used his trowel to scrape away enough earth from its side to see it clearly. I was only about a foot from it and tried to get crisp close-ups of the tip of the trowel scraping away the earth. Eventually, when I had got enough, he stopped and stood up. I asked, wiping the sweat away from my eyes, if that was it.

The seemingly casual reply was, 'Yes.'

Then, to my surprise, he said, 'Now we blow it up.'

Up to that point I had thought it was like the dummy ones we had dug up in Mozambique for practice.

I asked why there were so few children with limbs missing, compared to the number of adults.

'The landmines only blow the leg off an adult, but they blow children to pieces.'

Yet there were limbless children all the same, because there were other types of landmine that did not use explosive. Like a shallow pit lined with sharp stakes tipped in poison that ensured injuries festered and amputation was inevitable.

We were told that it would take a 100 years to clear all the landmines in Angola.

Perhaps the most upsetting part of the trip was the realisation that some of the children, who had been separated from their loved ones for several years, had formed close bonds with their adoptive families. We filmed as Joao Laurindo took leave of his adoptive brothers and sisters and mother. The tears flowed genuinely and freely. Joao himself seemed thoughtful because, although he was curious to see his parents again, he thought his dad only wanted him home for his earning potential. He knew he could be going home to a life of manual labour in the gardens while his adoptive family had given him the chance to go to school and learn.

His family lived in Mavinga and when we arrived I noticed that the community was surrounded by thousands of stakes coloured with red, yellow and white bands. Each stake marked the spot where a landmine lay buried. The colours showed what type of landmine it was. They all had to be destroyed and teams worked continuously to do this.

When the moment arrived for Joao to meet up with his family, it was obvious that he was not at all pleased to be home. In between the explosions of landmines being destroyed, he privately admitted he was thinking of going back to the 'real' home that he had just left.

Not all reunions were unsuccessful. Far from it. We witnessed near hysterical reunions between children and their parents that were heart-warming. Many more reunited families stayed together than did not.

Konnie had shown great compassion to all the children we had filmed and a genuine concern for their welfare.

At the end of the shoot we got to the airport early and checked in. I noticed with some alarm that there was a notice saying that no one would be allowed to leave the country with more than US$7,000 in cash. I had arrived with US$25,000 but because we were supporting the

(Far left): Military vehicle wrecked by landmine

(Near left): Konnie Huq wearing the protective armour worn by de-miners work of the British Red Cross and not incurring them any additional expense, they had refused payment for many things, like transport, which had been shared. I was left with about US$19,000, which I kept in my money belt. What could I do about it? It was too late to leave it with anyone. I feared that it would be confiscated but carried on, hoping that no one would notice.

They did. I was escorted by two policemen to a side room for questioning. They had seen the belt and were curious.

'How much have you?' a huge policeman asked as he indicated the money belt. By now there were about seven policemen in the room, obviously drawn by the thought of some unexpected bounty.

'About US$7,000,' I replied, trying to appear unconcerned. I felt compelled to lie on behalf of the licence-fee payers. I certainly was not going to give it away.

'Show,' demanded the officer.

I fumbled with the belt, half opening it before getting out my BBC identity card. It was contained in the leather wallet that I had bought off a policeman in Cambodia about a year earlier during another filming trip. I flipped it open to show the BBC card, coincidentally revealing the brass insignia labelled prominently 'Police Nationale' against the Cambodian lion.

'Police,' he announced to his companions. And then to me, 'No problem.' With that, they let me go. I had saved the BBC US$12,000.

I have often thought about that incident, especially when I have been forced to pay for filming items out of my own pocket because the BBC expenses system would not reimburse me.

11–21 March 2005
Vermont, New Hampshire and Canada

The editor of *Blue Peter*, Richard Marson, wanted a winter programme with lots of snow and he passed it to me. Vermont in the United States was the destination of choice and after some research I widened it to include the Mount Washington Cog Railway in New Hampshire and Niagara Falls on the border with Canada.

The programme had recently been joined by a former beauty queen of Northern Ireland with long blonde hair who also happened to be a qualified lawyer. Her name was Zoe Salmon and I had already made a programme with her about survival challenges. I knew that behind the strong but posh (Zoe was from Bangor) Northern Irish accent was a sharp mind.

Zoe was going to be joined by a very new Gethin Jones, who was not yet on the official list of presenters. Gethin was a diffident, good-looking Welshman. He had come close to becoming a professional rugby player and I thought he was just what the programme needed. I had

(Far right): Zoe Salmon with horse-logger Dave Fuller and Duke

(Near right): Gethin Jones with locomotive and crew at the Mount Washington Cog Railway

been surprised and exasperated when, during a straw poll at a programme 'away day', I was very much in the minority. The rest of the office favoured a candidate who would have driven the viewers mad with his hyperactivity. Several weeks later I was delighted when common sense prevailed and Gethin was recruited. He was going to join the programme later in the year and eventually take over from Simon Thomas.

I liked Gethin because he was easy-going and would be a good elder-brother role model to our young viewers. He also had some television experience having presented children's programmes for SC4 in Wales. I wondered how he and Zoe would get along.

Zoe arrived on location before Gethin and we filmed her 'horse logging' with Dave Fuller, one of the last horse-loggers in the state. He was a kindly man and very welcoming. His giant carthorses were Jake and Duke and he doted on them. A month before the shoot he had been concerned whether there would be enough snow. He needn't have worried. The day came and there was a blizzard. I have never seen so much snow. Zoe trudged through over a foot of it, driving Jake, who was dragging a 30-foot pine tree behind him on long chains. Dave explained that the great advantage of using horses to extract timber was that they could pick their way through the trees and so damage to the environment was minimised. It felt as if we were in the wilderness and I was surprised to learn that we were actually in someone's back garden. An American's idea of a big garden and mine were very different because I have never got lost in mine.

That evening Gethin arrived and the airline had lost his luggage. He wasn't thrilled at the prospect of borrowing my spare thermals.

Vermont in winter was beautiful, buried as it was under two feet of snow, and just a bit too cold for the maple bushes to produce any of their fabled maple syrup. The 'bushes' were really 80-foot-tall trees grown in huge plantations. The temperature had to be just above freezing for their sap to flow. We hoped that it would rise enough to allow us to film maple-syrup production before the end of the shoot.

The maple 'bush' was important to Vermont in many ways. While shops offered maple syrup, the local health spa offered a maple sugar scrub. It was too good to miss and in plush, spotlessly clean surroundings Zoe and Gethin stripped off to have liberal amounts of maple sugar rubbed all over their near-naked bodies. It all seemed a little weird to me but Zoe loved it. And I am sure the viewers did too.

The highlight of the shoot was just over the state border into New Hampshire where the steam-driven Mount Washington Cog Railway created huge clouds of black smoke as it hauled skiers to the top of the mountain.

I had been in contact with someone I had presumed to be the operations controller of the railway, and when we arrived at the Mount Washington Hotel (of the Bretton Woods conference fame) it wasn't long before I had a call to say that Mr Wayne Presby was waiting in the lobby. I was surprised and pleased to get the chance to meet my contact before the shoot, and hastened down to meet him.

Wayne wasn't in overalls, or covered in grease, or even smelling of soot. Quite the reverse. He was in a dark suit, white shirt and tie, and he invited me to join him for a glass of champagne. I offered to pay for the round because I thought it was only fair. After all, he was visiting the hotel to see me, but he reassured me that he was very particular about the brand of champagne he drank, and it was on him. We settled down to chat about filming arrangements. It was excellent champagne (not that I am any judge of these things) and Wayne was very good company. It transpired that he was, in fact, the owner of the Cog Railway in partnership with others, and whatever we wanted to do was fine by him. We talked about how he planned to convert the engines to run on diesel because he didn't think the black smoke was environmentally friendly. I put up a spirited defence of steam, although I could see his logic. I had to admit that there was a great deal of black smoke. An hour and a couple of bottles of Cristal champagne later, he asked if it would be all right for him to join us for the evening. He would buy the drinks.

At this point I was only just in charge of my senses and I gathered the team together to eat. The moment Wayne appeared in the dining room the head waiter came over and stayed with us. The flow of champagne increased. I cannot recall whether it was before or after another four bottles that we discovered that Wayne's business partnership also owned the hotel, which, somehow, wasn't a surprise. By the time we had consumed a fifth bottle and had moved on to some very fine red wine, he had confided that they also owned, or part-owned, the entire valley, including the popular ski slopes.

I make it a rule to never ever get drunk, yet by the time that night was over my hotel room spun unpleasantly every time I shut my eyes.

The next morning we all suffered. Mid-morning Wayne appeared with his daughter and looked none the worse for the night before. Gethin, who had been more sensible than the rest of us the previous night, bonded with the engine driver and shovelled mountains of coal into the firebox, sending huge columns of black smoke vertically into a pure blue sky. It stood out starkly against the white snow and the air was still and the sun shone. It was hard to believe that the smoke could cause any real damage because it was all so beautiful. The engine laboured slowly up the side of the mountain, snorting and chuffing like an old man battling with heavy luggage. The journey meant that the spectacle lasted for about twenty minutes and I knew that the shots would be a feast to the eye (and ear) when it came to the edit.

That night, content after a good day's shoot, we thought to treat ourselves to a bottle of the red wine we had tasted the night before. Steve Wagstaff, the cameraman, was a connoisseur and he thumbed through the wine list and then stopped short. The champagne we had consumed so liberally was all but US$400 a bottle and the wine about the same. Slightly embarrassed by our excess, we settled for a glass of beer, savoured the memory of our night in another world, and drank to Wayne's health and his continued prosperity.

(Top left): Gethin Jones and Zoe Salmon get stripped off for a maple sugar scrub

(Below): Gethin Jones and Zoe Salmon at Niagara Falls

The shoot ended with a flight to Buffalo and a short drive to the Canadian border, where we filmed a sequence about the famous Niagara Falls. The roar and splendour of the falls was a fantastic way to end the programme, and as the helicopter circled the falls, Gethin added a finishing touch when he put his hand on Zoe's knee. There was absolutely nothing between them but it added a frisson of interest when it was transmitted. Gethin had a job explaining his act of spontaneity to his girlfriend and it gave us all a good chuckle. Very generously he took it all in good heart. I suspected he had suffered no less during his rugby days.

From that moment Gethin and Zoe's relationship deteriorated. It was a disappointment because the chemistry between the presenters was vital to the programme's success. Any tension was hard to conceal. As it turned out, Gethin and Zoe were like chalk and cheese. Zoe described their relationship as 'cool and professional'.

They would both end up leaving *Blue Peter* at the same time, in the summer of 2008, to go their separate ways in the world of television.

33

The art of reality television

11–15 April 2005
Cyprus

Gethin had got his private pilot's licence the previous year so I decided to indulge his passion for flying by taking him to Cyprus to fly with the Red Arrows. For him it was the realisation of a lifelong ambition.

On arrival at RAF Akrotiri his enthusiasm was unbounded and the Reds took to him. His gentle charm and modesty meant he made friends very quickly and he had a great respect for the RAF's ace pilots. Squadron Leader Dickie Patounas was the new Red One, the leader. He was an old friend of the programme, having been on the team when Katy Hill had become the first civilian to fly in a practice display with the Red Arrows. It was the third time that I had been to Cyprus to film them.

Like Katy, Gethin had to do a 'shake down' sortie to make sure he would be comfortable flying in the Hawk. I was intrigued how he would get on because he had told me that, despite a hundred hours of flying, he had no experience of aerobatics. From the ground Gethin watched the team roll and bank, and I could see that doubts had begun to cloud his heady optimism.

When at last he climbed into the cockpit he looked decidedly pale, and as I filmed from the ground and another Hawk flew in formation to film from the air, Dickie put the Hawk through its paces. About nine minutes into the flight, poor Gethin was violently airsick. It was a deep disappointment for him.

Although it was good television, the airsickness episode raised a wider question. I thought that Gethin had a tendency to talk himself into failure. He would imagine the worst, dwell on it, and then the worst would happen. And I noticed that if I criticised his performance it would produce self-criticism that would make him even more uncertain. Something had to done about it.

The answer came in two stages. The first was a film with the Blades Aerobatic Display Team led by my old friend Andy Offer, a previous leader of the Red Arrows. We discussed the possibility of using hypnosis to overcome Gethin's fear of airsickness. Stage two followed several years later.

5–6 October 2006
Sywell

Sywell Aerodrome, Northamptonshire. The base for the Blades Aerobatic Display Team.

Andy took Gethin up one blustery day and flew him about until he began to feel a bit queasy. He then landed again before he was ill and had a prolonged session with a hypnotherapist. He was taught to squeeze his forefinger and thumb to summon up positive thoughts of enjoyment. As he did this, he learnt to recall the words 'What the mind believes the body achieves'. After about two hours of hypnotherapy, he went up for a second flight. Andy rolled, looped and flew upside down, while Gethin squeezed his thumb and forefinger and thought positive things. Much to his delight, he wasn't airsick.

Gethin wasn't the only presenter in the history of *Blue Peter* who had to overcome personal difficulties. Here are just a few of them.

Yvette Fielding had battled with the demands put on her. Her panic attacks were very real in the 1990s, even if her confident performance on television since has shown no sign of them.

Mark Curry was uneasy with heights, so it is odd that one of his most famous moments on *Blue Peter* was when I strapped him onto the sail of a windmill in Surrey and filmed him as he revolved. Mark has since wondered why we did it. Bizarre at the time, it was based on the folklore that you could not call yourself a master miller until you had been carried all the way round on the sails.

Romana D'Annunzio, despite her upbringing in Glasgow, always felt the cold and many of her early impromptu remarks were on the lines of, 'It's so cold.' Summer or winter, it was a line I knew she would utter at some point or another.

Zoe Salmon was a beauty and she had led a sheltered life. I don't think she had spent much time climbing trees, or riding a bike, when she was young. She was prone to say, quite truthfully, 'I've never done this before.' (Which I tried to ban after the novelty had worn off.) However, a huge advantage was that to me she seemed fearless because I assumed she had never known the pain of falling out of a tree or off her bike. She courageously did things that some of the other presenters had refused to do, like the cable-car rescue drill at the Heights of Abraham, and wing walking, and she did well. She was also the first female presenter to peel off her overall while acting as fireman on the 60532 Blue Peter locomotive

so she could get stuck in shovelling coal, her beauty-queen past forgotten as coal dust got the upper hand.

When he first joined the programme I noticed that Peter Duncan found it almost impossible to tell the viewers how he felt, whether he was canoeing in white water, climbing cliffs or skiing down precipitous slopes. He could tell the viewers what he was doing – which was obvious. But he foundered as he struggled to describe his emotions. So at the beginning we had long sequences of action that had to be covered with commentary because of his silence. Over time he improved considerably.

Diane Louise Jordan was quite fussy about where she stayed overnight. She used to bring her own bed linen with her on location. There have been occasions when I have wished I had done the same. Nowadays she doesn't bother.

Simon Thomas wrestled with being in direct competition with Matt Baker, who won awards year after year as the best Children's TV presenter. It was reminiscent of the time when Peter Purves felt the same pressures with John Noakes. However hard Simon or Peter tried, they were always topped by Matt (or in Pete's case John) and it rankled, even though the grown-up part of both of them screamed, *Why does it matter?* Just as Peter was John's friend, Simon thought of Matt as his best mate, which made the problem all the more difficult:

> Matt was one of the nicest and best presenters I've had the pleasure of working with. We were genuine friends, as we were with Konnie and Liz, and I think that it was the biggest reason for the success of the show during the period we were together. However, the nature of the job means there's always going to be a competitive edge to those relationships. It goes with the territory, and it was no different with myself and Matt. The problem for me was that Matt is without doubt one of the most talented people I have met, and as he proved from the day he joined the show until the day he left there is almost nothing he cannot turn his hand to. This was great for the show but for me at times I'm big enough to admit it was hard. Whatever film I did, I nearly always felt Matt could have done it and probably done it a lot better, and as Matt's continued success proves, he really is one of the best and most versatile presenters the BBC have. Whereas Matt won awards and was praised for his talents, I was often praised for my professionalism. It was hard at times not to look on with envy. As people have said many times, I was the new millennium's Peter Purves to Matt's John Noakes. Brilliant fun, so much to enjoy, but at times a bit tricky.

Joel Defries came to the programme as scatty as could be, which had an impact on the presentation team like a nuclear bomb. While he was incomprehensible on occasions, he exploded with entertaining fun and excitement. His greatest plus was that he was himself. Reality is everything in television presentation and audiences are quick to spot a fake.

(Above): Mark Curry goes for a spin to re-create an ancient ritual

His delivery to camera was a problem because he never used the same words in the same order more than once and this made him harder to direct. When we discussed it he made a big effort to learn the words so I could help him deliver them more convincingly. I explained that television presentation is very hard work if you are to get it right. I enjoyed his company and found him a pleasure to work with.

And some problems shouldn't have been problems at all. Andy Akinwolere suffered from being just a bit too nice. When he first joined the programme he wanted to please (like most presenters initially), so he changed his manner, chameleon-like, to meet every situation. It was frustrating because at first the viewers never knew who the real Andy was. Andy almost needed to be pushed to the limit for his real emotions to shine on camera.

We discussed this more than once and his defence (as if he needed one) was quite reasonable:

> I am the first black male presenter to be on the show. My 'niceness' came from being completely intimidated by my new surroundings. It was never my intention to be a pre-senter and I find myself on this middle-class show which I never really watched as a child. I was not the stereotype. Nominated twice for a BAFTA, I'm a different person now to what I was then.

And there is no arguing that he was a joy to work with, and his tolerance of other people's failings is remarkable. More on that later.

All these foibles, though transient, had to be taken into account. Much time was spent discussing how to cast presenters in films so as to bring out their personalities. It was no accident that the producers chose action films because it was only through testing challenges that the real personalities could be seen and empathised with.

Blue Peter viewers loved the programme because they had the chance to share extraordinary adventures with presenters they had come to regard as role models. That some were more successful than others was inevitable.

(Right): Liz Barker had more than one exploit in the Royal Navy. This is her in the fin of HMS *Vengeance* with Commander Stephen Upright, RN

The battle for viewers' hearts and minds

It had been two hundred years since the Battle of Trafalgar and the Royal Navy planned to celebrate Lord Nelson's success in style. We planned to do our bit, too, and make a whole programme about the sea and the Royal Navy. Gethin would tell the story of the Battle of Trafalgar from the deck of HMS *Victory*; Zoe would get wet with the Newfoundland water-rescue dogs; and Liz would spend a week on board an aircraft carrier, HMS *Illustrious*, which was on exercise in the North Atlantic.

It would have been tempting to put Gethin on the aircraft carrier but, in true *Blue Peter* style, we thought that Liz might find a more interesting angle on life afloat. We would not be disappointed.

11–14 June 2005
HMS *Illustrious*

We flew to Stornoway where a Royal Navy Sea King helicopter picked us up and flew us out to the carrier. HMS *Illustrious*, or 'Lusty' to her crew, was a fantastic sight as she steamed along with her escort ships. We landed on the main flight deck in a flurry of rain and buffeting wind and were taken below. We were billeted in various cabins and everyone but me had to share, which made a pleasant and unexpected change as it is usually the presenters who get the preferential treatment. On this occasion Liz had to bunk in with the crew because it was part of the story. Later, in the wardroom, we could feel the ship moving gently in the seas.

Liz seemed very out of place in the Royal Navy. She was a natural comedienne and everywhere we turned there was something that tickled her fancy. Her desire to treat it all very seriously – which she did – only made things worse. I hoped fervently that I was the only one who noticed. In uniform she learnt to salute and make a call on the boatswain's pipe, both the sort of routine activities that gave an insight to the traditions of the Royal Navy. Watching her carefully, I thought that they both left Liz puzzled. More confusion followed as, below decks, she fought an imaginary fire. The only thing she had to fight was her amusement. We got down to the serious business of an aircraft carrier on the flight deck in the nick of time.

The Royal Navy Harriers made an ear-splitting noise and created a body-buffeting blast with their jet exhausts as they took off. When they thundered down the deck the unwary could be blown over. Liz later told me she found the experience exhilarating.

Her job was to give the pilots a *Top Gun*-style thumbs-up to take off as she was blasted with all the noise and turbulence. She gingerly edged towards the madly revving jump jet that waited for her signal to take off. She duly obliged on cue, giving the all-important thumbs-up and then leaning into the direction of the expected onslaught of wind and noise. The five-tonne aircraft hurtled down the flight deck, hit the angled take-off ramp and leapt into the air. Liz was left in a maelstrom of engine fumes and black smoke. As the roar faded, she turned to camera, eyes rolling, and shook her head. 'I don't even know how to tell you how that feels.'

And it was quite an experience for the crew, too. While Steve Wagstaff filmed the take-offs from the centre of the ship, I crouched by the side of the ramp on the bow. The Harrier jump jets accelerated down the deck under full throttle, with black smoke billowing from their exhausts. Even though we were protected with ear protectors under a hard hat, the screaming noise was overwhelming and the force of the back blast as they passed within a few feet was extraordinary. I used all my strength to hold down the camera and it was hardly enough. In the

(Near right): Sound recordist Barry Smith and cameraman Steve Wagstaff filming Harrier take-offs on HMS *Illustrious*

(Far right): Liz Barker, Barry Smith and Steve Wagstaff on the flight deck of *Lusty*

eyepiece the aircraft filled the frame and every part of my body thrilled with the sight and sound. It was like being on the cusp of disaster when anything could have happened.

On the last day, early in the morning, we filmed Liz on the ramp (near the bow on the flight deck) where she tried to deliver a piece to camera. *Lusty* was belting along at 20 knots in grey skies into a 20-knot headwind so it was like filming in a 40-knot gale. I looked up to the bridge and waved. About 20 seconds later the great ship turned to port and headed back the way she had come. Instantly the wind dropped to zero and, very gratefully, we recorded the piece to camera and retired from the flight deck. *Lusty* resumed her original course and her escort (some four other ships) turned back with her. Her captain told me later that 'unexpected manoeuvres were good to keep the escorts on their toes'.

Liz had recently returned to the programme after the birth of her first child and going away on location for more than a day or two might have been a big strain. Later that summer, after a hazardous day's filming 'cheese rolling' in Gloucestershire and for the sake of her young family, she decided to leave. We were all very sad to see her go.

12–13 July 2005

Commando Training Centre Royal Marines, Lympstone, Devon

Keeping fit was always important for both presenters and producers, and Richard suggested that the Royal Marines' final green beret test might be worth a whole programme. He was, of course, right. Recruits had to carry full kit and a rifle and speed-march or 'yomp' 30 miles across Dartmoor in less than eight hours. I had filmed it once before with Peter Duncan for *Duncan Dares* in 1984 and Peter had failed to do it. The journey had been quite emotional because it is a severe test of physical endurance. This time there would be double the anxiety because I knew that Gethin, who was by now looking for a tough challenge, would give it his all.

Nothing upsets the military quicker than a civilian in uniform, but Gethin looked the part. I could tell that Sergeant 'Dibbs' Dyball and PTI Taff Evans, both burly and uncompromising in the best no-nonsense way, approved. Dibbs was Gethin's mentor and he took his job very seriously. They took him on a road run around the lanes that border Woodbury Common, and after four miles of marching and running they gave their verdict. He needed to be a lot fitter. They gave him a training regime and he returned to London. He took everything to do with the challenge very seriously indeed. A favourite exercise was a run around Richmond Park carrying a heavy log instead of a rifle. He had just two months to make a difference.

21–24 July 2005

Scapa Flow, Orkney

While Gethin pounded himself into fitness in the south, Matt went to Orkney and Scapa Flow in the far north. It was an odd experience because we had joined an obscure group from the Ministry of Defence who were draining the fuel oil out of HMS *Royal Oak*, a battleship that had been sunk by enemy torpedoes in 1939. The oil had begun to leak out, causing concern to fish farmers.

Fuel oil was not the only danger. The *Royal Oak* had gone down loaded with explosives and they were still inside. The ship was upside down on the sea bed. If there was an air pocket, there was a chance that some of the explosives could still be dry and therefore very unstable. They had been stored near the skin of the hull and now could be hung up; a slight vibration could theoretically dislodge them. So 70 years on any movement could potentially still set them off. The explosion would flatten Kirkwall ten miles away.

(Above): Alex with Matt Baker in diving suit above the wreck of HMS *Royal Oak*

Matt was intrigued. 'For some bizarre reason we laughed it off and carried on. I was told that if they went off I'd never know anything about it. I kept asking myself, "I wonder if we are dead yet!"'

On the recovery vessel moored just above the wreck, we were told to wear rubber-soled shoes and not to run; otherwise it was business as usual. Statistically it was unlikely the explosives would go off. At least, that's what I wrote on the risk assessment.

Matt watched and reported how the oil was being pumped off and tried on a diving suit. They lowered him into the sea and we thought they might have relented and let him dive on to the upturned hull. They hadn't, and he was brought back up again. Even so, Matt, being Matt, had made the most of it and even the quick dip was exciting. I asked for some of the oil to show in the studio and they gave me a litre in a large jar. It was very thick, almost tar-like. I put it in my luggage and we headed for the airport.

I was not reckoning on the thoroughness of the baggage check-in. They found the oil and banned me from taking it on board the aircraft. I had half a suspicion that it might have been because it was off the *Royal Oak* and they wanted it for themselves. I rang a contact from the museum and explained my predicament. A few minutes later my contact arrived and grabbed the jar with excitement.

I struck a bargain. He was to let me have half of it by sending it by airmail in the post. Fittingly, it arrived in a whisky bottle a week later.

12–14 September 2005

Dartmoor, Devon

Returning to the Commando Training Centre Royal Marines, Gethin was geed up and ready to go for his 30-mile ordeal. We set off for Okehampton Battle Camp on the edge of Dartmoor, a bleak place with lines of wooden huts left over from the Second World War. Because of the early start, we all stayed at the camp and filmed Gethin and the other Royal Marines as they prepared for the test. The barrack room was heavy with olive-green webbing, weapons and the smell of embrocation.

The recruits were at the peak of their physical fitness and I could sense both their dread of the test to come and their determination to pass it. Gethin was welcomed like a lamb to the slaughter and was allocated a bed in the open-plan dormitory. He was understandably subdued as equipment was weighed to make sure every man carried the same weight. Vulnerable spots like heels and toes were carefully taped up.

I had budgeted for three camera crews, including myself. One would film from a helicopter that I had booked at vast expense from the Ministry of Defence. I had decided to try out a new stabilisation system for the camera to get rid of the rotor vibration, and the cameraman seemed happy to try it out.

While they experimented in the helicopter we filmed the rest of the troop, who relaxed and stripped off. It wasn't unusual to see a stark-naked body in the back of shot and much reframing was needed to keep it suitable for family viewing. Lack of inhibition and nudity were part of the culture and we got the full frontal of it.

That night Gethin, thoughtful and resigned to his fate, bunked up with the rest of the troop and we, the film crews, bunked up next door with the directing staff. Any regret at leaving the army when I did (in 1973) was banished in a cacophony of snores and the smells of male bodies. The smell of embrocation was, to me, as significant as the sight of warpaint.

There was general apprehension in both dormitories at the physical horror to come. In the calm before the storm I was as anxious as anyone. Even though I had directed some five or six hundred films, I was still on edge. Deep down I knew, however hard I tried to plan, that something would go wrong. So during a sleepless night I wrestled with the machinations of juggling three crews and worked out what to do if there was a heavy mist or if Gethin gave up between camera positions. Wake-up call came at a deathly 0400 hours.

At 0500 hours, after a full breakfast and more greasing of private parts to prevent chafing, Gethin and his troop, fidgeting with anxiety and loaded with kit, set off into the darkness. They headed for the moor, where most of them got lost. We drove around the edge of the moor to the first checkpoint and waited. An early morning fog hadn't helped and they were very late. So much for marching by compass, I thought. I asked about timings. 'Won't they now fail the test?' I asked.

'We'll give them another 40 minutes to make up for the time they were adrift,' came the reply.

I had hiked across the moor in my youth, training for Ten Tors at school, and I remembered the torment of trying to keep up a rhythm as ankles were unexpectedly bent between tussocks in the heavily rutted ground. In those days we were lightly laden. In this exercise all the recruits, including Gethin, were carrying the equivalent of a heavy suitcase in their webbing. I knew from my army days that it jarred with every step, ripped muscles, and wore blisters into the skin.

At checkpoint one Gethin was coping well and after a quick slurp of water he was off again with his syndicate. He had found the pace and had fitted in well.

By checkpoint two the mist was thicker than ever and it swirled about the clumps of heather and rocks in the bleak moorland. They arrived in their groups and bolted bananas and a pasty. Pain now written all over his face, Gethin was told to eat, even though his body rebelled. He was beginning to suffer more than the others and he needed the energy. He was near crisis and I wondered how long he would last. By way of encouragement Sergeant Dyball told him that the worst of the uneven ground was over but I don't know if Gethin really believed him. They trundled off into the mist, heading for the next checkpoint and more hours of pain.

Eighteen miles in, at checkpoint three, Gethin was ten minutes behind the others and on his last legs. Sergeant Dyball had stayed with him and they came in together at a steady pace. He was very close to giving up. The mood of the staff was uncompromising – like it or lump it, he was in it to the end. They treated him like any other recruit and part bullied, part encouraged him and did anything to keep him going. He was now in obvious pain and I wondered if he would make the final checkpoint six miles away. The weather was clearing but it was still very overcast and I was concerned that the film crew with the helicopter had yet to put in an appearance.

As the grim-faced group of commandos set off at a jog, there was a moment of light relief. Ever looking for the extra camera shot, I tried to keep pace with them, running backwards while filming with the heavy camera perched on my shoulder. And while I was fired up with adrenalin, my sound recordist, Barry, wasn't. Even though he was on a flexible cable, it wasn't long enough. I was brought up short when he fell straight on to a wet cow pat. Even Gethin had to smile when his syndicate cheered.

Checkpoint four was humming with activity but there was no sign

(Left): Gethin Jones at Okehampton Battle Camp, contemplating the 30-mile green beret endurance test

of Gethin. One recruit was in a bad way and an ambulance had been called to take him away. The blue lights had just disappeared from sight when we got the first news of Gethin.

'He's about 40 minutes behind and still going,' someone shouted as they set off, bananas in hand.

And indeed he was. Through sheer will-power he was still going and the crisis was past. He was going to finish, even if it meant going it alone. At the final checkpoint he reached for yet another banana and I saw the fire of determination and the will to win that only years of club rugby could harden.

A small party of medics and instructors gathered around him and they set off for the final six miles. The weather cleared just enough for the helicopter to take off. It sped to the scene and we heard it faintly as it circled Gethin's group.

At the finish Gethin was only 20 minutes outside the eight hours, which meant he had failed the commando test. Yet he passed a much bigger test in the eyes of the Royal Marines. He hadn't given up. The corridor of Royal Marines who had already completed the test clapped him jubilantly as he crossed the ancient stone bridge to the finishing line. I tried to edit out his tears at the finish to save Gethin from undeserved embarrassment, and was overruled. He captured the hearts of at least half the audience and the other half gave him the benefit of the doubt. He was crippled with exhaustion and unable to stand. It was some days before he could walk without pain. Sergeant Dyball said, 'For a civilian to come down here and get to the end of a 30-miler is fantastic, and he's earned all my respect.'

He was among the very few civilians who have ever been allowed to take the test and, unlike Peter Duncan, he had finished the course.

Against all the odds, and a forest of metalwork of launch brackets recently used for a missile-firing exercise, the helicopter cameraman managed to get some shots of Gethin and his companions. They were just tiny figures against the great expanse of the moor. It may have cost a great deal for just a few seconds on screen but the aerial images helped give a sense of scale to the most gruelling of tests, one that puts the Royal Marines in a league of their own.

Gethin had more than proved himself in the best of the programme's tradition as a *Blue Peter* action man. He still proudly describes his achievement as the toughest challenge of his life.

(Top) Gethin Jones is applauded as he crosses the finish line

(Above): Total exhaustion

(Right): Digging deep

(Above): Zoe Salmon and
Matt Baker at the Great
Pyramid, Egypt

35

Temples, tombs and tummy trouble

As if a major shoot in the Far East wasn't enough, the programme bosses must have thought I didn't have enough on my plate and decided to spring an unexpected surprise in the Middle East.

So, hard on the heels of the all-important summer expedition to Japan in 2005, I was tasked with organising an equally complex but potentially exciting expedition to Egypt in October.

I got on with it post-haste in case someone changed their mind. The shoot would be for about two weeks, including travel, and I had a free hand. I contacted my old friend John McIntyre, who had been the underwater cameraman in Belize. We met just down the road from Television Centre at the Balzac Bistro at the bottom of Wood Lane, the venue for many an informal BBC huddle. Over coffee and a bite, we pored over the map of Egypt and made a plan.

As a former BBC News correspondent with a passion for scuba diving, John had an excellent eye for a story and suggested a dive over the wreck of the *Thistlegorm*, a Second World War armed freighter built in the UK. It was also one of the world's top dive sites. He worked regularly in the Red Sea and had very good contacts with a travel company that could organise the travelling arrangements. We set up some dates to do a recce.

John was a relaxing person to be with, perhaps because of what I imagined to be the bedlam of the BBC newsroom. There's nothing like a regular dollop of panic over many years to evoke the opposite reaction.

28 August–3 September 2005

Egypt

We flew to Cairo and I got my first lead. The in-flight entertainment featured a report of a new discovery in one of Egypt's ancient tombs and the archaeologist was a colourful character called Dr Zahi Hawass, who was Minister of State for Antiquities Affaires. Grey-haired, wearing an Indiana Jones-style hat, he had a deep rich voice and a passion for his work. On screen he was pure entertainment and at our first port of call, the pyramids, I began my enquiries.

'Yes, Dr Hawass is here and, no, he isn't at this minute.'

'You must talk to his secretary.'

'He is a very busy man.'

The people who worked with him were either very protective or terrified of him – or perhaps a bit of both. Either way I knew he was the key to any film about the pyramids and I was not about to give up.

Egypt turned out to be welcoming but hamstrung with paperwork. I had taken a small video camera to get background shots and, whenever possible, I filmed away.

'No, you can't film inside the Great Pyramid without a permit.'

'You will need separate written permits for filming on the station, another on the train, and another for the station where you get off.'

We travelled to Luxor and toured temples and tombs, and the nightmare continued. We joined the Brooke Hospital for Sick Animals to watch a village clinic in action. I sprinted off to get shots in the market and was hauled back by the chief of police, a charming man with a sense of humour, who was keeping an eye on us.

'You must realise that within a hundred metres there is someone who would kill you if they could,' he warned us. 'You must not film without me to protect you.'

I promised faithfully to stay close. I had momentarily forgotten that Egypt was under a cloud from the brutal attacks of extremists in the past.

There was a chink of light in the organisational gloom. At dawn the next day we went hot-air ballooning over the temples and the river Nile, and afterwards met the owner of Hod-Hod Soliman balloons, Mohamed Ezz el Dinn. He was an extraordinary man; larger than life, bombastic, charming, with a black beard and an accent that would have found a home in Hollywood. We talked about *Blue Peter* and he explained that when he wasn't piloting balloons he was farming and that his second wife was English. I reckoned we had struck gold but as usual there was a sting in the tail. 'You will not be able to film in the balloon without a special permit.'

We arranged to come back and film – whatever.

We travelled north to Lake Burullus. The lake was full of fishing dhows and it looked calm and peaceful. The sky was blue and the people friendly and the dhows glided to and fro with their sails set, gleaming in the afternoon sun.

Again came the now familiar refrain, 'Yes, you can come fishing with us if you get a permit.' We began our drive back to Cairo and at the side of the road we noticed a colourful encampment. There were dark, low tents patched like quilts and stretched by guy ropes, and we stopped to investigate. These were *rahala*, nomadic people who moved their flocks as necessary to graze on harvested stubble. We joined them for a cup of tea sitting cross-legged in our socks on exotic carpets laid on the hot earth. Yes, we could film and no permit was required. 'Why?' I asked warily. 'You are the first people to ask,' came the reply. I thought we were home and dry, but come the day there was trouble, not only because we did not have a permit but because the local authorities were far from happy about us filming such people.

12–26 October 2005
Egypt and the Red Sea

Two months later we set off for the shoot with Matt Baker and Zoe Salmon. The Egyptian travel company we had enlisted to cut through the bureaucracy had been driven mad by the permit application process and I was exhausted with having to answer so many detailed questions. No one had wanted to offend, so it all had to be just right. Our persistence paid off and the shoot began at the Great Pyramid, and with the elusive and colourful Dr Hawass.

The doctor's office was close to the pyramid and the curtains were permanently closed against the heat. Fear permeated the building. Dr Hawass ran a very tight ship and nothing happened except when he wanted it to. We introduced ourselves and explained the nature of the film. Dr Hawass was utterly unimpressed. I tried flattery because we desperately needed him to paint a picture of the ancient culture that built the pyramids. I needn't have bothered. Luck had it that a local Egyptian TV crew turned up. They wanted to shoot a profile of Dr Hawass for Egyptian television and our presence gave them a good storyline. He would film with us if we could do everything in two or three hours. I readily agreed, even though I knew it would be a real sweat.

We began the filming overlooking the three pyramids and then moved to the Great Pyramid itself. We had a permit (at enormous expense) to film inside for one hour only. But we had not reckoned with Dr Hawass, who was now on our side. He swept towards the entrance and announced to the queue and the guard outside that 'The pyramid will be closed for two hours. Let no one inside'.

We filmed in the entrance tunnel that sloped upwards and the sweat poured off me as I struggled to keep the action moving. Then we entered the main gallery and Dr Hawass paused for dramatic effect (and to get his breath).

'This in my opinion could be the best architecture piece ever created by a man in history.' He looked genuinely affected and his rich bass voice quivered to add greater effect to his words. 'If you look at it you'll feel that your heart is trembling and you will believe that those people did this for immortality.'

We entered the King's Chamber and suddenly the second TV

(Above): Alex films as Dr Zahi Hawass describes to Zoe Salmon and Matt Baker how the pyramids were built

crew, which had been invisible, was invisible no more. I mentioned this and to my astonishment they were summarily dismissed. I felt quite sorry for them. It was a savage reminder to stay sharp or we would be out as well. We filmed by the empty sarcophagus and Dr Hawass was determined to tell a deeper and more significant story about the empty Queen's Chamber in another part of the pyramid. He indicated a small opening in the side of the otherwise perfectly geometrically built stone-walled room.

Speaking slowly and with great significance, he continued, 'A short while ago we sent a remote camera into this opening and what do you think we found?' He had all the skills of a great storyteller.

Matt and Zoe were intrigued.

'They found a secret door.' Dr Hawass paused to increase the suspense. He went on, 'And then they sent another camera past that door and into the passage beyond. And what do think they found?' Matt and Zoe joined in the drama and looked spellbound. The pause was unbearable. Very slowly Dr Hawass announced: 'They found a second door.'

The triumph in his voice was unmistakable. He continued, 'Who knows what lies behind that second door?'

Matt speculated. 'Maybe the missing body of the Pharoah?' It was a good question.

Dr Hawass was conspiratorial and emotional. 'Maybe Cheops' chamber is still hidden inside the pyramid…you never know what [secrets] the sands of Egypt might hide.'

The rest of the day was an anticlimax and as darkness fell we boarded a coach to take us to the airport, where we flew to Sharm El Sheik on the Sinai Peninsula to join a luxury dive boat named *Tempest*, which would be our home for the next four days.

That night I was exhausted. It had been an extraordinary first day and Dr Hawass had taken us on a vivid journey. He had brought stone to life with his powerful presence and passionate description of the ancient Egyptians. I was so glad that I had persevered to get him to appear on the programme even though he had pushed me to my physical limit, carrying my heavy camera and tripod in the heat.

It was the *Tempest*'s maiden voyage and, apart from the crew, we were the only passengers. We could scarcely believe our luck. Brand new, about sixty feet long and gleaming with polished mahogany fittings, she was the latest in a line of high-end dive charters. There were enough en-suite cabins for us not to have to share. Zoe had only a minor part to play in Matt's diving adventure, and spent each day scantily clad and sunbathing on the sun deck. Matt was happy, Zoe was very happy, and the weather held.

After four or five dives and several tests, including how to cope with underwater emergencies, Matt passed his PADI Open Water certificate. We steamed across a flat Red Sea eating a salad lunch painstakingly prepared by the crew, for whom life on a dive boat was far more rewarding financially than the daily grind in Cairo. Egyptian dive guides enjoyed even greater privilege. Ours was a constantly smiling,

(Right): Matt with his dive buddy, Yasser Abd El Shafy in the Red Sea

enthusiastic instructor called Yasser Abd El Shafy.

Our main dive was the *Thistlegorm*, a British freighter that had been bombed by the Luftwaffe in 1941. They had mistaken her in the moonlight for the *Queen Mary*, which had been reported to be bringing reinforcements for the battles in North Africa. The *Thistlegorm* had been sunk in about a hundred feet of water with her cargo of vehicles and other military supplies. Sixty years later she had gained a name as one of the world's top dive sites because she remained largely intact. We hove to above her and joined half a dozen other dive boats that attached mooring lines to parts of her bridge far below.

I stayed on deck with my camera and covered the melee of circling dive boats on the surface while Matt and his instructor, Yasser, sank beneath the waves. Much later we viewed the tape in *Tempest*'s stateroom.

The *Thistlegorm* was an imposing sight and Matt and Yasser swam between the decks in the company of several lionfish and turtles. They floated over lorries packed with waders and other stores. Rows of BSA motorbikes lined one deck and, incredibly, a steam engine was still mounted on the upper deck. It was jaw-dropping stuff and did much to explain Matt's excitement when he resurfaced, saying in his infectious Geordie accent, 'And to think it was built just down the road from where I was born just makes it even better.' It was only after the dive, when Matt confessed what had really happened, that I realised there were some situations that were not only beyond my control but were truly dangerous. Matt recalls:

> My regulator malfunctioned and I sucked water into my mouth 30 metres down. Yasser saved my life by putting his regulator in my mouth, giving me the chance to use my spare. It wasn't a case of heading for the surface as we were too deep. Luckily things turned out OK.

(Left): The team in the wardroom of the *Tempest*. From L to R: underwater cameraman John McIntyre, Nicola and Matt Baker, safety diver Jo Ruxton, a crew member and sound recordist Barry Smith

Out at sea we were safe from the reality of being visitors to Egypt, but back on dry land the seriousness of the extremists struck home. As we set off for Luxor we had to share our coach with two guards wearing Showaddywaddy-type jackets that concealed Heckler and Koch sub-machine guns. We travelled in convoy with about fifteen other coaches and I wondered if it was all a bit extreme. But terrorist attacks had happened in the past and I was reminded that the authorities had to assume they could strike again. As it turned out, the journey, which took place at night, was uneventful and our guards stayed with us until we had finished filming in Luxor.

Mohamed Ezz, our colourful balloonist-cum-farmer, was very pleased to see us and when he saw Zoe his eyes positively gleamed. We spent the day on his farm and Zoe tried to milk a camel, saying (as she was wont to), 'I've never done this before,' as she squeezed the flaccid teat; the visual double-entendre was not missed by Mohamed Ezz. With great pride he showed them his herd of exotic goats and then watched Zoe with keen interest as both she and Matt herded and fed his massive flock of geese and turkeys.

It was very hot and uneventful until Matt began to hose down a water buffalo. Tethered as it was to a large cast-iron plough, it wasn't going anywhere and obviously loved the cold water in the hot sun. I advanced with the camera and while it looked at me suspiciously it continued to enjoy its bath. 'Just a low-angle shot with the water dripping,' I said, and lowered the camera to look up at the beast from behind. Its head turned, its eyes flared in terror and it was off, plough and all, missing me by inches. I marvelled at the strength of the brute and my lucky escape as it rampaged on until the plough got stuck between two tree stumps.

'That's the end of the washing sequence, then,' joked Matt.

The next morning, while it was still dark, we set off to go hot-air ballooning with Hod-Hod Soliman Balloons. The flames of the gas burners lit up the red light of dawn and, as the balloon canopies filled and stood upright, Mohamed Ezz arrived, larger than life. The flowing robes of the farmer had been replaced by the crisp uniform of a balloon pilot captain. He clasped Zoe very warmly and was genuinely pleased to see us. He had obviously given what he was about to say some serious thought during the night.

'I give you 20 camels for Zoe,' his deep, raspy voice boomed. 'I need another wife.'

Zoe didn't know what to say and looked slightly alarmed. He mistook our silence as a bargaining ploy. 'I give you 30 camels…' he paused '…and a house in Luxor.' And gave her a loving squeeze. It was difficult to know if he was serious or not and I thought he might have been up to his usual tricks and was teasing us, yet he had obviously taken a shine to her. We all laughed and I said that she couldn't leave the programme because she was under contract. Mohamed looked very disappointed because he knew all about contracts. We took off with great celebration and chanting from the helpers on the ground.

(Above): The balloons were inflated before dawn

During the flight Mohamed Ezz continued to show Zoe great attention and selected her to help fly the balloon. The Nile stretched out beneath us and the green fields on either side became clearer as the sun rose. Every few seconds the gas jets roared a few feet above us and for those who were hatless, the heat was scorching. We flew high one minute and skimmed the tops of the sugar cane the next. It was so peaceful and there was hardly a breath of wind. Mohamed Ezz enjoyed putting the balloon through its paces and was always the perfect gentlemen with his lady co-pilot. I overheard Matt explaining that Zoe had no choice. 'She has to come back with us because the children of the UK would miss her.' And that was perfectly true. Matt commented:

> He was a proper wheeler dealer with his farming and ballooning. I knew his offer for Zoe was a bid too far and at the end of the day I reckoned I would get lumbered with the camels and frankly I didn't think they would last long up in the Durham Dales!

Zoe found the heat overwhelming at times, and a tummy upset didn't help. At Abu Simbel in the far south, she excused herself to the call of nature and vanished for what seemed like an eternity. In fact, she went missing for three whole hours. I had no alternative but to carry on without her, assuming that she could not have gone very far and the tummy upset might have been too difficult for her to control.

When she did reappear we learned the truth. She had gone to the

(Near right): En route to Luxor

(Far right): Matt and Nicola Baker

lavatory and then back to the coach to lie down for ten minutes in the air-conditioning. She had fallen asleep and when she'd woken up she hadn't known where she was. The driver had taken the coach to a less salubrious side of town for his lunch and she had been stranded until he returned.

She was repentant and I was not best pleased. However, what was done was done, and I let it go.

Zoe excelled herself a few days later when it was time to spend the afternoon and evening with the *rahala* people who had been so welcoming. I wished that our police entourage of some dozen of all ranks had felt the same way.

In Egypt the *rahala*, who were nomadic Nile dwellers, were thought of in the same way as gypsies in Britain. They could not understand why we should wish to film them. The police objected, saying it was not good for Egypt to feature them. It all got quite heated and as the minutes ticked by so did our chances of completing the sequence I had planned.

Then, by some miracle, the argument ended and we were allowed to continue, and Zoe and Matt entered a world that few have ever experienced. They danced, trilled, fought with sticks, tried on exotic headwear, and pet geese were brought for their inspection. And because it was Ramadan, we had to wait until the sun sank to the horizon before we could join an evening feast, sitting cross-legged on huge carpets. There was laughter, music, and as food was brought in on huge plates, the last rays of golden light filtered through the palms. As darkness closed in to envelop us they lit a huge fire, and Matt and Zoe joined in to sing and dance around it.

'Thank you for making us so welcome...*Shukran shukran*,' Matt cried, as the flames flared and finally died away, marking the end of a memorable two weeks criss-crossing Egypt to witness its many ancient and colourful wonders.

Blue **Peter**

Film: Melbourne
COST CODE: PAD-6871-FILM

RX Date: 16th – 29th November 2005
TX Date: TBC

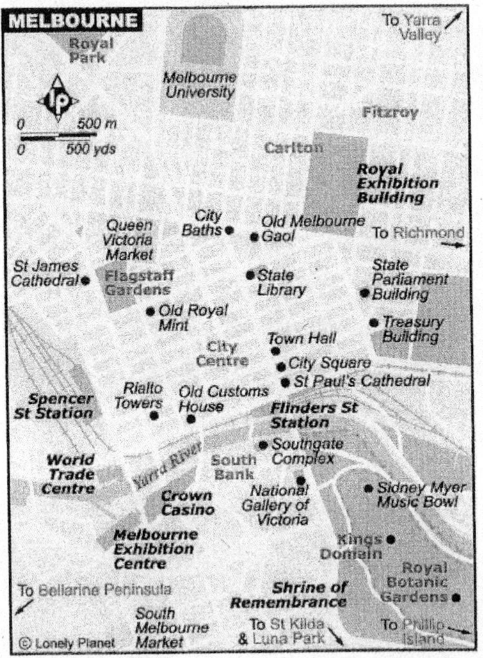

Director	Alex Leger
Researcher/Director	Mignon Aylen
Camera	David Hudspeth
Sound	Joshua McIvor
Editor	Chris Groom
Presenter	Matthew Baker
Fixer	Sharon McGrath

(Above): *Blue Peter* filming schedule for Melbourne

36

My secret *Neighbours* addiction

17–28 November 2005
Melbourne, Australia

In my younger days I dreamt about travelling the world and seeing things and places that the tourists would never see. I imagined myself tirelessly living that dream. By 2005 I found myself occasionally having to pinch myself as this had become my reality. Egypt had been an eye-opener. So had Vermont, New Hampshire and Niagara Falls, Cyprus, and Angola, not to mention the excitement of the flight deck on HMS *Illustrious*.

Now, having just returned from a hectic couple of weeks in Egypt, I had less than a month before I was off again. This time it would be to Melbourne, Australia. It was all too much – I was exhausted. It seemed ironic that my youthful ambitions had all come true when I was no longer a youth.

However, I had things I wanted to do in Melbourne and there was no better time to do it than before the BBC finally ran out of cash. Matt Baker had been asked to commentate at the World Gymnastics by BBC Sport and I had to supervise him making a film about his role and the England team. I also had to make a whole programme about Melbourne itself.

I am at an age when I am no longer embarrassed to admit to being a closet fan of the TV soap *Neighbours*. I have watched it for years. I watched it with all my children and so did my wife Lynn. And I watch it now. For me it's an enforced break in the middle of a busy day. People who know me avoid calling when *Neighbours* is on – even visitors to the edit suites in Television Centre. If I was seen watching it in the office there was a collective cry of 'How can you watch that stuff?' Well, I do.

So Melbourne was no hardship. I was going to make a film about *Neighbours* and for me it would be a pleasure.

I also had to think of some other things to put in the programme.

Under pressure I settled very grudgingly on Australian Rules football, even though I had absolutely no interest in it, and the zoo at Healesville, where we would help behind the scenes. For this I had a very able assistant, Mignon Aylen, who was Australian and had been working for the programme in London.

Mignon was keen to prove herself and went to enormous lengths to help. She located a 'footy' club, the Hawthornes, and a professional player who turned out to be a very good foil for Matt. She even organised a 'barbie'.

The Healesville Zoo was her film. I would act as cameraman and give advice if needed. By delegating, I could devote all my energies to Matt turning his hand to being a commentator, Aussie Rules football and, my favourite bit, *Neighbours*.

It wasn't easy to persuade the producers of *Neighbours* to let us intrude, but after much flattery they relented. Stingray, or actor Ben Nicholas, was incredibly quick witted and very funny, and it was agreed that we could follow him for a day.

Stingray's day began at dawn. Creeping along in a hire car to the front of his bungalow where he lived with his mum, Matt and I whispered to each other to keep quiet. It was all quite absurd because the morning chorus of kookaburras and heaven knows what else was truly deafening.

He came to the door in his dressing gown. He explained he was a bit hungover because he had been to a concert in Sydney the previous night. His eyes sparkled with the fun of it all. He reminded me of a mischievous Peter Duncan but more so. At 17, he was a born television presenter as well as actor.

Rather like John Noakes, who could entertain by just being himself, Stingray (I found it very hard to think of him as anything else) found humour at every turn as we toured Lassiter's, the general store and the studio set. Paul Robinson's front room became the set for an impromptu scene between Stingray and Matt. We all took photographs of ourselves sitting on the deep red settee.

We later met Paul Robinson (actor Stefan Dennis) and far from the evil he personified on television, he was charming. He told me that he was a big fan of *Blue Peter* and had a *Blue Peter* badge from when he had appeared on the programme years before. Steph Scully appeared with her children and was full of welcoming smiles. Stingray's on-stage mum made an appearance too, and I got a bee in my bonnet about something so we did a sequence with her about four times. I stopped when I saw the exasperation on her face.

The studio and set were just like every drama set I had ever seen. It looked good on camera and not so good off it. However, I did not expect their offices to follow suit. I was amazed how tatty they were, like 1960s architecture that had not worn well. I thought the BBC was pretty ropey, yet it was luxury compared to the *Neighbours* studios.

All too soon the day was nearly over and we finished the filming in Ramsay Street; I hate to spoil the illusion but its real name is in fact Pin Oak Court. As the sun began to dip behind the roofs, Matt thanked

(Right): Paul Robinson (*Neighbours* actor Stefan Dennis), Stingray (Ben Nicholas) and Alex

Stingray for being such a great contributor. He gave him his own *Blue Peter* badge and no doubt he showed it proudly to Paul Robinson the next day.

I briefly met the producer of *Neighbours*, Peter Dodds, in the lunch queue and reassured him that he had millions of devoted fans in the UK. To my surprise he was even older than I was. How he survived the treadmill of producing five programmes a week I will never know.

Back on the floor of the World Gymnastics, Matt was settling in uncomfortably between the incumbent commentators, Mitch Venner and Christine Still. I felt a bit sorry for Mitch, who seemed uneasy at this turn of events. Matt, as the new boy, had to mind his Ps and Qs and Mitch had to look to his laurels. What puzzled me was that the BBC had sent just one assistant producer to organise their side of things. There was a picture editor too, Chris Groom, who had been installed with his edit suite in the Hilton Hotel, a five-minute walk from the main arena. Chris's editing skills were sought after in Children's Programmes; even so, the BBC Sports production staff of one looked very hard pressed. One night the commentary sound feedback to the UK was cut because of an overrun, and they had to do it all again. It meant several hours of extra work late at night. I felt things were stretched to the limit and I offered to help.

The main video coverage could not cover the England team's pre-event nerves or the aftermath, so I offered to work on the arena floor as a cameraman. For three afternoons, and in my time off, I filmed the main events and behind the scenes and greatly enjoyed myself. I progressed around the arena hot on the heels of the competitors, like a middle-aged groupie, as they changed exercises. It was unreal to watch Beth Tweddle and other international stars perform their routines less than twenty feet away and know that the footage would be seen back in the UK. I had no idea that my movements were being noted by Matt:

> I will never forget seeing Alex in a luminous bib more or less under the apparatus, blissfully unaware of competition protocol and in true *Blue Peter* style getting as close to the action as humanly possible. Probably the most personal and

(Left): Matt Baker in the commentator's position at the 2005 World Gymnastics

close-up action shots of our British gymnastics team ever. It was my commentating debut yet I couldn't take my eyes off him. It was good to have him around.

I was told that my shots were used but whether they were appreciated or not I never found out.

Home again, and Christmas came and went with the speed of light. I had to do penance for my travels with weeks in the edit suites, cutting together the films I had made in Egypt. It was the best part of two months before I could scout about for more ideas.

Then a challenge came along that was achievable, looked safe – and suddenly wasn't.

13–15 July 2006
Hull

The Royal Marines were aiming to abseil 400 feet from the top of the Humber Bridge. It was billed as the highest abseil ever in the UK and Andy Akinwolere, who had just joined the team, was volunteered to do it. Andy was from Nigeria and being the new boy he was willing to please. He was a chick magnet, being good looking, athletic and cool. The snag was he had a fear of heights. However, remembering how he had excelled himself bungee jumping during the summer's expedition to America, great things were expected of him as he faced his fear once again.

I had worked with the Royal Marine mountain leaders before and knew them to be an experienced and helpful bunch.

(Above): Abseiling the Humber Bridge. Andy Akinwolere can be seen as a tiny figure, bottom right

My concerns grew on the recce. I found out that it wasn't a seasoned mountain leader group but a territorial unit, and the mountain leader element was one or two experienced men. There were lots of relatively inexperienced helpers, and this was a big project. The plan was to play safe and put down just two ropes. I pointed out that we would need a third rope for the cameraman or we would not be able to make the film. This was refused. For a few days I assumed that the shoot was off. Then there was a sudden change of opinion. A third rope was accepted as part of the plan. I was puzzled. How could this be safe now when it wasn't before?

I asked Rob Franklin, an abseiling cameraman, to film on the way down while Steve Wagstaff would film from the top. I would film from the ground.

The day arrived and after a morning of securing ropes we broke for lunch. A very worried Rob Franklin approached me.

'It's not safe,' he told me. 'Look at this.' He showed me a photograph of a frayed rope.

'They didn't lag the rope properly and when the first man went down it frayed on the sharp concrete parapet.'

There were other reasons he explained, which I didn't understand. 'I want an expert to check it out before I go down.'

Three hours later, expert Robbie Shone began his inspection.

An uncomfortable exchange took place between the Royal Marine colonel and Robbie, who explained what was wrong. I feared that *Blue Peter*'s previously excellent relationship with the Royal Marines was in jeopardy. It appeared that what had always worked for the Royal Marines was no longer safe for civilians because regulations outside the military had been tightened. In an atmosphere of necessity, a compromise was reached.

We were told to wait until the end of the day when all the sponsored volunteers had abseiled for charity. Then, as the sun got lower and redder in the sky, we began our abseil. There was hardly any wind and the late afternoon sun reflected off the sheer concrete columns of the bridge. It was beautiful and uncompromising but time was running out, with only half an hour to go before the sun disappeared below the horizon. I knew it would be a close-run thing.

With Captain Jason Milne beside him, a terrified Andy inched his way over the parapet and began his descent. It was all far from ideal. Because of the need to double up on ropes, Rob could only follow about a quarter of the descent, so for most of the abseil we had to rely on a helmet camera. I didn't know it at the time but there was trouble there too. There were so many delays when getting started that it ran out of tape within five minutes of going over the edge. There was one bit of good news, though. Robbie, our safety adviser, hung off a supporting cable and looked back at the bridge with a palmcorder. He got a stunning image that saved the day.

Andy just about held it together as he made his heart-thumping descent. He was unable to speak. Jason encouraged him to say something, to no avail. He spoke not a word.

When I looked at the rushes much later I realised just how close we had got to not getting a film at all.

For Andy it had been a baptism of fire in more ways than one:

> This was the first time I had been in contact with a very British director whose idea of film-making resembled the colonial BBC approach seen the world over. Very direct in speech and very matter-of-fact about everything. Contrastingly, he also had a softer side. He truly cared about my well-being and this I appreciated. Abseiling down that bridge was hell. The wind picked up and swung me left and right. I swore blindly all the way down. I realised at that moment that in order for the audience to get to know me they had to invest in me as a presenter and that included my high and low points.

Blue Peter will always seek to film with the Royal Marine mountain leaders, and especially their more extreme challenges. The Humber Bridge abseil and all its problems was a sign of the times and from that moment on risk assessments became a major part of every film I made, much more so than ever before.

4–10 January 2007
Blantyre, Southern Malawi

Blue Peter's 43rd annual appeal was called the Shoebiz Appeal. The aim was to collect 500,000 pairs of shoes to be recycled to raise funds for play areas for children living with HIV and AIDS in Malawi. As a follow-up to our filmed reports from Malawi that had already launched the appeal, Andy and I, with sound recordist Martin Huntley, found ourselves flying overnight and sleeplessly via Johannesburg to Lilongwe, the capital of Malawi. Our task was to report to the viewers what had been achieved.

It was six months since Andy's abseil from hell in Hull and he had come a long way. Even so, he would find the subject matter a test of his ability to deal with sensitive issues, as we all would. I knew that Andy's empathy with the contributors would play an important part in the storytelling.

The AIDS issue had not been fully addressed on the previous visit and I was under orders to clarify it once and for all. We needed to drum up support for the appeal, which had lost some of its impetus. I would be treading the tightrope of hammering home the hard facts without making the programme seem uncaring. The success of the trip rested entirely on being able to film the right children. We left the UK with the names of four possible children whom the host charity UNICEF had approached and who had agreed to be filmed. There were two girls and two boys.

From experience I knew that young African girls were hard to interview because they were not used to the attention usually reserved for the boys. Shyness could strike without warning and it could render them almost mute. Yet my brief was unequivocal – we needed to hear loud and clear about the terrible disease that was ravaging the country.

We had just six days to get there, film and get back.

The flight out was sheer torture. We had been given the cheapest tickets and flew through the night to wait for hours in Johannesburg airport, comatose with fatigue, for our connection to Lilongwe. By the time we landed in Malawi we were totally exhausted.

No soft bed awaited us, because our travelling was far from over. Our misery continued and the second day turned into afternoon as we waited for a connection that would take us to Blantyre in the south. It failed to appear. Hallucinating from lack of sleep, I began to wonder if Andy would be capable of remembering who he was, let alone the complexities of the script. We had about sixteen hours before we were due to start filming at our first location. Andy remembers the moment well:

> As an African, this was like coming home. I hated the fact
> that we had come over to my continent to see people dying.

> I was nervous at not being able to deliver as a presenter.
> While I'd seen so many *Blue Peter* presenters do appeals
> well, I think they sometimes failed to convey true emotion.
> That is why I really wanted to do this piece.

While Andy brooded on the challenges to come, the connecting flight landed. It was four hours late. In a deeply pessimistic mood we flew off and into a huge bank of fog. We circled in perpetual cloud over what we were told was Blantyre airport. The pilot might have sensed our impatience because he then played a game of 'dare' with the runway, only chickening out at the last second when he failed to see it.

After a few near-misses, when wisps of tropical rainforest were glimpsed only feet below the wing, he banked and approached the airport for a fifth time. By this time I was on my feet, trying to attract the steward's attention. I wanted to tell him that I really didn't mind if we didn't land. A nice safe arrival anywhere else was preferable. I sensed we were on the brink of an ignominious end, and with no more than a dozen passengers for company we wouldn't even get a mention on *BBC Breakfast* (then Britain's first morning national television show) if the worst should happen.

Thankfully the pilot bored of his game and we returned to Lilongwe airport with 11 hours to go.

After less than four hours' sleep in the airport hotel, we were on our way again, by road this time. For five hours we bounced from pothole to pothole through vistas normally reserved for coffee-table tour guides. They were wasted on us because we were all sound asleep.

And so it was that, curiously refreshed, we trundled into our destination an hour before we were due to set off for our first location, a school just outside Blantyre.

Travelling the road into Blantyre was a grim experience because here more people than usual traded with death. As if we needed reminding of what the film was all about, we passed shop after shop selling nothing but coffins. Not the result of reckless flying accidents but of that silent killer, AIDS.

Up until this moment I had been deeply pessimistic about filming at all but unexpectedly I felt I could survive a few more hours. I looked anxiously at Andy and he seemed buoyant. He agreed that we should carry on. Grasping the moment, I suggested we stick to our schedule. Our fixer looked hugely relieved, and in hindsight it was not hard to see why.

The school was expecting us and my dread of finding nothing special to film disappeared in a trice. We arrived to a fantastic sight.

Imagine about a hundred parents dressed to the nines in brightly coloured reds and yellows and singing their hearts out. In three lines mothers stamped in unison and swayed back and forth as a raucous four-part harmony washed over us with contagious energy.

From the moment Andy stepped out of the vehicle he was at one with the celebrations. All signs of fatigue gone, he fluently described his excitement at the warmth of the welcome. We all felt the same and, lifted by the intoxicating music and dance, we powered through the day. Once again, as on so many overseas shoots, disaster had been averted and we were on track once more.

The next day we visited a really nice young lad I will call 'H'. He lived with his aunt in a small mud and leaf house in a small community about forty minutes' drive from our hotel.

We arrived in our little convoy of two vehicles and created much excitement among the children of the village. Curiosity was at fever pitch and yet we were to film with discretion.

H was HIV-positive and no one in the village knew this. And for his sake we had to film without letting on. I wondered whether or not it was possible, but the cover story was swallowed whole, helped no doubt by the fact that no one spoke a word of English.

Andy bonded with H very quickly because it was obvious that he cared about him. He later admitted that it was because he had a brother who was about the same age and he 'hated seeing Africans in this kind of way'. This made the subject of the filming much easier for him to empathise with, which was just as well because it wasn't long before the thorny question about what it was like living with AIDS came up.

Both of H's parents had died of the disease a few years before, and we could feel his grief. I wondered how to bring it out. I believe that his aunt sensed this too. She knew only too well how life for H could turn for the worse, because she was a nurse who worked at the local hospital.

We sat ready for the all-important interview on the baked mud patch in front of the mud cottage that was his new home. We had already filmed him helping around the house, sweeping the yard, washing up and tending the garden vegetables. He knew that some tough questions were about to come his way. While we set up the camera, Andy, sensitive to the end, touched H occasionally on the shoulder as he shared his anxiety.

Then the interview began.

'When did you come to live with your aunt?' Andy was reassuring.

The interpreter worked between them and I filmed the whole of H's reply before focusing on the interpreter, who spoke in English.

H's answers were to the point and matter-of-fact and there was little emotion. I had briefed Andy to lead with easy questions before asking about his memories.

'Have you made friends here?'

All the while I moved the camera between H and the interpreter's reply so it would be possible to overlay the English interpretation under H's Chewa language.

'What do you miss most?'

H thought for a while and said he missed his family. The moment we needed to hear and see was approaching.

'And what was your family like?'

H began to talk and shake with emotion. Tears began to flow down his cheeks. I noticed that Andy, too, was crying. It was a dreadfully poignant moment and we all felt quite shaken by H's misery. Despite our intrusion into H's sensitivities (good or bad, I couldn't tell at that moment), I knew this was the response that our viewers needed to see in order to understand the devastation that AIDS left in its wake.

Andy conducted the same interview several times, exploring more and more of H's feelings and his regrets. Filming is a methodical business and I had to set up the camera from several different angles so the editor could cut the best sequence together in the short time that would be allowed on screen.

Each time we filmed the interview the tears flowed, and more and more of H's emotions were revealed until I knew we should stop.

In a thoughtful mood we moved on to other subjects.

The district nurse arrived by bicycle to check H's health and to deliver his medicines. His visit was routine so some normality returned. Andy was now very much in H's confidence and his replies had become very open and descriptive. Even I was unprepared for his response to one of Andy's final questions.

'What would you like to be when you are older?' It was a question that in any other circumstances would have been considered a 'filler'.

H's reply was as chilling as the look in his eyes. 'I would like to become a policeman so I could lock up bad men who harm children.'

Much later, several weeks after we left Malawi, we heard from the aunt.

In a letter to UNICEF she reported that H was now much happier. She added that up until our visit he had not said a word about his mum and dad. Andy, by asking some very probing questions, had released the grief and it had done him some good.

Andy commented:

> I think the reason why this worked so well was because I was a black man who did not resemble any of the attributes of the black men he might have come across. And as an interviewer my mission has always been to make the camera invisible to the subject.

H had benefited from our visit, even though we had ventured where sometimes it is not wise to go. I was hugely relieved. He had Andy to thank for his cathartic experience because it was only Andy's caring nature that had lanced a boil in H's soul that could have otherwise poisoned many years of his life.

Back in the UK, Andy's reports were hard hitting and focused on the real need for children in Malawi and across the whole world. And that was a deeper and lasting understanding of what living with AIDS was all about.

For me the experience had been less traumatic. Having filmed refugee camps in Ethiopia during the 1985 famine, the potato famine in Peru and the ghastly effects of dirty drinking water on young children in Cambodia in 1988, I found that H's situation, while dreadful, did not shock me. Like it or not, I had been brutalised by these and other memories. And the way I now worked did nothing to sensitise me. 'Self-shooting' meant I watched the drama unfold through the camera's viewfinder and it did not have an impact on me in the same way. My attention was divided, between listening to the action and deciding on frame composition, and both needed my attention.

Whether or not this is good for today's viewers is hard to say. I have noticed the tendency in recent years to 'keep rolling' when the tears start falling, while in the past the camera would have been cut on command.

24–26 January 2007
Gosport, Hampshire

The risk assessment was a major part of filming the submarine escape training tank at Gosport, where the Royal Navy trains its submariners. This is a 30-metre column of water in which sailors enter the tank from depths of 9, 18 and 30 metres. They then float rapidly up to the surface, breathing out as they do so. It is simple but dangerous.

Most of the training is being shown how to blow out using a whistling technique, because to forget to do so is fatal. Air expands as it rises to the surface and if trapped inside the body, the lungs rupture. The budding submariner might be alive when he reached the surface but would die of asphyxiation while frantically breathing God's clean air into his ruined lungs.

This was the second time in seven years we had decided to film the training. Simon Thomas had been the first to survive the challenge and now it was Gethin Jones's turn.

On the risk assessment I wrote, 'If Gethin does not do what he is told, he will die.' He enjoys telling this story, yet the threat was real. When the time came he did exactly as he was told and was a model student. Not for the first time I noted that he had grit.

Diving instructors hung motionless in the water at different levels to check each volunteer as they passed on their way to the surface. I asked the supervisor why.

'If they see someone not breathing out properly, they punch them in the stomach.' It wasn't the response I was expecting.

It is very unlikely that any other future presenter will follow in Gethin's footsteps. The navy now trains its submariners to expect rescue and the escape aspect is less important, so it isn't regularly practised.

The submarine escape tank was familiar territory. My next big project wasn't, and yet again it would endorse my overused passport with an unfamiliar entry.

(Above): Andy
Akinwolere and Gethin
Jones with novice Shaolin
monks

37

Chinese whispers

My mother had regaled me with intriguing tales of her youth in China, where she had lived within walking distance of the Forbidden City in Peking (now Beijing). I had heard that the Chinese could be obstructive without ever actually saying no and China, the country with so many connections to my family, was where I was headed.

Richard Marson had commissioned the shoot before he handed over to Tim Levell, the new programme editor. It was a time of turmoil. The programme had been reduced from three shows a week to two and its budget had been cut back. Tim, the new editor, had a remit to make dramatic changes to the programme style, and action films were to be its new life blood.

A central feature of the new-style programme was the splitting of all action films into two parts, with a recap at the start of the second part. I relished the challenge because it would mean I would get more air time. In practice this meant trying to make two short films out of one action sequence. Sometimes it was successful but often it wasn't. After a year of trying, we went back to single films.

China was to follow the new pattern and I was determined to make it work.

The new China looked Westernised yet beneath the futuristic facades still lurked the ghosts of old. The marble pavements and skyscrapers of Chengdu looked like Herculean attempts to blot out everything that was old or substandard. I thought that the Chinese desperately wanted their share of the modern world and there was no affection for their past.

Nothing, however, was as it appeared and I knew I would have to make it up as I went along.

19 March–2 April 2008
China

I set out with Gethin and Andy to make five films (to be made in ten parts) to be shown during the run-up to the Olympic Games in August 2008.

During a previous visit the year before, I had discovered that to understand the Chinese you needed a different mindset. I was told that while they would honour an arrangement, it was not wise to expect too much.

It had not helped that the BBC had upset the authorities with a documentary on the anniversary of the notorious Tiananmen Square demonstration, which to this day remains a festering indictment of communist rule.

I found that filming some things, like gymnastics, or any sports to do with the Olympics, was difficult to organise. No one ever said no, it was just impossible to get anyone to say yes.

Yet I felt an affinity with Beijing through my mother. We have many pictures of China in the 1920s and 1930s and our house is full of inherited memories, mostly featuring wide-brimmed hats and ox carts. When Lynn and I visited (I paid for Lynn to join me) we found a modern, functioning city and wherever we ate, the food was very good. I am not a fan of Chinese cooking in the UK, so it was a pleasant surprise.

Western influences were taking their toll. Whoever described the new China as a country with a thousand identical cities wasn't far wrong. It was disturbing to see how the hutongs, or side streets, were being demolished to make way for brand-new office blocks and shops. We searched in vain for my mother's old house near the Forbidden City and although we found the street, the site had become a school.

It wasn't just the destruction of some of the ancient parts of the city that upset me. The pollution in the air was another horror. Getting off the aircraft at Beijing airport at three o'clock in the afternoon it was so dark that it could have been early evening. The greyness was everywhere. It hardly ever lifted and it caught at the back of the throat. Beijing was literally choking on chemicals. When it came to the filming the following year, the air was cleaner. Faced with massive complaints, the authorities had shut down all the nearby factories.

Ning, our Chinese fixer, was pragmatic. He had devised a packed timetable of non-contentious things to do. He was a charming man who was tall and good looking, and on the surface seemed more British than Chinese. The presenters took to him immediately and I incorporated him into the action in front of the camera. Gethin, fresh from his *Strictly Come Dancing* triumph, loved the mid-morning ballroom dancing in the park and Andy got dressed up as an unlikely Chinese emperor to have his photograph taken. Sadly, neither sequence made the final cut – not because they weren't any good, quite the reverse – there was just not enough air time to show them. Instead, we showed Andy flying kites in the fabled Tiananmen Square and Gethin working as a part-time rickshaw driver.

We visited the Bird's Nest Stadium and were unable to get any closer than a distant viewing area where we had to shoot between coachloads of tourists. We were more successful with the Water Cube (the Olympic swimming pool) and were allowed inside for a couple of hours. I marvelled at the honeycomb construction but not much else. We embraced the Olympic ideal about a thousand miles from Beijing in Chengdu where, I was reassured, the authorities were co-operative.

Pragmatic as ever, Ning had interpreted my request for a stadium filled with frantically exercising students into a stadium with a couple of dozen volunteers. I knew he had done his best but, as so often happened, our schedule did not match theirs. We staged our own mini-Olympics nevertheless. Both Gethin and Andy threw themselves into the contest and I heaved a sigh of relief. In the true style of all *Blue Peter* presenters they made the most of the javelin, hurdles and 100 metres sprint. They are both naturally competitive and Andy was just that little bit fitter. It was a fight to the end and Gethin, good-natured as ever, had to admit defeat to the younger man.

I noticed a big difference in Gethin. From the new presenter who had lacked confidence and looked for reasons to fail, he had become quite the opposite. His participation in the peak-viewing Saturday night extravaganza that is *Strictly Come Dancing* had changed him. He had been runner-up and had successfully overcome a major internal battle. During the show, Camilla Dallerup, his lithe and glamorous dance partner, had criticised him and he had not crumbled. She had turned a shy young lad, uncertain of the world, into a very confident man who was in a mood to move on. The world was out there and Gethin had at last found his feet – literally.

Just when I thought that his new confidence might have overwhelmed some of his natural charisma, we travelled to Guilin, where he had to spend the day with a very poor fishing family who had a difficult son. Gethin saw the problem and worked hard to make friends.

The dad made a living fishing with trained birds and so continued a long Chinese tradition. The birds were cormorants, similar to the ones seen around the coast of Britain, and, despite tales of cruelty, they took pride of place in the family. The front room was home to newly hatched chicks and the family took it in turns to make sure they were kept warm and fed.

They lived on the banks of a circular lake with large islands in the middle. Incredibly beautiful jagged mountains towered all around, typical of that part of China. The scene is featured on one of their bank notes.

Gethin was kindness itself and paid a lot of attention to the errant son, who even deigned to go fishing with us. We set off on two bamboo rafts and headed down the lake to find a good spot. The ideal fishing place had long been devoid of anything worth catching. The lake had been all but fished out and our fisherman was looking for somewhere shallow instead.

For the purposes of filming, he demonstrated the fishing technique by throwing dead fish into the water and then releasing his birds while shouting incomprehensible words of encouragement. The cormorants used their long hooked bills to scoop up these tasty offerings. But for them it was all in vain because their necks were tied with a piece of raffia so it was impossible for the birds to swallow the dead fish.

(In reality, when there were fish to be caught, fishing would take place at night and a lamp used to attract the fish. The cormorants would then dive and chase the fish as they tried to flee and quite often they would succeed. The fisherman would then deftly scoop the birds out of the water as they tried in vain to swallow their catch and retrieve the fish.)

It sounds cruel yet I don't believe it was. They were a pampered lot. One look into their bright green eyes and all I could see was the hot anger of being spoilt rotten. Gethin helped lift the unresisting birds out of the water to retrieve the 'catch'. It looked great, but as I struggled to get all the shots I needed, I managed to upset Ning.

Filming between boats was never easy and on this occasion we were either out of touch or too close together. I shouted to Gethin to come back and he would signal the fisherman to steer back. Or it was 'Too close, Geth, back off a bit' and so on. After about an hour of this pretend fishing, I thought we had filmed enough and we motored back to the house.

Ning was in a very strange mood and I asked him what the matter was.

'You are so rude,' he complained.

Surprised, I replied with concern, 'How?'

'You shout and it's very rude to shout,' Ning informed me.

'But how can I communicate across the water without shouting?'

'It is very rude to shout in China.'

I was suitably admonished. I had committed a breach of etiquette and quickly apologised. I asked him to explain my ignorance to the fisherman and say that I was genuinely sorry. Meanwhile, the others were astonished. Gethin quickly leapt to my defence.

'It's not rude in Britain. It's the way we get things done,' he argued.

Ning replied, still looking like thunder, 'No matter. In China it's very rude. I am ashamed.'

It took Ning a long time to forgive me, even though I stressed that I would do nothing to knowingly upset him, or anyone else for that matter. When I asked him several years later he could remember the incident but not what had caused it. Perhaps I should have resorted to Chinese whispers.

At the hotel in Beijing at the end of the trip we all were woken up at three o'clock in the morning for two nights in a row by ladies telephoning to ask if we would like a massage. With exhaustion setting in and anger replacing every other emotion, I remembered Ning's words and kept a

(Above): This tethered cormorant is used for fishing

(Below): Gethin Jones and Andy Akinwolere at the Shaolin temple

calm voice as I explained to the receptionist that if it happened again we would first call the police and then leave the hotel. I am not sure whether it was because I hadn't raised my voice, or because of my threat to call the police and leave, but, either way, the nuisance stopped.

Meanwhile, largely unknown to me, Andy was finding it hard to cope with the Chinese lack of understanding about the world outside their borders. Being black, he was treated with curiosity, and worse:

> China was not my ideal location as I had heard horror stories of the Chinese lack of cultural awareness. My amazement of the enormity of China was marred by the constant stares of people on the streets. I remember brushing past a woman at the Shaolin temple and she pointed and screamed at me as if I was a creature from outer space.

At Chengdu we visited the famous panda sanctuary and thanks to an American researcher, who recognised the value of the publicity, we were given every chance to look behind the scenes.

Gethin helped clean out the night cages, removing and weighing vast amounts of what sounded like 'Peow peow', (probably 'chou chou', which is Chinese for panda poo), and Andy watched, as a worker, clad in protective clothing from head to toe, weighed out the vitamin-enriched cake. The slightest contact with humans, it was explained, was to be avoided at all costs. Imagine my surprise when an hour later we saw a family posing for photographs cuddling a baby panda. And there wasn't a pair of rubber gloves in sight.

'Could we do this, please?' I asked, thinking it would make a fabulous pay-off to the film. There was a pause.

'Regret not. The authorities do not allow it.'

If you paid for the privilege then a few moments with a baby panda was possible, but not if it was going to be seen on television.

The Panda Research Institute at Chengdu did remarkable work breeding the endangered species and we watched the little ones play and being played with. Their human playmates were heavily protected, shrouded in white suits, boots and gauntlets.

Andy, again, had an unpleasant surprise, which would astonish people in the UK. To his credit, he maintained his composure:

> At the panda sanctuary I remember a lady saying she could make money by painting my eyes white and getting tourists to have their pictures taken with me – a black panda. I did not find this remark funny.

It was the kind of regressive, ignorant racism that used to be dressed up as humour in early 1970s sitcoms in Britain. Thankfully, it's a thing of the past in many parts of the world.

The adult pandas lived in large arenas designed to be like their natural habitat, with rocks, tall plants and sturdy wooden sleeping platforms. At prescribed times, Andy and Gethin fed them lumps of 'cake' by hanging them from the end of long poles, which they held over the deep ditch separating visitors from these cuddly icons. To give the pandas some exercise, they encouraged them to stand up and walk about as they reached for the tasty morsels. Only the greedy fell for it. Most lay on their backs and crunched up bamboo. They looked very contented and between meals they did what they did best – sleep.

The Institute's breeding programme was the envy of the world. Their secret was to replicate their living and mating conditions in the wild as closely as possible. And from what we could see, they had a winning formula.

A year later there was a disastrous earthquake in Sichuan. Luckily, the research centre in Chengdu was unscathed. Another field centre further up country was not so lucky. Several pandas and two of their keepers were killed.

Before we left China, Ning arranged a surprise for us. He had a friend who was a prominent member of the Beijing Opera and Andy and Gethin spent the day dressing up and taking lessons from the master. In full regalia and make-up, they glided around the practice room, using tiny steps, and twirling swords with surprising agility. The real test came when they were told to sing.

It was just a single word, '*Ni hao*', which means 'hello' in Chinese. Mr Wen Ru Hua demonstrated in various keys, each higher than the last, much to the amusement of the boys. When they imitated him, we all got a good laugh. It was just a small moment but the sheer ludicrousness of it, combined with Andy's and Gethin's willingness to throw themselves into it, made it one of the highlights of the trip.

I wanted more from China, but because we had not been able to stray far off the tourist track we had not witnessed first hand the areas of the country that remained trapped in the past. Our tight filming schedule and limited filming time had put paid to this. If I ever go back, my aim will be to go further afield and find the old China that my mother might have known.

If there was one lesson that I had learnt from China, it was not to expect what you ask for, yet, if you can be courteous and very patient, it was sometimes possible to glimpse the secrets of an ancient world trying hard to make friends with the rest of the world. There's probably a Chinese proverb for that.

38

Creating a buzz

31 March–10 April 2009
Royal Air Force Brize Norton

The best stories come around again and again as audiences move on.

Tim Levell had decided that, during this series, each presenter should have their own big challenge. Joel would learn how to scuba dive, Helen Skelton would attempt to run 72 miles in 24 hours in the Namibian desert, and five years after Simon Thomas had overcome his fear of parachuting, I suggested that Andy Akinwolere attempt a formation skydive with the whole of the RAF Falcons Parachute Display Team.

At a meeting with the RAF Falcons I found out that a larger-than-life character from Simon's challenge had been promoted to team coach. With completely shaven head, uncompromising, eloquent and with an East End accent, Toby Goodchild was the ideal contributor. He was also a fan of the programme. Now, as the Falcons' team coach, he would be our main point of contact and Andy's instructor. I thought it was too good an opportunity to miss.

Toby had a plan. He suggested that if we went out to America a week before their scheduled training in California, he could teach Andy to freefall parachute without interruption. When the rest of the team arrived at the end of his training, Andy could then attempt the formation skydive with the whole of the RAF Falcons. It promised to be a spectacle to remember.

I had no doubt that with Toby at the helm it would happen. All I had to do was square it with the Ministry of Defence.

The way these filming events were organised had changed at the MOD. Long gone were the days when all you needed to do was ring up the unit and fix a date. With wars to pay for in Iraq and Afghanistan, the extra cost to the RAF was an important issue. And in 2009, even though no one denied the positive publicity that would result, the

MOD was facing money battles that were just as fierce as the ones at the BBC.

Six weeks before Christmas, negotiations began as the cost of everything from insurance to hire of equipment was added up. A major part of the costs was the numbers of RAF personnel needed to comply with tightened safety regulations. I was at the eye of a storm, with cost and risk at its centre. The MOD's costs spiralled into outer space and completely beyond the programme's budget. In short, we could not afford it. At the same time the programme editor, Tim Levell, had allocated transmission slots for each phase of the challenge, despite my warning that winter was not a good time to go parachuting. The first slot was in mid-January and I was told that the dates could not be changed.

We decided to knock the overall cost issue on the head until after Christmas and focused on the four-day static-line course at RAF Brize Norton scheduled for the first week of January.

The cost of this course was modest and we were given a contract to proceed. Uneasily we began the filming because, overall, the cost was still far too much. Unable to go back, it was an act of faith. Unless the costs came down, we could be held to ransom.

Andy began his ground training with 60 others. During the first two days he learnt how to fall without breaking anything. He bent his body into a banana shape and, on command, rolled onto the mat to simulate the direction the wind might take his parachute.

'Side right landing – go!' And 60 bodies collapsed to the ground in unison. In other exercises they jumped off ramps, fell from swings and then jumped from the exit trainer 20 feet up. It was good to watch and Andy did well.

Doubt began to set in when, dangling from the hangar ceiling in a parachute harness, he practised the flight drills, including the moment his feet would hypothetically hit the ground. But it was the emergency drill, when he would have to cut away his main canopy and operate his reserve, that was an all-too-vivid reminder of the danger. Up to this point, Andy had not fully considered the possibility that his parachute might fail, and it began to prey on his mind. It didn't help that the paratroopers on the course revelled in the risk. As Andy reached the end of the course he had the appearance of a man about to face a firing squad.

Then what I most feared happened. There were no aircraft. The MOD needed all the Hercules they could lay their hands on for the war effort in Afghanistan and Iraq. Number One Parachute Training School was low on their list of priorities and the Hercules aircraft was cancelled. Andy relaxed and went for a kickabout with his friends.

Then I got a phone call from the office.

'Andy's twisted his ankle. He thinks it might be all right but he says it's a bit painful.'

This was awful news and I knew that we couldn't brush it under the carpet. Toby confirmed my fears: 'He's got to get checked out. We can't risk his ankle. Wreck it now and the whole project's off.'

We sent him off to have it thoroughly checked out.

Then the weather took a hand because the country was suddenly blanketed in snow and everything ground to a halt. All static-line parachuting was postponed. But so far we had lost nothing and the consultant reported that Andy's foot would need a week to recover.

Remembering Simon's crisis of confidence, I decided that Andy should spend time in the wind tunnel, a freefall simulator near Bedford. Simon Thomas had given up because he had not felt confident in freefall and I thought that if Andy learnt how to do it before going to America, he would have one less thing to worry about. The vertical wind tunnel was not affected by vagaries in the weather. It was something we could film and we would meet the January deadline in the process.

Built on an old Ministry of Defence testing site, Bodyflight was an eight-metre circular space with a powerful fan that created a hurricane of air that flowed from the base to the top. Skydivers could practise balancing on this airflow by leaping out of a door about halfway up. It was so powerful that the whole freefall display team could balance on the airflow at the same time.

The Falcons were frequent visitors. Every two-minute session was the equivalent of three skydives. Skydivers took it in turns to dive on to the airflow. Half an hour of wind-tunnel time was the same as 45 freefall parachute jumps.

Andy took to it instantly. He picked up the technique quickly and his confidence soared. Toby was delighted with him. And because there were no landings there was no pressure on his healing ankle. Yet I could see that the prospect of doing it for real loomed large in his mind.

Meanwhile, the battle to agree costs with the Ministry of Defence continued. Estimates hurtled back and forth. One moment the figure was impossibly large and another almost affordable. There was determination from both sides to come to an agreement. With just a day or two before we were due to depart, a figure was agreed that would not break the bank of either party. It had been an exhausting process and I heaved a sigh of relief. But my problems were not over because I had issues with the operators of the drop zone in America.

The 'at-your-own-peril' contract for the airfield at Lake Elsinore in California was not resolved easily. The Americans had devised what an expert in the BBC insurance department described as 'one of the most pernicious contracts he had ever seen'.

I had seen such contracts before and had shut my eyes and signed because there had been no option. It was the way business was done in America and there was no moving them.

We were told by the BBC's lawyers not to sign. And despite my pleas, the Americans would not alter their document. I was almost resigned to the fact we might not even make it on to our flight to Los Angeles. The hours ticked by.

Pragmatism was no longer a part of the BBC. In 2009 there were levels of management that embraced, even relished, conflicts. Muscles were flexed and there was much posturing, and all the while I wondered why we bothered. The result was inevitable. If we really wanted to make the programme, we had to sign.

By the time we climbed wearily up the aircraft steps, I was all but emotionally exhausted. All the energy I should have stored up for the shoot had been dissipated in the battle to set it up.

I remembered the days, especially in the 1970s and 1980s, when producers fought their way through impossible situations; we had been the buccaneers in a media war that had no end. Now all sense of buccaneering had ended with that great American invention of all time: 'No win, no fee'.

30 March–10 April 2009
Lake Elsinore, Los Angeles

For the first two days Andy lay on an oversized skateboard and learnt skydiving drills. Manoeuvres in the air were simulated by sliding about on his belly with Toby and another of the Falcons, Spence, on either side of him.

His first jump went well. Andy coped, even though he still battled with his anxieties. But once in freefall, and unlike Simon, he looked confident. The time he had spent in the wind tunnel had paid off. Andy was reflective:

> I was unexpectedly quiet through the parachute filming because for the first time I realised the pressure there was to complete the challenge. Especially one of this magnitude. The money spent on it and the fact we had travelled so far meant I felt I needed to do it. Simon Thomas failing six years previously gave me extra motivation to succeed.

The shoot was different in another way. For the first time ever, the Ministry of Defence allowed the Falcons more money to spend on food than the BBC did. Yet we had to eat. After a couple of visits to very average restaurants I realised that, unless I was prepared to foot the overspend myself, we would have to change our eating habits. We agreed on the only affordable course of action. We would visit the local shopping mall, buy what we could afford and eat in our rooms. Even so, when the time came for me to be repaid (I had to pay all the bills), I was still out of pocket.

Meanwhile, Toby looked at the weather. We had a strict timetable and every day counted. I had been losing the battle to film every sequence as thoroughly as I would have liked because Toby did not have time to repeat the actions for the camera. We had to fit in with aircraft availability. I began to wonder how I would catch up. Then, with only three jumps completed, the wind picked up and parachuting was cancelled for the day. I seized the chance. Toby fretted, Andy relaxed, and I pushed them to re-enact sequences that we had lost in the rush to 'go jumping'.

(Right): Andy
Akinwolere begins a
tandem skydive

(Bottom right): Andy
in tandem freefall. It was
always important to try to
ensure *Blue Peter* badges
could be seen while
filming such challenges

I had to gauge carefully how much to push this extra filming. Parachuting is dangerous. Too much pressure from me and I could cause an accident. Andy was stressed, and Toby was equally uptight worrying about the days slipping by. Some cross words were exchanged. I could see that they were both very highly motivated and I reconciled myself to their fragile temperaments. I became insensitive to Andy's anxieties in my determination to succeed. It was my weakness even after thirty-odd years of directing.

The atmosphere was not helped by the arrival of the RAF Falcons' chief rivals, the army's Red Devils. There were dozens of them and Toby felt outnumbered. His pride was vulnerable and he told me that I filmed them at my peril. Even so I was surprised that there was virtually no communication between the teams.

The penultimate day arrived and so did the rest of the Falcons.

While they prepared, we watched the weather anxiously. Gone were the cloud-free days for which California is famous. Instead, banks of cloud frothed all around. Impatiently, we waited for gaps and blue sky.

After seven days' training and with minutes to spare, we did it. For a few precious seconds Andy flew in formation with the RAF Falcons and the challenge was over. The video coverage was just enough to cut a sequence together. We packed in a rush and headed for the airport. I knew for certain that, sadly, it was the very last time I would ever film a parachute jump. I was sorry to leave the competitive atmosphere and camaraderie of the Falcons.

However, that frisson of uncertainty I loved so much was never far away.

4–5 June 2009
South Molton, Devon

There were always some film ideas that were just a bit too risky. The 'beard of bees' was one of them. In this exotically named event, honeybees were encouraged to swarm around the queen, which was placed in a small wire cage and hung under the victim's chin. As they swarmed, the bees hung from the face, beardlike, just as they would from a branch on a tree.

As a beekeeper myself, I knew it could only be done safely in early summer when bees swarmed naturally. It also had to be a warm day with no rain.

Bees are sensitive and while they can be very peaceful, if aroused they could sting their victim to death. So the choice of presenter was literally a matter of life or death. And that is why year after year the idea had been turned down.

In 2009 the programme editor, Tim Levell, had more faith in me than perhaps he should have done. Bowing to my age and experience he had enough confidence to give me the go-ahead. It was only possible because Helen Skelton had joined the show as a presenter. She was courageous and cool, and nothing fazed her. I felt confident she would be safe.

Helen had never been stung by a bee before so I had absolutely no idea what would happen if she was. Anaphylactic shock, when the flesh goes rigid, was the big danger. If she was stung on her neck, and she got it, she could suffocate. I consulted my youngest brother, who is an Exeter GP, and he advised that it would be unlikely for Helen to have an adverse reaction the first time she was stung. Providing the emergency services were standing by, it was a reasonable risk. I set up the challenge with the Quince Honey Farm in South Molton in Devon.

The Wallace family have been running the honey farm for 60 years and I had visited it on and off since I was six, taking breaks on family expeditions to Widemouth Bay and Bude in North Devon. I

(Left): Toby Goodchild (shaven head) debriefs Andy Akinwolere after a jump

was fascinated by the spectacle of thousands of bees busy at work, as well as their complex social behaviour. It was this that had inspired my own interest in beekeeping and I enjoy tending the three hives at the bottom of my garden, not to mention the benefit of producing my own honey. I often take time to watch the bees and their comings and goings.

The owners of the honey farm were a likeable father-and son-team, Paddy and Ian. When I telephoned it was Ian, the son, who answered the phone, and he agreed to my request. It had been a lucky break. Father and son were both quiet and sincere, and I believed every word they said. Paddy, the father, admitted to me later that if I had spoken to him first the answer would have been no – it would have been just too much of a risk. The previous year a sheep had wandered into a small collection of Paddy's hives and had been stung to death within minutes.

We decided that Helen should get to know about bees in general before they got too close. Fully protected in bee suits, we were warned not to wear anything black. Black was an enemy colour and the bees would attack. Unfortunately for me, the mesh of the face veil was black and would have severe consequences when I was operating the camera.

The day before the 'beard' shoot, Helen was given the chance to look at the bees in their hives and see how swarms were moved to new locations. Even though the bees buzzed angrily, no one got stung. Except for me. When I put my eye to the viewfinder, the black mesh of the face veil was pressed against my forehead and nose, and the bees had a field day. I was stung fourteen times and that did nothing for Helen's confidence.

Unperturbed, the next day, we progressed to the grand finale – the 'beard of bees'. Paddy borrowed a domestic swarm from a friend because they were less aggressive. A St John Ambulance ambulance arrived and I alerted the local surgery. Helen took her bee suit off and applied Vaseline to those parts of her face that needed to be bee-free, like her upper lip and eye sockets. She also put cotton wool in her ears and nostrils.

Then the bees, all 20,000 of them, put in an appearance.

They were less adventurous than the wild bees, and they hadn't read the script. They were only slightly interested in swarming. Paddy encouraged them to move from their box and follow the queen, but they refused to take the hint. Instead of heading for Helen's chin, where their queen was running about in her cage, they crawled all over her shoulders and front. As Paddy quipped, it was not so much a 'beard of bees' as a 'shawl of bees'.

Helen had been warned that she would feel a sort of tickling as the bees looked for footholds on which to build their honeycomb. For half an hour she waited patiently as thousands of bees explored every part of her upper torso – except her chin. It was impressive and we all knew that this could not go on for ever. Maybe they sensed her growing impatience, maybe two bees had an argument – whatever the reason, she was stung and the waiting game was over. Smoke was urgently puffed over the restless swarm and they began to leave. Three more stings followed

(Right): Helen Skelton didn't complain despite being stung four times

before she was bee-free. Helen took the pain without complaint.

I knew that the film would make compulsive viewing. I was, however, worried that Helen's face would swell up because she was due to be photographed for the *Blue Peter Book* the following day. I wondered what she really thought of it all. As I drove home the stings on my face took full effect and I began to feel as if I had a mild bout of flu. My phone bleeped and it was a message from Helen. 'Just to say thanks for a really fun two days! Hope you don't swell up too much!'

I had been surprised to be allowed to film the beard of bees but it had been done safely and no one had been hurt. The risk assessment had been a work of art and we had employed the right experts. At worst, if anything had gone seriously wrong, I would have been morally liable.

In 2009 there was a tendency to think of the risk assessment as a 'get-out-of-jail-free' card. If all actions that could be taken to ensure safety are taken, it was all right to go ahead. To my mind this is very dangerous ground, especially when working for *Blue Peter*, which prides itself on taking calculated risks to make exciting television.

(Above): Helen Skelton
achieves the 'beard of bees',
if not quite the full set

39

How many *Blue Peter* staff does it take to change a light bulb?

25 January 2010
Topsham, Devon

I was on standby to join Helen Skelton, whose highly publicised Amazon adventure was a very bold departure from normal programme practice. At the time she was intending to paddle down the mighty river in a canoe, and she would miss 14 editions of *Blue Peter* in order to do it. However, through the magic of satellite, the programme would see every nuance of her trials and tribulations. If she succeeded, she would become the first woman to paddle down 2,010 miles of the river, and she admitted it would test her to the limit. She was doing it partly for *Blue Peter* and partly for Sport Relief.

I wasn't disappointed to be left out. Seven weeks of being cooped up on a river boat did not appeal. Even so, I knew that if the call came because of sickness or injury, I would be as excited as anyone else.

I had other challenges up my sleeve. I had plans for presenters to replace the light bulbs on top of the spire on Salisbury Cathedral, climb the Old Man of Hoy, and fly with the first woman member of the Red Arrows. Thirty-five years with *Blue Peter*, and the variety and interest were as rich as ever.

Reliving the past has been a roller-coaster of emotions and memories, and has made me think about what I have endured and enjoyed in equal measure. I have seen the programme change out of all recognition, and to the 'true believers', from those halcyon days when there were six to eight million viewers, the change has been traumatic.

Even so, to the new generation of viewers, *Blue Peter* still strikes a chord.

In the past we believed, *If it isn't broken, don't fix it.*

Yet, without a doubt, it has been necessary to change the programme as viewers' expectations have changed.

In the production team, the greatest change has been caused by the age of the producers and directors. They have been getting younger. In 1975 it was unusual to find a director younger than 28. In 2010 young directors are in their early twenties, and instead of experience in the theatre, radio or as a studio vision mixer, they have a university degree and little else.

There is a saying that 'content is king' but in 2010 I thought more time appeared to be spent on the look of the programme rather than what was in it. And young directors are much more excited by this than older ones. In the past, video-editing technology was not as advanced and so the options were very few. Nowadays, video editors use every tool they have to make the look of the programme as exciting as they can. And sometimes they are distracted from the storyline. Too many young directors focus on image and neglect the message. And it is an increasingly competitive world. Yet good ideas and storylines win in the end.

12 April 2010

Eurobait, Nottingham

When Petra, *Blue Peter*'s pet dog, died in 1977 I had frivolously suggested that we make a film of her being recycled by sending her remains to a maggot farm. Biddy's response was predictable. Without even looking up from her scriptwriting, she had said dryly, 'I somehow think it would not go down well with the viewers, darling.'

Some fellow directors smiled at my black humour and all dismissed it. Yet the idea remained on my list of promising items.

The opportunity came 33 years later when *Blue Peter* was told to produce four programmes in a week of 'horrible histories'. There were four ages – the Vikings, the Tudors, Medieval and the Victorians. I got the Victorians and the horrible aspects of Victorian medical remedies. Maggots were back on the menu. I remembered that they were used to clean wounds in Victorian times and further research revealed they had been a remedy for tuberculosis of the lung. I seized my chance.

The maggot farm just outside Nottingham looked hellish and had a sickening smell. A haphazardly built brick and corrugated-iron construction did not look like the home for millions of maggots. I arrived by car with my son Henry (who had been given the job of animating some graphics to describe some of the unpleasantness) and the stomach-churning odour was so bad we gagged even before we opened the car doors. I reached for the jar of Vicks I carried for such occasions and we smeared a liberal layer of the stuff on our upper lips. Even so, the smell prevailed and I wondered if this was a challenge too far. We made our way into the farm office.

Fifteen minutes later we emerged, clad in blue disposable overalls and wearing nothing of our original clothing other than our underpants.

The smell, we had been told, would render our clothes unwearable – for ever. We entered through a door that led to a dimly lit narrow room filled with concrete vats (or pits as they are known in the trade) lined with meshed crates of maggots. They had been stacked so the maggots could crawl out of the piles of raw flesh that they had been eating and drop into the pits.

But it was more than just the smell of ammonia produced by the maggots in Eurobait. There was yet another smell that was equally unpleasant, an underlying smell of something that had died some time before, and it caught at the back of our throats. And all the time tears rolled down our cheeks as our eyes struggled to cope.

I carried my camera to judge how it would 'see' in the low light and, trying to ignore the smell, I fiddled with the focus and exposure. Henry was hunched in his personal struggle with nausea. And then we entered the fly room.

Unexpectedly, the smell wasn't that bad, and my years of filming in the tropics had hardened me to the close inspection of flies trying to find moisture. Even so, the numbers were overwhelming. They got everywhere – down your neck, in your eyes, and settling on every inch of exposed flesh. We were told that there were three million flies in that one room and they were there to lay their eggs. This was the source of the 5,000 gallons of maggots that the farm produced each week.

I knew I had struck gold. I made a mental note to make sure that the presenter wore white coveralls so the flies would show up and, momentarily, I forgot about the smell.

28 April 2010
Nottingham

Come the day, the presenter Joel Defries, coped remarkably well as he nearly choked on the flies crowding his lips as he tried to speak. His horror was genuine and he made the maggot farm a moment for us all to cherish.

There was an aftermath. I had not reckoned on the cloying smell permanently affecting the camera equipment. We had filmed as fast as we could. No one wanted to spend more time in that place than was absolutely necessary, and the sound recordist came near to collapse with the pungency of the ammonia. Even so, the foetid smell of maggots lingered on the metal and rubber surfaces, despite repeated wiping with Dettol and other remedies. The canvas camera bag was almost beyond help and it stayed in my garden shed for several months.

(Left): Joel Defries and proprietor Mark Hammond share a room with three million flies at Eurobait's maggot farm

7–8 October 2010
Salisbury Cathedral

One of the many secrets of *Blue Peter*'s success lay in revisiting memorable storylines. And one of the secrets of my longevity of employment was to remember what those were.

Changing the light bulbs on the top of Salisbury Cathedral spire (the tallest in Britain) was one such moment, and it had been one of the best. The film was last made in 2000 with Simon Thomas, and the bulbs were due for another change because they would blow after about ten thousand hours of lighting up the night sky.

I rang the cathedral, wondering how they would react to the idea of us returning. I needn't have worried because they remembered us very well, and their memories were all good. The cathedral staff had been so impressed by Simon that the doors were flung open to us for a second time. It was yet another example of the wisdom of always parting on good terms. We gave the challenge to Helen and, excited as ever, she wrote:

> We have an infamous director who's been on the programme
> since Biddy Baxter's days, so whenever you see on your rota
> that you're doing a shoot with him you know that it's going
> to be something that involves fear or danger.

Meanwhile, for me, the prospect of such a shoot was a moment for rejoicing. Or so I thought.

Salisbury turned out to be a turning point in my relationship with *Blue Peter*, because I soon discovered that there was not really enough money in the programme budget to support such ambitious films, except on rare occasions.

The programme's cash had been steadily whittled away until there was much less of it about. I knew this but I assumed, incorrectly, that such a spectacular film, one that could be shown again and again, would be exempt from these pressures. I was deluding myself. The high production cost was an important issue and, spectacular or not, the money had to be carefully accounted for.

I was in luck. The *Blue Peter* production manager may have looked worried but I got the green light. A proposed January shoot had to be moved, quite sensibly, to March in the hope of more certain weather to avoid cancellation fees. The shoot was then moved again into the next financial year because there was no money left in the programme's coffers. Again this was understandable because it was not unusual for things to become tight at the end of the year. The cathedral staff, patient but anxious that we were losing interest, were mollified when we agreed to pay for the bulbs (£600) because they had already been acquired on our behalf. It seemed that the cathedral's coffers were similarly depleted and anxieties built up on both sides.

To make matters worse, the new filming dates then unexpectedly clashed with Helen's availability due to a prior event, and the climb was moved yet again, into the early summer. Surely this would work? I thought. Unfortunately not. It had to be moved yet again because the programme's summer expedition had been unexpectedly brought forward. In despair, I chose a date in October, hoping to avoid any overspill problems from the summer expedition filming. This time my scheduling was spot on, but a new problem appeared. The crew, who had been booked and postponed several times, had lost faith in me. They became unavailable!

Grasping the nettle, I decided to fix the date of the climb and make it work with whatever crew I could persuade to save the day.

Thankfully, my climbing cameraman, Rob Franklin, cancelled his other job, then promptly announced that new health and safety regulations meant that he would need not one but two back-up climbers. He was an old hand, having climbed the spire twice before, and he knew what was essential for his safety. Even so, the narrow top of the spire was going to be a crowded place and the production cost rose.

Additionally, and spurred on no doubt by all the cancellations, Rob and his support team asked for full payment whether or not the shoot went ahead. This was unusual because it was customary to pay half, and then only if the cancellation was with less than 48 hours' notice.

As we forged ahead, the cancellation fee was renegotiated back down to half, and then we discovered that Rob, who usually used a conventional tape camera, had changed to a tapeless model. He was ahead of his time and, it appeared, ahead of the BBC post-production department. I was told that we could not cope with the new technology.

I conferred, pleaded, and in the end had to agree to let Rob use his new toy if, and only if, he found a way to transfer the material on to my own Avid edit system in Devon.

By now my bête noire, the risk assessment, seemed reasonable in comparison. With helicopter time booked and flight plans logged, we were locked in. All we needed now was for the weather to be on our side.

The weather changed. Rob helpfully pointed out that the day before would be better for the climb. The weather was against us and we had no option but to swap the dates. The only person who couldn't make it on both days was the sound recordist. Untried and untested, his understudy would have to do the big day. Too numb to care, I thought it was worth a risk.

The day of the climb began well. The clear blue skies were warm and inviting – unlike the steeplejack, Brian Moor.

'We've got to get this done and be off the spire by one,' he announced with a sense of gloom the moment we arrived. The weather front had been predicted to arrive earlier than previously forecasted.

This would give us two hours less than I reckoned we would need. I flew into a controlled panic.

Yet rush was exactly what we could not do. Helmet cameras (more tapeless headaches) and back-up sound recorders (which turned out to be too big to carry) had to be carefully set up – and climbing harnesses adjusted for comfort. And how the huge team of support workers would arrange themselves in the close confines of the spire had to be thrashed out. If something – anything – didn't work, it would all be in vain. I felt the stress rack my body as I pretended not to worry. And outside I could see clouds piling up on the horizon.

At long last the climb began and we took our pre-planned camera positions: one crew on the top of the tower, looking up the spire; and me (with two cameras) on the ground on the cathedral green. Rob would climb with Helen, carrying his tapeless camera. I was joined by half a dozen news reporters and stills photographers. If anything went wrong, it would happen in front of the media.

The hours ticked by. One o'clock came and went yet the weather held. Brian was in his element, philosophical and reassuring as the team of cautious technicians left the safety of the tower and began to make the climb to the top of the spire.

Helen demonstrated her usual nerves of steel as she climbed out through the weather door on to the roof to tackle the final 12 metres using special metal hoops set into the masonry. She remembers it well: 'I reversed out, shaking, and I didn't want to look down. The drop was so steep.'

I thought we were over the worst when both the radio mics failed as their batteries went flat. I listened in with horror from my spot several hundred feet below on the cathedral green as first there was no sound from Brian and then, minutes later, no sound from Helen. We were close to disaster. Not only was Helen cold but the wind was freshening and the helicopter crew were keen to finish the job and get back to London. Fretting, I knew there was no option but to send down for more batteries.

I cursed that my preferred sound man was not there. I had never ever, in 36 years of location filming, had two radio mic batteries fail in half their expected life. With just ten metres to go to the top, we waited while a safety climber returned to the base of the spire to collect fresh ones.

It was 40 minutes before sound was re-established and by this time Helen was shaking with cold and the weather was breaking. Rob, unperturbed, thought Helen should go down and warm up, but she refused. She could see that a glorious moment might be lost for ever. She found the extra strength to clamber to the top, where she and Brian changed the light bulb. I heaved a sigh of relief.

It was Brian Moor's last-ever such climb and spirits lifted with the historical moment. It was a triumphant team that returned safely to the ground. We rushed Helen to the waiting helicopter so she could do her opening speech hovering over the cathedral. As the light faded the helicopter dropped Helen off at Old Sarum airfield and headed back to London.

The next day we were in a buoyant mood as we returned to take shots of the cathedral's exterior. Much to our surprise, we recognised the steeplejack's van parked at the base of the tower. Brian and his team were back and he was preparing to climb – yet again. We thought he had retired. What had gone wrong?

The previous night the all-important aircraft warning lights we had changed had not worked. Panic had swept the cloisters because the safety of the building was at stake. The lights had to be fixed – and because they had worked before our arrival, the BBC was culpable, if not wantonly so. For me, it was a ghastly end to a problematic shoot.

A break in the wiring was diagnosed. A misplaced boot from the many pairs of feet had inadvertently broken a connection and urgent repairs were needed. And the BBC would have to pay for it.

Caution, additional safety regulations, a reducing budget and delays brought on by money worries and presenter availability had finally culminated in additional cost and even more worry. I was exhausted and relieved that the shoot had succeeded, if only on the television screen. We were still on speaking terms with our contacts at the cathedral, which was a huge relief.

What should have been a breeze in my experience had turned into a harrowing occasion and I wondered if it was all worth it.

But it wasn't all bad. On the plus side the film was a joy to edit and it turned out so well it moved Tim Levell to tears when he first saw it. I have no doubt that when he saw the bill we received for the extra cost of repairing the damaged wiring, it had the same effect.

Helen rated the experience as in her top three achievements on *Blue Peter* to date.

I, however, was raw with frustration and I knew we would almost certainly never attempt to change the light bulbs on Salisbury's Cathedral spire (or anywhere else as inaccessible) ever again. The cost, both in stress and the programme's finances, was just too much.

Even though I know I should never say 'Never again' I knew, deep down, it was time for me to leave the television business.

(Above): Helen Skelton at the top of Salisbury Cathedral spire

(Right): Helen demonstrates nerves of steel as she nears the top of Salisbury Cathedral

(Above): Helen at the door to the Salisbury Cathedral spire

40

Rich pickings in paradise

9–26 January 2011
Solomon Islands; Honiara, the capital

As I have already explained, the recce is an invaluable part of the filming process, especially when large amounts of licence payers' money are at stake. This could not have been more true than when it came to the grand finale I was planning for my time at *Blue Peter*. With just six months to go before leaving the BBC, I intended to return to a part of the world I had loved as a young man and where a decade earlier I had already made a couple of successful programmes.

This time around, though, the Solomons had changed. Sadly, they were no longer 'The Happy Isles'. I remembered that there had been piles of refuse lying about before, but the memory of it had not been seared into my mind. The capital, Honiara, with its unattractive main street of ugly, dilapidated and dirty buildings, had now become more like a civic amenity refuse disposal site. There was litter ankle deep everywhere. To make matters worse, the plastic bottles, wrappers – all the detritus of a consumer society – were splattered with bright red betel-nut juice. A newcomer might have been forgiven for thinking that the streets had been the scene of a recent and violent bloodletting.

I was amazed how seemingly normal, intelligent people – accountants, government workers, priests, almost everyone it seemed – chewed the betel nut with lime and leaves which produced a bright red liquid that hideously disfigured their mouths and teeth. I was told that the narcotic effect was similar to that of a pint of beer, but unlike beer this vice turned a pleasant smile into an evil-looking grimace. Talking business with a betel-nut chewer was an unsettling experience.

And there were other changes too that were equally disturbing. Mobile phones, Walkmans and other trappings of the digital age, had become an essential part of the islanders' way of life. Yet there was not enough money about to support this new addiction.

Young thieves now worked in gangs along the main street and in the afternoon of my first day my camera was expertly stolen from a shoulder bag. A visit to the police station revealed that thefts were quite common and I began to notice posters on public buildings offering rewards for the return of cameras and other stolen possessions. The police sergeant described how youths had learnt to watch at cash dispensers and wait for elderly people to withdraw cash. They would then follow their victims, knock them to the ground, grab the cash and scatter so pursuit was impossible. For those young people at least, respect for age was a thing of the past.

Yet when I first went to the Solomons in 1966, theft of any kind was unheard of. At Alangaula School, where I was a volunteer teacher, 'sharing and borrowing' of possessions was a sign of friendship; shirts, umbrellas or what-have-you would disappear but they would always be returned in due course.

Tragically, Western values in the form of money had become one of the important yardsticks of *mana*, the spiritual power that was once attached to physical possessions. And *mana* was at the centre of pre-Christian Melanesian culture. In the old days a chief was deemed to have *mana* by the number of pigs he possessed. Now it seemed the white man's trappings had a greater authority, and the pursuit of this modern influence was more ruthlessly pursued than ever before.

My contact and fixer for this expedition was a pupil I had taught when I was 19. Stephen Waiwori exuded confidence and goodwill. With a bit of a paunch through too little exercise (because of a dodgy knee), he sported a pair of sunglasses that he seldom removed. Now, over 60 years old, he was prone to repeat himself and, because of his injury, we had to take taxis rather than walk. He was very proud of our previous lives as master and student in our teens, and spared no opportunity to tell everyone about it. I began to realise that my presence gave him increased status. I wondered if I was evidence of what might have been called *mana* in centuries past, or nowadays his authority or influence.

I took him as a trusted ally because I had used him to provision and organise the *Blue Peter* filming in 2001 (which he had done well). Ten years on it appeared that there had been changes, and now, as never before, he was employing his quick intelligence to make a living. I surmised that, as the time came for him to retire and return to his village, the need for status (and therefore increased *mana* or influence) had become urgent. And it was at his village that my programme proposals were based.

In a nutshell, the proposal, discussed with Stephen, was to teach our newest presenter, Barney Harwood, how to rub sticks together to make fire, build a shelter, fish and look for food in the bush, and in general learn the art of survival from the experts. A second programme would follow when we would maroon him on his own desert island and he would struggle to survive for a few days. It was an ambitious project, as a suitable desert island had yet to be found.

Stephen came to meet me at the airport and, dazed with jet-lag, we drove in a taxi with a cracked windscreen and torn seats and headed for the Chester Rest House, the cheapest and friendliest self-help hotel in town, run by my old friends the Melanesian Brotherhood.

A couple of hours later we walked to the Mendana Hotel, a much posher place on the sea front. Stephen had found out that there was an 'all you can eat' buffet at a fixed price, and he was keen to impress. It was not long before I found the reason why.

'Alex, I wish to talk to you about a small matter,' he confided as we began to eat an eclectic mixture of boiled kumara, pineapple rings, salad and tinned tuna fish at £22 a time.

'The BBC team cannot go to the toilet on the beach like the rest of my village so I have built one especially for them. Perhaps the BBC can pay me some small monies for it.' He looked at me anxiously.

'How much?' I asked, equally anxiously.

'Two thousand three hundred dollars.' This was about £230.

'That's an awful lot for a squatting pad,' I complained, thinking of the usual hole in the ground covered by a concrete lid with convenient places to put one's feet.

He defended the expense, insisting, 'This is a toilet with a water flush.'

My mind boggled. In a place where the houses were built of leaves and there was no water on tap I reckoned this was the first flushing loo in the village. And then I wondered if Stephen was keen to show the villagers modern ways. Reluctantly, I had to admit that he had a point. I paused and imagined the alternative – dropping one's pants and doing the necessary into the sea in full view of the men of the village. It would not go down well with the team.

'I will pay the money but I do not think that the BBC will repay me. This is something I shall have to pay myself.' I wanted to nail any thoughts that the BBC had an open cheque book. I began to regret that I had emailed him from the UK reassuring him that he would not be out of pocket as a result of my visit.

The toilet was the beginning of a series of requests for cash or 'small monies'. Everything and anything was a reason to ask for 'small' money. Although justifiable, every job, like washing a shirt or carrying my rucksack, meant yet more Solomon dollars.

In the following days he was a willing and efficient guide, always turning up promptly at my request. He was helpful and introduced me to the right government officials who would need to grant filming permits. Even so my meagre funds from the *Blue Peter* office soon began to look inadequate.

There was another complication that was going to make mincemeat of my plans to check out a suitable island for our castaway.

In nearby Australia, Brisbane and half of Queensland were under water and the cyclone that had caused the flooding lurked menacingly somewhere south of the Solomons. The sea was so rough that all inter-island traffic by outboard motor and canoe had stopped. The search for the 'castaway island' would have to be put on hold. We agreed that the trip would not be possible while the seas raged and whitetops filled the horizon.

(Above and below): Natagera village, Santa Ana, Solomon Islands

Meanwhile, we boarded a small tired-looking aircraft and were hurled around the sky as we headed for Stephen's island of Santa Ana.

Santa Ana was very hot and humid, and in the centre of the island there was virtually no wind. With a porter lugging my rucksack, I marched along with the energy one has only in the first few days of arrival from a much cooler climate. We had about two miles to go and, thinking to take advantage of the walk, I asked to make a detour and visit a nearby village. I wanted to get a taste of what the island was like.

I was aghast.

The plague of litter, usually unheard of except in Honiara, had spread to the attractive leaf houses that sat on the edge of a lovely white sand beach. And there was another horror. That universal blight of every developing country, corrugated-iron, had arrived in strength. The village was an unruly collection of mismatched buildings that did not fit my ideal of a primitive society where we could teach our presenter the secrets of survival. I dreaded seeing Stephen's village, which was 'just around the corner'. My spirits sank and I walked with a heavy heart and considered calling the whole thing off.

Forty minutes later (it was a big corner) and after a frank discourse on my views on litter to my companions, we arrived at Stephen's village of Natagera. To my astonishment, there was very little litter and, heaven be praised, there wasn't a sheet of corrugated-iron in sight! My spirits rose and, surprised, I was forced to admit that this was an attractive village in the best traditions of Solomon Island culture. Could this change of fortune last? I wondered.

I should have known it could not. The colourful warrior welcome and community singing that had been promised had been cancelled because there had been a sudden death, and there could be no filming or celebration of any kind until the period of mourning was over. Sinking back into negativity, I felt that the trip was doomed after all. Meanwhile, the seas crashed violently on the beach and the white-topped waves confirmed that inter-island hopping was impossible.

We settled into Stephen's house and within minutes he was expounding how he would expand the premises and build more bedrooms for the crew before our arrival. I replied with caution because, while no money was mentioned, I felt it would only be a matter of time before it was. That evening I wandered around the village, conscious of the constant wailing coming from the home of the departed. It fitted my mood.

By 11 o'clock the following morning the funeral was over and normal life resumed. Dozens of naked, woolly-headed children played the fool in excitement whenever I pointed my small camcorder in their direction. Pretty leaf houses fronted the beach while others bordered the village square, which also served as a football pitch.

I was introduced to Peter, the village's youngest chief. To my delight, he spoke good English. He was a clever man who quickly understood the problems of filming. He had once worked for the tourist commission and was eager to come up with helpful suggestions.

I was encouraged by the friendliness of everyone I met and I began to feel that I could produce quite a creditable programme from the village. I rubbed fire (literally, by rubbing two sticks together) for the fourth or fifth time in my life. The first had been when I was 19 years old. We also went hunting for coconut crabs at night, toured the skull house, where the bones of their ancestors were kept in model canoes and tuna-shaped coffins, and generally filmed everything in sight. While the heat and the humidity were oppressive I felt that if we could only find an island for our would-be castaway, then the project could go ahead.

Always on the lookout for a compromise, I took a walk around the island with Chief Peter. It did nothing to convince me that, if necessary, we could cast our presenter away on the other side of Santa Ana. The entire coastline was pitted with the burrows of land crabs and a night excursion had revealed two snakes in less than an hour.

'Are there many snakes?' I asked my companion.

'Very many,' he replied with enthusiasm.

'Are they poisonous?' I asked with a sense of the inevitable.

'Some are very poisonous. They live in the trees and come out at night. I have been bitten several times.'

This was not what I wanted to hear. And meanwhile the heat and humidity had brought out an attack of prickly heat on my arms and back. I was in torment trying not to scratch.

In my agony I wondered how any presenter could survive on a land swarming with land crabs (harmless but alarming) and poisonous snakes when it would take all his will to overcome the heat and humidity. I was a great believer in 'upping the ante' when it came to presenter challenges, but this seemed unnecessarily dangerous. If he wasn't bitten by a snake he would have his work cut out just to survive the climate, even with a constant supply of fresh water. Using a satellite telephone, I began to let the office know of my misgivings.

In the meantime, the wild sea opposite the village had died down and soon became a flat calm. My pulse quickened. Surely this would be a good moment to begin our quest for a desert island away from the land crabs and snakes?

Stephen looked alarmed. Several weeks before my arrival he had been sent £700 from the office (by Western Union) to pay for the canoe and petrol because, he assured us, he needed to secure the arrangement in advance. But no money had changed hands. The money was still in a bank account in Honiara. He would now have to go back there to get it. Worse still, there was only one flight a week, assuming the weather held.

The thought of waiting another week in the village while he disappeared to spend yet another £240 on an airfare did not appeal. I talked to Chief Peter and asked him if he would be prepared to accompany Stephen for the much-needed recce to the islands further up the coast after I had gone. I thought that the opinion of two was better than one and to my relief he agreed. It might be weeks before the canoe trip was safe but we could not commit to the filming without first-hand evidence that it was feasible.

Back on board the battered Otter aircraft of Solomon Airlines, we left Santa Ana in bright sunshine and then, within seconds, we were in a thunderstorm. The weather had changed in minutes without warning – which was why canoe journeys during the period from January to April were so dangerous. I praised Stephen for looking after my welfare because it would have been very unwise to have made the journey along the coast, as I had bullishly suggested. Through thick cloud and rain we landed at Henderson Airport on Guadalcanal.

Back in Honiara and wading amongst the litter and leaking sewers, I got to grips with the vessel that we needed to carry us between locations if the filming went ahead.

The *Kopuria* was a wooden cargo vessel with six bunks in three cabins. Maintained for years by the Church of Melanesia, it had recently been sold to a shipping group based in South Malaita. We had hired it with great success ten years previously and it had proved a comfortable home, albeit a little spartan, as we'd travelled around the islands in 2002. My contact was Fox Irokalani, who was honest, reliable and a good friend. When I had taught at Alangaula School on the island of Ugi in 1966, one of my fellow teachers had been his elder brother, David Lillimae. I had no doubt that Fox's word was his bond.

Fox looked worried. Over a lunch of rice and chicken curry (£3.50 a plate) I found out why. The price we had negotiated was lower than they had wanted (because it was all the BBC could afford), and yet recently the price of oil had gone up. He wanted to increase the total price for 15 days' hire from $198,000 (Solomon) to $200,000 (about £18,000). One look at Fox's open and honest face and I readily agreed. I made a note to take a

look at the MV *Small Mala*, as she was now called, as soon as possible.

I found her berthed alongside the quay, preparing to load up for another voyage. The years had not been kind to her. She was in constant use, ferrying cargo and people between Honiara and South Malaita, and the living facilities were not what they had once been. The shower did not work and the toilet was unpleasant to visit but functioning. The overall impression was one of dirt. All the living quarters needed a good scrub. I left thinking that we should buy some cleaning materials and a broom. I was reassured that she complied with all safety regulations needed for inter-island work.

Back at the Chester Rest House on the hill overlooking the town, I received some surprise visitors; two old friends who had been brothers, members of the Melanesian Brotherhood, the monastic order universally admired throughout the islands. We sipped cold water in the best air-conditioning in town, at the Lime Lounge, where expats who needed a taste of civilisation took refuge. They looked at me uncomfortably.

'Why do you use Stephen Waiwori?' one asked.

With sinking heart I explained that it was Stephen's village that we were going to film, that he was available to make the arrangements, and that he was an old pupil so I had known him for a long time.

'The brothers think he treats you like a damson tree loaded with fruit and he wants to pick as much of it as he can.'

This was not a surprise because the brothers followed strict rules based on generosity and giving. Stephen's meticulous expenses would have appeared alien to them. I was touched by their loyalty and told them not to worry. I wondered what to do.

A couple of days later I left the Solomons with strict instructions to Stephen to do the recce for the castaway island as we had planned, and report back. I even bought him a cheap digital camera so he could take photographs and send them to me. Setting down in Brisbane, I rang the *Blue Peter* office.

'Couple of bits of bad news.' My trusted and very capable assistant, Louise, was pleased I had rung. 'We have just received an email from the Santa Catalina Development Association via half a dozen government ministries in the Solomons and the British High Commission. They want to charge £50,000 for the spear-fighting ceremony and another £3,000 for kite fishing.'

I reeled with shock. Stephen and I had discussed filming these activities but we had been unable to meet the people of the nearby island of Santa Catalina to discuss it. They had got wind of our request before we had made one, and their message was hostile. Both fees were far beyond anything we could afford and there were reports about how a film crew had had to be removed by police for not going through the official channels. I instantly decided to give the island a miss, even though it left a huge gap in our second programme.

This news revealed a fundamental lack of understanding in the Solomons about how much they could charge for filming fees. I had an uneasy feeling that more difficult negotiations might begin in other locations after we had arrived for the shoot, by which time it would be too late to back out.

The second piece of bad news left me gasping. Our new presenter, Barney, was prone to travel sickness! How would he survive 40 hours rolling and pitching on the Coral Sea before we began the shoot? And how could I ask anyone to share a cabin with him? Things looked serious.

3 February 2011
Plymouth, Devon

Bishop James Mason, once the Bishop of Makira in the Solomons (the area in which we intended to film), read the letter from the Santa Catalina Development Association. We were in the front room of his modest house in the parish of Plympton, just outside Plymouth, in South Devon where he was the vicar (on loan from the Solomons). I watched for his reaction. After a minute or two there were gasps, sighs and the odd 'Wheeee!' Finally he looked up.

'I am shocked,' he said. 'This is very bad and it has never happened before.'

I recounted my experiences aroung the islands and the general change in attitude to money that I had seen since my last visit ten years ago. He listened attentively. When I had finished he sighed. 'The contents of that letter will be known by everyone in Makira Province by now. Every village will think that they can charge large fees for filming. You cannot go.'

It was what I had already feared.

'What if you came with us?' I asked.

'Alex, I have problem with my visa. I cannot go anywhere until it is solved. I am sorry.'

He went on to explain that he knew the person who had written the letter. He was an educated, respected man and it seemed he had taken it upon himself to protect the people from exploitation. His day job was as the Archbishop's private secretary and he was now involving himself with other work apart from his diocesan duties.

Letters now went back and forth with no firm result and I received no evidence that Stephen and Chief Peter's search for a desert island had been successful. I concluded that however much I wanted to believe in my old friends and a place far away on the other side of the world that I hold dear, the financial risks were too great.

After a lot of soul searching and with a heavy heart, I decided that the only right course of action was to cancel my proposed filming expedition to the 'Happy Isles'. I felt terribly let down and disappointed that the islands had not only lost their innocence but had in this case begun to adopt the worst excesses of life in the so-called civilised world. In the 46 years since my first visit, their world had changed so much for the worse. I knew I could no longer admire it as a place that I once believed could have set an example to the rest of us.

But the project did not end there. A few weeks later I was persuaded that there was nothing wrong with the idea and I should continue with it as a single programme in a location nearer home. My eyes strayed to Scotland and the Isle of Mull.

With the expert help of ex-SAS survival expert Paul Johnson, with whom I had already made a survival-orientated programme six years before, I devised a journey from the craggy wilds of Beinn na Croise overlooking Loch Buie and down to the sea and rescue.

To my delight, Barney Harwood stood the test well, resorting to his memories as a Scout. Under Paul's guidance they built makeshift shelters for his overnight stops along the way; swam in a freezing loch; made fire by rubbing two sticks together using a bow and drill; plucked, gutted and ate a pheasant; and made a coracle with a 'green' cow hide (not yet a week old) and hazel sticks.

Perhaps one of the most memorable moments was skinning and cooking a deer in a pit of hot stones. By this time, after four days of near-starvation, Barney had lost his inhibition for food that had not been cooked in a hygenic kitchen. His delight as he sank his teeth into the roasted flesh was a sight to remember.

I prided myself that, yet again, I had pushed the boundaries of what information was acceptable to our viewers. I had literally showed the bloody entrails without emails of complaint. Even the blood-chilling sound as the deer's hide was ripped from the flesh, which made the programme editors tense with anxiety, passed unnoticed. It confirmed my faith that our young viewers are curious about life in the rawest sense, and not exclusively absorbed by the products of our exploding digital age.

So while it was not the Pacific, it was still a severe test for Barney, and, most important of all, the programme had broken new challenging ground fearlessly, just as it had always done, and made an impression on its young viewers. Not a bad way to end 36 years of programme-making.

(Above): Barney makes camp for the night in the best of *Blue Peter* traditions

(Left): Survival expert Paul Johnson and Barney Harwood about to skin a deer

Epilogue

During *Blue Peter*'s extraordinary 54-year history there have been hundreds of memorable moments. And every so often the production team have had the luxury of choosing their top selection, like the '*Blue Peter* top ten', which was shown in 2012. My memory is longer than most and I thought it would be fun to share my top moments with you. They are in no particular order.

John Noakes in the mast-manning ceremony at HMS *Ganges*

John had to climb up the mast at HMS *Ganges*, the shore-based training academy, and stand up straight on the 'button' on the very top. It was an extraordinary feat and hard to watch if you had a fear of heights. Today the risk assessment would be worth reading and I doubt it would be allowed. John bravely made it to the final part of the mast, but ran out of steam trying to shimmy the final few metres to the button. It was testimony to the risk-taking spirit of *Blue Peter*, daring to go where no other television programmes would.

John Noakes 'the long fall'

A whole programme was devoted to his parachuting challenge, which was to freefall from 25,000 feet, a drop of four miles. They used film 'gun' helmet cameras to capture the freefall, which was trailblazing at the time, and earned John a place in *The Guinness Book of Records* as the first civilian to make such a jump. He also became the first person to talk to camera in such a dramatic style, although I can reveal that his actual words were drowned out in the rush of passing air and had to be 'post-synched' later in the dubbing theatre.

Lulu the elephant

This was probably the funniest moment in the history of the programme and arguably the most repeated clip of all. It happened because, I am told, Biddy did not like the way the keeper prodded Lulu with his pointed stick. Because it looked cruel, the stick was banned, and as a result the keeper lost control of the baby elephant.

Concorde's inaugural transatlantic flight

Concorde, the world's first supersonic passenger plane, was a potent symbol of Britain's share in the future. Its inaugural flight was covered live and we filmed Lesley Judd as she climbed aboard. The departure was pre-recorded and was featured on the programme. Its arrival in New York happened while the programme was on air live later that day.

Lesley emerged and walked on to the apron below Concorde, and to my astonishment looked up directly to the camera and delivered one of the most precise pieces to camera I had ever seen her do. Lesley's presence and professionalism made me realise that there was lot more to television than I could have ever imagined.

The 1977 Spithead Review

We had about half an hour to rehearse on HMS *Ark Royal* before the live transmission. Peter Purves stood on the flight deck and while the *Blue Peter* drum roll and the signature tune were played, the helicopter-borne camera slowly zoomed in from a wide shot of the fleet down to Peter who, as the music ended, said hello to the viewers. It was a camera move easier to describe than do, and it took half an hour to rehearse.

Transmission came almost immediately and the camera zoom was perfect. The programme went back to the studio in London and John or Lesley linked to a pre-recorded item with Percy Thrower in the *Blue Peter* garden. Back in the outside broadcast scanner, the director set in motion Peter's rehearsal of the guided tour of the ships. About two minutes into the garden VT, it crashed.

The director, John Vernon, immediately offered shots of the fleet while Peter skilfully improvised, using his research from earlier that morning. For something like four or five minutes Peter kept up a fluent commentary about the ships that John selected and even told stories about them. It was a salutary lesson to me to never to underestimate the presenter's ability.

The first phone call from the Transglobe Expedition from Antarctica

We had pledged to keep in touch with the expedition as it circumnavigated the world via its polar axis and I was given the job of finding a way of doing it. There were no satellite phones in those days so communication had to be by radio. Portishead Radio monitored all shortwave communications from around the world and luckily for us there were fans of the programme who worked there. They agreed to listen out for Sir Ranulph Fienne's wife Ginny, who was the expedition's communications expert, and ask her to radio in at a certain time so they could link her through to us.

To my surprise, it worked and we had several live phone calls reporting the team's progress. At the time it was a breakthrough and yet another first for *Blue Peter*.

Pelé

The great footballer appeared on the programme dressed in a suit and wearing black shoes because, despite requests, he had not agreed to kick a football. He did not reckon with Biddy's determination. The presenter, Simon Groom, was dressed to play and wore football boots. Halfway through the interview someone threw a football on to the set. Pelé could not contain himself. His reaction was instinctive and the rest of the interview was conducted with a ball continuously in play.

The Great Bring-and-Buy Sale for the Orphaned and Abandoned Children of Romania

By the end of this appeal *Blue Peter* viewers had raised over £6 million and in monetary terms it was the most successful appeal ever. The programme influenced the way orphaned and abandoned children in Romania were taken back into the community. It laid the foundations for the major UK charity Everychild. It changed the lives of hundreds of children in Romania who would otherwise have been forced to live in the nearest thing to hell on earth.

Kilimanjaro

I have to put this in because it was the best programme I ever made. It was an expedition to the roof of Africa and is described in Chapter 26.

Beard of bees

Helen Skelton didn't know anything about bees yet had faith that it would be all right. She had a calm manner and a determination that had already been tested when she had run 72 miles in 24 hours in the Namibian desert. The beard of bees was uncertain and therefore possibly dangerous. Despite both of us being stung, it was memorable because it looked amazing and we had gone about as far as we could with risking the safety of a presenter.

Helen Skelton's first report as she began her Amazon challenge

This had everything. It was emotional, gutsy and pioneering. For the first time, what happened halfway around the world could be seen as well as heard in the *Blue Peter* studio, live. Helen's presence on the show was sorely missed and without the live satellite links, even for a few moments in every other show, the damage done by her absence would have been much greater.

Not on screen...

There was another memorable moment that the viewers didn't see.

Stuart Miles was learning how to parachute and freefall with the RAF Falcons Parachute Display Team. We were in the desert near El Centro, in southern California, and the round of practice jumps had come to an unexpected end because the C130 Hercules transport aircraft had gone unserviceable. Filming out in the desert had been hot and thirsty work and the thought of a break was a welcome relief. En masse we headed for the Desert Inn just outside El Centro for an unscheduled lunch. We all began to unwind from the pressures of film-making and the ice-cold American beer was the best I can remember. To keep the building cool there wasn't a window in the place and we played a sort of giant shove halfpenny with wooden discs and ate and drank for the rest of the day. I cannot remember ever feeling so relaxed on location.

And finally...

For me, 36 years on, the programme has been a voyage of discovery that has taken me to destinations most people could only dream of. It has shown me how the poor and underprivileged the world over survive. It has given me glimpses into cultures that have made me grateful for the life I lead in Devon.

I joined *Blue Peter* partly because of my enjoyment of manageable danger and risk-taking. The presenters knew this. But for all the scary moments, even to the point of putting their lives at risk, I can now finally breathe a sigh of relief that I never lost a single presenter.

Four months after I left the BBC I invited a hundred guests to a farewell reunion. There were colleagues from the 1970s to the present day and they had been carefully chosen for their selfless contributions to the programme. They represented the core of a team of 'true believers' committed to the ideals laid down by Biddy Baxter, Edward Barnes and Rosemary Gill in the early 1960s. They had made *Blue Peter* a focus for enquiring young minds for over fifty years and had given them inspiration. And, above all, they were my friends.

(Above): A photo from my farewell party. From L to R (back row): Tina Heath, Stuart Miles, Simon Thomas, John Leslie, Joel Defries, Anthea Turner, Clare Bradley, Peter Duncan. (Front row): Katy Hill, Janet Ellis, Alex Leger, Sarah Greene, Diane Louise Jordan

Index